CARRIE FISHER

A LIFE ON THE EDGE

CARRIE FISHER

A LIFE ON THE EDGE

SHEILA WELLER

SARAH CRICHTON BOOKS
Farrar, Straus and Giroux
New York

Sarah Crichton Books
Farrar, Straus and Giroux
120 Broadway, New York 10271

Library of Congress Cataloging-in-Publication Data
Names: Weller, Sheila, author.
Title: Carrie Fisher : a life on the edge / Sheila Weller.
Description: First edition. | New York : Sarah Crichton Books/Farrar, Straus and Giroux,
    2019. | Includes bibliographical references and index.
Identifiers: LCCN 2019021323 | ISBN 9780374282233 (hardcover)
Subjects: LCSH: Fisher, Carrie. | Actors—United States—Biography.
Classification: LCC PN2287.F495 W45 2019 | DDC 791.4302/8092 [B]—dc23
LC record available at https://lccn.loc.gov/2019021323

Designed by Gretchen Achilles

Our books may be purchased in bulk for promotional, educational, or business use.
Please contact your local bookseller or the Macmillan Corporate and Premium Sales
Department at 1-800-221-7945, extension 5442, or by e-mail at
MacmillanSpecialMarkets@macmillan.com.

www.fsgbooks.com
www.twitter.com/fsgbooks • www.facebook.com/fsgbooks

1   3   5   7   9   10   8   6   4   2

To feminists—whether "badass" or earnest, private or noisy, second or third wave or #MeToo and #TimesUp, or any combination thereof—everywhere. And to everyone struggling with bipolar disorder or any mood or mental challenge.

The best I have been . . . is when I have been mildly manic . . .
my liveliest, most productive, most intense, most outgoing
and effervescent . . . I am a hard act to follow.

—KAY REDFIELD JAMISON,
An Unquiet Mind: A Memoir of Moods and Madness

CONTENTS

CARRIE FISHER

A LIFE ON THE EDGE

FAMOUS FOR SIMPLY
BEING HERSELF

On December 23, 2016—right before her favorite holiday (for a long time, she had a year-round Christmas tree in her house)—as the day was just starting in London, Carrie Fisher boarded United Flight 935 at Heathrow Airport. The plane was scheduled to leave London at 9:20 a.m. and arrive in L.A. at 12:40 p.m. (local times). With Fisher was her constant companion, Gary, the baby French bulldog she'd adopted from a New York shelter a few years earlier. She took Gary everywhere: to talk shows (interviewers happily gave him his own director's chair), to restaurant dinners, and now to his own seat in the first-class cabin of this plane. The damaged, not-very-housebroken mutt, whose hot-pink tongue invariably hung sideways out of his mouth ("It matches my sweater," she once told an interviewer, pointing to her own hot-pink top), was like her canine twin. They were sweet survivors together: he, of a puppyhood of neglect; she, of several things. First, she'd survived a Hollywood childhood of glamour, popping flashbulbs, and headline-making scandal when the marriage of her parents, Hollywood's sweethearts Debbie Reynolds and Eddie Fisher, blew apart under the spell of the gorgeous, just-widowed Elizabeth Taylor, with whom Eddie fell in love. Then Fisher survived early, sudden, international mega-fame—at age twenty, in 1977—as Princess Leia, the arch-voiced galaxy-far-away heroine in that flowing white gown and those funny hair buns. Despite Leia's storybook royalty; her silky, almost-parody-of-feminine clothing; and a touching, repeated plea—"Help me, Obi-Wan Kenobi, you're my only hope"—made all the more plaintive because she uttered it as a hologram miniature, she was the fiercest hero of them all: ironic, tart, yet positive, and already a Resistance leader who could deal with her own survival while her twin brother, Luke Skywalker (Mark Hamill), was still a mere farm boy and her later love Han Solo (Harrison Ford) was a cynical gun for hire. She was the only girl warrior among the boys, and she could hold her own better than they could. If second-wave feminism had a science fiction stand-in, it was the Princess Leia created by Carrie Fisher.

As Fisher and Gary settled into their plane seats for the long flight home to Los Angeles, if Fisher had wanted to use the hours in the sky to mull her accomplishments, she had plenty about which to feel satisfied.

More seriously than surviving huge early fame, Fisher was a survivor of inherited drug addiction and of major bipolar disorder—the latter an incurable, biologically rooted mental illness that causes changes in the way one's brain processes the chemicals the body naturally produces. Fisher's version—the more serious bipolar one versus bipolar two— could come on unpredictably, and for her, enduring it was like living "with a war story." She talked about both of these problems so frankly and so helpfully to others that in the early years of the twenty-first century "she completely kicked the stigma of bipolar disorder to the curb," says Joanne Doan, the editor of *bp Magazine*. Expert after expert would gratefully agree: nobody took the shame out of bipolar disorder the way Carrie Fisher did.

Of course there was more, much more. Fisher had a brilliant, sage honesty and madcap personality—a crazy joyousness—pretty much unequaled in Hollywood. During the three-year run of her self-written one-woman show *Wishful Drinking*—her autobiographical late-career tour de force—she started sprinkling the audience, and her friends, with glitter. Actual glitter. She did it backstage at the Oscars; she did it at restaurants. She became such a glitter aficionado she had special glitter-holding pockets sewn into her coat. Many years earlier, on her honeymoon with Paul Simon, she'd brought the bridesmaids who traveled to the Nile with them silly fairy costumes to camp up their visits to the ancient catacombs. Her house, tastefully decorated though it was with antiques and folk art, was also chockablock with felicitousness: the tiles in the kitchen were embossed with linoleum images of Prozac bottles; one of her bathrooms contained a piano (didn't *all* bathrooms have pianos?), and a series of what she called "ugly children portraits" hung over her bed.

Her bons mots were epic. During an Equal Rights Amendment march in the 1980s with her friend the screenwriter Patricia Resnick, Fisher had wisecracked of a small weight gain, "I'm carrying water for Whitney Houston." When she first dated Paul Simon—who was almost as short as her five feet one—she'd remarked, "Don't stand next to me at a party. They'll think we're salt and pepper shakers." When, with her fluent French, she had saved her friend, the world-famous security expert Gavin de Becker, from the Hotel George V concierge's outrage because Gavin had made off with the bathrobe from his room, she eyed the straight-arrow boy she'd known in high school and said, "I didn't know you were a thief." Pause. "Now that I do, I'll take you traveling with me more often." When, late in the first decade of the twenty-first century, men started weight and age shaming her on social media, she bounced back with "You've just hurt one of my three feelings." When her father, Eddie Fisher, wrote of his dislike for her mother, Debbie Reynolds, in his second memoir and falsely accused Debbie of being a lesbian, Carrie, hurt and angry, nevertheless riposted, "My mother is *not* a lesbian." Pause. "She's just a really, really bad heterosexual." Most recently, when, six weeks before she boarded this plane, it was revealed that the presidential candidate Donald Trump, whom she despised, ogled only beautiful women, she tweeted, "Finally, a good reason to want to be ugly."

It wasn't just snappy wisecracks that were her forte; she was good at substantive aphorisms. She knew from the up-and-down (including the *very* down) career moments of her parents that "celebrity is just obscurity biding its time." And she warned about the toxic nature of competitive Hollywood. "Resentment," she liked to say, "is like drinking poison and waiting for the other person to die." Fisher's main maxim for her complicated life was "If my life wasn't funny it would just be true, and that is unacceptable." It *had* to be funny, and she *made* it so.

Fisher was gifted with a quicksilver tongue. "She is the smartest person I know," many of her friends said about her. "Charisma" is an easy word to throw around, but she possessed it. In her book *The Princess Diarist*, she wrote that as a girl she had longed "to be so wildly popular" that she could "explode on your night sky like fireworks at midnight on New Year's Eve in Hong Kong." Many would say that Carrie Fisher had achieved this goal. She was "irresistible," said Albert Brooks; her friend Richard Dreyfuss called her a subject of "worship" among their friends. "I am a very good friend," she once told Charlie Rose, in a way that didn't sound conceited, because she'd been brutally frank about so much else. She was a "loyal, alert, fierce, vulnerable friend," she'd said. "I can go the distance with people."

"Vulnerable?" Charlie Rose asked, beaming at her easy wit. "Everyone told me I would *love* you."

"Unfortunately, yes," she'd answered, adding, with tart self-knowledge, "I can do wrong better than anyone."

The night before she'd boarded the plane for L.A., she'd had dinner with another one of her best friends, the author Salman Rushdie, and Fisher's newer and younger friend, the Irish actress and producer Sharon Horgan, whose wacky-bitchy mother-in-law she played on the TV series *Catastrophe*. She and Sharon and their co-star Rob

Delaney (who played Sharon's husband) had just filmed one of the final episodes of the third season of their jubilantly profane comedy about a hapless marriage.

The three—Rushdie, Horgan, and Fisher—had had a good restaurant dinner, full of laughter, while Gary the dog farted, Horgan recalled. Says Rushdie, who'd had a twenty-year friendship with Fisher and cared deeply for her (and sometimes worried about her, as did many of her friends), "She seemed hale and healthy, and she ate heartily. She'd bought a house in Chelsea, which seemed to lift her spirits." Fisher, a gift giver of wit and thoughtful specificity (and an opinionated matchmaker of Rushdie with women), handed the writer a tiny chocolatier's box over the dinner table. He opened it, and "there were a pair of . . . chocolate tits!" He laughed, of course, and vowed to devour the luscious breasts slowly over the following nights. (He never would; they're still in his freezer.) Fisher gave Horgan a lovely antique pin. *No one* gave presents like Carrie Fisher.

After the dinner, Fisher returned to her hotel for a good night's sleep before her flight. She had packed a lot into the previous two months: she'd filmed her part in a glamorous sci-fi movie called *Wonderwell* in Italy and zipped over to London to shoot several episodes of *Catastrophe* while buying the house in Chelsea. She'd also flown to L.A. and back for a few-weeks-late sixtieth birthday party that her mother, Debbie, had insisted be a big deal, including inviting Brownie and Girl Scout troop alumnae as well as all of Fisher's close celebrity friends. Fisher worried deeply about her eighty-four-year-old mother's health; Debbie had suffered two strokes in 2016. But Reynolds was, like her famous movie character, unsinkable: insistent on never slowing down. This workaholism had been passed on to her daughter.

The weeks before, Fisher had also been busy promoting *The Princess Diarist*, which disclosed the secret affair she'd had with Harrison Ford while filming the first *Star Wars* and the intense vulnerability she had felt at nineteen. It was her seventh book and, like all the others, a bestseller. She hadn't been feeling particularly well. "She'd lost some spring in her step" during November, Sharon Horgan had noticed. In fact, she was almost ill enough to cancel a TV show hosted by one of her many English best friends, Graham Norton, to promote the book, but she had decided—just as her mother would have—that the show had to go on, so she went through with it.

The plane took off, arched over the Atlantic Ocean, nipped the lower tip of Greenland, entered Canada, and zoomed over Montana, Idaho, and Nevada, approaching California.

During the eleven-hour flight, two young performers, a comedian named Brad Gage and his girlfriend, the YouTube personality Anna Akana, happened to be seated near Fisher and Gary. Huge fans (Anna had just read *The Princess Diarist*), they were amazed at their luck. Fisher slept for much of the flight, but as the plane began descending toward LAX, at thirty thousand feet, she woke abruptly and started violently throwing up. She said she couldn't breathe. For decades, she had worried about sleep apnea—a serious sleeping disorder where breathing can stop, dangerously. Now here it was.

Passengers who were nurses rushed to her side and administered CPR.

"Don't know how to process it but Carrie Fisher stopped breathing on the flight home," Akana tweeted. "Hope she's gonna be OK." Akana has a large Twitter following. This was the first news anyone, even Fisher's family, heard about the emergency. "I'm in complete shock," Gage tweeted, backing up the account.

Not long before the scheduled landing, Fisher went into severe cardiac arrest. The pilot radioed and "coordinated [for] medical personnel" to meet them at the gate. The pilot told air traffic control, "We have some passengers, nurses assisting the passenger, we have an unresponsive passenger."

According to a log from the Los Angeles Fire Department website, documenting real-time emergencies, at 12:11 p.m. a fire department truck full of paramedics rushed over to gate 74, waiting for the flight's arrival. When the flight did arrive at 12:25 (two minutes before its revised and sped-up scheduled arrival), the paramedics "provided advanced life support and aggressively treated and transported the patient to the local hospital"—UCLA Medical Center's intensive care unit.

It wasn't long until all the major websites lit up with versions of this shocking headline: "Carrie Fisher Suffers Massive Heart Attack on Plane."

Fisher's millions of fans were anguished. She meant so much not just to those who knew and personally loved her but to anyone who'd watched *Star Wars*, read her books, seen *Wishful Drinking* onstage or on HBO, or seen her outwitting everyone on any talk show.

For three days, a virtual news blackout on her condition had media and fans on edge. Many suspected it was only a formality that Fisher was being kept on life support. *People* magazine, holidays be damned, called in staff and freelancers to produce an all–Carrie Fisher special memorial issue. The magazine put out such special issues only very rarely. But this was merited and would sell, the editors knew.

On the morning of December 27, Simon Halls—the spokesperson for Fisher's daughter, Billie Lourd, and Billie's father, the CAA managing partner Bryan Lourd—announced, "It is with a very deep sadness that Billie Lourd confirms that her beloved mother Carrie Fisher passed away at 8:55 this morning. She was loved by the world and she will be missed profoundly. Our entire family thanks you for your thoughts and prayers."

"I cried when I heard Carrie Fisher had died," wrote the author Karen Karbo in her book *In Praise of Difficult Women*. Karbo—a contemporary of Carrie's—knew she was not alone; she remembered that moment of national pain. "People all across the galaxy did. *Star Wars* nerds, avid readers of her novels and memoirs, mental health advocates, self-proclaimed killjoy feminists." And, of course, Fisher's friends: Meryl Streep, J. D. Souther, Helen Fielding, Laurie Anderson. "I can't believe she is gone," Salman Rushdie, Richard Dreyfuss, and the producer Bruce Cohen each told this author, even weeks later. In the acknowledgments of her memoir, the recent president of HBO Documentary and Family Programming, Sheila Nevins, said she would "miss [Carrie] as long as I am able to miss." "She was so real it was dangerous": that's how Sharon Horgan described her. The words had an accidentally poetic meaning: Carrie Fisher's personality, expressed directly and through her body of work, was so candid and intimate it made her vulnerable and made others feel that way as well. Most of us have filters. She was famously unfiltered, but not trivially so; several close friends felt there was pain she kept to herself and soldiered beyond. Says her close friend Richard Dreyfuss, "Shakespeare said in *Othello* something about throwing a pearl away. We often throw our pearls away. Carrie *didn't* throw her pearls away. She was going to eat life like a great meal—the good and the bad: *all* of her life. And she did."

The major obituaries of Carrie stressed her revolutionary sensibility as Princess Leia. Dave Itzkoff in *The New York Times* said she "brought a rare combination of nerve, grit and hopefulness to her indelible role . . . as a damsel who could very much deal with her own distress . . . Winning the admiration of countless fans, Ms. Fisher never played Leia as helpless." And they also noted that she went well beyond that role (which she often affectionately mocked) and became that rarest thing for a woman: as Josh Rottenberg put it in the *Los Angeles Times*, "famous and beloved for simply being herself: an author, actor, activist and personality, armed with acerbic comic flair and an admirable, if occasionally unnerving, tendency to tell the truth."

Famous and beloved for simply being herself.

Social media went wild with grief and awe, with Paul Simon, Mark Hamill, and Harrison Ford just a tiny handful of those close to Carrie chiming in, with virtual tears in their tweets. To soothe their pain, young, mostly female writers popped up short web pieces on Fisher's best tweets and witticisms. They wrote about the movies they hadn't known she had script doctored (very few people knew this calling of hers before the obituaries). There were pieces on the words of wisdom and encouragement she gave to her fellow bipolars—to *all* people with mental illness. It became clear she had been a multifaceted hero hiding in plain sight. No one had taken her for granted when she was alive, exactly, but with her death came a torrent of appreciation. No wonder that when the women's marches were held in January 2017, thousands of women—including girls who weren't even born when *Star Wars* was released—hoisted Princess Leia posters high.

Fisher's life story—which she told and retold—started, of course, with her mother, Debbie Reynolds, the irrepressibly wholesome 1950s darling who sang and danced "Good Morning" with Gene Kelly and Donald O'Connor in *Singin' in the Rain* and who was nominated for the 1965 Oscar for *The Unsinkable Molly Brown*. Older Americans knew and adored Reynolds; they recalled her as the lovely Tammy, singing wistfully of the "cottonwoods whisperin' above," and as the profoundly sympathetic, ponytailed victim of her husband Eddie Fisher's rapid-fire infidelity, his cat-eating-the-canary-proud dumping of her, the mother of his two toddlers, for Elizabeth Taylor. Middle-aged Americans knew Reynolds as the game, financially hapless, reliably sequined nightclub singer and casino owner and actress. She was a devoted collector of Hollywood memorabilia: a glamorous member of studio-system old Hollywood who refused to let age get in her way. Debbie Reynolds was a survivor, and those who followed industry awards knew she'd won, in the last eighteen months, the Academy's Jean Hersholt Humanitarian Award and the Screen Actors Guild (SAG) Lifetime Achievement Award: very richly deserved.

But these days, mostly everyone knew her foremost as Carrie Fisher's mother, and everyone knew Carrie Fisher as Debbie Reynolds's daughter. "Hollywood royalty": the term followed them everywhere. (In truth, Fisher didn't mind that and stoked its glamour and ironies, to much laughter.) They were rare in America, this mother and daughter—*both* icons, *both* full of life and likability, *both* so present in the culture, yet so different. ("Debbie had been America's sweetheart, but as American values changed, that job was no longer open, so Carrie became America's cynic," says a close friend of Reynolds's.) And through the thicket of humor that Carrie had often showered on her mother—whether, with name changed, in her first book, *Postcards from the Edge*, or later, more frankly, in *Wishful Drinking*—people knew one thing for sure: *they loved each other.* Deeply if complexly. (And what mother-daughter relationship worth its salt is *not* complex?)

Debbie Reynolds was as physically fragile as a human being could be, and the public's pain at her daughter's death carried over to concern for the frail eighty-four-year-old. How do you take it when your child—even a woman of sixty—predeceases you? People's hearts were broken when they read Reynolds's Facebook message, posted shortly after the official announcement of Fisher's death: "Thank you to everyone who has embraced the gifts and talents of my beloved and amazing daughter. I am grateful for your thoughts and prayers that are now guiding her to her next stop. Love, Carrie's Mother."

The next day, December 28, the public received an agonizing piece of news both shocking and unbelievable but also something that might have been predicted—by Shakespeare or the Bible. Carrie's mother had been rushed to the hospital with another stroke.

And then the headline: "Debbie Reynolds Dies."

People said to one another, "There are no words."

Every news organization in the country reacted to the heightened melodrama of a beloved famous mother dying one day after her beloved famous daughter. The history of the family was paraded out in all its Hollywood-royalty glamour, pathos, scandal, and sweetness: much, much sweetness. (A famous Lawrence Schiller photograph of tiny Carrie sitting in the Las Vegas wings, watching her mother perform, particularly caused lumps in throats.)

Debbie wanted to be with Carrie, Todd Fisher simply said. Later he would say that his sister's death surprised him but their mother's, a day later, did not. What didn't get told amid the tragedy, pain, celebration, and love swirling through the media accounts was that, as a close friend of Debbie's put it, Debbie had braced herself for a "call about Carrie" every day for decades.

Carrie Fisher was a rare woman in American culture, one who embodied wit, honesty, originality, complexity, and feminism: "famous and beloved for simply being herself." How could such a charismatic, quick-witted creature—adored by fans and best friends alike—be so vulnerable as to incite such worry in her mother?

Here in Carrie Fisher's extraordinary life lies part of the answer to that question.

ONE

HOLLYWOOD BABY

In September 1957, Carrie Fisher was an eleven-month-old being tended by her nurse in the back of the bright living room of her house—her parents Debbie Reynolds and Eddie Fisher's house—on Maple Drive between Lomitas and Sunset, in Beverly Hills. She was a plump-faced, wary-seeming, unsmiling baby, as if aware—and why would she *not* be?—of the number of cameras already pointed in her face (not to mention her mother's face), a situation that would continue and intensify, much later turning into material for great, witty irony. If a baby can have a sense memory of the milieu, the atmospherics, of her life, perhaps these days, this surrounding world, provided the makings for her.

It was one of those perfect, sunny, humidity-free days for which the Southland was famous, just before Indian summer—and a still one: no cars drove by those quiet streets; the only sound came from the occasional buzzing of the hummingbirds and the lawn mowers powered by the "Spanish" gardeners. You could smell the sweet fresh-cut grass, along with the jacaranda and the bougainvillea that twined the homes and gave the street such color. Inside the windows of the close-together houses (Tudor and Spanish and what was then called Early American), one might catch a glimpse of maids cutting the crusts off the peanut butter and jelly sandwiches they were making for snacks as the children walked home from Hawthorne, the public elementary school, five blocks away. Hawthorne was the school that the raucous Michael DeToth, the son of the actress Veronica Lake—she of the unsurpassably sexy blond hair—attended. Hawthorne was also where one would find Rita Hayworth's daughters, Rebecca Welles (daughter of Orson) and Yasmin Khan (daughter of Prince Aly Khan). Or the children were dropped off by school bus from the private schools: Harvard for boys, and Marymount and Westlake and Marlborough for girls. The boys wore little suits and ties; the girls wore pinafore uniforms. The littlest children had already been delivered home, by parent or chauffeur, from the tiny, exclusive Miko's nursery school: Tyrone Power and Linda Christian's daughters, Taryn and Romina, and Zsa Zsa Gabor's daughter, Francesca Hilton, were recent alumnae. The Miko's girls wore Peter Pan–collared, puffy-cap-sleeved dresses and black patent leather Mary Janes with pretty white socks folded at the ankle. Tiny Carrie Fisher, blooming into toddlerhood, would soon wear such dresses.

A movie magazine writer—her pen name Helen Gould—who lived around the corner on Elm Drive had come to deliver her article to Debbie about her storybook marriage to Eddie Fisher and the rumors, which turned out to be true, of her pregnancy with a second baby. Answering the doorbell herself and standing at the front-door landing, Debbie looked more beautiful in relaxed-face reality than in the sentimentally smiling photographs of her that were so often circulated. She graciously thanked the writer for the carbon-copy-papered story, which was typed, as everything was back then, in the uneven font of a manual typewriter. And in a voice with the gentlest touch of a lisp but all her El Paso childhood vanquished, Debbie said she would read it for accuracy. Directly across the street from Debbie and Eddie and Carrie lived Louella Parsons, the queen of gossip columnists and the woman Debbie trusted so much she called her "Mother." Debbie would go over the story with Louella, one of them crossing the slender, curving swath of blacktop to the other's house, as neighborly as if this were Mayberry.

These were the "Flats"—the neat twenty-two-block stretch of Beverly Hills, from Whittier on the west to Doheny on the east, Little Santa Monica on the south to Sunset on the north, with evocatively Spanish-named cross streets: Carmelita, Elevado, and Lomitas. Carrie would claim Beverly Hills as her own for most of her life. And in time, she and her family would move west, to the fancier Holmby Hills area. But what was special about the Beverly Hills Flats in the years of Carrie's earliest childhood was the combination of its innocence, intimacy, and unpretentiousness, on the one hand, and the glamour and the secrets it was hiding, on the other hand.

On these streets, movie stars lived like regular people, picking their morning *Herald-Express* and *Los Angeles Times* off their dewy front lawns in their bathrobes. The neighborhood, with famous names and faces tucked into the mix of doctors and lawyers and songwriters and screenwriters, had a coziness to it in those years before Hollywood—as glamorous as it was—was called "the industry." In those now-forgotten days, the very few morning and evening national television shows (transmitted on rabbit-eared sets) emanated from the Place That Counted: New York City! Jill Schary Robinson (the daughter of the director of production at MGM, Dore Schary) once recalled that schoolchildren in Los Angeles at the time read textbooks full of pictures of the tamed and formal-looking grassy rolling hills of the far-off East Coast. That landscape was the "normal." Jill aptly used the term "those workbook trees" for a New England look—a place of the supposedly "real," proper, historic America—unknown to Angelenos. It was so different from the unsung lovely Alhambran Spanish buildings, the palm and eucalyptus trees, the looming dirt-brown mountains, and the serpentine canyons that marked *this* place, in which tiny Carrie Fisher would grow up.

Thus, the Beverly Hills in which Carrie was a toddler was full of movie stars but also—in those years when regular folks took very few coast-to-coast plane trips—curiously hidden by this focus on that more "real" America. Her world had a normal, now-quaintly 1950s feel. The white-uniformed Adohr man delivered proudly "pasteurized" milk in glass bottles to people's back porches. The Wonder Bread Bakery, a factory where workers actually *made* the bread, sat on Little Santa Monica between Elm and Foothill, just over the railroad tracks, where a small freight train toot-tooted as it rumbled through several times daily. The smell the bakery gave off was heavenly! Kids could race across the tracks with their nannies, who ingratiated themselves to the foreman, and buy warm white bread straight from the ovens. Uniformed maids made family dinners in chafing dishes and pressure cookers. Couples went out to dinner at Chasen's; dolled-up grown-ups had grand evenings at Ciro's, the Mocambo, and the Crescendo—the nightclubs where elegance ruled along with occasional liquored mayhem—on Sunset; and families dined at the one Chinese restaurant (Chinese food was exotically new), the classy and intimate Ah Fong's on Beverly Drive, just south of Little Santa Monica Boulevard.

It was safe for kids as young as ten to walk after school "into Beverly"—the unassuming shopping streets, Beverly and Canon, between Santa Monica and Wilshire. You could buy knickknacks at Livingston's, have milk shakes at Whelan's drugstore counter, read *Archie* comic books, and listen to 45s in glassed-in booths at the Gramophone Shop. And when you got fitted for shoes at Children's Bootery, your foot was routinely X-rayed; nobody worried about the danger of X-rays any more than they worried about the danger of cigarettes or the nonexistence of car seat belts. Your mother bought you pretty, girly clothes at Bobbi Teen and Pixie Town; God forbid she should be sensible, or gauche, enough to purchase them at Lerner's. (Don Loper was the glamorous, urbane adult store—"boutique" was not yet in parlance—for women such as Audrey Hepburn, whom you wanted to grow up to be like.) The Gramophone Shop, Bobbi Teen, Pixie Town: you couldn't beat those names for an almost desperately wholesome snapshot of the moment in time that baby Carrie's America's sweetheart parents, Debbie Reynolds and Eddie Fisher, were beloved across the country.

Carrie's immediate neighborhood was quietly full of movie stars—some of them the most earnest upholders of those 1950s values, others hiding big secrets deeply against the grain of that morality. Right around the corner from Carrie and her family, on the southeast corner of Elm and Elevado, was the comedian and entertainer Danny Thomas and his family. (Thomas's eldest daughter, Terre Thomas, always had a line of suitors parking their cars in the family's circular driveway.) The Lebanese Thomas was a fervent Catholic. An elaborate Nativity crèche was mounted on the family's lawn every Christmas, and it drew pilgrim-like visitors from far-off—poorer—neighborhoods. (No one else in Beverly Hills had a Nativity crèche. Christmas there was cheerfully nonreligious. Santa's sled and reindeer were strung high across various points on Wilshire Boulevard, and Bob Hope sent glorious Mission Pak mega-arrangements of fruit and candy to every local gossip columnist and press agent.) Half a block south of the Thomas home was the cottage of Elizabeth Taylor's mother, the retired English actress Sara Sothern. Two doors down from Sothern was the home of Robert Young, the genial patriarch in the TV series perfectly named for the satisfied sensibility of the times: *Father Knows Best*. His house seemed Connecticut-like in its propriety. Every day at shortly after 3:00, his long-legged, shiny-haired daughters would bound through its white picket fence in their saddle shoes and Marymount pinafores.

Just down from the Robert Youngs, on the northwest corner of Elm and Carmelita, was the lovely one-story house Loretta Young occupied. Loretta was so proud to have adopted her daughter Judy from an orphanage that she once had a birthday party—movie magazine flashbulbs popping—for other notables who also had adopted children. But in fact Judy was Loretta's natural child by her married secret lover, Clark Gable. As fervent a Catholic as her neighbor Danny Thomas, the shocked, shamed newly pregnant Loretta Young had gone into hiding early in her pregnancy. She had secretly given birth to the baby girl, put the baby in an orphanage for several months under an assumed name, and then officially adopted her as a single mother Good Samaritan. It would be many years before anyone knew the truth.

On Palm Drive, one street east of Carrie's Maple, lived Esther Williams, star of all those lushly choreographed MGM swimming musicals, and her Latin-lover actor husband, Fernando Lamas. How passionate this couple seemed to be! Their next-door neighbors could often hear them trilling, high- and low-voiced—"Darling!" "Dahlink!"—as if they were chasing each other through their home to find and embrace and sexually devour each other. Years later, Williams would say that Lamas kept her captive in that house of theirs.

Several blocks west, still in the Flats, lived the Farrows, including their daughter Mia; and the Bergens, including their daughter Candice. Both girls, ten or so years older than Carrie, would become, respectively, Carrie's admiring co-star and her dear friend. More darkly, on nearby Bedford lived the femme fatale and noir movie queen (*The Postman Always Rings Twice* "made" her) Lana Turner, originally from northern Idaho (so many movie stars of that era, like Debbie herself, were from the provinces), who had famously been "discovered" sipping a soda at the Top Hat Cafe on Sunset Boulevard as a teenager. Lana—formerly Judy—Turner had already been married to and divorced from four men, including the bandleader Artie Shaw (who had also been married to Ava Gardner and, over time, to *six* other women), and would soon commence a romance with a handsome young hot-tempered bodyguard for the gangster Mickey Cohen named Johnny Stompanato. In a year and a half—April 1958—the jealous Stompanato would threaten not just Lana but also Lana's daughter by the restaurateur Steve Crane, the young teenager Cheryl Crane. Cheryl would take a kitchen knife and stab Stompanato to death. That national-news-riveting killing (some wondered, had Lana done it and Cheryl taken the blame?)—so close in time to the nonviolent but nevertheless viral news scandal that would catapult Carrie's parents and Elizabeth

Taylor into nonstop headlines—was a major Hollywood melodrama. (After her brief time in juvenile detention, Cheryl Crane would return to Beverly High, and her fellow students would try not to act as if there were anything different about this pretty, too-self-conscious sophomore when she walked into homerooms with a clipboard for the teacher as an attendance monitor.)

So this was the first neighborhood, and world, that the very young Carrie Fisher lived in.

"I came from simple folk—people of the land," she would say, decades later, opening her *Wishful Drinking* show by strolling around the stage, backed by the blown-up photographs of multiple movie magazine covers featuring her parents and her tiny self. "From simple folk": this line made the audience howl with laughter.

Even Carrie's birth—in Burbank during Debbie's pre-stardom days—had seemed so significant that both its imminence and it were trumpeted in the newspapers. "The baby was born almost three weeks ahead of time," *The New York Times* announced, in a breathless one-paragraph article, a day after her October 21, 1956, arrival. "Eddie Fisher, singer, and his actress-wife, Debbie Reynolds, became parents of a daughter today after a hectic dash by car from Palm Springs. The couple left there at midnight for the 120-mile drive to the St. Joseph's Hospital here." The brief article was titled, aptly male-focused for the mid-1950s, "Eddie Fishers Have Daughter."

By the time Carrie was born, Debbie Reynolds had had roles in fifteen movies, including 1952's *Singin' in the Rain*, which made her a star. She had been pregnant with the baby when she filmed the saccharine *Bundle of Joy*, co-starring with her new husband, Eddie. No movie or TV couple (Eddie's twice-weekly *Coke Time* was one of the most popular shows on television) so embodied the American dreams of the desperately conventional 1950s. Both stood for wholesomeness and patriotism: Debbie as an adorable actress, not a sex symbol like Marilyn Monroe or Rita Hayworth; Eddie as the boyishly handsome Jewish American version of a teen idol crooner. Debbie was a Girl Scout who wanted to be a gym teacher; Eddie had served his country during the Korean War, albeit mainly stateside at Fort Hood.

They came from disparate backgrounds. Eddie was the son of émigrés from the Pale of Settlement, raised in Philadelphia with the freedom to be genuinely assimilated. (He didn't like his father's shul-attending religiosity; he considered himself "culturally Jewish.") Debbie—Mary Frances "Franny"—Reynolds was born into the fiercely strict and pleasure-denying Nazarene Baptist religion in El Paso, Texas. She didn't know what a Jew was before she moved with her family, as a girl, to Southern California. In an era when people didn't marry out of their religion, their wedding—on September 26, 1955—gave their fans a gratifying sense of participating in the breaking of barriers of provincialism and bigotry that was just beginning in America.

What they had in common was childhood poverty, intense even for Depression upbringings. Mary Frances's family was so poor she shared a bed in her grandparents' house with her brother and three uncles. ("My brother and I slept with our heads at the top of the bed, my uncles with theirs at the foot. I woke up every morning with toes in my nose.") The house had no toilet or tub; the family used the nearby gas station to bathe and relieve themselves. And "our kitchen," she wrote in the first of two memoirs, "was a hot plate." Her mother—the emotional, needy Maxene, who bonded closely with her daughter—took in laundry to pay for groceries. Her father—the taciturn, enterprising Ray, a carpenter for the railroad—had dust-bowl-typical dreams of moving his family to the Golden State. Forgoing even dime-a-night lodging to save every cent he could, Ray Reynolds had slept on a bench in MacArthur Park to be able to buy a Burbank house for his family of four.

The Nazarene Baptists were as fundamentalist as rural Christians got, except for the Pentecostals. "No drinking, no smoking, no partying, no gambling, no movies, no dancing, no nothing," Debbie recalled. But somehow, from this childhood of staunch denial bloomed a tough, game, spirited girl who "cussed like crazy" and who, when Maxene locked her in the closet, asked for water because "I spit on all your shoes and now I'm out of spit."

Fortunately, the Nazarene minister in Los Angeles was more liberal than his counterpart in El Paso. Once they moved to Burbank, Mary Frances was allowed to audition and entertain. Renamed Debbie by her studio, she was signed first by Warner Bros. after becoming Miss Burbank in 1948; then she moved to MGM, known for its dazzling musicals. (Debbie's love for those MGM musicals would define her life and give her a heroic second career as a rescuer of vintage props and costumes.) In 1950, she had a hit record with "Aba Daba Honeymoon," from the movie *Two Weeks with Love*. Her freshly learned tap dancing, performed between the masters of the art Gene Kelly (who worked her ruthlessly) and Donald O'Connor, won her fame in 1952 in *Singin' in the Rain*. (Learning to dance so well, from scratch, was one of the hardest things she'd ever done, she said.) And her wistfulness, while singing the ballad "Tammy," as the star of 1957's *Tammy and the Bachelor*, gave her an earned gravity that deepened and complicated her sweetness. She was wholesome, yes, but she was lovely looking, her face often affecting a poignant expression. And she'd picked up a classic style of dressing. She wasn't trivial or kitschy. She was the girl next door whom you respected. And she radiated an integrity. Like an American Julie Andrews, she used her likable, lightly dignified persona to star in musicals from those early 1950s hits to the highly successful *The Unsinkable Molly Brown* in 1964 and *The Singing Nun* two years later.

The poverty in which Eddie grew up, while in a totally different milieu, was almost a match to Debbie's. As the fourth of seven children in Philadelphia, the son of an immigrant mother and father who married at, respectively, fifteen and eighteen, he was forced to drop out of school to support his family. "Ripe tomatoes, ten cents a peck!" he and his brother called out as they drove a truck through the Philly alleys.

Curly-haired and handsome in a boyish way, Eddie was called

Sonny Boy by his family. He had a smooth, appealing tenor voice and a deeply sincere delivery on ballads. If you were Jewish and looking to launch a career in entertainment and you lived on the East Coast, you either tried to land a spot in a New York nightclub, on a few choice television variety shows, or at the family resorts in the Catskills. Of these, Grossinger's was the best attended and most famous. (It has been memorialized in movies and TV series, from *Dirty Dancing* to *The Marvelous Mrs. Maisel*.) Eddie Cantor—a likably hammy performer, singer, dancer, comedian, and actor—was a mainstay at Grossinger's, and it was he who "discovered" Eddie Fisher there. Grossinger's made Fisher a star.

Eddie already had two hit records when he was drafted into the army in 1951. When he was signed to be the singing host on TV's *Coke Time*, renamed *Coke Time with Eddie Fisher*—a position that lasted from 1953 to 1957—his charm turned charismatic. His signature hits "May I Sing to You" and, especially, "Oh! My Papa" were too filled with genuine artistry to quite feel off-puttingly sentimental. And he had a twinkle of danger in his eye. He might have *looked* like the nice boy every Jewish mother wanted for her daughter, but he knew he wasn't, and he got a great kick out of the deception.

Once Eddie became famous, he traveled with an entourage. He had careless romances with many beauties; the night of his first date with Debbie, in 1954, the actress Pier Angeli also thought she had a date with him, and the two women nearly collided. Most significant, he was an early patient of Max Jacobson, MD, the infamous "Dr. Feelgood," who gave "miracle tissue regenerator" shots—featuring amphetamines, human placenta, and animal hormones—to a slew of famous performers. Later, for several years, Jacobson injected the presidential candidate and then president John F. Kennedy. As Eddie became in demand, journeying around to concerts in 1953, he flew Jacobson in to give him an injection of what was essentially the substance we now call speed before almost every performance. "It was like a wave of sunlight passed through my body, rejuvenating my voice," Eddie said of the addictive sensation. "Those of us who believed in Max didn't understand the danger. And once we understood it, we didn't believe it. And once we believed it, we didn't care."

Eddie would go on what were called "insane buying sprees": clothes, cars, gadgets. Nobody knew then that wild buying sprees were a sign of manic depression (which was later, in 1980, renamed bipolar disorder), with which Eddie almost undoubtedly lived. With manic depression/bipolar disorder, the patient experiences mania: periods of higher-than-normal energy levels; restlessness and inability to sit still; decreased need for sleep; and increased self-esteem, confidence, or grandiosity. The patient's mania alternates with periods of depression, and in between the two are interims of even, balanced moods, called euthymia.

Eddie would live with a mild version of this condition, but his daughter would experience it far less mildly. As studies conducted in 2006 would show, genetic factors account for 60 to 80 percent of bipolar disorder; Carrie inherited it, and her version would be pronounced. As for Eddie's other curse, addiction, experts now believe that about 50 percent of the risk is genetically based. Todd Fisher would be spared these two inheritances, but Carrie would inherit a double whammy from her father and would struggle mightily with it. For decades, Debbie would unwaveringly blame Carrie's problems on Eddie.

Eddie recalled meeting Debbie initially, very briefly, in 1951, when both were entertaining wounded soldiers at the Walter Reed Hospital. Despite her later enmity for him, Debbie remembered Eddie in 1953 as "the heartthrob of America, bigger, for that moment, than Sinatra, bigger than all of them—until Elvis." Movie magazines, which were the *People* magazine (and, one might say, the Instagram) of the day, and Hollywood columnists became, in effect, the couple's matchmakers. That same year, when one such publication asked Eddie who was the girl he'd most like to meet, he answered, "Debbie Reynolds." Debbie, within months, would be named by *Modern Screen* America's most popular young actress, ahead of Grace Kelly, ahead of her MGM school friend (and eventual saboteur) Elizabeth Taylor, ahead of Marilyn Monroe. Yes, it was all a bit hype filled and, from this vantage point, borderline tacky, but such were the times in popular entertainment and its media.

With the unflagging energy that would go on to characterize her whole life, Debbie was busy that year, making four movies. Although she was still living with her parents in Burbank, she had finally morphed from Mary Frances to Debbie: the studio-christened name now *felt* like her name. For his part, Eddie was smitten by "the most famous virgin in America!" for whom he had already fallen, "along with about a million other GIs," when he had watched *Singin' in the Rain* on the big screen in the leaky entertainment tents during the time he was stationed in Korea.

Debbie remembered first meeting Eddie in a substantive way in 1954, when he visited the set of the romantic comedy *Athena*, in which she co-starred with Linda Christian and her dear friend Jane Powell. MGM was wooing him, and he was about to open at the Coconut Grove. Though most of the songs are forgotten now, he was on his way to the seventeen Top Ten hits he would score by 1956. The easy-listening half decade of *Your Hit Parade* was his fertile pasture. Debbie thought him "adorable." So did her mother, Maxene, from having watched him on television; at least that's how Debbie reported it in her memoir. When Eddie called Debbie at home the next day, asking her for a date, Maxene supposedly said, sarcastic and disbelieving, "Eddie Fisher?! Sure, and I'm Lauren Bacall."

It was a columnist-covered but up-and-down romance. Frank Sinatra gave an indirect and generalized warning to Debbie, saying, "Very difficult life, to be married to a singer . . . You're not aware of what you're getting into, Debbie. It's a very hard life." Religion was discussed, but warily. "You're a Christian, do you think you can handle it?" Fisher asked Debbie because of the anti-Semitism to which he was acutely sensitive. She said she could. They married at the Catskills home of Elaine Grossinger, the daughter of the resort's owner.

However kitschy the America's sweethearts love story, the back-story was genuine. These two impoverished children made their own fame, and they did it from talent, charm, and resourcefulness. Debbie was particularly plucky: on movie sets, she danced when she was seven months pregnant. She filmed *Tammy and the Bachelor* during her pregnancy, as well as the hokey *Bundle of Joy*, which so perfectly advertised the couple's own situation that its studio, RKO, bought a full-page newspaper ad for the movie the day after Carrie was born.

So Carrie entered the world in a mid-1950s pop culture version of a merchandisable royal birth. And during the first seven months of her life, numerous influences were manifest: she became accustomed to life in hotels. And whether she sensed it or not, there was Debbie's unhappy awakening to her husband's problems, along with the media's focus on the very real tension between them.

There was also something else: an unmistakable father–baby daughter bonding. Carrie's middle name came as a rhyming match to her mother's—Carrie Frances, Mary Frances: the twinning was unmistakable, especially because, for the first almost two years of her life, Carrie was *only* called Carrie Frances, all four syllables. It was Eddie who chose the name Carrie. He chose it, he told *Modern Screen*'s Helen Gould, for its timeless, old-fashioned quality. Eddie's choice of that then-unusual name, and his thoughtful reason for it, indicated a pensive charm out of character for a braggadocios rapscallion.

Carrie's eyes were the shape of Eddie's, Gould reported in one of the earliest interviews the family gave, when Carrie was five months old, published two months later. Gould was describing her visit to Carrie Frances's nursery room in the Tropicana hotel, where Eddie was in the midst of a five-week engagement. Though the eyes were currently blue-gray, Debbie *insisted* that "they're going to be brown" like Eddie's.

The infant and toddler Carrie Frances Fisher became a prop for the selling of these magazines. She was on the cover of the August 1957 issue of *Modern Screen*—fat-faced and unsmiling, in pale pink, propped between her two parents, who wore matching hot-pink shirts, both cupping one of her tiny hands in one of their own. The inside photo showed Debbie lovingly pressing her baby daughter's head to her cheek, across from a black-and-white photo of a thoughtful (or sullen) Eddie, head down and arms crossed over his chest. The fraught nature of Carrie's later life was previewed by the article's large captions, describing what fickle America was likely wondering: "Is Debbie a good mother?" and "Will Eddie settle down?"

Barely crawling, Carrie was the star of the article. Here is a baby being raised, for five weeks, in a Las Vegas hotel! "You walk down a blue-carpeted white-walled hall to rooms 148-49-50. You open the door to 150, and you're in a nursery. A nursery just like in that nice house on Shady Lane, Anytown. Complete with baby. There's a play pen inhabited by a couple of pink cuddly lambs. Carrie Frances herself is lying in her bassinette, holding tight to a rattle in her sweet, sturdy fist, regarding it with great interest out of her brown eyes."

Eddie's affection for his baby daughter is clear in the article: Eddie "said, 'Where's my girl?' and shot into the next room like a rocket. Came sounds of lots of father and daughter stuff that concerned just the two of them . . . They were having a ball."

Debbie spent much of the interview defensive about the media's intense attention to changes in weather in their marriage, and she hewed to the 1950s party line that Eddie's career was more important than hers. *Tammy and the Bachelor* was in theaters, and the theme song would become a huge hit. Still, she was turning down pictures to defer to Eddie's touring schedule. "Every girl does that when she gets married . . . I just don't leave my husband to make a picture . . . I'd rather be a wife than an actress," she declared. But togetherness was also important to quiet the media skeptics who had fiercely turned on the couple and now looked at every short separation as a sign that the marriage was in trouble. To quell the rumors, Debbie would soon leave Carrie with Maxene to vacation with Eddie after his two weeks at the London Palladium. She had considered leaving Carrie for such a trip when Carrie was four months old and was glad she had not done so; it would have been a capitulation to those who "jumped to the usual conclusion: that we'd had a quarrel," she told Helen Gould.

Debbie was blunt, even brusque, in refusing to exactly deny the possible cracks in the marriage. Asked about rumors of their quarreling, Debbie told Helen Gould, "I won't discuss it; I won't discuss it," adding, "One person cannot change another, so there's no use trying." And "over the father-daughter talk still going on in the bedroom," as Gould put it, "[Debbie] said, vehemently, 'Eddie hasn't changed. The difference is that before he was a bachelor. Now he's a married man.'"

Three months later, Louella Parsons, arguably the most powerful Hollywood columnist, came to interview Debbie for the same publication. The photo that accompanied the article—"Debbie Tells Louella the Truth About Our Marriage"—was unctuous. Eddie, in a pink-and-white-striped shirt, avidly hugged Debbie, in a similar pink-and-white-striped shirt. Her smile is genuine; his seems exaggerated, as if he were saying, *I'm doing this B.S. because I have to, suckers.*

Like a bolt of early feminism, Louella had come to lecture Debbie for her own good: Stop deferring to Eddie! Stop ignoring your own career! "*Debbie,*" she said, in an italicized warning she posted as an open letter. "*I think the time has come when you'd better start minding the store.*"

Why was Debbie continuing to put Eddie's career first and turn down roles? She fought with her "mother" Louella. "I think you are completely wrong," Debbie said, and when Louella protested, Debbie cut her off: "No. Let me finish! Eddie's career is the most important in the family and it will always come first. I have no intention of giving up my career, however . . . But to me a career can't possibly be as stable as a marriage." Was this Louella-Debbie fight a gimmick, to make Debbie look heroic? It's easy to infer thus today, but on the page the candor seems genuine and laced with 1950s values and Nazarene earnestness.

Carrie Frances was, again, the melodramatic pinion of the article.

Debbie talked of moving to a one-story house because, she fretted, "pretty soon Carrie Frances will be toddling and I worry about stairs and places where she might hurt herself." In her putting-marriage-first move, Debbie had just spent two months in Europe with Eddie, away from her child, and now it bothered her. Debbie told Louella, "Carrie Frances didn't recognize me when I came home. Honest, she didn't . . . For a few days my heart was broken. She'd go to my mother or the nurse, but she'd just look up at me as though saying, Who are you? And *where* have you been? I don't see how I can ever leave her again . . . I've missed two wonderful months out of her life."

Debbie's old MGM classmate, the sophisticated and insuperably beautiful Elizabeth Taylor, was still married to her second husband, Michael Wilding, with whom she had two young sons. But Taylor and Eddie's mentor Mike Todd met and fell madly in love. Elizabeth was twenty-four; Todd was forty-seven. He had long been divorced from his second wife, the actress Joan Blondell. He had just produced the winsome and artful (and expensive) *Around the World in 80 Days*, the film adaptation of the Jules Verne novel, starring David Niven and Cantinflas, in a hot-air balloon. It won the 1957 Academy Award for Best Picture.

Born Avrom Hirsch Goldbogen, the son of an Orthodox rabbi in Minnesota, Todd was an aggressively self-made man with brio and tough-Jew sex appeal. He was a room rocker, a glamorous overspender, a bet maker and bet *winner*. He was the kind of man who easily merited the cliché, which Debbie bestowed on him, "larger than life." Eddie, who worshipped him, called him "a rogue and a gambler and a dreamer, a promoter and a perfectionist, a man of great taste and outrageous demeanor." Elizabeth had had two civilized, coddled husbands; the hotel heir Nicky Hilton had preceded Wilding. Todd could eat Hilton and Wilding for breakfast. Elizabeth Taylor fell for that; other men were too easy for her. "In Mike," Eddie said, "Liz finally found a man who could dominate her."

Debbie was shocked at the tempestuousness of Elizabeth and Mike's love affair. Mike Todd called Elizabeth insulting and obscene names; he bragged about "fuck[ing]" her in mixed company. He *struck* her. But Elizabeth seemed to . . . *like* it. There was much that this Nazarene girl did not know, even after years of stardom. (The physical violence Elizabeth Taylor seemed to enjoy even shocked Eddie, who at least attempted a more sophisticated outlook.)

Elizabeth became pregnant with Mike Todd's baby, and in exchange for the house they lived in together and much else they had maritally shared, Michael Wilding obliged her with a quickie divorce. Eddie was Mike's best man at the couple's Acapulco wedding on February 2, 1957, and Debbie, the matron of honor, washed and set Elizabeth's hair before the ceremony. In August 1957, Elizabeth bore Mike Todd a daughter, Liza.

Debbie had become pregnant again in May. According to Eddie, whose account of their marriage is enormously cynical, he had recently come back from a singing engagement in Israel, and he was ready to move out and divorce Debbie when she announced, "I am with child." On February 4, 1958, when Carrie was a little less than a year and a half old, Todd Emmanuel was born. "Todd came into the world smiling," Debbie said. His disposition would remain easygoing, while his older sister's was complex and intense. He was named after Mike Todd. The Jewish religion forbids naming a baby for a living person, but Eddie loved Mike too much to follow custom.

A month and a half after Todd Fisher's birth, on March 22, Mike Todd was en route back to his bride in L.A., aboard a private twin-engine plane he had hired. Overloaded and flying at the wrong altitude in bad weather, the plane ran into peril, lost an engine, and crashed in New Mexico. Todd and the three others on board were killed. Elizabeth was waiting for him at their Beverly Hills canyon home on Schuyler Road when she learned of his death. Hysterically bereft, she and Liza were quickly, temporarily, secreted into her mother's English cottage on the 600 block of Elm Drive. These tree-filled blocks were usually impeccably quiet, bearing no traffic. But on the days after Todd's death, reporters' cars blocked the street. The media sensed this tragedy was very big. Did they have a sixth sense that it would get bigger?

As one of Mike Todd's closest friends, Eddie Fisher consoled Todd's widow while Debbie was preoccupied with her new baby and toddler. She thought that she and Eddie were finally making their marriage work. Industry rumors whispered of an affair between Eddie and Elizabeth, beginning in August, but Debbie seems to have not believed them.

While Eddie and Elizabeth were carrying on clandestinely, the Reynolds-Fisher family gave another cover story to Louella Parsons at *Modern Screen*. "Our Family" idealized the 1950s family of four: a loving Debbie holding little Todd and an equally cherishing Eddie holding Carrie, who is (as usual in these pictures) strikingly unsmiling as she pats her baby brother's head. The article started, as usual, with Carrie, ecstatically jumping up and down in the swimming pool, calling, "Daddy! Dad-dy!" and displaying her brand-new "tiny teeth like pearls." In her caption accompanying a heartbreakingly sweet image of Eddie and Carrie, Louella wrote, "Here's one family I have a strong feeling will never be separated for any length of time."

Yet Eddie and Elizabeth were both in New York in late summer. On a night in early September, Debbie was at Edie Adams's house for a dinner party, she recalls in her memoir *Debbie: My Life*. She overheard one guest whisper to another, "Does Debbie know?" Debbie went home and called Eddie at his hotel, the Essex House. The phone in his room rang numerous times before she hung up. She guessed Elizabeth was staying at the Plaza, and after calling that hotel and asking for Miss Taylor and getting an operator's "I'm sorry but there is no answer," Debbie toughened up and switched gears. She called again, imitating a secretary's voice and said she was calling Eddie Fisher for Dean Martin. It was the middle of the night in New York. Eddie answered the phone in Elizabeth's room, jovially greeting a supposedly insomniac Dean Martin.

"It's not Dean, Eddie, it's Debbie."

"Oh, shit."

Eddie arrived back home the next day, professing his love for Elizabeth. An angry Debbie said, "She doesn't love you. She'll never love you. You're not her type." Debbie did not want to give up on their marriage, and Eddie reluctantly agreed to see a marriage counselor, and with the press now assembled in front of their house, the two ran through a neighbor's yard into a car to get to the appointment. After the fruitless session with the counselor, Debbie conceded. A studio publicist arrived at their house and announced to the assembled reporters, "A separation exists between Eddie and Debbie. No further action is being taken at this time."

While Maxene took care of baby Todd, Debbie grabbed Carrie and dashed off with her to spend the night at the home of the dancers Marge and Gower Champion. She still had Todd's diaper pins pinned to her blouse, and the photograph of the wronged wife and good mother went the 1958 version of viral. Eddie claimed this was a deliberate play for sympathy; Debbie denied it. In the glare of the cameras and emotion, Carrie Frances Fisher, so long a prop for her perfect family, was now a surrogate for her mother's humiliated abandonment but refusal to end the marriage. "I do not intend to file for divorce," Debbie said to the television cameras.

Eddie left the house abruptly—she sent him his clothes—"but he never came by to see Carrie and Todd," Debbie said. "I didn't want them to notice. I wanted them to love their father, no matter how I felt." Debbie much later said that she could forgive Eddie any number of things, "but not that he didn't come back and see the children." She told her children the reason "was that he was out earning a living to support us."

In fact, after two months of receiving child support, Debbie got no further money from Eddie. She has explained it this way in her memoir: "Eddie wanted the divorce right away," and "he wanted to pay alimony, not child support, in order to get a tax break." Debbie wrote that she refused to give him the quickie divorce, and that refusal was the reason he stopped sending money altogether. She apparently never took him to court over the presumed breach. This was a pattern that would continue for the rest of her life. When it came to husbands and money, Debbie would always get the short end of the stick.

The scandal made headlines for months. At one point, there were so many paparazzi camped out in front of their house that Ray Reynolds took to standing on the lawn, shooing them away Texas-style: with a rifle.

On February 19, 1959, Debbie and Eddie were officially divorced. On May 12, Eddie and Elizabeth married at Temple Beth Sholom in Las Vegas on the heels of one of his nightclub appearances. Elizabeth had converted to Judaism through Rabbi Max Nussbaum of Los Angeles's Temple Israel, and the Las Vegas wedding was extolled, in *Modern Screen*, by Eddie's good friend and secretary Gloria Luchenbill. Mike Todd Jr. was the best man; Elizabeth's three children—Michael and Christopher Wilding and Liza Todd—attended. Carrie and Todd did not. The article was so cloyingly happy—so full of family and folksiness ("I'll take good care of him, Mom," Elizabeth said to Eddie's mother as they left for their honeymoon in Europe)—that anyone reading it as a proxy for two-and-a-half-year-old Carrie Fisher might have felt hurt by it.

Some months later, *Modern Screen* ran another article. Eddie and Elizabeth were in England, and the article included paragraphs relating Carrie's excitement when her father would make transoceanic telephone calls to her and her pleas for him to fly back and see her. When he said he couldn't yet, she'd "nod a brave little nod and say, 'Yes, Daddy, not today.'" The article concluded with the end of one such conversation. "About Todd she says, 'He eats his cereal. He plays with me sometimes. He walks now, Daddy.'" And, "'I take your picture and I kiss it . . . I ask Nurse to play the record you made, and you sing for me, for Carrie.'"

However enhanced that anecdote might have been, there was truth in it. Debbie said that one day, Eddie made a date to see the children and didn't show: "Carrie, just three years old, stood on the couch looking out the window for her daddy who never came." Many years later,

Todd Fisher's wife, Catherine Hickland, would tell a friend of Carrie's, "Carrie said that her parents' divorce *almost killed her.*" When she embarked on deep acting training with Marilyn Fried, after being cast as Princess Leia, Carrie tapped into the wounds of her childhood: "His leaving affected her terribly!" exclaims Marilyn, recalling their sessions. In late adulthood, Carrie and Eddie would forge a relationship. It would not be a typical father-daughter relationship; it would be something more edgy, poignant, bizarre, generous, and cynical. Nevertheless, a part of the very adult Carrie would, with it all, remain a child. She wrote in *The Princess Diarist,* "I knew in my heart that the only rationale he could have had for leaving was because of how big a disappointment I must have been."

Debbie started dating Harry Karl, a homely but extravagantly wealthy self-made shoe-empire magnate, about a year after the divorce and following a brief romance with the actor Glenn Ford. Karl had already been married to three different women, and one of those wives he had married, divorced, remarried, and *re*-divorced.

Debbie met Harry through the charity she co-founded, the Thalians, devoted to children's mental health and attached to the new Cedars-Sinai, the high-profile melding of two of the biggest L.A. hospitals: the older Cedars of Lebanon, which at the time was *the* hospital in L.A. (its imposing, V-shaped building is now the headquarters of Scientology) and the newer Mount Sinai. She went on a date with Karl to the Luau, a Beverly Hills restaurant owned by Lana Turner's husband, Steve Crane, in hopes of soliciting a large Thalians donation from him. The starstruck and impetuous Harry, who at forty-seven was almost twice Debbie's age, proposed on that first date. When she said no, he turned around and abruptly married Joan Cohn, the widow of the president of Columbia Pictures, Harry Cohn, and *they* divorced after twenty-one days of marriage. This was the Hollywood of the late 1950s and early '60s—multiple marriages, status matings, bizarrely overly quick marriages, no such thing as merely living together for people of a certain age—and eccentric, self-made wealth: Harry Karl had a barber come to his house daily to groom his hair, and he had two hundred pairs of shoes. He had been—at least as the story he told Debbie went—a literal orphan, rescued on the street by his adoptive mother, whose husband, Pincus Karl, was a cobbler turned shoe manufacturer. The gossip columnists who had championed Debbie after the breakup with Eddie now cautioned her not to marry Harry. "He gambles," Hedda Hopper warned. But after a sufficient length of time spent proudly rebuffing Harry's many-times-a-day phone entreaties and his apology gifts for having married Joan Cohn on the rebound, Debbie decided to marry him. "For the first time in my life I felt lonely and frightened," she wrote. "I had a big career and I knew not one thing about business. I had children to bring up. I felt I was in a very exposed position. Harry was older and urbane and wealthy and thoughtful. I wasn't deeply attracted to him physically. But I wasn't unattracted to him either, because he was so kind and loving and companionable."

Harry's money—and Debbie's presumption of its legitimacy—was a comforting advantage to her. Debbie seemed to love bragging about the unnecessarily large staff of servants she had with Harry; Carrie chalked it up to her mother's childhood poverty. Debbie used to go, alone, to her little-sister-like friend Elizabeth Ashley's parties, thrown with Elizabeth's husband, George Peppard. The difficult George liked Debbie; she razzed him about his drinking, and he enjoyed her chutzpah for doing so. There, Debbie would breezily say, as Ashley recalls it, "Uncle Shoe isn't here because he's out there making money." Debbie would prove to be very naive about this assumption.

TWO

A COMPLICATED CHILDHOOD

Did your mother ever put you to bed?" Carrie asked her new English friend, the fellow Central School of Speech and Drama student Selina Cadell.

Selina was surprised at the question from "the American girl"—no one knew much about Carrie—whom she had first met when that seventeen-year-old girl was in a very vulnerable situation.

"Yes, my mother put me to bed," Selina answered.

"What did she do when she put you to bed?" Carrie wanted to know.

"I said, 'She told me a story.' I could see this look in Carrie's eye"—envy and surprise. "I said, 'What happened to *you?*' Carrie said she and Todd would often sit on the stairs waiting for someone to remember to put them to bed. She said she fell asleep on the stairs quite often. And"—embellishing the point that Carrie's was an oddly privileged *and* wanting childhood—"she asked me if my mother could teach her how to cook."

Though Carrie was probably exaggerating about the number of

nights she fell asleep on the stairs, "Debbie's life"—after the divorce from Eddie and beyond her marriage to and divorce from what would be a disastrous second husband—"was not that of a normal mother," Selina deduced. Toward the end of her life, Carrie admitted, with typical irony, that the only way she was sure to be able to have any time with her hardworking mother (who, still tied to the factorylike MGM studio system, was making four movies a year on top of nightclub performances) was to create an unusual sleeping arrangement. She would sleep not in her own fairy-tale-lovely bedroom but on the floor—on the "white carpet on my mother's side of the bed [that Debbie shared with her husband, Harry Karl], huddled under my pink blanket." The experience was funny from the distance of decades. The house was "a multimillion-dollar mansion," the older Carrie wrote, but cramped on the floor next to her mother, "we lived in it as though it was a shack in the Appalachians." In Selina Cadell's fielding of Carrie's strange questions, she saw the sad part without the irony. "Carrie's need to be loved was simply way overlooked—not on purpose. Debbie adored Carrie, but she didn't put any boundaries on her," Selina would come to understand from many conversations with Carrie. "And there were vacancies—gaping abysses—in Carrie's childhood, things she never had."

Carrie told another friend that when Debbie would come home after a long day's labor and young Carrie craved her mother's attention, an exhausted Debbie would sometimes give her daughter half an adult tranquilizer to quiet her down. Or, because young Carrie, according to her brother in his book *My Girls*, always had a hard time sleeping, Debbie would sometimes give her an over-the-counter sleeping pill. Even very young, Carrie was intense. Debbie recalled that once, when Carrie was four, she hit two-year-old Todd on the head with a plastic baseball bat and, according to Debbie, "knocked him out." But brother harbored no bad feelings for sister, and he opened his eyes with a smile on his face. It went deeper than that. As Todd Fisher would put it in his book, "Since Carrie was a child, the constant noise in her head had made her prone to being overwhelmed by her own mind." This was the unnamed, nascent bipolar disorder—from the insomnia to the voices in her head—that would plague Carrie throughout her life.

Carrie's was a complicated girlhood lived in, and bigger than, the sweet small town that was Beverly Hills in the early 1960s. She attended the Paul Henreid Cotillion, where the kids learned the cha-cha and the waltz and, as if it were 1955, the boys had to dress in suits and ties, the girls in white dresses and white gloves. She had ice cream at quaint, tiny Wil Wright's on Beverly and Charleville, where each scoop was accompanied by a single macaroon in a cellophane packet, and at Blum's around the corner, which featured the rich Almondette sundae. Between the two stood Jax, where stunning, skinny beatnik-influenced actresses bought their Geistex sweaters and next-gen toreador pants, and down the street was Lanz, whose tender 1950s nightgowns and blouses were its opposite. Carrie, and others, did all of this just before the culture flipped to the political activism, drug use, and rock-hero deaths of the late 1960s.

But she was also always Debbie's daughter. "And when Debbie walked into a room, everybody stopped eating their hors d'oeuvres and it was, 'My God! Debbie's here!'" says Donavan Freberg, whose sister, Donna junior, would be in Carrie's high school friendship circle. The Frebergs—the satirist and advertising eminence Stan and the producer Donna senior—were close to the singer Rosemary Clooney, who was married on and off to the actor José Ferrer and raising their brood of five, including Miguel and Gabriel. Both couples were close to the Boones, the Christian country-pop superstar Pat Boone (who had been the "good boy" heartthrob pitted against the "bad boy" Elvis in the 1950s) and his wife, Shirley, and their kids: this group was a safe haven of family feeling in Beverly Hills.

They were moral people. All three families—the Frebergs, Ferrers, and Boones—adamantly refused to sign the secret anti-Negro restrictive covenant that customarily attended house purchases in Beverly Hills in the 1950s. (When Johnny Mathis bought his mansion on Elm and Sunset during that decade, the wealthy and gentle hit-making bal-ladeer had to have his white manager, Helen Noga, officially purchase it for him.) Donna Freberg Sr. and Rosemary Clooney were feminists before their time—"the dames of Hollywood; they didn't take shit from men," says Donavan—and strong mothers whose doors were al-ways open to the needy or troubled friends of their kids'. The three families kept links through the next generation: Donna junior mar-ried her teenage sweetheart Todd Fisher, and Donavan became Todd's kid-brother-like sidekick for years. Gabriel "Gabry" Ferrer married his childhood sweetheart, Pat Boone's daughter Debby; they are married still. Miguel Ferrer became one of Carrie's lifelong best friends. Then there was Gavin de Becker.

At ten, Gavin had witnessed his mother trying to shoot his step-father, and at sixteen he had watched his mother die of a heroin overdose. Thus violently orphaned and gravely wise beyond his years, Gavin was taken in as a permanent part of the Ferrer family for sev-eral years and then by the Frebergs for two years, and soon he spent so much time at Carrie's house he almost lived there, too. There weren't supposed to be orphans in Beverly Hills, but they existed. The Fre-bergs, Ferrers, and Boones were a buoyant, anchoring group, and Deb-bie and Carrie and Todd were part of it, emotionally and by marriage.

But Debbie was always the scene-stealer, Donavan Freberg noticed. Debbie's fame—in 1965, she was nominated for a Best Actress Acad-emy Award for her starring role in *The Unsinkable Molly Brown* and the third U.S. manned space capsule was officially named *The Molly Brown*—made Carrie a kind of second-fiddle daughter to her mother.

Carrie developed her theatricality. When she was four and five, she began performing little plays she'd written, in her closet, for Todd and Debbie. By the time she entered elementary school at El Rodeo, "Carrie was charisma personified—always the center of attention," says Nancie Lewis Levey, who was on the painful outer edge of Carrie's school clique. "She never talked about her celebrity connections; she was always try-ing to be normal. But she would do things like talk about movies she saw—like *Buona Sera, Mrs. Campbell,* starring Gina Lollobrigida—that weren't for kids. Everyone was transfixed with her sophistication. She was always whispering things to her cronies, things that us lesser forms of girlhood were not privy to. It was just the kind of thing I wanted to be part of but never was."

When Princess Margaret visited Beverly Hills, a motorcade was planned in front of El Rodeo, with the students and teachers standing behind a rope line. While waiting for it, Carrie entertained her class-mates by singing and letting a few of them know that as far as celebri-ties were concerned, *her* family had access to many as famous as the princess.

"A lot was expected of Carrie," says Lynn Pollack, Harry Karl's niece. "She was supposed to be the really cute, really good Hollywood movie star kid, and although big perks came with that, which she took advantage of, so did a lot of pressure and difficulty and anguish. I felt jealous of her *and* sorry for her at the same time."

Lynn, one year older than Carrie, saw Carrie and Todd as somewhat neglected. Although Debbie wrote sincerely of Harry's devotion to his two stepchildren—and photographs reflect that—there was this: while Harry bought and was refurbishing for the family a large house on Greenway Drive, on the western edge of Beverly Hills, the new family of four technically lived in *another* Karl house on Sunset, but, as Lynn recalls, Harry and Debbie spent most nights at the adjacent Beverly Hills Hotel. Carrie and Todd were left in the nearly full-time care of a governess named Dottie Wolf. "She was a proper, old-school govern-ess in a tidy white uniform. You wouldn't dare call her something as insulting as a nanny," Lynn says. Dottie was a strict disciplinarian "and a little crazy, and she had a very short fuse. She would smack Carrie and Todd around when they were bratty—which was probably a lot. Really! When the children 'misbehaved,' Dottie chased them around and beat them with a wooden spoon."

Years later, Carrie spoke with gruff candor of Dottie's toughness and that of her grandmother Maxene. "When I was young, I was raised more by my grandmother and this nanny named Dottie Wolf—who was just like that name makes her sound. They both used to say just awful things to my brother and me." Maxene was especially hard on Debbie—"What are you, still asleep?" Carrie would remember Maxene ragging Debbie "when she'd done two shows the night before." And, "when my brother was two years old, I remember him saying to my grandmother, 'Do we do anything right?' So that's the climate we grew up in. My mother would go away and do a film and we'd stay," she said, in an atypically (but perhaps admiringly) tough characterization of the grandmother for whom she otherwise showed affection and respect, "with those two bitches."

For a while, Carrie and Todd and Debbie and Harry had Friday night dinners with Lynn's mother, Harry's sister, at her enormous house on Sunset and Hillcrest. Maxene and Ray Reynolds attended. Even though the Karls and Pollacks were Jewish, Christian prayers were said with heads bowed before forks were lifted. "Carrie rolled up her eyes at it," Lynn recalls. "She rolled up her eyes a *lot*. She loved to get out from the dinner table with all these people talking, so we'd go and play a game called Chocolate Ears—a make-believe game, looking for a chocolate bunny. We would put on makeup and do our hair and sometimes get a jar of Vitalis, grease our hair, and pretend we were boys. It was stupid stuff, less for her to play with me than for her to irritate the governess."

Debbie and Harry's own house on Sunset was lavish. When the filmmaker Lawrence Schiller was starting out as a photographer, he trained his Leica on Debbie at the Sunset house and then, excusing himself and going to the bathroom, saw "the most incredible Renoir, ten inches opposite the toilet," he says. "I said, 'Debbie, why do you have a Renoir in the bathroom?' And she said, pointing to another painting, 'Look at this Picasso! When people come to the house they always get so goddamn drunk they never appreciate the paintings that I love, so I put them in the bathroom, where they'll *have* to see them.'" Schiller saw a different Debbie from the perky Tammy he'd expected. "I felt her strength. I'd felt strength from Bette Davis and Deborah

Kerr. But here was an unexpected strength in Debbie. You knew that Bette Davis and Deborah Kerr were run over by a lot of Mack trucks, but now Debbie got run over by her first Mack truck—Eddie—on a lonesome highway. She'd toughened up."

Debbie invited Schiller to Las Vegas, where she was appearing at the Riviera, and it was here that he snapped the now-iconic photograph of little Carrie just offstage, seemingly adoringly watching her mother perform. Debbie went through many costume changes—a clown one moment, a tuxedo the next—"and I'm in the wings and all of a sudden I see a nanny bringing Carrie, and Carrie is peeking around the curtain," Schiller recalls. "So the woman brings the stool and Carrie climbs up—and I aim my camera." Right after that, Debbie, as she often did, took Carrie by one hand and Todd by the other and brought them onstage to introduce them to her fans. "Debbie is talking to the audience about her kids and," in a telling act of childhood anger, "Carrie is *dragging* her mother offstage," Schiller recalls.

"I had to share [my mother] and I didn't like that," Carrie later said. First, there was sharing her on the stage. Then, "when we went out, people sort of walked over me to get to her." Schiller spent the rest of the evening photographing Carrie riding her tricycle up and down the hotel hall before going to sleep in a room with her preschool paintings taped to the wall. From babyhood on, Vegas hotels were a second home. And from girlhood on—whether pulling her mother offstage or joining her *on*stage—she was part of her mother's Vegas show.

The house at 813 Greenway, overlooking the Los Angeles Country Club, was actually two joined houses. It was avant-garde "modern" and forbidding on the outside: stacks of open cubes of white marble connected by horizontal and vertical planks. Carrie, who would eventually become a serious collector of warm and witty folk art, thought it offensively impersonal. "It looked more like a place where you'd get your passport stamped than a house," she said. The property was a behemoth, with edgy architectural details that made it resemble, she said, an "air conditioner." The house was always filled with people—assistants, a concierge couple, Harry's butler, and maids, all uniformed—and music: show tunes, sound tracks, people at the piano.

"What a house!" remembers Nancie Lewis Levey, the girl on the outside of Carrie's social circle. "Very sharp angles, lots of rooms, beautiful furniture—*a castle!* Outside there was a swimming pool. There was pool water all around the house, where everything flowed into the big pool through skinny little moats. Carrie's bedroom looked like something out of Buckingham Palace, a canopied bed, girly all the way. And she had a tree in her house, a fake tree with all long branches." Carrie's grandfather Ray had built her a log cabin in the back as a retreat. Carrie wanted for nothing. "Her room was filled with 'troll dolls'—Barbies were history. Carrie had such a vast collection of troll dolls, which we girls called 'dammit dolls'—nobody had more dolls than Carrie—that I was green with envy." But when Nancie, then a plump and somewhat ungainly girl, tried to touch one of Carrie's "dammit dolls," Carrie said a resolute *no*. There was a mean-girl streak, as well as a woundedness (perhaps flip sides of the same coin), in Carrie.

Debbie loved to give parties, and as Todd Fisher recalls in *My Girls*, the "family friends" who flocked to their Greenway house included old Hollywood legends: James Stewart, Judy Garland, Cary Grant, and Groucho Marx. A frequent guest was the distinguished actress Agnes Moorehead, thirty-two years older than Debbie and a very close friend.

There are four lower-to-middle schools (then called elementary schools) in Beverly Hills, going up to eighth grade. Hawthorne and El Rodeo are north of Santa Monica, where the sometimes elegant but close-together Beverly Hills Flats homes and the grander homes north of Sunset exist. Horace Mann and Beverly Vista are south, below Charleville, where the smaller houses and the apartment houses are. In Beverly Hills, living north of Santa Monica was long considered a somewhat cliché status-delineating marker: north was wealthy; south was poorer. By the time the eighth-grade graduates from all four schools merged together as the entering freshman class of Beverly Hills High—a lovely, blocks-long English Norman building set on a massive tiered front lawn on the elegantly curved Moreno Drive—the cruel but democratic values of teenage life would usually take over. Whether you were the child of an entertainment eminence or millionaire industrialist and his wife, or of a single-mother secretary or hairdresser (and these women, living in rental apartments, often mothered the prettiest girls), what mattered was what mattered in any high school: how cool and attractive and peer-group appealing you were.

But at the time that Carrie and her friends were entering El Rodeo elementary school, in 1962, a certain degree of deference was starting to be paid to the children of celebrities, and there were many of them. Among Carrie's fellow students were Karen Caesar, daughter of Sid Caesar; James Coburn's daughter, Lisa; Buddy Hackett's son, Sandy; and Lee Grant's daughter Dinah Manoff. Dean Martin's kids attended a nearby private school, and Jamie Lee and Kelly Curtis, daughters of Janet Leigh and Tony Curtis, went to Hawthorne. Still, Carrie's life as an El Rodeo first grader was normal; Carrie and Todd rode their bikes to school—roughly two blocks from their house—at least until the December day in 1963 when Frank Sinatra Jr. was kidnapped, and celebrities' children became presumed targets.

On Carrie's ninth birthday, Harry Karl's ex-wife Marie McDonald died of an overdose. Harry and Marie had two adopted children, Denice and Harrison, and a biological daughter, Tina, close to Carrie's age. Debbie rushed over and saw how needy Tina was. Debbie would view her, as she put it in *Debbie: My Life*, as someone she wanted deeply to help. Over Harry's objections, Debbie moved Tina into their home. With stagy flippancy, Carrie described it this way in *Wishful Drinking*: "Marie ended up overdosing and passing on. But now there are three children left. 'What shall we do with them? Ah! Let's send them to Harry and Debbie . . . Let's put [Tina] in *Carrie's* room.'"

The line evoked huge laughter. But it wasn't a laughing matter, and perhaps Debbie might have better predicted the inevitable clash between the privileged and intense Carrie, already vying with fans for her busy mother's time and attention, already sleeping on the floor just to be next to her mother, and the more chaotically raised Tina, who begged Debbie to let her call her "Mother," too. Tina's relationship "became a competition with Carrie," Debbie recalled of what might have seemed an inevitable outcome. "Whatever Carrie wanted, Tina wanted, too. If Carrie learned a certain piece on the piano, Tina would learn it, too."

A classmate of Carrie's who later became a clinical psychologist saw the cobbled-together family—Debbie, Harry, Carrie, and Tina—eating ice cream at Wil Wright's one night and could see something was wrong: there seemed to be a tense or unpleasant atmosphere. Another friend of Carrie's at the time says that Tina and Carrie butted heads a lot, and Carrie, at nine, "was already getting unhappy with her mom's marriage to Harry."

"Tina was treated like the black sheep," says Lynn Pollack. "She was a troubled child, and a big animosity started. She was a victim of Carrie. Carrie was mean to Tina. Actually, I wouldn't say Tina was *that* much more troubled than Carrie. She was just more open about it. My mother tried to help her. My mother loved Tina." At around this time, "when I'd visit Carrie on Greenway, I'd come into her room and see her writing feverishly in her diary. She could *really* write."

"Words saved me from a lot of stuff," Carrie later said of this fraught time. "Books were my first drug. I was called a bookworm, and not in a good way."

In the midst of this unusual upbringing, Carrie became the most cheerfully all-American thing: a Brownie and then a Girl Scout. Debbie was the leader of Carrie's Girl Scout troop. Having loved being a Burbank Girl Scout, Debbie felt it was very important for her to perpetuate the tradition, so much so that she arranged to get Wednesdays off from the filming of her movie *The Singing Nun* to be able to preside over meetings at the Greenway house. In jeans and a ponytail and strumming a guitar, Debbie would lead her slightly eye-rolling daughter and her daughter's less sardonic friends in old-fashioned hymns—"White wings, they never grow weary; they carry us cheerily over the sea"— and the pop hit of the 1940s "Mairzy Doats." The girls adored her, and scout leading seemed to bring out an essential, pre-fame Debbie. The troop sold thin mint and peanut butter cookies door-to-door, up and down the streets of Beverly Hills, from Carmelita to Sunset, and they spent overnights at a seminary bunker and toasted s'mores over a campfire. Another troopmate's mother came and gave them sewing lessons.

And they had perks that other Girl Scout troops didn't have: not-yet-released movies in the Greenway screening room. There were visits to film sets, weekend trips to Carrie's houses in Malibu and Palm Springs, troop photos taken with Debbie's friend Omar Sharif. For the troop's "flying up" ceremony—where a Brownie acquires wings and "flies up" to become a Girl Scout—Debbie rushed into the auditorium rented for the event wearing her *Singing Nun* costume—a proper religious habit—and stormed onto the stage, handing out diplomas and sashes. "Debbie was a photo bomber before they invented the word," Lynn Pollack says, "and Carrie resented her for it."

Having a movie-star mother was difficult and would become an abiding issue between them. But Carrie had her own diva moments. One was at her ninth birthday party, Nancie Lewis Levey recalls. It was held at the other Karl house—Lynn Pollack's parents' house—on Sunset. "It was a big brown-and-white Tudor building on a lot of property," remembers Nancie. "You came in the gates and there was a manufactured forest. There were paths and trees and rocks, and in the middle of the forest was a big hollowed-out seating area, with seats built into the rocks; it truly looked built for royalty. All the presents filled up this whole large table. And Carrie got a puppy, a Dalmatian named Natalie.

And"—this was the imperious Carrie—"you didn't touch that puppy. You didn't go near her. *'Don't you put your dirty hands on my dog!'* Carrie's attitude was like a dictator." So, other than the girls in her core group of best friends, "we didn't touch the puppy, and we were not allowed to venture beyond the forest until our parents came." Nancie suffered other unhappy moments from Carrie. Once, at the Greenway house, Carrie was particularly difficult. Not only did she tell Nancie there were monsters in the pool and Nancie couldn't go in, but in the large kitchen "Carrie got a step stool and reached up to the cookie jar and took out ten Oreos. I asked her if I could have one. Carrie said, 'No, they're my special snack.'" Nancie burst into tears. Debbie's assistant, Connie Freiberg, came downstairs and straightened out the conflict, as she often did. "She said, 'Carrie, you have to share with Nancie.' Carrie gave me an if-looks-could-kill look and said, 'I don't have to do anything I don't want to.' Connie got Carrie to come around. Connie was a lovely girl who was a very big influence in keeping Carrie sane and making things right." Connie, one of Carrie's closest, most loyal friends for decades, has said, "Carrie was more interesting than any [adults] I'd ever known."

Later, in their freshman year of high school, Carrie did something unusual. She went out of her way to seek Nancie out. "I want you to know I owe you an apology for the way I treated you," Carrie said. Nancie had moved on and become more confident. She was defensively cool in response; Carrie *had* hurt her deeply. But in retrospect, Carrie's apology seems like an uncommonly mature, decent, and classy gesture for one so young, indicating an empathy that would flourish later.

In second grade, Carrie would become lifetime best friends with May Quigley, whose father was the producer of *The Hollywood Squares*. Like many Beverly families, May had one Jewish parent (her mother) and one Christian parent (her father)—the opposite of Carrie, but the same mix. They lived close to each other, May in a beautiful house in the canyon, and would remain living close to each other through much of their adult lives.

At El Rodeo, Carrie and May were "hilariously funny," a mutual friend says. When they were eleven, in 1967, they performed "Do You Love Me?" from *Fiddler on the Roof* for the class talent show, dressed in old Jewish shtetl costumes. "Carrie and May had something called a 'goddess' pact," this friend says, proclaiming their specialness.

Aside from the ever-important May, Carrie's preteen posse consisted of three girls who emulated her and imitated her. Kathy Avchen, Kimme Brunk, and Alison Roden flanked Carrie. These four were the popular girls, with Carrie easily the most popular of all. "They were such a clique, you could run their names together—Kathy-Kimme-Alison-Carrie, with Carrie always at the center," say Nancie Lewis Levey. Carrie, with her sand-colored hair, was the only blond in the group. Kathy, Kimme, and Alison dressed like Carrie (eventually, bouncy miniskirts and white kneesocks and ballet-type slippers) and wore their hair like Carrie: center-parted and straight (sometimes with the help of a straightening iron) and far past their shoulders. Carrie's hair flowed down to the high middle of her chest in waves, and she "ratted" it—back combed it—at the crown, as was the style. Carrie, at twelve and thirteen, had such a good figure (as the compliment went at the time)—full breasts, tiny waist, five feet one, and always so tan she seemed olive-skinned—that she could pull off a bikini like a starlet. With her round, serious brown eyes, upturned nose, and heart-shaped face, she was distinctive looking and "cute" at once.

Many of the boys at El Rodeo seemed to have crushes on Carrie. These included Willie Breton, who eventually became an ultra-Orthodox rabbi in Israel with, one friend estimated, ten children; and Michael Lubell, considered the cutest boy in the school, who, failing to land Carrie, tried to use Carrie to get to Kathy Avchen. There was also Richie Stone, who was short and "had a laugh that could shake trees," a classmate says. But Carrie held off. "Only someone like Morgan Mason," the handsome and prematurely adultlike son of James and Pamela Mason who eventually married Belinda Carlisle, the lead singer of the Go-Gos, "would have been good enough for Carrie," a friend says. There might have been another—graver—factor in her holding off on a boyfriend. In her early thirties, Carrie told her acting coach Alice Spivak that Eddie had reentered her life at about the end of her elementary school years "and had approached her sexually." Carrie's words to Alice—according to Alice—were, "He finally came back into my life—and the first thing he did was make a pass at me." Was Carrie exaggerating for effect? Carrie herself described the incident thus: After the years of waiting for him when he didn't show up and resigning herself to the fate of the father-rejected daughter, he looked at her during a rare walk they took together and said, "I see you're developing breasts." In reporting this in *Shockaholic*, Carrie's usual sarcasm deserted her: "It was awkward, to say the least."

At El Rodeo, Carrie's singing talent was noticed. Eloise Haldeman, the school's head of music teaching, nurtured Carrie and made her the star of the school assemblies. Mrs. Haldeman was very conservative, as were other female teachers there, like Mrs. Schenkel, who seemed to have eyes in the back of her head and could *tell* if a girl was wearing forbidden makeup and would turn around and order her into the bathroom to wash her face. As opposed to some of the faculty, the students were staunchly liberal. "It was a rich-hippie school," a classmate remembers. "It was the era of the Vietnam War protests. We sang the song 'Abraham, Martin, and John'"—about the assassinated Lincoln, King, and Kennedy—"at assembly."

Anyone entering a liberal high school in 1969 saw the culture change. There was Woodstock. Much closer to home, there had been the heinous Manson murders, which cast a pall of terror on the entire film community. The edgier kids at El Rodeo were doing drugs, and everyone was listening to FM radio, then an esoteric pipeline to hipness. Carrie became an enormous fan of Joni Mitchell, whose decorous Canadian–turned–Laurel Canyon plaintiveness and long-skirted-maiden presentation could not have been more different from her own Beverly

Hills movie-star-daughter panache. But there was the sharp beginning of a common-sensibility bond (that would, much later, blossom into a two-tough-broads friendship). In two years, when Joni's masterpiece, *Blue*, was released, Carrie would find herself playing and replaying Joni's mournful and self-deprecating Christmas song, "River." She listened to the song repeatedly on the record player and played it herself on the piano. The refrain of "River"—"Oh, I wish I had a river I could skate away on"—had the same wish of self-erasure as the Mark Strand lines that Carrie later used as the epigraph to one of her books: "In a field / I am the absence / of field . . . / Wherever I am / I am what is missing." It would mirror Carrie's dark sadness and self-destructiveness back to her.

For now, another song—and a singing duo—were seizing her attention. Paul Simon and Art Garfunkel were two boys from Queens who had specialized in thoughtful songs that took soft rock up a few elegant notches. Together, they were the voice of sensitive upscale young male seekers. Their 1966 hit "Scarborough Fair," with its courtly first lines—"Are you going to Scarborough Fair? / Parsley, sage, rosemary, and thyme / Remember me to one who lives there / She once was a true love of mine"—represented the pre–Summer of Love moment when still-somewhat-hidden young members of the counterculture took on the clothes, affect, and romance of earlier centuries. So respected had Simon and Garfunkel been by the staunchly Bay Area–loyal Grateful Dead that in 1967 when the L.A. music producer Lou Adler was trying to entice the fervently anticommercial Dead to appear at the Monterey Pop Festival, it was Paul Simon whom Adler sent as an emissary; Paul was *that* authentic, that unslick. Short, Jewish, book smart, the stably raised son of a professor (and musician) and a schoolteacher, Simon was the writer of the pair, while tall, curly-haired, offbeat-handsome Garfunkel had the far more affecting singing voice: high, romantic, yearning, like a Jewish choirboy. Their second hit, the theme song "Mrs. Robinson" for the 1967 movie *The Graduate*, was wittier and less earnest than "Scarborough Fair" and represented a buoyant side of the anti–Vietnam War movement, as, subtly, did the movie. Dustin Hoffman's star turn had echoed Paul Simon's singer-songwriter eminence. Short, unconventionally handsome young Jewish men: this was a new kind of "star" for a more open-minded era.

In January 1970, when Carrie was thirteen and in eighth grade, Simon and Garfunkel released their next album, *Bridge over Troubled Water*, and its title song, with its distinctly gospel sound, became an enormous hit. Simon wrote the song for the woman who would soon become his wife, Peggy Harper. She was from a background very different from his own: working-class, southern, rural. It was intellectual white man's soul, with the same vibe of gallantry as "Scarborough Fair." "When you're weary, feeling small / When tears are in your eyes, I will dry them all," it began. And it was unabashedly hymnlike. In fact, the first time Paul Simon heard the line "Like a bridge over troubled water, I will lay me down," which he *himself* had written, after having adapted it from a gospel song by the Swan Silvertone Singers, he was surprised to find tears in his *own* eyes. Thirteen-year-old Carrie heard in the song a poetry that touched and impressed her. (She would feel equally impressed, a year later, with what would be considered by many the best Simon and Garfunkel offering, "America," with its similarly courtly, grave opening line: "Let us be lovers, we'll marry our fortunes together.")

In the spring of 1970, under the music teacher Eloise Haldeman's guidance, the eighth-grade El Rodeo student Carrie Fisher made "Bridge over Troubled Water" her choice to sing at the schoolwide assembly. She belted heartily, a different take from the original version. The kids were knocked out by it.

When Carrie entered Beverly High in the fall of 1970, the school was at an acme of political activism. After a couple of school-closing protest days, the dress code had been revised, allowing girls to wear pants rather than skirts whose hems fell no more than two inches above the knee, and the lowest-riding, widest-legged Landlubber hip-huggers were now seen on most of the girls. The students had also shut the school down for a more serious cause—antiwar protests. And a program was soon in place to bus in kids from a black neighborhood, albeit an affluent one, Baldwin Hills. There was so much hippie-dippie ecology-mindedness in the air that a student actually "married" a tree on the front lawn. And a large group of Beverly upperclassmen (they called themselves the Stoners) would spend after-school time at the park on Beverly and Santa Monica, getting high on the joints or the diet or sleeping pills they cadged from their parents, popping in and out of Morley's Drugs across the street to use the bathroom. At least one student in this group eventually died of a harder-drugs overdose. During a time when drugs were so in the air, however, it is notable that Carrie Fisher was not on drugs, or not to any discernible excess. That scourge for her would come later.

The two incoming freshmen Carrie now seemed to be best friends with were Donna Freberg and the stunning Gina Martin (Dean Martin's youngest daughter). All three—Carrie, Donna, and Gina—were so thin—"all skinny arms and skinny legs"—that the Stoners referred to them as the Spiders.

"Carrie, Donna, and Gina were popular girls. There was definitely a celebrity aspect to their appeal," says Stephanie Charles, a lawyer now, a Stoner then.

"They were the cool rich kids: 'I've got a lot of money and I'm gonna have a lot of fun,' attitude," says another student. "I remember Donna Freberg for a $17,000 car she got when she turned sixteen; that seemed glamorous."

Carrie also retained her friendship with Kimme Brunk and a girl named Laurie White. Fredrica "Fredi" Duke was a Beverly High girl three years older than Carrie. She watched the girls enter high school as wildly charismatic freshmen. "They were these adorable new girls, and they'd known each other from Brownies and Girl Scouts. I remember on the first day of school Carrie and Laurie White were wearing knit caps like Ali MacGraw wore in *Love Story*. They looked like twins. I asked, 'Why are you wearing them?' They said that they had gotten horrible haircuts and wanted to cover their hair." What they had were actually the first "shag" hairdos, which would soon become the rage.

Carrie and Laurie seemed far too sophisticated to be freshmen. "I was going to ditch school one day—a cool thing to do—so they wanted to come along, and we all ditched together," says Fredi. "We went to Nibbler's"—a popular Wilshire Boulevard coffee shop—"at eleven in the morning." Fredi was knocked out by Carrie in the way that so many people would come to be. "She was ridiculously adult and bright and clever and witty. I don't know if she grew up fast because of her mother and her life story, or if it was all just *in* her, but Carrie was something I had never witnessed before."

Carrie took drama, chorus, and singing classes at Beverly. Lynn Pollack "was now *so* jealous of Carrie," she recalls, "because our family friend, the school's drama teacher, Bill Corrigan, would come over to our house and *rant* about how talented and how fun Carrie was. I was so angry I would leave the room. But he was spot-on."

By her sophomore year at Beverly, Carrie's charisma was soaring. "You'd see her in the hallway there. She stood out," says Jeffrey Sherman, now a producer and a freshman at the time. "She was adorable and sort of outrageous and had this absolute aura about her. I took drama class just to be around her."

Gavin de Becker—whose mother was on food stamps and who lived in a home full of violence—and another male classmate would cadge Carrie's schedule from the office so they could hang out at the door of her class when the period-finishing bell rang. She'd walk out, and, as in a Debbie musical, they'd all burst into song and dance to "Puttin' on the Ritz." Carrie's love of the old Hollywood that her mother was moored in—Carrie had a Cary Grant obsession and felt that Debbie's reviewing, with her, of such vintage gems as *The Philadelphia Story*, *It's a Wonderful Life*, and *Bringing Up Baby* was the equivalent of everyone else's "teddy bears"—was part of her enchantedness. Carrie was also a consummate pianist. "The first time I touched a piano was at Carrie's house when she was playing an Elton John song," recalled de Becker.

"The first time I had sex was also at Carrie's house," he has said. "It wasn't with Carrie, but she arranged it. She let the piano lessons slide, and I stuck with the sex."

When he wasn't living with Rosemary Clooney or the Frebergs, Gavin was essentially living at Carrie's. "There was no one like Gavin de Becker. He is the most brilliant person I ever met," Donavan Freberg says. "Because of the violence in his home, he became a grown-up at eleven, always 'managing' us. Gavin, at fifteen, would say, to cops, 'It's okay, Officer, they're with me,' if one of us was doing something like smoking. He was so square he was hip. He had a mustache before it was a 'thing.' At seventeen he was wearing a suit, like the Secret Service." (Today de Becker is the most noted—and most successful—personal safety authority in America. He devised MOSAIC, which safeguarded the Supreme Court judges; he tailored protection for many celebrities; he wrote the decades-long bestselling book *The Gift of Fear*; and he was the inspiration for Kevin Costner's character in *The Bodyguard*. Most recently, he has been advising and protecting the head of Amazon, Jeff Bezos.)

Two others who would remain friends for life entered Carrie's circle around this time, Charlie Wessler and Griffin Dunne. Charlie would become a film producer (he was part of the team that won the 2019 Best Picture Oscar for *Green Book*). Griffin was a handsome young would-be actor and director/producer, and the son of the then producer (and, later, *Vanity Fair* writer) Dominick Dunne, as well as a nephew by marriage of Joan Didion. He would become Carrie's best friend and her traveling companion, roommate, and running buddy when she moved to New York in the 1970s—and long after.

Like Carrie, Griffin was the child of a sophisticated family full of theatricality, and eventual tragedy: In 1982, Griffin's younger sister Dominique was strangled to death by her psychopathically jealous boyfriend, John Sweeney, a chef at the trendiest restaurant in town, Ma Maison. Sweeney would receive a shockingly light sentence, his crime legally labeled voluntary manslaughter. Pain and fury over that injustice would launch their father, Dominick, into a crime-writing career.

Humor and show-business bonhomie constituted much of Carrie and Griffin's early bond. When she died, Griffin said, "I think every time we were together we thought we were on a show. We would break into song and tap dance." Everything was a performance. Describing their daily repartee, he sang operatically, "'I'm in the baaaathroom . . .' We didn't have a serious moment in all those years."

Carrie was wildly attractive to Gavin and Miguel and Charlie and Griffin, and other boys. Charlie has remembered that he and "about ten" boys would be in the living room of her house after school, "waiting for Carrie to come out of her [log cabin] playhouse," all of them "deeply in love with her, all trying to get her attention. She was the most sexy, adorable fourteen-year-old—cute like you can't believe . . . We'd all be waiting and then we'd hear this deep belting voice singing some show tune, and then she'd come out and say, 'Okay, let's hang out.'" But Carrie gave back, through a blazing generosity that would come to characterize her all her life. Charlie has recalled that she treated her teenage crowd to piles of appetizers at the Luau, the popular Polynesian restaurant in Beverly Hills. And Griffin remembered her paying for his ticket from Colorado back to L.A. and for a room at a hotel for a night with his girlfriend. Carrie always had access to her mother's money and was very generous with it.

Despite how adorable the boys thought her, much later she would deny that she'd felt attractive. She would put the development of her strong personality in modest and self-deprecating terms, describing it as compensation for the belief that she wasn't beautiful. "I knew with the profound certainty of a ten year old that I would not be . . . the beauty that my mother was. I was a clumsy-looking and intensely awkward, insecure girl. I decided then that I'd better develop something else—if I wasn't going to be pretty, maybe I could be funny or smart." For an "intensely awkward, insecure girl," she had a lot of bravado and admirers. Still, her sense of not being a beauty was real. In an unguarded moment, she had harshly snapped, some years later, to a friend, "I know I'm not pretty. I don't need anyone to tell me that." Her woundedness was clear. And insecurity against her mother's sparkling prettiness dogged her.

As Selina Cadell, who would meet Carrie a few years later, says, "If Carrie and Debbie both walked into a room, who were you going to pay attention to? Debbie, of course, not Carrie."

Carrie was immersed in the entirety of classic Hollywood, not just from her mother's life and friendships but also from what would soon be Debbie's new obsession: collecting (literally saving from the dustbins) the costumes and memorabilia of classic musicals. When Carrie was fourteen, MGM, under the new leadership of Kirk Kerkorian, began to unceremoniously off-load its "old" costumes, and Debbie, who had loved those costumes and the movies they represented, was on a mission to preserve them. With Harry Karl's money (really Debbie's money, which Harry had been purloining), she bought a cache of the most delicious garments and accoutrements that had had Americans swooning in their theater seats from the 1940s on. Among them: Audrey Hepburn's white Ascot dress from *My Fair Lady*; Charlie Chaplin's trademark bowler; Julie Andrews's guitar and the von Trapp children's clothes from *The Sound of Music*; a come-hither-to-Rhett-Butler hat Vivien Leigh wore as Scarlett O'Hara in *Gone with the Wind*; Judy Garland's magic red *Wizard of Oz* slippers; and the most famous victim of subway wind spray of all time, Marilyn Monroe's white halter dress in *The Seven Year Itch*. And more. Debbie warehoused these and looked in vain for a venue for a museum. Carrie breathed the air of her mother's passion, and for the rest of her life she would live with old movies blaring from her bedroom TV on Turner Classic Movies (TCM) and old movie anthems issuing from her lips, and her friends' lips, as she sat or walked or danced or got stoned with her friends.

Carrie and Todd had been casually part of their mother's Las Vegas nightclub routines ever since their toddlerhood, when Debbie (in top hat and jaunty shorts) would walk them onstage from the wings. When Carrie was twelve, Debbie started to officially include them in her act.

The children practiced with their mother in the music room of their home on Greenway, with Debbie's friends—a musical director and a choreographer—rehearsing the three of them. Todd reports that Carrie loved the idea of performing, while he preferred to be a cameraman.

Carrie and Todd were temperamentally different. Where Carrie was complex and intense, Todd was simple and easygoing. Where Carrie was intellectual, Todd was driven to engines and tools and mechanics. Says Donavan Freberg, "He'd accompany Debbie to the soundstages, but he wasn't attracted to the stars or interested in hanging with the directors. He was curious about the sound guys. 'Why are you hanging that light over there and what are those props?' He took a shine to the cinematographers and gaffers. And later, if you were with him and your phone would go out, he would go outside and climb up the telephone pole and fix it. He had almost a blue-collar work ethic." But he was also a privileged movie star's kid who got away with having guns in his car because he knew all the Beverly Hills cops and was best friends with Clint Eastwood's son and Michael Landon's son. Todd would spend the entirety of his adult life working for his mother in a hands-on way: on her dance studio, memorabilia collection, and hotel purchases.

Debbie was hustling hard for money now. She had overspent—and would continue to do so—on the memorabilia. She had lost a TV show, *The Debbie Reynolds Show*, because she refused to take cigarette advertising. (She was ahead of her time; two years later, in 1971, such ads would be made illegal.) She was working hard because she *had* to work hard: she was taking roles in a few forgettable movies and had her nightclub act—in Tahoe and Vegas—as well as the *All New Debbie Reynolds Show* (on which Carrie made her TV debut, belting her now-trademark "Bridge over Troubled Water"). Those kept her solvent, while the memorabilia purchases would tear at that solvency.

Summers for Carrie and Todd were now always Las Vegas. "It was fun" having the casino town as her "summer camp," Carrie said. "I was a good mimic, I could do a perfect Streisand, a perfect Garland." But she was different from her peers. As she told Arsenio Hall on his hit

TV show, "As a child, you want to fit in. And that did not enable me to fit in—I was doing nightclub work during the holidays instead of skiing. My mother's world was a quarter of a century older than mine. So I was sort of lost between all the worlds. I was decidedly without a generation."

"The rest of us were marching for Angela Davis, and some of us were getting into trouble and having to transfer to Rexford, the local 'reform' school," says a female classmate. By contrast, "Carrie was dancing and singing with Debbie on vacation. I wonder if some of her problems wouldn't have existed if she had loosened up and rebelled earlier than she did. Then she might have gotten it out of her system"—the antiestablishment sensibility and the untethering from her mother's other-generation world—"and not had to rebel so hard in her twenties."

More than the alienating effect of being separated from her hip contemporaries at Beverly, Carrie seemed to feel deeply insecure about her talent, especially next to that of her razzmatazz mother. "If I made any mistakes," she once said to a friend in reference to her mother's nightclub routine, "it would kind of eat me up." She suffered tremendous stage fright before each performance.

A casual friend of Carrie's saw her torment. Lisa Karlan was a popular Beverly junior with a car when Carrie was a freshman, so for about a year Lisa drove Carrie to their mutual weekly dancing lesson at Elle's (pronounced Ell-ie's) Dance Studio in Westwood. "Carrie wasn't a great dancer; I expected her to be, but there were clearly things she couldn't do. She had two left feet," Lisa says. Lisa was a student body cheerleader as well as a member of the school's elite dance troupe, the Terpsichoreans, better known as the Terpsies. To Lisa, "Carrie was somewhat reserved. She was always turning things over in her mind, deciding what to say and what to withhold." This is certainly very different from the fabled adult Carrie, the wildly boundaryless one. "She was very introspective," Lisa says.

Carrie invited Lisa Karlan to come to Las Vegas to see her, Debbie, and Todd (who accompanied his mother and sister on guitar) at the Desert Inn. It was spring break 1971. "Carrie and I hung out in the daytime and went to Circus Circus," a casino and theme park. "We were stupid teenagers. We went to the pool, we got kicked out of the casino, and we lost track of time and only realized at the last minute it was almost showtime. We made a mad dash to the Desert Inn and got there in the nick of time for Carrie to change"—to a lovely, long, romantic, tight-bodiced dress—"and go onstage with her mom. To Carrie, performing with her mother seemed more of an annoyance than anything. Debbie introduced her and said, 'Carrie can't dance, but she *sure* can sing. Well, I guess Eddie did *something* right.'" Laughter! "Then she sang 'Bridge over Troubled Water.'" As so many others had been, Lisa was flabbergasted: "She had an amazing, rich voice. I thought, I can't look at her the same way anymore, the next time I drive her to dance class. She's a star!"

What Lisa didn't see from her seat in the audience was the trembling and panic that always preceded Carrie's performance, which had to be allayed by Debbie or Todd hugging her to quiet her terror before she stepped onto the stage. But, Todd said in his book, "once the lights would hit her, the terror would transform itself into sheer joy." Great insecurity, then great satisfaction.

"I don't think Carrie *wanted* to be a star," Lisa Karlan says. "She didn't want to be a singer! At least it didn't *seem* that way." Debbie had thought that Carrie wanted to follow her right into the business. "When I first did my act in Vegas, she learned every step, every line," Debbie had said. That Carrie had felt "without a generation," and that the fun was mixed with resentment and a sense of loss, might have been hard for Debbie to grasp. Some footstep following is ambivalent; it feels complexly pre-ordained, seductive, and comfortable, based on almost genetic family knowledge and desire. But it is also involuntary and confused, while a rebel, inside, is crying to escape and find herself. In a few years, Carrie would wisecrack for reporters who had come to love her wit that she had a terror of being "the oldest living child at the Tropicana belting out 'Wendy.'" But that terror seemed less witty back when Lisa Karlan drove the pensive Carrie to dance class, and it seemed real. Looking back on the teenage Carrie, Lisa saw a hint of what slightly older Selina Cadell (and others in London) would see a few years later. "Carrie seemed lonely," Selina says. "It seemed like there was something deep in her that she didn't share. I would even say that she was tortured. Yes, *tortured*."

There was an even better reason for that "tortured" sense than the ambivalence about performing with her mother. In 1970, Harry Karl had lost $3 million by gambling in a fixed card game at the Friars Club. He continued to gamble and lost more and more; Carrie knew the broad outlines of the disaster. "He was now losing sums of money to the kind of people who don't send a collection agent around when you're overdue—they send a hit man," Debbie wrote in her memoir *Debbie: My Life*. He asked Debbie for money, and she had only $300,000 from a settlement she had made with a corrupt business manager. Harry told her he needed that $300,000 as collateral against a business loan. They argued about it; he won. On a dire hunch, Debbie went to the bank and discovered that Harry, despite the shoe stores and other property he owned, was flat broke.

In short order, Carrie would learn the hurtful news that Harry had employed hookers; this was the real function of the "manicurists" who came to their home. Carrie and Todd discovered this fact when—as Todd reported it—Todd and a friend elaborately set up hidden video cameras and monitors around the house, waited for the doorbell to ring, and watched as the "manicurist" was let into the house, went into Harry's bedroom, took off her clothes, and appeared to be sexually servicing Harry.

But there was far more consequential news: Harry had blown through the $21 million that he'd had when he and Debbie married, as well as the money *Debbie* had made, which had gone to him as well. "The enormity [of that loss] would take time to comprehend," Debbie wrote in her memoir. Debbie confided all of this tearfully to her close friend and former drama coach Lillian Burns Sidney and to Agnes Moorehead. Both of them, older female veterans of imperfect marriages, counseled Debbie to stay with Harry.

Debbie had taken Carrie and Todd on a trip to Europe—Carrie's first—along with Harry. It was 1971, and Carrie was a young teenager. During time in Madrid, Carrie had been privy to a conversation her mother had with a man who asserted that Harry owed him almost $2 million. According to Debbie, Carrie asked her some questions about it, but Debbie gave her vague and optimistic answers. She didn't want Carrie to worry. She didn't want Carrie to cry for her mother the way Debbie had cried for Maxene when Maxene, in Texas, had told young Mary Frances how lonely and unhappy she was. But Carrie was too smart not to worry, and she'd had a bad premonition about her stepfather all along. "She nailed Harry right away," Lynn Pollack recalls. Much later, Carrie told Arensio Hall, "I was aware of my mother's bad taste [in men] at fourteen. She said [Harry] was cheating on her and he spent all her money. That was astonishing." Significantly, and movingly, Carrie had continued, "I remember [Debbie] said, 'I can tell you because you're the strong one and your brother is the open wound.' And I said, 'No! You've completely got that wrong!' But, you know, I *was* the strong one. Maybe my strength was born of weakness. We grow into our expectations." That concept might be thought of as Carrie in a nutshell, and she would repeat versions of it later. Her honesty about her problems gave her a strength—empathy toward and relief for others with problems; a unique, wise humor that would grow over the years. "In my weakness there is strength," she would much later say—an almost biblically formal statement, uncharacteristic for the usually irreverent Carrie. But she meant it, and others *felt* it.

Still, strong or not, she was mad at her mother's mistakes and at her mother's line-crossing candor with her. "We *did* fight," Carrie said. Debbie "had a lot of problems and I urgently needed her to be right." A daughter needs her mother to be right, and having a husband lose all your money is not right. And as much as Carrie's radar made her know something big was wrong in her mother's marriage, and even though she might have asked, she didn't want the responsibility for the truth dumped on her. "Carrie and I were always buddies," Debbie said. "I was never the boss." But it is hard being "buddies" with your mother, especially one who is prettier than you, who is wildly famous (and enjoys attention), who was rejected by the same man (Eddie) as you, and who has just confessed that she was extorted, very badly, by another husband, with consequence to you.

In her memoir published in 1988, Debbie wrote that she "lost" Carrie over the awfulness of what happened with Harry Karl. The fighting between Debbie and Carrie would grow more intense. "Carrie and I were [soon] driven apart by [the financial ruination of the Karl marriage]. She had seen her mother, who always handled everything, suddenly wanting to take a drink and sit in a corner by herself. She didn't respect me any more." Debbie's next words about Carrie say a lot: "Perhaps I was subconsciously pushing her into adulthood so that she could help me deal with the problem."

Carrie rose to the occasion. As a young girl, she had used writing as her "first drug"—her relief, her clarifier, her refuge. She was always writing in diaries and writing short stories. She read the great writers; to be a writer was her unexpressed but latent dream. Now she would use writing for another purpose. Debbie recalled that one day shortly after New Year's 1971 Carrie handed her a notepad and said, "Read this." It seemed to be an essay on "personal sacrifice." Debbie felt proud of her daughter's dutifulness in taking on a civics essay. Then she realized that Carrie had written the passionate, staccato screed *for* her mother and *about* Harry, with Carrie making a perceptive, literate, and poignant case for her strong opinion that Harry was using her and was insincere and that his problems were his *own* doing. "You owe no debt . . . Your guilt is unfounded," she told her mother.

Carrie gave her mother what Debbie's mature friends were too weary and old-school to deliver to her: Moxie. Self-esteem. Permission. Carrie might have been materially spoiled and not always nice, but beneath that almost inevitable response to her upbringing were wisdom beyond her years, and compassion. Carrie's lifelong friends would rave about the wise advice she always offered. That gift might have first surfaced here. Debbie thought, "I was almost forty years old: My fourteen-year-old daughter was living in reality and I was living in a nursery rhyme."

Shortly thereafter, when she turned fifteen, Carrie asked her mother to put her into therapy. "Why are you here?" the therapist asked. According to a friend, Carrie said she responded, "Because I want to stop crying so hard."

In 1972, Debbie made plans to leave Harry and to accept the starring role in the Broadway remake of the 1919 musical *Irene*, about a scrappy Irish American girl in New York who is swept up in love with a society man. She took the role in order to start earning back the money she and Harry both owed. Working hard was the Nazarene way. It was also, distinctly, Debbie's way.

Debbie would leave Todd and Tina with Harry. (Debbie's brother Bill, a chip off their parents' block, turned down her request to take Todd into his own home, citing Todd's "spoiled" upbringing.) And she would ask Carrie, then a sophomore in high school, to join her in New York. Beverly High peers and their parents, who witnessed the saga, would gossip and fret about it. One friend distills what the story was at the time: "Debbie pulled Carrie out of Beverly to take her to New York and help her earn money she needed to cover her and Harry's debts." But Carrie has indicated that she didn't get pulled out of school by a needy Debbie so much as "slid out" of school, as she put it to one friend, implying her own willingness. However it happened— whether because of her mother's financial crisis or because of her own restlessness—Carrie dropped out of Beverly High at fifteen. In New York, Debbie put Carrie—a girl "without a generation," a girl who enjoyed and relied on partnering with her mother as much as she painfully *didn't* enjoy it—in the play's chorus, where she sat, at least in one scene, literally at her movie-star mother's knee.

THREE

FROM BROADWAY TO BEATTY TO BRITAIN

arrie and Debbie left for New York in the fall of 1972. Debbie rented a town house on East Seventy-Fourth Street, and Carrie, somewhat reluctantly, went along on the mad dash of rehearsals and chaotic out-of-town previews of *Irene* in Toronto and Philadelphia and the intermittent emergencies, starring her mother as dramatically beleaguered focus puller. There was panic and exhaustion—and Debbie involuntarily slimmed down to under a hundred pounds. "You're the only mother I know who works right through a nervous breakdown," Carrie would later say admiringly. But the play had a successful opening at the Minskoff Theatre in New York in March 1973, to good reviews. As Carrie would later put it, "My mother taught me how to sur-thrive."

Todd called long-distance one morning from the home he was sharing with Harry Karl. "Mother," he said, "I don't want to bother you, but there's no food in the house." Carrie watched as Debbie frantically wired her son $600. It wasn't long before Todd joined his mother and sister in New York.

The transition wasn't seamless. At fifteen, Todd was already a gun aficionado. One evening, he accidentally shot himself in the knee. He'd been absentmindedly playing with a Colt .45, twirling it around, Western-style, when it went off. It was loaded with full-load blanks. They may not be actual bullets, but they can do plenty of damage. Debbie rushed Todd to the emergency room, where she was arrested, because her son was a minor.

"Todd wouldn't brush his teeth, so Mom shot him," Carrie joked to reporters.

Debbie was arraigned and released. All charges were dropped.

Carrie had been at a disco club, the Continental Baths, when Todd shot himself. The club had become a kind of home for Carrie. Gay culture was jubilantly everywhere, and disco music's infectious slickened funk flattened now-quaint folk rock like a steamroller. There was something narcotic-like in its lack of any pause between tracks. It was almost campily operatic, with its swirling strings and glossy urbanity.

At the Baths, everyone solo danced to Barry White and Love Unlimited, on a tropical-plant-filled floor made to resemble a Roman *caldarium*, with a pool in the center. Men who five years earlier had worried that they could be arrested in "those kinds" of bars, or beaten senseless if they had misread a cue and reached out to touch the wrong hand, ambled around naked but for towels wrapped around their waists, and they moved from the private sex rooms to the public area. There, a sequined disco ball revolved overhead, mesmerizing one and all as the room oscillated from darkness to light and back and forth and back again. Women in stacked heels and hot pants and men with wide lapels and long sideburns danced amid their towel-clad brethren.

Much of Carrie's social life revolved around the men in the *Irene* chorus or singer/dancers she had met with her mother in Las Vegas. There was a handsome young dancer named Albert, from the musical.

He was gay, but they would make out, with flirtatious innocence or near innocence.

Debbie encouraged the friendships, perhaps because the men seemed like perfect chaperones. One was the actor Brian Freilino, who eventually had a role in *The Godfather: Part III*; he worked in Italy with Sergio Leone. Freilino had a wonderful, Carrie-compatible sense of humor. "Brian was her best friend in New York" during the *Irene* months, remembers their mutual friend Alfa-Betty Olsen. Brian was a stabilizing influence over Carrie, Alfa-Betty says. "Carrie could be out of control and Brian pulled her back. Once they were in a store, and she just grabbed this fur jacket impulsively. Brian had to remind her that they had to pay for it."

Ted Pugh was another enduring male friend from the show. Debbie was taken by Ted because he looked like a cross between her old dance mates Gene Kelly and Donald O'Connor. "Ted Pugh was like a father figure, and Carrie loved him; she called him 'Puppet Face,'" says Selina Cadell, who a year later would get to know Pugh well enough to stay with him in his apartment near the Café des Artistes, on the West Side of Manhattan.

Years later, Carrie wrote that she became quite "obsessed" during these years with "homosexual men," but "since their inaccessibility was already established before I came along, I couldn't take it too personally."

Bette Midler, eleven years older than Carrie, was the refreshing star of the moment. Friendly looking but not a classic beauty, wildly funny with a big, wry, squinty-eyed smile, Bette was a Jewish girl from Honolulu who'd tried for a break in New York for years while living in a tiny apartment on Barrow Street in the Village. Suddenly she was "Bathhouse Betty" (she had to keep reminding everyone her first name—Bette—was *one* syllable), the queen of the Continental Baths, taking the club and the new culture mainstream with her buoyant hit "Friends."

Bruce Vilanch, who had been writing patter for Debbie, was now writing for Bette, and, he recalls, "I brought Bette to see *Irene*. That's how I met Carrie. Carrie decided I was okay—a big thing in her book; you have to make the grade with her. That night we became friends. Bette and I went backstage after the show, and all of a sudden there was a bucket of Colonel Sanders chicken and Debbie grabbed it and stood by Bette and pointed both of their faces to the camera and said, 'If we take this picture, they'll give us free chicken for a month, to feed the kids in the show.'" Debbie, who was making $15,000 a week but still in debt, "knew every angle, and Carrie was rolling her eyes, like, *My mother is such a howzer*—that Yiddish word for when you squeeze every penny. *She's so embarrassing! Get me out of here!*

"Carrie's whole attitude," Bruce continues, "was 'This is the squarest thing in the world, this show I'm doing. What I really want to do is what Bette's doing.' Not that kind of balls-out performance but being a hip recording artist.

"Carrie was a *huge* Joni Mitchell fan. She wanted to be like Joni, as different as they were." (Later, in 1978, when they were doing a *Star Wars* TV special together, Bruce recalls that Carrie wanted to use Joni's ballad "River" in the show. "Carrie sat at the long piano and played it. She loved it. But when we called Joni to ask her permission, Joni gave us, in her laughing, silvery voice, a big 'Nooooo!!!'")

"Debbie was Miss Sock Boffo with Carrie," Bruce continues. "She was very, very busy trying to get Carrie into the record business. Everyone who was in the music business was steered by Debbie into Carrie's arms—'Please, please, evaluate my darling daughter! Do you think she has a future doing this?'" Debbie's proactive, sometimes desperate hawking of Carrie would continue for years. Much of Debbie's seemingly ham-handed stage mothering might have stemmed from a genuine belief that this was what Carrie wanted, and she knew that Carrie was too quirky and ambivalent to effectively go after it herself. Debbie believed in Carrie's talent, and show business was the only life that Debbie knew. Debbie also knew her daughter was emotionally very vulnerable. The sleepless nights, the voices in her head, the high-strung nature, the roiling complexity so opposite to that of easygoing Todd:

Debbie wanted to do everything she could—even if it was pushy and undesired—to make sure Carrie was okay. Years later, Debbie would write in her second memoir, *Unsinkable*, words that ring true for any mother of a complicated adult child: "It's heartbreaking to watch someone you love struggle so. As a mother, I find the hardest thing for me is to love my daughter and not to intervene in her life. I want to do everything humanly possible to keep my girl out of pain, to pick her up when she's down." Emphasis added: "*If I could, I would suffer for her.*"

Carrie seems to have been ambivalent—even annoyed—about her mother's efforts on her behalf. "I don't want to be like Liza [Minnelli]!" she'd say to friends. Liza Minnelli had a singing career like her mother, Debbie's good friend Judy Garland. But while Liza was successful, Judy Garland was a hard-to-equal legend. It would be understandable that Carrie wanted to steer a course different from that of her own legendary mother. But it was not simple: Carrie was also half enjoying the performing career she'd now shared with her mother for so long it was second nature, and especially as a sixteen-year-old high school dropout with few other options handy, she was not ready to deny contact with the door-opening celebrities and handlers Debbie planted in her path.

One of the people whom Debbie used to help open a door for Carrie was her dear friend George Furth, an actor, a librettist, and a playwright. George was a frequent backstage visitor, and after Debbie took her final *Irene* bow for the evening, "my mother and George sat up and talked and drank—my mother liked to drink," Carrie told the author Suzanne Finstad in a private conversation. "I was an age where otherwise I would have steered clear of my mother, but I liked to listen to some of [their talk] because George wrote *Company* and that was very interesting to me." Debbie eschewed the use of four-letter words, which made Carrie sure to make her mother wince by peppering her conversation with the occasional "fuck." Furth got the picture of the hip daughter wanting to rebel from the proper mother.

During a break from *Irene*, Carrie flew to Paris to visit Furth. "I drank champagne and ended up in a room with George and his boyfriend with an open door, and maids were looking in with furrowed brows" at the girl and the two men, innocently socializing. The impression Furth had of Carrie as a tough-talking, worldly, but virginal girl chafing against her mother was intensified. It so happened that Furth's friend Warren Beatty was in the final stages of casting the movie that he and Robert Towne had written for Hal Ashby to direct. It was called *Shampoo*, and it was about a handsome, motor-scooter-riding, but unaccountably hapless Beverly Hills hairdresser, George Roundy, who had multiple girlfriends: a nice current one played by Goldie Hawn; a wily, sexy ex, played by Julie Christie; and a scheming, rich older married woman, played by Lee Grant.

Its action took place six years earlier, in 1968, on the eve of Richard Nixon's election. Roundy, looking to finance a hair salon of his own, attends a Republican Party fund-raiser as the guest of a hoped-for benefactor who is actually the husband of one of his lovers. Everything goes awry, and during an evening of partying in which all of his lovers appear, much adventure with drugs and sex ensues, and George loses both his business opportunity and the woman he loves the most. The movie, Lee Grant says today, was socially significant, for under its Rodeo Drive mufti *Shampoo* was a feminist table-turner. "The movie was an interesting reversal" of the usual sexual politics, Grant says emphatically. "It was not Warren who was after *us*; it was *we* who were after *him*. He is trying to please us sexually—trying to please *us*, in every way—and in the process he loses everything."

Beatty was looking for an actress to play a small but vital role: a swaggering Beverly Hills teenage girl who wants to get back at her mother in the strongest way imaginable: by having sex with her mother's paramour. George Furth called Warren from the Paris hotel room during his time with his boyfriend and Carrie, while Carrie was drinking with them and throwing the *F* word around with sophisticated abandon. "And George suggested that I would be good in *Shampoo*," Carrie said. "So champagne got me *Shampoo*."

In the spring of 1974, Furth brought Carrie to the set. Not unlike the movie, the set was in real life abuzz with female gamesmanship. Though Warren was still romantically involved with Julie Christie, Michelle Phillips, who had recently broken up with Warren's close friend Jack Nicholson, asked to be able to watch the filming. Beatty was segueing from one gorgeous girlfriend to another when Furth introduced him to Carrie, whom Beatty was well aware of, because Debbie was friends with his older sister Shirley MacLaine. "I was a little too young to notice" the Michelle-and-Warren dynamic, Carrie would later say. "And," touchingly, "I was a little scared of those people. It was like, 'Get me out of here!'"

Carrie had met Warren before. "Everybody in town had met him before; if you lived here, he is sort of like the LaBrea Tar Pits," she told Suzanne Finstad. Everyone knew that he was the playboy every young woman wanted to reform, but when Carrie went to the *Shampoo* set with Furth she was under no illusions that he would be interested in her. "It would be silly," she said, realistically; she was a cute seventeen-year-old, not a Christie or a Phillips. She knew that expecting romantic interest from him would be "tragic," she said. "He was a seducer, a collector, as well as a very talented person," and every woman wanted to do what many years later Annette Bening would do: domesticate him. "I knew I would never have any chance of" being considered a serious lust object by him, she said. Still, because she was that tender age and had a complex personality, her realism was twinned with resentment: "I was like a kid angry that I wasn't worth more of a try from him."

Carrie wisely defended herself from that insecurity by playing tough, idiosyncratic, and uninterested in the role. Coming to the set that day with Furth, she was wearing "Marcel Marceau whiteface makeup and old clothing. I was going to be this person that he could *not* charm." Smart of her!

"George knew I didn't care if I got the role, and I remember George introducing me to Warren and Warren looking up at me and saying, 'Perhaps wash your face.' I remember saying to *him* something like, 'What makes you think I would want to be just like the others?'"

Her I-don't-give-a-damn attitude was persuasive. Warren hired her on the spot. Did she do an audition? "No." Read any lines from a script? "No. Nothing. He just listened to me talk for a while," Carrie told Finstad. "I was very precocious. Certainly the 'I am nothing like my mother' thing might have come up. However, though I may have used a four-letter word, I in no way was suggestive in my manner. I was a virgin. I mentioned that to him. I liked being the foulest-mouthed virgin anyone ever met.

"And he liked that. And, soon after"—once they started shooting—"he offered to alleviate the incredible burden of my virginity." (He made that offer four times, Carrie would later say.) At some point, Carrie could not help but regret not yielding to the subsequent invitations. "I probably should have done it because it was so random." But she *also*, even more firmly, believed that if he had been *really* serious, if he wasn't just kidding, "he would have made a bigger play for me." And kidding he *was*. "He told everybody on the set that I was a virgin." Carrie was embarrassed by this, but she also liked the attention.

Because she was underage and because Warren knew and respected Debbie, he insisted on coming over to their house and playing the piano for both of them as part of wooing Carrie for the role. "It was very sweet," Carrie said. "He was very charming to my mother."

Carrie's character Lorna Karpf was the daughter of Lee Grant's Felicia Karpf, a woman married to the wealthy wheeler-dealer, played by Jack Warden, from whom George Roundy wants to extract salon-starting money. Felicia is having an affair with George. Scheming, jealous, sexually intense, Felicia is (by those years' ungenerous standards) an "older" woman desperately looking for a path back to youth. Grant's skill and nuance softened the unlikable role and would earn her the Best Supporting Actress Oscar.

Lorna hates her mother and she propositions Roundy—boldly. In the script, she says, "Wanna fuck?" and these words were brought up to Debbie when Warren made his house call to the family. Debbie spent much time, during Warren's visit to their house, trying to get Warren to change "fuck" to "screw," but Carrie and Warren both resisted. Debbie finally gave in. "She went 'okay'" to the more explicit word, Carrie told Finstad.

Carrie did her major scene in a tennis outfit (braless, Warren decided) with white knee socks and a tight scarf pulled low over her forehead and tied in back of her head, as was the style that year. Lorna is standing next to a tennis pro at her parents' court when George arrives. She tells him her mother is not home, escorts George into the kitchen, informs him she knows he is having an affair with her mother and that she is *nothing* like her mother. Then it comes: "Wanna fuck?"

After every one of the various takes in which those words were uttered, Warren laughed, "and so did everyone else," Carrie said. But Lee Grant, whose role was so key to Carrie's (and vice versa) and who depended on Carrie to play off, didn't laugh at the ingenue's charisma and competence. Lee remembers today, "I was shocked at how ephemeral and beautiful Carrie was, and how strong and direct and honest she was. She was only a kid; just seventeen! But she was so sure of herself in the way she communicated. And her arms and legs and face were so white at a period when everyone else was baking in the sun; her whole being was the opposite of what a glamour girl was supposed to be in that period, and she was comfortable with that, confident. Here was an actress; she played it so straight, so honest." Lee Grant pauses. "Carrie *owned* it."

On the heels of the "Wanna fuck?" proposition, Carrie did a scene in which she, as Lorna, is sitting on her bed, barefoot, and Lee, as Felicia, walks into her daughter's bedroom just as George is coming out of the bathroom. Lee and Warren heatedly debated what Felicia's reaction should be. Lee *knew* Felicia would know her daughter has slept with her paramour, while Warren wanted her to redo the scene as a woman in denial. Lee threatened to quit, saying, "No one ever told me what I was thinking!"—meaning she'd already made up her mind about her character's motivation. Warren conceded, "Play it your way. What do I know? I'm a man."

Being a method actress, Lee Grant stayed away from socializing with Carrie during the shooting (but spent much quality time with her friends Goldie and Julie). "Carrie's character was *my* character's competition, and"—again making the feminist-role-reversal point— "*she* was the aggressor" with Beatty. "*She* was the 'boy' and *he* was the 'girl.' Carrie was extraordinary in the movie," Lee says. And Lee, as the mother of a daughter (Carrie's onetime schoolmate Dinah Manoff), caught the authenticity. "She was playing a daughter of a certain age, and a daughter of a certain age hates her mother; it just happens. *Later* they love their mothers."

The wrap party, on June 12, 1974, was so full of marijuana—Hal Ashby's idea—"that," Carrie once recalled with a smile, "it was almost like Haight Ashbury." Much later, Carrie would be surprised to learn that some of the film's music was written by Paul Simon.

Carrie attempted to get several roles in major movies after filming *Shampoo*. She utilized her access to Beatty to audition for Mike Nichols's *The Fortune*, starring Beatty and Nicholson. Stockard Channing, like Carrie a newcomer with an elite background, got the role of the young heiress instead. At some point later, Carrie auditioned for a role in *Grease*, which was released in 1978 and made Olivia Newton-John a star and in which Dinah Manoff memorably played Marty Maraschino. Carrie's most disappointing near miss was *Days of Heaven*—a dramatic, substantial, arty movie directed by one of new Hollywood's most revered auteurs, Terrence Malick. Carrie did a reading with John Travolta (who'd just become a star on TV's *Welcome Back, Kotter*). It would be interesting to picture these two starring, so against their now-long-established "types," as scheming émigrés to the 1916 Texas Panhandle. Carrie would later blame the loss of the role on the fact that Travolta, with whom she had good chemistry, was contractually unable to accept the part and that when she auditioned with Richard Gere,

"let's just say," she said, "our beakers didn't bubble with compatibility."
Gere and Brooke Adams got the roles and established themselves by
way of the film. Carrie had two different sets of agents during this
time period: Thomas Chasin at Chasin-Park-Citron, and Rick Nicita
and Johnnie Planco at William Morris. It's not clear why she lost the
roles.

A month after the wrap party for *Shampoo*, in July 1974, Carrie was
in London. Debbie had accepted a three-week engagement at the London Palladium, and Debbie, Carrie, Todd, and Ray and Maxene moved
into the Savoy hotel several days before the July 30 start date. Carrie
had agreed to share the stage with her mother and perform several
solos in her own style, not as Debbie's mini-me. They were directly following the last-night engagement of Cass Elliot, doing her first solo act
after leaving the Mamas and the Papas. *This* was a generation to which
the "girl without a generation" related. Cass was a very close friend and
Laurel Canyon neighbor of Carrie's idol Joni Mitchell. Carrie would
eventually move there, too—her first of three Los Angeles canyons.
(Benedict and Coldwater would follow.) Most important, Cass Elliot
had been for six years now what Carrie would soon be for thirty: the
connection-making head of the coolest celebrities' salon in town and a
highly valued advice giver to its highly creative members.

Cass Elliot's last Palladium performance, on July 29, ended with a
prolonged standing ovation and an after party in her honor at Mick Jagger's town house. Cass invited Debbie to come, and Carrie was more
than thrilled to tag along. But when they got there, Jagger told Debbie to keep the young 'uns downstairs. Upstairs, Debbie, shocked and
certainly disapproving, encountered a huge bowl of cocaine. This was
a substance, among others, to which Carrie would soon become tragically susceptible.

Carrie and Debbie returned to the hotel, preparing to get a good
night's sleep for their Palladium performance. In the morning came
the news: Cass—only thirty-two and mother of a daughter, Owen, almost seven—had just died of a heart attack at Harry Nilsson's house.

Poignantly, she had just written a letter to her daughter—"Dear Owenski, I miss you!"—before she suffered the fatal attack. The entire entertainment world and the now-maturing counterculture were steeped in shock and grief.

That night, preparing for her performance on the heels of Cass's death, Carrie experienced almost paralyzing stage fright, and it lasted the length of the engagement. "Every night before she went on, Carrie was a wreck, almost throwing up," Debbie said. "I'd spend two hours before each show giving her glasses of water, calming her, and getting her dressed."

Perhaps it was in part due to her high anxiety, which turned itself into poignant affect, that Carrie "killed," Debbie proudly recalled of the success of her Palladium performance. "She was brilliant and wonderful in"—as Debbie put it—"her *Piaf* way, the opposite of me." The days of Debbie and Carrie teaming, which had worked well in Las Vegas, were past. When bubbly, beaded Debbie left the stage after "singing and dancing and chattering away," Carrie would walk out in a high-contrast serious mode. She belted out "Mean Time" and "Being Alive" and other songs. Carrie got a standing ovation; Debbie sobbed with pride. "The umbilical cord was never cut," Carrie would say later. Debbie's tearful gratification was one of countless instances of that stubborn truth.

Variety raved, "The dramatic power and depth of [Carrie's] young pipes mark her as a strong bet in the immediate future. All-pro at 17 years of age, she appears to have all the ingredients of a powerhouse career." Another reviewer decreed that daughter topped mother: "Debbie Reynolds is the gold of vaudeville. She has presented us with her daughter, Carrie Fisher, the platinum."

But Carrie wanted to be an actress, not a singer or nightclub performer like her mother (and father). And among those in the Palladium audience was George Hall, head of acting at London's Central School of Speech and Drama, long the "second" drama school in London after the prestigious Royal Academy of Dramatic Art (RADA) but catching up to RADA now, and quickly. Lyall Watson, a Central teacher who would go on to head up RADA, was there in the audience with George, and he remembers George going backstage to, in Watson's sensing, be "vetted" by Debbie. Debbie wanted Carrie to apply to Central, and Debbie was checking Hall out. The reason for the vetting? Carrie had already auditioned for RADA and had been turned down. Central might have to prove itself to *not* be sloppy seconds.

Central was not the school one would automatically pick for a movie star's cosseted daughter. It was known for its left-wing leanings, and it had a talented, competitive, but decidedly non-elite student body: tuition was cheap; it was state subsidized. But now, under George Hall's direction, everything was changing. Its reputation was suddenly overtaking that of the reigning RADA. As one former Central teacher, Alan Marston, recalls, "In 1974, Central emerged as the crème de la crème of drama schools. It was definitely the best training for any young actor."

Its methods—both radical and empathic—had a lot to do with it coming to favor. "Central wanted its students stripped down and natural," recalls Christopher John, who would become a student with Carrie and is now a theater director in South Africa. "During the first year, they took us back to 'neutral.' Girls wore no makeup, boys no sideburns or facial hair. We worked our bodies and our voices. We studied and imitated animals. They sometimes cast us against type in order to challenge and stretch us. Only the year's students observed each other's work—the teachers creating a safe space to explore without the pressure of authorities' judgment. Although it was based in Stanislavski training, our training at Central made very limited use of jargon. There was a big emphasis on speaking literature, vocally shaping ideas, working with heightened language. We engaged the Western theater canon by working on plays by Shakespeare, Shaw, Noël Coward, Ibsen, Chekhov, Tennessee Williams, Eugene O'Neill."

George Hall *was* Central, and he was beloved (as was his much younger life partner, John Jones, a gossipy charmer who was also on the staff). Clare Rich, who would be a student contemporary of Carrie's there, says, "George was an inspirational, charismatic man who was passionate about teaching, passionate about theater, and passionate about *musical* theater." Hall and Debbie had much to talk about, and he seems to have charmed her.

Central was a product of the 1930s Bristol Old Vic school, "which produced the young actors that shook up the postwar theater. It was very left-wing working-class, not this glamour thing, not this MGM-back-in-the-day thing," says Christopher John. Its cachet was its selectivity—it accepted only twenty-six freshman students a year—and its effective emphasis on getting students jobs. Rare for England at the time, "Central achieved about 95 percent employment of students within a year of graduation," John says. "At the time, in the U.K., you couldn't join Actors' Equity unless you were already employed with the regional repertory theater companies." But Central somehow solved this catch-22 and *got* its graduates *into* rep companies. Clare Rich says, "At the end of our three years we wanted jobs, and Central made that happen. Most of us went straight from school to rep. We weren't rich, so working right away was huge."

"There weren't many blue bloods at Central," Alan Marston recalls, and those who were snobbily class-conscious were very much disliked. The elite Rupert Everett had recently caused a stir by brandishing his class status and by insulting the school's prejudice against the highly born. But students also included the daughters of Laurence Olivier, Richard Burton, Jessica Tandy, and Hume Cronyn, and Clark Gable's daughter with a Spanish actress.

Central was situated in the old Embassy Theatre in a section of London known as Swiss Cottage, not far from the Irish Republican Army's stomping grounds, and the 1970s was the time of the IRA protests and bombings and cease-fires. Vanessa Redgrave, a Central alum, and her brother Corin Redgrave would come to Central to give impromptu speeches as members of the Workers Revolutionary Party.

Central's audition process involved two speeches—a Shakespeare monologue and a contemporary one—followed by a series of improvisations. At the end of the improvisations, you learned whether you had been accepted.

Carrie traveled to Central for her audition, and she got a sense of the school. There was the infamous Canteen, the hub of activity between classes, run by the matriarchal Marianne, a strongly accented Romanian scolder (when you were in her café, you behaved yourself!) who served "fairly disgusting" coffee, as one alum recalled it, and liver sausage rolls and cheese and tomato rolls, wrapped in cellophane. And there was her more accommodating husband, Gerry, who ran a proper but drearily menued restaurant upstairs. Marianne and Gerry's was where *everybody* congregated. The food was crap, but there was little choice, except to walk down to the Cosmo, the Eastern European café on Finchley Road.

Shampoo was not released yet—that would come in February 1975—but George Hall knew about Carrie's role in it. Still, her audition was handled, as all Central auditions were, by the proprietary head of admissions, an elegant elderly woman known simply as Miss Grey, whom the actress Deborah MacLaren, then a Central student, recalls wielding great power but being "tiny, birdlike, imperious, with a gray chignon; she looked like she'd just stepped off a ballet stage. We had all these fantastic old eccentric ladies fluttering around, and Miss Grey was a major one." Miss Grey gave Carrie Fisher the official good news: she was "appointed" one of twenty-six students entering Stage '77. (The classes were named for their graduation date, three years hence.)

Carrie's response was not uncomplicated. Initially, she was gratified. Still, in the late summer of 1974 there might have been fear of the unknown. Drama school in London was a good choice; it meant *Don't be a movie star's daughter. Take acting seriously!* But this would bring out her insecurity, and she might well have sensed this.

And perhaps she understood that an epic showdown with her mother was what their long push-pull relationship was heading toward and that fighting over attending Central was a handy igniter. What-ever the reason, shortly before she was set to fly from L.A. to London for Central's orientation week, Carrie told Debbie, "I'm not going. I've decided to stay home. I want to stay in Los Angeles and decide what I want to do."

Mother and daughter had a whopper of a fight. Debbie in New York screamed at Carrie in L.A. that she had "no training and no education." Those five words would pain Carrie for a long time; she was, she would later admit, "very insecure [that I] dropped out of high school to be a chorus girl." Still, Carrie dug in her heels: I am *not* going!

"No," Debbie retorted. "You're going to do this or you're going to have to support yourself."

Carrie, eventually, angrily conceded.

"She was so angry" when she boarded the plane. "I felt sick," Debbie said. "I'd lost my little girl."

And, in a sense, she had. This began a period where Carrie kept at arm's length from her mother and put her down (while relying on her). Whether in Beverly Hills or New York, they had always lived together. No longer. Debbie would tell Oprah Winfrey many years later, in a dramatic exaggeration, that she and Carrie didn't talk for twelve years. ("We talked really badly," Carrie clarified.)

Carrie sort of *sidled* into Central," Deborah MacLaren, who was a year ahead of her, says, remembering the early September 1974 first day of school. (Today Deborah is a working actress with her own British production company.) "We knew she was going to come—the 'Holly-wood starlet.'" There was reliable rumor that she'd already shot a few scenes in a yet-to-be-released major movie. "So we were all slightly ex-cited and wondering what she was going to be like. I remember looking at her staring at the notice board to see what the next set of casting was in this rabbit warren of a building. She came past me and she was all covered up. It was a warm day, but she was wearing this drab raincoat and this knitted hat that looked like a tea cozy, terribly unflattering. My feeling was she was hiding and wanted to be the least significant person there."

"She just kind of *mucked* in," says Lyall Watson of Carrie's unprepossessing entrance. "There wasn't anything 'I am Debbie Reynolds's daughter!' about her. She was very quiet—mouse-like. Not in a bad way—some Americans come over to the English drama schools and attack them, and she wasn't like that. Carrie was vulnerable."

"I was the youngest student there," Carrie has explained, something that others noted, and "it was the first time I actually lived on my own. I was finally away from my mother (whom I'd happily live *off* but not with) . . . where no one could be disappointed in me." She also arrived, she said, "carrying more freight" than the other students, because people knew she was a movie star's daughter. She said she consciously tried to minimize that.

But beyond the attempt at minimization, there seemed to be genuine insecurity. "She was a *lost* girl—I felt that very strongly," MacLaren continues. "She wasn't a smiler; she *never* seemed to smile. She was a solemn little thing, not the sassy American we were expecting. She looked as though she needed a bloody good hug, and I don't know how good Central was for pastoral care. Here we all were, middle-class students from Labour families. I got the sense that she was at sea—surrounded by confident young folk, singing, sitting on stairs, kissing the teachers, in the middle of IRA territory—we were doing that. It was the '70s! I got the feeling she wanted to hide."

Whereas most of the students lived with their parents or with roommates in ramshackle make-dos, Carrie had a lovely apartment she'd sublet from a friend and was often driven to school by a chauffeur (something she has said she was embarrassed by and hated). She visited her mother's friends in London—the photographer Michael Childers and his boyfriend, the masterful filmmaker John Schlesinger (*Midnight Cowboy* and *Darling* were two of his praised movies). She and Childers would keep up their friendship, and Childers would photograph her many times over the ensuing years. "I adored her; she was totally original," Childers says. "She had such style and taste and talent, even that young." But she was in a distinctly rebelling-from-Debbie mode, "and she had made up her mind *not* to be a singer—'Both of my parents are canaries; isn't that enough?' she said. The Debbie-Eddie thing was repellent to her."

Carrie became friends with a stunning girl named Lucy Gutteridge who was intense and emotionally complicated. In the casting-specific way of Central, Lucy was Stage '77's "'beautiful girl' and Carrie was the 'ordinary girl,'" Christopher John believes.

Carrie began giving parties at her London apartment, inviting everyone at the school. This approach—brandishing great, indiscriminate generosity—was unusual at Central and caused curiosity and opportunism. Who else *did* this? the Central faculty rhetorically wondered. "I remember the parties she used to throw in Chelsea," says Barbara Griffiths (known to one and all as Bardy), the voice teacher who taught a very eager Carrie "standard English." "Carrie was an extremely lively, very likable person. She had a twinkle in her eye, and what stood out was her youth," Bardy says. Bardy was gobsmacked by "Carrie's *innocence* in giving those parties. Nobody else had parties where they invited everyone in school!" Deborah MacLaren saw the contrast strongly. "She was a lost girl who also had these glamorous parties; the party thing was part of her neediness. I thought, 'What is she doing? Wafting around in that silly hat and throwing these lavish parties!' It was about wanting friendship. I don't know who her real friends were, aside from Lucy."

Carrie's indiscriminate generosity was promptly taken advantage of. Right before Christmas, she gave a big party, and one rowdy fellow picked up the grand piano in the apartment and pushed it out the window! Fortunately, no one was standing on the street in the wee hours of the morning when the massive piece of furniture hit the sidewalk with life-crushing force. But a large monetary fine was inflicted on Carrie, as well as police attention. The incident buzzed around the school the next day, with the students "thinking it was a huge joke; 'oh my God, how naughty, how hilarious!'" says MacLaren. But the young instructors who attended—Bardy, Lyall Watson—felt worry, shock, and sympathy for naive Carrie.

The day after this catastrophe was when Selina Cadell met Carrie for the first time; "ran smack-dab into her" might be a better description of their encounter. Selina happened to walk into one of the school's cloakrooms and was stunned to find "the American girl," which was all she knew about this young student, "crumpled in a heap on its floor, crying her eyes out." Selina was hit in the face with Carrie's pain, and that dramatic first encounter would color her feelings about Carrie from that day forward. "People tended to exploit her because she was so wealthy," Selina would later say, those people's attitude being "'Well, who cares if we spill champagne on the carpet or push the grand piano out of the window?' I sympathized with her and I think she found that unusual. I didn't know about her background when I was smoothing her ruffled feathers. She never played a grand game or pulled rank. She was just a lovely person with this amazing sense of humor. And she was immensely generous." After they became good friends, in one of many gestures "Carrie paid for me to come stay with her in the U.S. when I had absolutely no money." For years Selina was fighting off Carrie's reflexive generosity. "We think of sharp, witty people as being very resilient, but she had a striking softness and vulnerability."

Selina helped Carrie deal with her very unhappy landlord over the grand piano incident, and after Christmas, Carrie wrote Selina a thank-you note and took her to tea at a tea parlor on Finchley Road. The two became virtually lifelong friends.

Carrie thought she could learn what a "normal" childhood was like from Selina's family. For some reason, she pictured Selina's elegant mother, Jill, as an "earth mother." Once, visiting the Cadells' country house in Highgate, England, Carrie sat at the kitchen table, raptly watching Jill at the stove. "Could I make that, do you think, Jill?" she asked of a simple recipe, which turned out to be shepherd's pie (a name that made Carrie laugh). She followed Jill along, kneading the pastry dough, doing things that the constantly working Debbie Reynolds, aside from leading the Girl Scouts, never did. The simple act of being in a kitchen, cooking—something Selina took for granted—had meant "a huge amount" to Carrie, Selina saw.

After an endless raft of presents and treats that Carrie would bestow on her over time, Selina, whose father was a well-known actors' agent, reciprocated by giving Carrie an heirloom brooch. "Tears welled up in [Carrie's] eyes" when Selina gave it to her. "You're giving this to me? It belonged to your family?" she said through her tears. That's how accustomed she was to being the giver, *not* the receiver. For all her bravado and charm, Selina says, "Carrie was as fragile as a butterfly."

"She had the *biggest* heart, and she was so easily hurt," Selina theorizes, "that she built a survival suit of great humor and wit to keep guard over this massive desire to be loved and give love back."

Carrie had a boyfriend at Central, Simon Templeman. He was her first real love, and they had a quiet, close relationship for much of her time there, says Christopher John, who remained friends and theatrical colleagues with Simon for some years, in England and New York. (Templeman has a significant career in Los Angeles, with a recent recurring role on *Modern Family*.) "Simon was a hunky guy—people compared his look to Mick Jagger," John continues, "and he was a nice guy, but he had a slightly morose and sometimes monosyllabic quality. He was shy. He was very close to Carrie and very guarded about the relationship and we did not pry—we were very British." Carrie said she and her "English boyfriend [would] smoke and have these yellow stains on our fingers and do Chekhov and Ibsen and fencing."

Deborah MacLaren became Simon's girlfriend after his relationship with Carrie was over. And "I loved him so terribly and I was very, very jealous of Carrie" because of Carrie's hold on his heart even after they broke up. "They loved each other in that first-love kind of way—it was real—and they were very important to each other. He was from

suburban England from a very, very normal family. He may have provided a bit of calm for her."

It is to Carrie's credit that at Central she spoke little to nothing of
her role in *Shampoo*. There, hanging out with the others at Marianne
and Gerry's between classes, she was just a student—in a city she had
fallen in love with, enduringly, and at a school where "I got real acting experience," she said, adding pointedly, "Something that I'd never
had." Christopher John improvised with her; Alan Marston supervised
her "animal studies," an important part of the curriculum. The students went to the London Zoo every week and first closely observed
and then "became" their self-appointed animal. Carrie chose the "bush
baby, a little animal from Australia, very cuddly but with very sharp
claws, which is probably a bit like Carrie," Marston says. He'd divined
that "she liked to manipulate people. She was a marvelous egocentric
who was happy in all states." And Bardy taught Carrie standard Shakespeare text: one of Carrie's favorite classes.

Most significant, London gave her privacy. She has said several
times, "It was the only time in my life that I was unobserved." And,
"for the first time, I was with people my own age. Twelve hours a day
of acting, fencing, voice, movement, everybody with one common interest. I was blessed." She added dryly, if it hadn't been for Central,
"I might have stayed a Hollywood kid, dressed in sequins and flinging
mike cords for the rest of my life. I could have ended up in the Tropicana lounge."

In *My Girls*, Todd Fisher recalls that the few times Debbie visited
her daughter in London, Carrie treated her poorly. Even though Carrie enjoyed the school, she was still angry that she'd been forced to go.
Todd said that Debbie would return home after such trips shaken and
sad. But friends of Carrie's at the time felt "Debbie was the 'problem,'"
as one close female friend says. "It was hard having a beautiful mother.
Debbie would say things like 'Darling, why do you drag around like
that?' Or, 'Darling, don't you want to do something with that hair?' *I*

had a beautiful mother," this friend says, "and they're mean in a subtle, even unintentional way. Or you can attribute meanness to them." Debbie was always "the 'real' star," said the friend. Even after *Star Wars*, "Carrie was always trying to get her approval."

Shampoo was released in early February 1975, when Carrie was still at Central, "hiding," she would say, from the impact of the classy commercial smash that reminded so many of Mike Nichols's *Carnal Knowledge* and that would soon evoke comparisons to Robert Altman's *Nashville*. It would become the fourth-biggest box-office hit of the year. It received mixed reviews; interestingly, the East Coast reviewers were more smitten than the weathered locals. *The New York Times'* Vincent Canby called it "the American film comedy of the year, a wittily, furtively revolutionary comedy of manners." In *The New Yorker*, Pauline Kael (charmed by Beatty, some said) raved that it was "the most virtuoso example of sophisticated kaleidoscopic farce that American moviemakers have ever come up with," whereas Roger Ebert called it a "disappointment," overpraised and not as "funny," "savage," or "poignant" as it should have been. One of the deadliest reviews (and a rebuttal to the enthusiasm of the other reviewers in her city) was from *The New York Times'* Nora Sayre, who had wanted to like it but found it a "glossy farce [that] never levitates." However, Sayre did single out one performance for praise: "Carrie Fisher makes a deft, cool debut as a hostile adolescent. Somehow, the daughter of Debbie Reynolds seems more at ease in the movie than some of her hip senior colleagues."

Carrie flew from London to New York, introducing journalists to her precocious wit. "Are you a magician?" she asked *Newsday*'s Jerry Parker, taking a leisurely drag on her Benson & Hedges and sipping the Coke that would be her beverage of choice forever after. "Could you possibly make me look like I have cheekbones?" What's wrong with your face? Parker asked, playing along with her self-deprecation. "Facial flesh denotes extreme youth," she declared with mock grandiosity.

"I am a *celebration* of adolescence." Comparing herself to her character Lorna, she said, "I probably am sophisticated, which is a terrible thing to be." The former was true; the latter, a Carrie-ism she was branding. In the same way that this guise had worked with Warren—he'd cast her on the basis of it—"it was crucial that I appeared to be a kind of nonchalant citizen of the weary part of the world," is how she'd later see her pose. "I did my best to come off as this kind of ironic, amused, disenchanted creature." (Soon she would grow into it.)

To the press, she defended Eddie Fisher, with whom she was back in touch. He'd taken such flak for leaving her mother for Elizabeth Taylor, only to have Taylor dump him for Richard Burton. Eddie, back on cocaine and painkillers, had had two lovely daughters, Tricia and Joely, with the actress Connie Stevens, whom he had divorced in 1969, and was in the midst of what would be a short fourth marriage to Terry Richard, a Miss Louisiana who was—Carrie would later roll her eyes at this—just three years older than Carrie but called Carrie "dear."

Carrie proudly said that Beatty had recommended her to Mike Nichols for a role—in *The Fortune*—but that she was "too young." She wisely didn't mention the roles for which she was passed over and said that she'd been "turning down a lot of Linda Blair roles where they ask you to be raped or murdered."

When Carrie returned to Central, she resumed her romance with Simon Templeman. And her classes. Elocution class with Bardy was particularly important. Carrie, who had that *intentionally* arch and ironic way about her, was determined to master compatibly arch and ironic English diction, and she had a special love for attacking the tongue twisters that were a staple of Bardy's curriculum—such as "All I want is a proper cup of coffee made in a proper cup of coffee pot! You can believe it or not but I want a proper cup of coffee in a proper cup of coffee pot! *Tin* coffee pots, *dime* coffee pots, they're of no use to me if I *can't* have a proper cup of coffee in a proper cup of coffee pot . . . I'll *have* a cup of *tea*!"

Then she heard about an audition in L.A. for a Linda Blair–like role that *did* seem worth considering, if for no other reason than for the serendipity of the title. The movie was about a vengeful teenage reject. It was called *Carrie*—who could beat that?—and it would be directed by Brian De Palma. It was worth flying back to L.A. for Christmas vacation for the audition. Sissy Spacek would eventually get the role, but the trip proved fateful all the same. Hitching a ride on De Palma's casting call was his friend George Lucas, the director of *American Graffiti*, who was casting a science fiction fantasy, an outlier in this era of sophisticated, urban films like *Shampoo*, *Nashville*, *Midnight Cowboy*, and *Carnal Knowledge*—or *Days of Heaven* and *The Fortune*. Carrie was strongly recommended to Lucas by Debbie's friend Fred Roos, Francis Ford Coppola's casting director, a man considered a genius in the field. As Furth had championed Carrie with Beatty, Roos now did with Lucas. Lucas was resistant; he wanted a "beautiful girl" for the role, and Carrie Fisher was not that. But Roos pushed, and Lucas gave in.

Carrie boarded her plane armed with her Bardy-trained, smoothly confident, just-elite-enough voice and the "sophisticated" hauteur she'd cutely proffered in her *Shampoo* interviews. These were fine tools to have in her arsenal because Lucas wanted a cool, sardonic, strong woman in this role. His movie's name—with a first word that would later be dropped—was *The Star Wars*.

FOUR

PRINCESS LEIA BECOMES THE TOAST OF YOUNG NEW YORK

During her trip to L.A. from London over Christmas vacation 1975–76 for Brian De Palma and George Lucas's casting call, Carrie was one of the last to be auditioned. De Palma had finished casting *Carrie*, so she was auditioning only for Lucas, with Roos advising him closely.

Three big roles were to be cast, and Lucas wanted very young, relatively unknown actors for all of them. In his complicated epic film—set in a galaxy "far, far away" and peopled by warriors known as the Jedi, who wield a power of good called the Force—the young woman's role was key. Princess Leia Organa is the secret leader of the Rebel Alliance—the major "good guys," trying to disable the space station, called the Death Star, of the evil Galactic Empire. The Death Star is able to destroy an entire planet, and Princess Leia, embarking on a civil war against her Galactic foes from her planet Alderaan, has been cannily and passionately trying to keep this from happening. She has found the recipe—the "plans and specifications"—for the destruction of the planet. She has hidden them inside a lovable robot, an "astro-mech droid" named R2-D2. (The residents of this galaxy are a mixed bag: humans; large, bizarre animal-like creatures; *and* droids.) But before Leia can effect her plan, she is captured by the ultimate villain, the Galactic Empire's Darth Vader, a fearsome Jedi-gone-very-evil in a metal suit and face helmet who is threatening to kill her.

Meanwhile, R2-D2, the holder of the precious codes—having escaped Vader with C-3PO to planet Tatooine—is captured and sold to a family of farmers that includes young Luke Skywalker, who (this fact is kept secret until a later movie in the franchise) is actually Princess Leia's twin brother. Luke gets drawn into the action by running after the missing R2-D2. In the course of trying to find the droid, Luke gets captured, only to be rescued by coming upon the ultimate Jedi master, Obi-Wan Kenobi, an elder living as a hermit who was the one meant to receive the Death Star plans. When he finds Luke, he does not yet know about Leia, but she is seeking him to help the rebellion. "Help me, Obi-Wan Kenobi," the tiny shimmering image of the yet-uncast Leia will say, repeatedly, in her embedded capsule. "You're my only hope."

Aside from Leia and Luke Skywalker, the third main character is a smuggler and bit of a scoundrel named Han Solo. He was a street kid in a gang and then became the co-captain, with a large, hairy creature named Chewbacca at his side, of the *Millennium Falcon*. Princess Leia will cajole Han Solo to join the Rebel Alliance along with her and Luke.

The young woman who got this part would be a damsel-in-*controlled*-distress: an aggressive heroine. It would be a star-making role.

During the interview with Lucas, Carrie was nervous talking to the seemingly "impassive" director, whose initially discomfiting enigmatic nature she would eventually come to see as "discerning" and "shy." When she was given her scene to take home and master, she would later write in her final book, *The Princess Diarist*, "My heart pounded everywhere a pulse can get to." She brought home the script segment—repartee between haughty Leia and a snarky Han Solo, whom she's hiring to complete the mission.

She had the shrewd idea to practice it with her good friend Miguel Ferrer. The Beverly Hills family group was still intact. Todd was now dating Donna Freberg, and Gabry Ferrer was dating Debby Boone; both couples would soon marry. Miguel was different from his gentle brother Gabry. He was "sharp tongued," not unlike Carrie. "You didn't want to fuck with him," says Donavan Freberg. Miguel reading Han Solo, a rakish smuggler with a bounty on his head, seemed a good fit. As for Carrie reading Leia, she brought all she'd learned at Central into her personification.

When Carrie arrived at the studio to audition, she was assigned to read with an actor whom Lucas actually didn't want in the film because he'd already been in a Lucas film, *American Graffiti*, and, anyway, he was too old—thirty-three. His name was Harrison Ford. Married with two young children and ironic and undemonstrative by nature, Harrison was a Hollywood hipster. He had worked as a carpenter and handyman to established actors and singers, and he hung out at the insider bohemians' West Hollywood restaurant Port's; he was a good friend of Eve Babitz, a writer who chronicled the sensibility of hip Hollywood in such works as *Eve's Hollywood* and *Slow Days, Fast Company*.

In their videotaped scene together—during which Carrie, as the princess, describes how she's hidden the "plans and specifications" and what her ploy is to get them to safety—Harrison is clearly flirting with her. Carrie, for her part, looks quite beautiful, with soft, darkened, styled hair and a long high-necked wool sweater. "You'll get your reward" when you finish the job, Leia assures the rakish Solo. She delivers her lines with a passionate hauteur and a lot of leaning in, as if she were pouring English tea while gently trying to talk a lordly peer into a smart but risky gambit. Bardy's elocution lessons had paid off.

The actress Amy Irving was also auditioning for the part, and she was paired off with the young actor Christopher Allport. She used a soft and stately near-English accent, not as confident and sharp as Carrie's. Carrie would later say that what persuaded Lucas to choose her over Amy, despite Carrie's lack of major beauty, was that she "wasn't a damsel in distress; she was a fighter." It's been said that Fred Roos's influence strongly affected the choice of Carrie over Amy Irving.

A week after her audition, Carrie got the news from Debbie's agent: "They called. They want you." In recounting her reaction in *The Princess Diarist*, Carrie says she ran down the street in the rare L.A. rain in near disbelief: "They would pay me nothing and fly me economy, but I was Leia and that was all that mattered." Later, during the filming itself, she would tell Simon Templeman, Griffin Dunne, and others that she thought the movie was nutty and bound to fail. But for now she felt triumphant.

Despite Lucas's initial reservations, Harrison was cast as Han Solo and a fresh-faced young actor who had been in wholesome network sitcoms, Mark Hamill, was cast as Luke Skywalker. Alec Guinness would be Obi-Wan Kenobi.

This was early 1976. Carrie was nineteen. Her contract ordered her to lose ten pounds for the role. Carrie withdrew from Central. Debbie was happy for her daughter, but in her movie-star-diva way, she was upset that Carrie had to fly coach, not first class, to the film site, which was Carrie's now-adored London.

Carrie lost the required ten pounds at a Texas fat farm that Debbie recommended; small weight loss was standard in contracts, especially for women. Carrie also knew she needed help embodying Princess Leia, so, upon the recommendation of friends, she called a highly regarded acting coach, Manhattan-based Marilyn Fried. Before flying back to England to start shooting, Carrie flew to New York. She spent several weeks meeting with Fried, who had a warm and welcoming presence and immediately adored Carrie. Marilyn would become a mother figure to Carrie. "Carrie wanted an acting coach—absolutely!"

says Marilyn. "She was excited. She came to me with such enthusiasm. She was so witty! So clever! I loved her! Who *didn't* love her?" Twice a week Carrie trundled to the cozy living room of Marilyn's Christopher Street apartment. "She came with the script and said, 'What do we do?! What do we do?!' And I said, 'We have to make Leia lovable, logical, and believable.'"

Together they created an inner life for the cardboard Leia. While "jingle-jangling with words and ideas—that's how Carrie is, and I utilized that," the two women set about figuring out "'What is her behavior? What is she like? What is her daily life?' I would say, 'She's not "Princess Leia"—let's make this personal: a girl, a woman.' It wasn't from the script; we were creating the backstory, which is really important. 'Was your mother a queen? Was your father a king? What year were you born? What was your education like?' We would find wonderful things that Leia would do during the day. Pleasurable things. And then we would find the obstacles in her life."

Carrie and Marilyn let their imaginations go while reading the script and picturing Leia as a little girl, an older girl, and a young woman—an identifiable female. "We had many sessions, here in my living room. We took the script and turned Leia into a person for Carrie to be. She'd lived a whole life until that moment when the movie began. An actor has to love a character, and by the end of our sessions Carrie loved Leia."

Thus prepared to inhabit her character, Carrie flew to the Borehamwood Elstree Studios in London to begin filming.

On the first day of shooting—March 22, 1976—came an important event: the creation of her "double bagel" hairstyle. Carrie's hairstylist, a jaunty Irishwoman named Pat McDermott, presented Carrie with a group of images of hairstyles for Leia, Carrie would later write. "This isn't a hairdo, it's a hair don't," Carrie would say at several of the choices in the exotic display. Although she would greatly laugh at it later—as would the public and her friends—Carrie thought what she called the "hairy earphone configuration" was better than most of the rest. When

Carrie pleaded with her good-natured hair stylist for a simpler style, Pat reminded her that it was an "outer space film" and she couldn't merely wear a ponytail. The hairstyle—originally worn by Mexican women in the previous century—was one that made Carrie feel "as if all I needed was a dirndl, a goat, and clogs to be ready to take my place in *The Sound of Music.*"

The filming had already taken some hits. Earlier scenes had been shot in Tunisia, and there had been problems with some of the visual effects: the front projection in the cockpit wasn't working, a storm had destroyed the set, and R2-D2 wasn't working. "George was under siege," recalls Jonathan Rinzler, author of *The Making of "Star Wars"* and a former staffer at Lucasfilm. Already, no one at 20th Century Fox except for Alan Ladd Jr., then president of Fox's film division, thought the movie—this fantasy of Lucas's—would be anything but a flop. Lucas had dreamed of this space opera for years, but the studio's business division had been invested in making sure it didn't get made; Ladd had virtually been its only champion.

Even Carrie herself had made fun of the movie when she got to the set. She called Griffin Dunne, long-distance, and told him, "Oh, God, I'm acting opposite a nine foot tall hairy fucking ape, and we hold these little ray guns and we're not even on a fucking set," he recalled much later, possibly exaggerating for effect.

Two months into the shooting, the crew had a party for Lucas's thirty-second birthday. Carrie was one of the few women at the party. In a then-"quirky" incident that would be considered deeply offensive today, the crewmen tried to get her drunk—and did. In *The Princess Diarist*, Carrie recounted the episode as a "kind of joke abduction"— "jovial" and "certainly not a serious thing," with a woozy Carrie spirited to an unknown location. Still, her head was hurting. When he realized she was reeling and the crew was making fun of her, Harrison, whom she'd perceived as remote and intimidating, played the savior. "Pardon me, but the lady doesn't seem to be very aware of what she wants," he said, heroically. Even though Carrie thinks her "rowdy" captors didn't have any seriously nasty plans, they were noisy and "Harrison was suddenly making a great show of saving me from what I can only guess at . . . What began as a kind of pretend stage-fight tug-of-war" between the crew and Harrison evolved into a seemingly genuine fight for, as Carrie later put it, her "wine sodden virtue." Carrie would present all this decades later with wit and understatement—and with no outrage at the randy crewmen.

That evening Carrie and Harrison grew tentatively intimate. They had dinner with a group of people, including a British actress, Koo Stark, next to whose beauty Carrie felt "incredibly self-conscious" and "awkward." A three-month affair with Harrison started that night. This affair was one that no one in the cast or crew knew about for decades. For Carrie, it was marked by such insecurity, which she revealed in real-time diary passages, that it stands in striking contrast to the sophisticated, world-weary "brand" she was putting out in interviews just after the movie was released.

Over the subsequent three months, Carrie and Harrison would have a "sleepover," as she put it—at her apartment—every Friday night. She was very self-conscious with him. "He was not a garrulous person; I inadvertently held my breath quite a bit" during their workweek together, deducing that "on our relative lists of priorities as we went about filming, I might have ranked as high as number fifteen on his agenda while Harrison was my number one." One can picture her pain. "It was all so confusing . . . Harrison made me feel very nervous. I got tongue-tied in his company, and clumsy."

During nights with him, she, such a talker, was frustrated by his "frightening awful silences," which she would "suffer" through. Like many other young women at the time, she was dying to be sexually sophisticated. Simon Templeman had been her only boyfriend, though Griffin Dunne had done her the friendly favor—something a non-romantic friendship could bear only at a tender age—of relieving her of her virginity about a year earlier. She had started the movie *wanting* to have an affair to bring her real life up to the level of her conversationally proffered one. But by choosing a difficult, withholding, married man fourteen years older than herself, she had set herself up for challenge and for misery. That misery miraculously vanished when she confidently emitted Leia's arrogance—"I recognized your foul stench when I was brought on board," she intoned in one scene, with what she felt was too much of a British accent. But that attitude hid her self-admitted "hopelessness" and "worthlessness" and her "vague sense of desperation" in a secret emotional vault that drugs would eventually assuage. (Carrie and Harrison smoked a good deal of marijuana together, but she was not yet doing other drugs such as cocaine and painkillers.)

Carrie knew her gifts, and she knew that she had chosen a less than appreciative recipient for them; "I could charm the birds out of anyone's tree but his." She called friends—as she would all her life—to talk through the frustration of the affair. But the talks didn't help; in such stacked-deck romances they rarely do. "I suspect that no matter what happens I will allow [the romance] to hurt me. Eat away at my insides," she wrote in *The Princess Diarist*. In many ways, Carrie was a typical nineteen-year-old in a disadvantaged love affair with a man who would never love her back. "I was with him when we worked in scenes together and I tried to avoid him otherwise so as not to annoy him."

Harrison would continue to make Carrie uncomfortable over the decades. When, in the last year of her life, she broke the news of their romance in *The Princess Diarist*, she worried what he would think of her revelation. She sent him a rough draft, and he never wrote her back. Two months before she died, when she was filming the movie *Wonderwell* in Italy, she confided to her co-star Vincent Spano that she was very concerned about Harrison's reaction: Had she made a mistake in spilling the beans? By then, Carrie was known as a confident, tough, ballsy truth teller. This concern and regret was unusual and poignant.

"I'm sorry it's not Mark [Hamill]," she'd opined at one point of her far more accessible co-star. In fact, Hamill disclosed years later that there was flirtation going on with them on set as well. "We *were* really attracted to each other," he said. "We got to the point where we were having our make-out sessions—and then we pulled back. A great way to cool any amorous feelings is laughter, and," even then, "Carrie had this sort of Auntie Mame desire to find humor in everything. We also realized that, if we did this"—had a romance—"everything would fundamentally change. Wisely, we avoided that."

But Hamill, the young son of a military man, was definitely fascinated with his Hollywood royalty co-star, and he let drop all his emotional caution once the movie was wrapped. "After we finished filming I did fall in love with her. I was completely under her spell," he confessed at her memorial service. "I went to Beverly Hills." At a party to which she had invited him, "everyone was somebody famous. I was the only one nobody ever heard of. This exotic life! I'd never met kids who grew up in Beverly Hills." Still, then and later Hamill realized, "I thought I couldn't handle her as a girlfriend. She was so high maintenance. She was so laser-focused on you when you were with her—you felt you were her *best* friend."

Wait'll you see it—this is such a stupid movie," Carrie had told her best friend, Griffin Dunne, while she was filming *Star Wars*. She also said this to her high school friend Miguel Ferrer (with whom she had practiced her lines) and his girlfriend, Fredi Duke, the girl with whom Carrie had ditched high school on one of her first freshman days. Miguel and Fredi were living together in Malibu, and Miguel was a drummer for his mother Rosemary Clooney, and when Miguel and Fredi went to New York to visit Carrie and Griffin at the end of 1976, all Carrie could do was make fun of the movie she had just made.

Carrie and Griffin were sharing a tiny apartment that he has described, literally or figuratively, as the "maid's quarters" in the Hotel des Artistes apartment houses on Manhattan's West Side. Griffin was moonlighting as a waiter at Beefsteak Charlie's while becoming a writer and producer. But Carrie was wrong about "stupid" *Star Wars*. "The minute we saw it," Griffin has recalled, "we knew Carrie's life would never be the same." Todd Fisher felt the same; everyone did. Which is interesting, because even a month before the movie's release, some executives at Fox thought it would tank. According to some accounts, they were ready to sell it to German investors until Steven Spielberg saw it and raved about it.

The public agreed with Spielberg. Upon the movie's release in May 1977, *Star Wars* was an immediate zeitgeist shifter. The movie completely reinvigorated Fox, and it changed the trend in Hollywood movies from serious adult social-issues pieces—*Klute, Serpico, One Flew over the Cuckoo's Nest, Dog Day Afternoon*—to special-effects-driven fantasy, a genre that previously had not seen innovation for twenty years. The special effects and the sound—designed by Ben Burtt, a physicist and "a poet of sound"—and John Williams's soaring music all made it something no one had experienced before: a genuine space opera. Lucas described his passionate intent: "I want to give young people some sort of faraway exotic environment for their imaginations to run around in. I have a strong feeling about interesting kids in space exploration. I want them to want it. I want them to get beyond the basic stupidities of the moment and think about colonizing Venus and Mars. And the only way it's going to happen is to have some dumb kid fantasize about it—to get his ray gun, jump in his ship and run off with this Wookiee into outer space. It's our only hope, in a way."

Star Wars would become—sequels abounding—a mega-brand. It was partnered with *Jaws* as the movie made for the new phenomenon, the summer blockbuster. The star of *Jaws*, Carrie's fellow Beverly High alum Richard Dreyfuss, would soon become her neighbor, fellow manic-depressive, and lifelong close friend. But *Star Wars* would end up being that much bigger: by December 1977, it surpassed *Jaws* by $1 million. (Steven Spielberg took out an ad in *Variety* to congratulate George Lucas.) By eleven months later, domestic retail sales totaled over $164 million, and as of today, says Jonathan Rinzler, the first *Star Wars* movie alone has totaled over $700 million worldwide.

Carrie attended the May 25, 1977, grand opening at Grauman's Chinese Theatre with her brother, who reported she was a "wreck" before the screening, chain-smoking and pacing. They took their seats, and they were, wrote Todd, left "speechless, wide-eyed, and . . . blown away" by the movie.

Carrie, Harrison, and Mark went on a whirlwind promotional tour, from May through July, for what *The Baltimore Sun* called the movie that was "as everyone this side of solitary confinement knows . . . a box office phenomenon of *Jaws* proportions. Armies of patrons are massing at movie theaters to experience *Star Wars*, then going forth and reigniting more legions." As the uproar loudened, George Lucas praised Leia's character as a new kind of woman: "I wanted someone tough because I didn't perceive the princess as just a damsel in distress"—that concept would frequently be reprised. "I knew she had to stand up to the bad guys. That's why I chose Carrie Fisher."

Carrie's initial dismissal of the "ridiculous" movie changed quickly and decisively. "The girl is not an alcoholic, she's not a prostitute; she's a normal, sophisticated young woman," she told reporters who noted that her role as the "lovely and gutsy princess also establishes her as something other than the daughter of Debbie Reynolds and Eddie Fisher." Yes, she couldn't help but be wry Carrie; she "wanted to say to these people" who praised it to the skies, "Lighten up, it's only a movie." But another part of her understood that her sarcasm and contrarian intelligence radiated truthfully: "I don't see myself as tough, but I'm fairly independent for someone my age." She now could appreciate the phenomenon it had become, although she put it in a measured way. "I knew *Star Wars* would have an audience," Carrie said. "But it would be megalomaniacal to think it would be this big. We knew it was going to be special, but we really couldn't have expected *this*."

Women and girls especially saw Princess Leia as a feminist action hero. "I was just hitting puberty when *Star Wars* came out and my friends and I were quietly knocked out," says Stephanie Wilson, a devotee who has worked at *Star Wars* conventions and shows. "She was supposed to be a victim—she was taken prisoner and she watched her whole planet get destroyed—but she *never* fell apart." While her captor (and father, though we do not know this yet), Darth Vader, has her in a cell and is trying to get information from her by torturing her (which is implied but off-screen), she *never* reveals the information. What she *does* do is put the specifications for blowing up the enemy in the droid R2-D2; hence, the hologram speech. The speech, which will become a classic, is "I've placed information vital to the survival of the rebellion into the memory systems of this R2 unit. My father will know how to retrieve it. You must see this droid safely delivered to him on Alderaan. This is our most desperate hour. *Help me, Obi-Wan Kenobi. You're my only hope.*"

"But she's not *crying* in the message," Stephanie Wilson recalls that she and her friends realized. "She's *not* begging. She's *not* nervous." She wants the Rebellion, of which she is leader, "to get the Death Star plans, whether she lives or dies." And she has the wit to ask, "Aren't you a little *short* to be a storm trooper?" when Luke Skywalker, disguised as a storm trooper, walks into the prison cell in which Darth Vader is keeping her. "She's like Rosalind Russell in *His Girl Friday*. She still has the power. Even though her planet was getting destroyed, she is *still* the princess."

Alyssa Rosenberg of *The Washington Post* would later write what many thought when they first encountered Carrie: "Leia's nerves as a revolutionary are clear from the moment she arrives on the screen . . . She takes shots at the Storm Troopers boarding her ship, gets stunned with a blaster in her hand, and has the audacity to make Darth Vader feel ashamed of himself." She also takes the destruction of her home planet, Alderaan, in a kind of stride, and she subtly bests the arrogant Han Solo. Carrie's Leia combined the classy toughness of Katharine Hepburn with the cool, vaguely aristocratic-sounding snark of Ali

MacGraw's Jennifer Cavalieri in *Love Story*, and she eventually paved the way for Jennifer Lawrence's characterization of Katniss Everdeen in *The Hunger Games*.

By the time Carrie finished her three-month-long *Star Wars* tour, she was not just Carrie Fisher of *Shampoo* and Debbie-and-Eddie. By now, Griffin Dunne recalled, speeding up the time frame for emphasis, "things happened very fast—the phones rang off the hook all day, all night . . . People would try to get ahold of me to find out how to seduce her. 'Just pretend you're not interested,' I'd say. Our deal"—their friendship—"confused the hell out of people."

In speaking to journalists, Carrie seemed very far from the vulnerable and insecure, even self-loathing, girl in the diary entries during her affair with Harrison. She seemed far from the desperately needy, openhearted girl that Selina Cadell and others saw and would continue to see over the years. *This* Carrie was aware of the Next Dorothy Parker image she was cultivating. Her distinctive persona was accentuated by the fact that, unlike most movie ingenues, she always wore writerly clothes: high-necked, long-sleeved, black. She spoke with the *New York Times* writer Anna Quindlen about wanting to work with Robert Altman. And she spoke of the thrill of having just worked with Sir Laurence Olivier and Joanne Woodward in her role as the scampish boarder in the home of an angry man and his unhappy wife in the stagy TV production of *Come Back, Little Sheba*, which she had quickly filmed right after *Star Wars*. Carrie kept her slightly Anglicized upscale accent in that presentation; the 1940s play had a period-appropriate formality. Although she didn't confess this until decades later, Olivier was intimidating to her, but he set her at ease by his touching perfectionism (did a midwestern man say "Mornin'" or "Good morning"? he asked Carrie). She also confessed that he was a dirty old man: he constantly asked her if she was having her period.

In interviews, she answered the obligatory questions about her infamous childhood—saying, for example, that Debbie had long ago made up with Elizabeth Taylor. But mainly, she made fun of herself—those *I-want-cheekbones!* jokes, and anecdotes about her ordinary looks. "When I went and saw *Shampoo*," she said, "I sat next to a woman who kept telling me"—Carrie, not her on-screen character—"to be quiet all through the movie." She threw around big words: there was a "visceral catharsis" about the tour that she and Harrison and Mark had just finished. Quindlen analyzed Carrie this way: "There is a serious side and a sarcastic side, and both are expressed in the same even voice, with a drop of pitch for a heavy goof."

A key adult friend of Carrie's at this time was Joan Hackett. The actress—sharp, opinionated, and sometimes difficult, best known for her role in *The Group*, and twenty-two years older than Carrie—had lived with Debbie and Carrie in the Seventy-Fourth Street town house during the *Irene* period. Carrie once described her as one of her parents' alcoholic next-door neighbors: "They had irony; and I just had a weirdly sophisticated life that didn't give me things in common with other people." But the flippancy hid the importance Joan held in Carrie's life. She would become one of Carrie's closest friends. Having Joan as a friend abated some of Carrie's anger at Debbie. Joan saw a value in Carrie's roiling complexity. She encouraged Carrie to keep a journal; she sensed that Carrie was a writer at heart. And she encouraged Debbie to get Carrie therapy in New York.

Their close friendship continued through the 1970s. The near quarter of a century of distance in their ages seemed irrelevant. "I knew Joan Hackett; she was a year or two older than us; Carrie and Joan were best friends," says Elizabeth Ashley, Debbie's friend, who would get to know Carrie well when they co-starred in Broadway's *Agnes of God* in 1982. Says Selina Cadell, "It was an untrammeled friendship. With Joan"—as opposed to with Debbie—"you didn't have to perform to be loved."

In her post–*Star Wars* interviews, Carrie was aware of how she came across: as the wry if inadequately educated commentator. "I know I'm getting a reputation for being flip with interviewers," she told Guy Flatley of the *Chicago Tribune*. "When I was younger they called me precocious, but now I'm too old to be precocious, so they either write that I'm a little glib or a little pretentious . . . All the interviews I've read make me sound so snide, so fashionably sardonic . . . They always say, 'She flipped,' 'She quipped,' 'She wisecracked.'" With the insecurity tucked aside, this was Carrie at twenty, and she reveled in it.

Others did, too.

Carrie bought a corner apartment on the twelfth floor of the Eldorado at 300 Central Park West, off Ninetieth Street. Richard Dreyfuss had an apartment there as well. "She lived in the back; I lived in the front," Richard recalls. "She had this apartment that looked small, but it got bigger as you went in. I don't think I ever knocked on her door without hearing a party within. Joan Hackett was always there. And Teri Garr." The bubbly actress and dancer, twelve years older than Carrie, who had been in Mel Brooks's *Young Frankenstein* and had played Richard Dreyfuss's wife in *Close Encounters of the Third Kind*, would soon be one of Carrie's best friends. Carrie was becoming a collector of on-site friends. When Mark Hamill called to say he was in town at a hotel, Carrie told him—as she would later in her Beverly Hills canyon houses say to *everyone* she liked—"Move out of the hotel and stay with me!"

Selina Cadell would visit Carrie in New York now, and she would stay with Carrie's "father figure" Ted Pugh at his large apartment near the Hotel des Artistes. "When Carrie behaved badly—she would sometimes not turn up for a dinner or theater date with us," Selina says— "Ted would tear a strip off of her for her rudeness. He'd say, 'Carrie, that is out of order! I won't come back tomorrow to see you!' Her little face would crumble, though later she would kiddingly say, 'Teddy told me off!' I came to understand that she had never learned that being on time can be a pleasant thing to do. *No one* had really taught her that. Sometimes she'd be two hours late to meet me and Ted; she'd been brought up as a spoiled child. But she also wanted love so much; she was always paying for everyone! *Ted* did tell her off. Ted taught Carrie an *enormous* amount. He loved her and she loved him, and he was kind to Carrie when Debbie was drinking."

Selina saw the difficulty of Carrie's relationship with her mother, the complexity of which was the subject of conflicting interpretations. "The only time I actually met Debbie was in her fifth-floor room at the Plaza Hotel," Selina continues. "Carrie and I had to put her to bed because she had drunk too much"—a stress-based problem Debbie has never denied. "Carrie did *not* want to put her mother to bed. But she did it. When I met Debbie I saw she was someone who demanded attention all the time, and Carrie wouldn't get a look from Debbie until she got her attention by being funny and witty. It was given that Debbie often drank too much. But," notably, "Carrie *didn't* drink." Selina adds, dryly, her theory about the reason for Carrie's avoidance of alcohol and the degree of Carrie's rebellion from Debbie: "If Debbie had been a drug addict, I think Carrie *wouldn't* have been."

The New York that Carrie moved to in 1977 was all about irony and creativity; there was a love for a certain kind of soulful hipness and darkness. The city was broke, and it had just gone through a summer of humid heat, an enervating blackout, and the terror of a mysterious murderer who called himself the Son of Sam. You could trip over bodies on the sidewalk, and there was so much crime and disorder that if you were moving your stereo from one apartment to another and set it down on the street to scratch your nose, a thief could pick it up and take it away. A young person could feel cool and spiritually virtuous just by choosing to forgo easier pleasures by living in grungy Manhattan, and many moved to New York for that reason.

It was also a time of thriving nightlife, fashion, and diverse female role models. There was the punk princess Deborah Harry—blond and beautiful, unsmiling and monotone—leading Blondie at CBGB and mingling coolly with boldfaced names at Studio 54. By contrast, Diane Keaton—with her winsome "La-di-*das*" and her wittily mannish outfits—was the new fashion icon. Upscale feminism was alive and well, even as young women were bombarded with mixed messages. Two elite Sarah Lawrence alumnae offered two distinctly different ideal paths: the singer Carly Simon, a sex goddess among the coolest men just years before, had settled down with her catch of a husband, James Taylor, and was having babies, while Jill Clayburgh would soon, in *An Unmarried Woman*, trumpet the self-reliance-building message that being without a man was better than being with even the most desirable of men.

The city was a good place for sophisticated, ironic Carrie Fisher to be.

Toward the end of 1977, Griffin Dunne introduced Carrie to John Belushi, the biggest star of TV's two-year-old *Saturday Night Live*. This would be an important but, ultimately, sadly significant friendship for her. John liked Carrie immediately because she made him laugh.

The show's writers and cast were in their late twenties to early thirties, and they were like one big incestuous family. Interestingly, at the time, the show had as many female as male writers. One of the three woman writers, Rosie Shuster, was separated from Lorne Michaels, the show's conceiver/producer; her father, the noted comedian Frank Shuster, had been Lorne's mentor, and she had been with the dominating, five-years-older Lorne since just before she was a teenager. "It was the sex, drugs, rock and roll—and feminist—'70s and I wanted to be free" was her reason for splitting from him. "Lorne was incredibly into the music and humor and culture of the times, but there was something in terms of a wife where he still was on the old software." She was now dating Dan Aykroyd, who, despite his genially ordinary looks, webbed toes, Asperger's, and mismatch-colored eyes, was a lady-killer. He had dated Gilda Radner, and he would soon date the fashion model Susan Forristal, who eventually became Lorne's second wife. Belushi—the brashest and most seemingly out of control—was the only one to have married and stayed with his teenage sweetheart: Judy Jacklin Belushi, who reined him in nicely. The *SNL*ers were a smart, young in-crowd, and Carrie fell right in with them.

After all, she was Hollywood royalty while the *SNL* people were on top of the world right now. That said, they were also provincial: From Canada. From Illinois. From the Midwest and the South. Even *SNL* people who had some connection to Hollywood couldn't help but be awed by Carrie's glamorous lineage and how she played it up so naturally. The show's talent booker Barbara Burns, who would become very close to Carrie, had a father who was the business manager for *Easy Rider*'s producer, Bert Schneider, himself the son of the president of Columbia Pictures. "Carrie grew up in a Hollywood we could only imagine," Barbara says. "She was the only person we *ever met* who had flashbulbs—from strangers, not relatives—in her face from childhood! Her family was like the Kardashians today: everyone knew everything about them. She knew every angle of dealing with that celebrity world, the Hollywood machine, past and present—it was ingrained in her. We might have been smart and arrogant, and we got successful so fast! But we had ordinary backgrounds. *She* had cameras trained on her since the day she was born."

SNL's venerated star writer, the sadistically dark-humored Michael O'Donoghue, was from Rochester, New York. He was older than most of the rest of them—thirty-seven now—and he deeply impressed the others because he had started a theater group based on the French absurdists and had published stories in the *Evergreen Review*. "Oh, what a mischievous dandy Michael was!" says Susan Forristal. "He was devilish and he could charm anyone." Michael lived with Anne Beatts, who was, along with Rosie and Marilyn Suzanne Miller, one of the three female writers on the show and the co-editor of *Titters*, the first collection of feminist humor. *Titters* was smart and snarky. O'Donoghue and Beatts affected an intimidating boho-intellectual élan together, and when Carrie came on the scene, she and Michael sensed each other's darkness. A part of Carrie badly wanted to be a literary writer, and O'Donoghue was one. He would become one of Carrie's best friends.

Carrie started including the *SNL*ers at parties in her apartment—dazzling parties. "Her parties kind of spanned the celebrity and literary worlds, all these witty New York types," says Rosie Shuster. At these get-togethers, Shuster recalls being "really amazed at Carrie and Griffin Dunne. The polish, the witty repartee: they could have been a movie. The way they operated together—I don't know how romantic it was, but it was really notable and striking. I had a really strong sense of the Nick and Nora Charles–ness of them. Carrie was so sophisticated—a little girl with such a big voice."

Whenever Selina Cadell visited Carrie in New York, she witnessed that Carrie-Griffin bonhomie as well. "I can remember singing in an open-top car with Griffin and Carrie in Manhattan," Selina says. "She sang a wonderful old Judy Garland song. (She sang Judy Garland songs a *lot*.) We were collapsing all over each other, falling all around; Carrie and Griffin had such free, unruffled moments of creativity together. Griffin would impersonate Carrie," whom he called Fuck-Face. "And she would impersonate him. And I would try—badly!—to impersonate both of them. With Carrie and Griffin, I would laugh until we wept.

"I can't say enough how utterly, utterly charming Carrie was," Selina continues. "Her ability to say things that other people did not say: she was so funny and so dangerous, and she took you to the very brink. She lit up a room when she came in. You could be at a party and you would be waiting for Carrie to come, and when she came in, everything changed because it was Carrie. She was very small and her little wrists and feet were tiny, but she was a 'pint pot'—that's an English term for magnetism. Her eyes lit everything up, and there was also her dangerous surprises. She was magnetic. You'd think you were on safe ground, but she could pull the rug out from under you with her wicked, wicked sense of humor."

One night, for example—because Selina was constantly telling Carrie she didn't want Carrie to keep *paying* for her—Carrie pulled a stunt on her friend. Carrie was having a birthday party for herself at Sardi's; at least two dozen people were coming. Selina made clear she would only come if she picked up her own tab. After the fine meal, the waiter arrived with the check—for the entire table. Carrie raised her wineglass and announced to all her guests that Selina was footing the whole bill. In the glare of the entire table, Selina, after a gulp, had no choice but to agree, wondering how the hell she was going to survive for the rest of the month. Then Carrie announced that it was a joke: she'd already treated everyone to the meal. "That was her wicked, impish humor," Selina has said. "Not cruel, just loving, and very, very naughty." A running joke between the two was Selina's gullibility. That Christmas, Carrie and Selina and Ted Pugh drove to Connecticut to pick out a Christmas tree "so deep green," Carrie said, "it was *blue*." "Blue? *Really* blue?" Selina had said guilelessly. The naive question of Selina's was, forever after, Carrie's sweet spot for teasing her. When Carrie would call Selina in the middle of the night—and, indeed, she would, a lot— Carrie would identify herself simply, with one word: "Bluuuue!"

When Selina had a role in *Uncle Vanya* in Birmingham, England ("the pits"), Carrie flew over and hired a car and driver, and no expense was spared. "The next day we drove into the Cotswolds, and Carrie insisted that my friends and I and she all spend the night in one of the most expensive hotels in England. I said, 'Carrie, no! No way can I ever repay you.' She wouldn't hear of not doing it. I think it came from the fact that when she was a child, people paid her with *things*, not affection. People did take advantage of that—as they had at Central. But I think she knew *we* weren't doing that—that we loved her." Those spurts of magnanimity alternated with her middle-of-the-night phone calls to Selina. Once Carrie called Selina at 2:00 a.m. and asked her to come over and comfort her. Selina, who was staying with Ted Pugh, rushed to get dressed and race the few blocks to Carrie's in the darkness. When she got there, Carrie "opened the door a crack," Selina recalled, "and said she had a man with her and I was no longer needed." Selina was incensed. "I tore her off *such* a strip the next day, and she never took me for granted again." In generous hindsight, Selina sees this behavior as part of Carrie's upbringing: she had somehow never learned appropriateness in that unusual childhood of hers.

Carrie was self-conscious about never having graduated from high school and leaving Central. She decided it was time to advance her education. But wanting and following through were different things. Carrie asked Griffin's friend the magazine writer Jesse Kornbluth if she could enroll in the New School for Social Research writing class that he was teaching. She gave herself the nickname Student Fisher to him (elsewhere, and to others, she would call herself Fishlet), but although she was happily accepted, she never showed up at Jesse's class. Charmed by his friend Griffin's famous and irresistible bestie, Jesse just sighed and said, "Student Fisher, take your A and go."

Similarly, she got herself into Sarah Lawrence College, which was barely an hour north of her apartment, but she didn't follow through on attending. Sarah Kernochan, a young director who was writing a musical for Joseph Papp's prestigious Public Theater, was a Sarah Lawrence graduate who helped talk Carrie into applying there. Tall, lanky, and blond, Kernochan, who had won an Oscar for the documentary *Marjoe*, had met Carrie months earlier, when Carrie and Mark and Harrison had just finished their *Star Wars* tour and were still a little delirious from it. Carrie and Mark kept jumping on their hotel bed, as Sarah recalls.

Sarah had heard from Harrison's friend Eve Babitz that Carrie had a beautiful voice, so she'd offered Carrie the lead in a musical about runaways, *Sleeparound Town*, which she was writing for Joseph Papp. Carrie, seeming not to care how bankable she now was, accepted right away. The new *Star Wars* star went down to the Public Theater and auditioned for Papp. "She gave a killer rendition" of Sarah's ballad "Mister Sloane," and "Joe was very excited," Sarah recalls. Sarah revisited Carrie at the Eldorado in the fall—"she had already started stocking it with the most amusing paraphernalia, an antler bed," woven out of willow branches—and when Carrie talked about wanting to go to college, Sarah pumped her up to apply to Sarah Lawrence. The college was noted for alumnae with elite pedigrees: Jill Clayburgh, Carly Simon, and Joanne Woodward—and Hope Cooke, who would become the queen of Sikkim. And the college was not un-proud of them. Carrie applied, and both she and the college announced that she was accepted. Carrie was proud of this fact. But rather than actually attending classes for more than the most minimal time, if any, she eventually hired a Sarah Lawrence teaching assistant, Mark Notturno, as a private philosophy tutor. Only an intellectually invested movie star's daughter with a superhit movie would do that. Notturno came to Carrie's apartment, and the two sat on her willow-branch bed and read the great philosophers together. (In very Carrie fashion, she made a point to tell Notturno, when they were reading Plato, that she'd been to the swingers' club Plato's Retreat.)

All of this—the intellectual interest (and insecurity); the family-name-value-stoked impressiveness; the preference for conversational or notes-based writing over hard, solitary writing work; the penchant for choosing small or offbeat projects arbitrarily rather than the big ones presumably enabled by her new star power; the expectation that people would come *to* her abode for play *and* work (all her books would be written by her sketching the words on a notepad while flopped on her bed, with editors often on the premises)—would be typical of Carrie.

Richard Dreyfuss—Carrie's neighbor at the Eldorado—had a little crush on her. He felt a "glow," he said, just entering her apartment, a mere two-minute inside-hallway walk from his own. In 1977, he was far more accomplished than she: he had starred in *Jaws* and *Close Encounters of the Third Kind* and had just given a sterling performance in *The Goodbye Girl*, which would imminently earn him the distinction of being the youngest actor to win the Best Actor Academy Award. Still, her charisma got to him and seemed to outpace his secret insecurity. "I loved watching how Carrie lived," Richard says. "You'd walk in and she made everyone feel at home. She had courage. She was smarter than anyone; *everyone could see it.* And she 'worked the word' in her sentences, turning a verb to a noun. Nobody talked like she did; everything was wordplay. She wasn't intimidated by anybody." (Actually, Carrie said she was immensely insecure at this time, but she hid it well.)

The two Upper West Side neighbors who'd been raised in Beverly Hills (they hadn't known each other at Beverly High; Richard was nine years older than Carrie) felt a kinship right away. Later they would realize that they were both manic-depressive, although neither had yet been diagnosed.

Early on, sitting in her apartment, Carrie acknowledged to Richard their sensed commonality—their shifts from hectic talking to quiet depression. "She said, 'You know, we're both from the same egg,'" he says. "That intimacy meant so much to me. It was her saying, 'You and I, no matter what: we share the root.' I absolutely needed that." From then on, Richard felt an undying loyalty to Carrie. "With Paul [Simon]"—to whom he would soon introduce her—"and, yes, he did hurt her, and, yes, it went on for a long time and they would both keep reopening the wound or the scab . . . and with her mother, Debbie, and her grandmother Maxene . . . with everybody, I was *always* on Carrie's side. Nobody's side but Carrie's." Dreyfuss tears up.

Many men were enamored of Carrie. One was the actor and producer Mark Metcalf, who was Griffin Dunne's and Amy Robinson's occasional producing partner and an actor in the play *Streamers* and the movie *Julia*. He met Carrie through a classmate of hers from Central when she was going back and forth to London to finish *Star Wars*. "I became infatuated with her," Mark says. "She was so magnificent, I broke up with Glenn Close," whom he says he was dating at the time, "to try"—unsuccessfully—"to be with Carrie." Mark also intensified his friendship with Griffin just to be near Carrie. "Griffin adored her, too; he was totally crazy about her. I don't know if they ever had a physical relationship, but he was capable of seducing anybody. He was also protective of her like a brother to a sister. Their closeness was so much— so much shared history and knowledge—that I wanted to be part of that fabric, that fluid. Carrie was impish and brilliant," but, Mark says, what was notable is that "she never sexualized herself the way other women do. She didn't wear makeup. Her seduction came from her brain and heart and sensibility. Her humanity. The whole time I knew her, she never played that sexuality card."

That said, she did use sex as part of her eccentricity or as proof of her sophistication. "She took me to my first strip club," Mark says. "She was nineteen or twenty—and she taught me how to slip a dollar bill into a G-string, and as a Christmas present she offered to buy me a hooker, which I turned down—I was drunk enough to go to sleep with my pillow." Carrie and Mark went to see *The Philadelphia Story* "six or seven times, and then we'd go around the corner to Glades, a hangout of mine on the Lower East Side, and do the Katharine Hepburn and Jimmy Stewart lines over and over. Neither of us was getting lost in a real love affair—sex never clouded it—but I loved her." She talked a lot about her parents, and, contradicting what some friends felt while validating what others said—and perhaps part of the whole messy push-pull—"she was always looking for her mom, comparing herself to her in some way. I don't know if she ever grew up and moved away from that connection to her mom.

"Carrie gave a birthday party for herself at the Café des Artistes," Mark continues. "It seemed like thousands of people came. She and I were on the opposite ends of the table, and we gave each other eye signals and crawled under the table and greeted each other in a dramatic, campy way after this 'long' separation. She was the center of gravity in that world of Central Park West. She had a kind of emotional heat. Her universe grew, and the party got bigger and bigger. And the wit never left her; it only got bigger.

"I knew her heart could be broken," Mark says. "I think it was broken many times, by her mother, by her father—not by a man yet, I don't think." He didn't know the Harrison Ford story. "She didn't have a boyfriend. But she was moving quickly through time and space in 1977, gathering up people who adored her. And later I would see that anyone she was with she turned into her sidekick—now, *that's* a skill! I'm sure she had all the insecurities we all had and even deserve, but at that age at that time she *didn't seem to* have them, although, as I said, you could tell her heart had been broken many times. She had been through a lot at a young age, and it was all so present tense in her: in her eyes, in how she talked about everything close to the bone—in that low, low voice. It *appeared* she was on top of it because she had this terrifyingly great sense of irony and 'control' about it all. But," he says perceptively, "she wasn't on top of it at all."

Guy Strobel came into Carrie's life in 1977, too. He was the musical director of *Sleeparound Town*, the Joseph Papp musical she had committed herself to. A handsome, wholesome, and talented young musical director and actor from Iowa, Guy had toured in *The Best Little Whorehouse in Texas* and *The Robber Bridegroom*. He had an empathic, upbeat, and even naive demeanor—he was a soother—and he came to see a lot of her vulnerability.

Carrie and Guy started to rehearse in late 1977. "I'd come to Ninetieth Street and I'd sit on her bed in her beautiful apartment, and Joan Hackett would be there or Teri Garr would be there or Richard Dreyfuss," Guy says.

But usually Carrie was alone when Guy came over. And they'd rehearse the *Sleeparound Town* song "Mister Sloane." "She had a beautiful low alto, very smooth and sensuous and powerful," Guy says. "We became close—soul mates." Carrie wasn't sardonic with Guy, he says. She seemed to appreciate his lack of irony enough to pack some of hers away and quietly drink deep of what he could give her: peace and normalcy. "She wasn't 'witty' with me. She called me Dr. Guy, because I tended to listen to people and fix things. Lots of people called me that.

Yes, once in a while she got, I guess . . . manicky. Her fast speech. But usually we just sat and played the piano and sang. She loved Keith Jarrett. She loved Chick Corea. She loved movie music. She would hear something she liked and burst into song, and I would sing along with her, and we sounded great together and were on the same wavelength. We'd go to the movies once a week. One time when we were preparing to go around the corner to see the art-house rerun of *Lolita*, which she was dying to see, she was so immobilized I had to carry her piggyback the *whole* way."

In retrospect, Guy now believes by that point she might have begun using Percodan, an aspirin and oxycodone pain reliever, what we would now call an opioid. It is very common for people who are bipolar to use opioids to try to blunt their racing thoughts, excessive energy, and urge to talk. No one knew then that Carrie was bipolar—or, as the term was then, manic depressive. But Guy *knew* she was in pain. "I asked her what she was in pain about; she never could say. I was her rock, in a way. And I was naive."

It didn't help matters that Eddie Fisher was staying in Carrie's spare bedroom. Eddie had come around, looking for money from Carrie. He was one year out of his fourth marriage, to the young actress Terry Richard. He hadn't had a nightclub career or an album in a long time, and he needed money and help. He had declared bankruptcy in 1970. At almost fifty, he had had a face-lift and now sported long hair and a mustache and beard, and he wore open shirts with medallions on chains bouncing off his chest. Carrie has explained her father's reappearance in her life—the first time since she was thirteen—this way: One night when she was tripping on acid with a friend, she called first Harry Karl and then Eddie; father-melancholy (even for her stepfather) had motivated her. In a flash, Eddie was on the next plane from L.A. to New York, moving in with his daughter.

Carrie now started what would be the long, erratic, unconventional, but ultimately poignant process of becoming, in essence, her father's guardian. She paid Guy to try to help Eddie fashion a whole new singing image for himself. "Carrie wanted him to try some new songs way past 'Oh! My Papa.' So we worked up Leon Russell songs," especially "A Song for You," "and Randy Newman songs; she *wanted* Eddie to succeed." The two men had sessions in Carrie's apartment once a week. "Eddie had the perfect instrument [voice], like John Raitt," says Guy. "I was arranging as I played and it made Eddie feel good. He said, 'Singing with you at the piano is like singing with a full orchestra.'" In Guy's view, "she was a daughter with money helping a father who didn't have any."

Perhaps Guy was particularly partial to Eddie because something Eddie said led to Guy's physical relationship with Carrie. "One night," after being grateful for Guy's help with him, "Eddie playfully said, 'Take my daughter—she's yours!' As if on cue, Carrie came running out of that little galley kitchen and across the room and *leaped* up into my arms, and I caught her and twirled her around. And that was the beginning of our romance." They slept together: "I loved her body; I loved her mind; I was sure she had feelings for me. It was a beautiful kind of happy, touchy, feeling—kissing, laughing. She did have big breasts. She wasn't insecure about that. She said, 'Everybody wants me because of that.'"

For the nightly Public Theater rehearsals of *Sleeparound Town* in December, Carrie would drive the Mercedes Debbie had bought her the forty blocks downtown to Guy's apartment. She would idle the car at Guy's Hell's Kitchen curb and ring his buzzer. "And then I would come down and take the wheel and we'd drive downtown" to the edge of the East Village, where Papp's Public Theater was.

"Joe Papp loved her in the starring role" of *Sleeparound Town*, says Sarah Kernochan. But Sarah started to notice that Carrie's work ethic was not at all what it should be. "The prospect of a month of rehearsals must have triggered a fit of overpowering laziness in her, such that you might feel standing at the base of Everest, looking up. Joe Papp wasn't that happy with her after he got the word that she wasn't cooperat-ing. The other cast members were pretty pissed because she seemed to be making fun of the play, which was her way of distancing herself.

"In retrospect, I kind of understand because I was treading water as an amateur; the play was not that good," Sarah says. Sarah and Carrie had a fight about how each was overworked, "and Carrie came up with a great line—'This isn't a suffering sweepstakes!' We both started laugh-ing. We *still* use that term in my house." (Sarah is long married to the Broadway librettist and director James Lapine.)

One day in early January 1978, after Carrie had been in L.A. for a few days, "she came into rehearsals looking like a cat who had swal-lowed a canary," Sarah recalls. Carrie announced, "I have a new boy-friend." Sarah asked, "Is he taller than you?" Carrie said, "Just barely."

Here is what had transpired.

On January 10, 1978, Richard Dreyfuss was in L.A. to receive the Los Angeles Film Critics Association Award for Best Actor in *The Goodbye Girl*, and Shelley Duvall was there to pick up her Best Ac-tress Award for *3 Women*, a Robert Altman movie. Paul Simon was ac-companying his girlfriend, Shelley. Huge-eyed and quirkily pretty, tall and thin, Shelley, twenty-eight, was having a big moment in quality movies. She was a favorite of Robert Altman's. She'd been a cosmet-ics salesgirl who had never left her native Texas when Altman met her on the set of his film *Brewster McCloud*, eight years earlier, and, as the story went, inveigled her to be in that film. She was ambivalent toward acting but quickly did a run of his highly touted films—*McCabe & Mrs. Miller* (1971), *Thieves Like Us* (1974), *Nashville* (1975)—and now, after a small supporting role in *Annie Hall*, she had starred in *3 Women*, for which she had just won the Cannes Film Festival Award. She was here with Paul to pick up this latest prize. Carrie was at the same event as part of the team receiving the *Star Wars* Best Movie award.

"I was staying at the new hotel on Burton Way, L'Ermitage," Richard remembers. "And I wanted us all to have dinner together. I don't know if I thought that Carrie and Paul would be so right for each other."

As Susan Forristal and others who knew Paul felt, Richard might have sensed Paul had a crush from afar. "Or if I was setting up a situation where I was somehow competing with Paul"—playing out his un-acted-upon crush on Carrie against a friend whom he deeply admired, just to get it out of the way and settle in his mind whether he should pursue his close friend romantically or not. He invited them all to the restaurant at his hotel. By intent or happenstance, "I was the yenta, the matchmaker."

Carrie certainly loved Paul's music. "Bridge over Troubled Water" had been *her* song, at El Rodeo, at Beverly, in Las Vegas, and at the Palladium. "If I could've ever been a fan of anyone, it would've been Paul, Joni Mitchell, and Cary Grant—go figure," Carrie has said.

The mutual crushes from afar became intense interaction in person. Even in the back of the car, going from the Film Critics award ceremony to L'Ermitage, Carrie and Paul were talking so absorbedly (and, according to Carrie, were so smitten with each other) that Shelley, with whom Paul had lived for two years, was sidelined.

"Paul's choice of women was very interesting," says one who knew him very well during those days. "They weren't particularly beautiful in the starlet sense, but they were smart. Because he's so smart and well read, Paul never felt he needed to go with the flow. Shelley was just really eccentric, bigger than life. Paul needed some fun people in his life because he was so self-controlled. He's a thinking man; you could see him thinking; he would almost stroke his chin. He was very disciplined in everything he did in life, very serious and sophisticated." One person who had dinner with Paul and Shelley during their time together thought "Shelley was the sweetest thing in the world, and he kept putting her down. He was hypercritical of her—he was nasty to her—and she didn't deserve it."

The main women in Paul's earlier life had very different backgrounds from his own. The love of the earliest adulthood of this solidly middle-class Jewish Queens boy was a gentle, stunning Welsh brunette named Kathy Chitty. She was a seventeen-year-old folk club employee in London when he traveled there at twenty-two, between his junior and his senior years at Queens College, looking to be inspired by the English music scene. Kathy helped him deal with his depression—something he would suffer from all his life—and she was the (differently initialed) "Cathy" he mentions romantically in "America," about a couple on a searching-for-America road trip. It was the song that made Carrie fall in love with Paul from afar in her youth. (She would excitedly quote those lines—"'Cathy, I'm lost,' I said, though I knew she was sleeping"—to a reporter when she and Paul got engaged.) His melancholic "The Sound of Silence"—starting with the line "Hello darkness, my old friend," and inspired by John Kennedy's assassination—was also a song of his that Carrie deeply admired.

In 1969, when he was in his late twenties, Paul married Peggy Harper. Peggy was tall, willowy, outspoken, and beautiful, the daughter of a troubled rural Tennessee family—a girl who had run away, young, to New York, to leave the downscale tumult for a bohemian urbanity. Paul met Peggy—a model turned graphic arts studio worker—when she was married to his manager, Mort Lewis, and he eventually lured her away from Mort. Peggy's relationship with Paul spanned some of his most musically fruitful years—"Homeward Bound," "Still Crazy After All These Years," and, of course, "Bridge over Troubled Water." The songs were eloquent and melodic, full of book-smart hopes and wistful longing. Many young men in the 1960s had that coloration to their souls, but few of their songs attained the perfection of Paul Simon's. He was one of the great songwriters of the last half a century—as his twelve Grammys, including a Lifetime Achievement Award, and his many other distinctions easily attest. In venerating his work, Carrie showed typical good taste.

Paul's wife, Peggy, "was cute and charming, a woman from the mountains," says one who knew them well during those years. "But she and Paul were so different; they were really a mismatch." His family was stable and bookish and liberal and Jewish; Peggy's was troubled

and highly fundamentally Christian. As justifiably famous and respected as he was during their years together, "Peggy wasn't worship-
ping Paul. Peggy would say things like, 'Why do you lie around all day?
Why don't you go to an office?' Which was good for Paul," the intimate
says. Peter Carlin, author of *Homeward Bound*, wrote that Peggy—a
gruff realist and two years older than Paul—"made certain, as their relationship grew, that Paul didn't let his pain, wealth, or power distance
him from the real world."

Once their son, Harper, was born in 1972—the early height of
women's liberation, with absolutism flaring—"Peggy Harper Simon became a staunch feminist," says a former confidante of Paul's, "telling
Paul he had to wake up in the middle of the night to feed Harper every
bit as much as she nursed him. They probably had some fights, but I
don't think of Paul as volatile. He's low-key and cerebral, high-strung
intellectually, and moody and brilliant and very self-absorbed and insecure and very complicated and very, very smart—always thinking." But
the fights brought home the issue of feminism, which suddenly in-
truded on many relationships and marriages—fixed, as they still were,
to prefeminist rules.

Another longtime Simon insider has stronger and less positive
things to say about Paul and Peggy: "It was a very volatile relationship.
She went through a Billy Idol–looking stage for a while. Peggy was
emotional and very southern. Peggy could push Paul's buttons. This
poor kid, Harper, would be riding in the backseat of limos, being fer-
ried around, with his parents not present. Paul was on the road all the
time, and Harper just kind of fell through the cracks. I almost never
saw Harper with either of his parents. Paul was never with him. Ian
[Hoblyn]," Paul's personal assistant, a dashing, charming young British
man who looked like Jeremy Irons, "was with Harper all the time." The
insider goes further: "Ian did and would later always do everything for
Paul. Bring him his toupee in the middle of the night. Paul was very
disciplined and brilliant, and these kinds of people have to be in control and have to have people do things for them. Paul would call Ian at

two in the morning to bring him something. And Ian would get up, get dressed, and say to the person he was with: 'Sorry. That was God on the phone—I gotta go.'"

A friend of Carrie's who knew Paul well defends him by pointing out the different expectations for men during that span of years. "The '60s and '70s were different times with fathers being in their kids' lives," says this friend. "Fame for a man; intense touring; becoming an icon—this was all-encompassing. Yes, people like Paul had assistants who picked up a lot of slack, including personal slack. But Paul loved his son."

After divorcing Peggy, and just as *Saturday Night Live* was start-ing, Paul went in a whole different direction. As opposed to the small-town, rural girls he had been involved with, he now began dating Edie Baskin, the show's official photographer and the heiress to Los Ange-les's Baskin-Robbins ice cream franchise. You couldn't be raised west of Robertson Boulevard in the 1950s through the '70s and not have a thrice-weekly Baskin-Robbins fix. Blond, fashionable, lanky, and so-cially connected, "Edie definitely had Lorne's ear," says an *SNL* insider. It was through Edie Baskin that Paul met Lorne, just before *SNL* pre-miered, with Paul as the show's first musical guest. Paul and Lorne became fast friends immediately. "This was the beginning of Paul's 'Hollywood period [New York version],'" the old friend says, demar-cating his time as a lauded singer-songwriter from his newer time as an Elaine's-going Manhattan A-lister.

After Edie came a few other women, and then, finally, Shelley Duvall. From outer appearances, Paul and Shelley were solid. Paul and Shelley and Lorne and Susan Forristal and Michael O'Donoghue and Anne Beatts would give "White Parties" at rented houses in the Hamptons, where everyone had to wear only white, parodying F. Scott Fitzgerald soirees. Susan and Lorne's house was a turreted, ten-bedroom affair. Life was chic, even if chic was being satirized and mocked by them.

During the meal that Paul, Shelley, Richard, and Carrie shared at

L'Ermitage after the Critics Awards event, a faux argument developed: Carrie said she was going to Sarah Lawrence, that she'd gotten in "through the philosophy department," that she'd always wanted to be college educated, given her history of dropping out of both Beverly and Central. ("I have always considered myself street smart," Carrie often said. "But, unfortunately, the street was Rodeo Drive.") Paul bet Carrie that she'd never go to Sarah Lawrence. Her career was in full swing; why would she take a pause for studies? He made a big point of this opinion. Carrie rebutted, "You don't even know me!"

The argument-cute was the beginning of their love affair. Right after they returned from L.A., because Paul was technically still with Shelley, Carrie and Paul tried to keep their romance a secret. An actor and nightclub performer named Greg Fleeman had met Carrie with Joan Hackett when he was performing at Reno Sweeney. Upper West Side neighbors, Carrie and Greg became friends. "She was undoubtedly the funniest woman I ever met in my life, and she had no boundaries," Greg says. One night in early 1978, Carrie asked Greg to take her to the movies on Eighty-Second Street. He happily obliged. "We go in and take our seats downstairs, and five minutes into the film she says, 'I gotta go!' and leaves. Paul Simon was waiting upstairs. I was the unknowing beard in the situation; they were still trying to keep the relationship quiet."

But soon it was out in the open, and Shelley Duvall went to England to film the movie *The Shining*, giving Paul and Carrie's relationship a long time to bloom. "It was definitely a super-duper infatuation," says Barbara Burns. Says Susan Forristal, "Paul and Carrie were very attracted to each other—just crazy about each other. And Paul was out to impress her. Early in their relationship, he rented a yacht that I think had been Aristotle Onassis's or Princess Grace's—it had some very romantic past. And they traveled to the Greek islands. Paul had Ian [Hoblyn] on board, and Carrie invited Craig and Melissa North," two friends Carrie had made from London and would keep for life.

After proudly telling Sarah Kernochan she was now dating Paul Simon, Carrie started missing rehearsals; she had bronchitis. But news of her evenings with Paul at downtown restaurants hit the columns, and Sarah and Joe Papp and the cast members were further annoyed. Of far more concern, Guy Strobel, who was still working with her, would see John Belushi showing up at the stage door at the end of rehearsals and very impatiently asking, "Where's Carrie? Is she done yet? Is she *done?*"

"John and Carrie had become very close right away," says Judy Belushi of her husband's platonic friend. "He didn't suffer fools. Carrie was very feisty." And they had something else in common: a predilection for cocaine.

There were rumors that Carrie and her *SNL* buddy were doing coke all night. This came to Joe Papp's attention, which displeased him greatly. Carrie panicked. "*Please* tell Joe that's not true!" Carrie begged Guy Strobel: "It's not true, it's not true! John's *not* doing that stuff! Will you come to Joe's office with me and be my moral support while I tell him that?" Guy said of course he would. He couldn't resist this hysterical plea from the girl he quietly adored. "Carrie and I went to see Joe Papp like you go to the principal's office, and I said, forcefully, to Joe, 'Carrie's my friend and what you've heard is *not true.*' Joe acted like he believed me." They had pulled it off.

Then, Sarah Kernochan says, just before *Sleeparound Town*'s autumn 1978 preview, "Debbie flew into town to the rescue." In her own life, Debbie was proactive. She had recently purchased an old post office building in North Hollywood and was turning it into the Debbie Reynolds Studios, with dance classes and rehearsal spaces. She seemed to welcome the chance now to help the daughter who had spurned her when she was at Central. "Debbie absolutely shaped Carrie up—no question about it," Sarah says. "They went through the whole script together. Carrie knew she couldn't do it unless Debbie showed her how. When Debbie was there, Carrie wasn't going to be taking drugs or letting her time with Paul get in the way. Carrie was nearly letter-perfect when we presented the scenes for Joe. Debbie was in the audience. I assume she rehearsed Carrie day and night."

Guy Strobel's feeling about Debbie was different. He didn't see her, as Sarah had, as the disciplined, no-nonsense saver of the day; he saw her as a difficult mother and a snob. "During the rehearsal, Debbie was sitting up in the bleachers with her hair all done, and she looked disapproving and judgmental. She wasn't being nice" was Guy's feeling. "The feeling I got from Debbie was 'Nobody can look as good as Debbie Reynolds.' And the feeling I got from Carrie was 'I can't be as good as my mother.'" Mother-daughter neediness is complicated and double-edged, with two women hiding sensitivity from each other. While several friends of Carrie's feel she felt less-than in comparison to her dazzling mother, and that Debbie's confidence and charisma heightened this, a friend of both women—especially of Debbie's— says that during this time Debbie sadly missed her closeness with her daughter.

Meanwhile, Carrie was growing increasingly fragile. She was spending a lot of time at Paul's stunning duplex apartment at 88 Central Park West near Sixtieth Street, its walls adorned by Helen Frankenthaler paintings. Paul and Lorne were literally next-door neighbors, their kitchen pantries connected by a secret door. Carrie would call Guy when Paul was out of town and she was under stress. Guy's naïveté was blasted away now; Carrie told him about the Percocet she was beginning to take in quantity. (Carrie's friends used the similarly named drugs interchangeably. Percodan is oxycodone. Percocet is oxycodone plus acetaminophen, also known as Tylenol.) The drug, by either name, was innocently called a painkiller then; today it is called an opioid, and we are aware of opioids' addictive properties. Guy continues, "She'd call and say, 'I'm bedridden at Paul's. Can you rescue me?'"

Let's pause for a moment and review what is now called bipolar disorder and was, when Carrie was a teenager and young adult, still called manic depression. The extreme form of bipolar—bipolar one—is a brain disorder, associated with cellular differences in energy processing, that involves episodes of mania with or without a major depressive episode before or after the mania. During the manic episodes, the person exhibits persistent euphoria, agitation, irritability, grandiosity, extreme happiness or anger, and racing thoughts. He or she might also have hallucinations or delusions, sometimes caused or worsened by lack of sleep. The manic episodes can last anywhere from several days to several months and are often severe enough to demand immediate hospital care.

Then there is bipolar two. It's not a "milder" form, since the depression can be as bad (the suicide rates for bipolar one and bipolar two are roughly the same), and the manic symptoms can feel very negative and make the depression far worse. Bipolar two looks just like depression but includes phases of hypomania: a less serious, more fleeting form of mania. A little hypomania can actually be a *good* thing. With hypomania, the patient feels "up" and has more energy than usual, and his or her mood is not out of control. Neither hypomania nor depression involves psychosis (a complete break with reality), but untreated mania can. And psychosis requires hospitalization. Both conditions—bipolar one and two—have no cure, but they are treatable, with early attention and vigilance. There is usually no risk of progression from bipolar two to bipolar one, but bipolar two can sometimes be prevented from turning into a highly recurrent illness with early treatment.

Carrie's description of herself as a teenager—"trying too hard . . . had to bowl you over with my wit and charm"—could be a normal experience or could be hypomania, says James Phelps, MD, clinical psychiatrist emeritus at Samaritan Mental Health in Corvallis, Oregon, and author of *A Spectrum Approach to Mood Disorders*. Dr. Phelps has seen thousands of bipolar spectrum patients. But here is the significant thing: he says it was very unusual to diagnose a teenage girl with bipolar two in the 1970s, when Carrie first went to psychiatrists, because "we knew *very little* about hypomania back then. We didn't even know much about hypomania in girls in the early '80s. Most girls like Carrie then would

have simply been diagnosed as 'depressive.' Because of how very little
we knew about hypomania, it took more overt manic behavior to get to
the diagnosis." And even if Carrie had manifested overt mania and
been diagnosed as a youthful manic-depressive (which was extremely
rare then), it is possible that she—and Debbie—would have rejected the
highly negative label. The term "manic depression" was *so* stigmatizing,
the negative words sounding unadorned, like mental illness, that young
patients, and certainly parents, would naturally recoil, and many did.

The change to the neutral name "bipolar disorder" (which was
coined by the German neurologist Karl Kleist in 1953) would make
the disorder much more easily accepted, but its official adoption by
American psychiatry, and the liberation from shame it conferred on
the patient, would not happen until 1980.

Dr. Dean Parker, a New York–based psychologist who has worked
with bipolar patients for decades, says, on the basis of a recent study,
"Fifty-six percent of bipolars"—whether diagnosed or not—"feel the
need to self-medicate. To calm down their mania, their raging thoughts,
to go to sleep. And they do it through opioids . . . Most take two a day."
Carrie would eventually admit to taking thirty a day.

Carrie would later describe what it felt like to live in her mind—
during the milder forms of mania—this way: "I will tell myself nine
stories about what I'm looking at . . . It can be fine because I'm never
bored, but you can't turn it off, so when it fastens itself on the negative
it's less pleasant. My drug thing was, if I tell seven stories about every
situation, [the drugs would help] to take it down to maybe a three."

In June 1978, there were previews at Roseland of the featured songs
in all the new prospective musicals that were candidates to be staged
on Broadway and off. *Sleeparound Town*—which Sarah Kernochan
wrote and of which Guy Strobel was musical director—was one such
play. Carrie had the lead, and she and Guy had been working on it for

months. Any play in tryouts was approved or vetoed by a panel of musical theater eminences according to how the songs were received. Carrie was all ready to sing "Mister Sloane." She and Guy had rehearsed
and rehearsed. "It was this introspective, haunting song, and she sang
it beautifully," he says. They now did the run-through: "checked the
mikes, checked the grand piano," which Guy would be playing. Carrie
expressed insecurity to Guy that she'd be performing among a group
of other singers who included Stephanie Mills, the young star of *The
Wiz*, "and she couldn't sing nearly as well as Stephanie Mills; she had an
inferiority complex."

They took a break for lunch. Carrie went to her apartment. Guy's
family was in town, and he lunched with them. "It wasn't like I had
orders: 'Guard her,'" Guy says. Just before they were to reconvene at
Roseland, Guy got a panicked call from Carrie. "I can't do it, I can't do
it!" she pleaded. "I'm just too nervous!" It was similar to the debilitating stage fright she'd suffered at the London Palladium. "I kept trying
to affirm: 'You're gonna be fine! You're gonna be great, Carrie!'" says
Guy. "But *she* kept saying, 'I just can't do it!'" Guy couldn't do what
Debbie had done: push Carrie past her crippling stage fright.

Tragically, despite how well she had mastered the song and how
long she had worked on it, Carrie didn't show up for the crucial performance.

Joe Papp had no choice but to cancel the play.

It mattered, and it also didn't. Carrie was still so considered the girl
of the hour in 1978 that when a goofy short film called *Ringo* was being
conceived—Ringo Starr would be featured as an L.A. map-to-the-stars
salesman with an adoring girlfriend—and the casting of an actress for
Ringo's adorable girlfriend came up, "Ringo and the producer and I
were tossing out names," says the film's director, Jeff Margolis, "and
after a couple of names we *all* said, 'Carrie Fisher!' at the same time.
It came about because (a) she was hot and (b) Ringo had met her. We
were hoping she'd be available." She said yes to the quick L.A.-based
shoot, "and we all loved working with her. It was a pleasure. She was a

doll." In the short, in which Ringo's father (played by Art Carney) is mad at him for his lack of ambition, she and Ringo spend much time in his car singing the song "You're Sixteen," which was a hit on Ringo's 1973 solo album after having been a 1960 hit for the singer Johnny Burnette.

Carrie's official, public connection with the *SNL* crowd came on November 18, 1978, when she hosted the show. She came out in her white Princess Leia gown, at first saying she wasn't going to wear it, then going into her I'm-so-ordinary-looking stance: if she didn't, no one would recognize her. After saying she'd merely tell a joke and then weaving humorously obscure and complicated *Star Wars* patter into her monologue (and getting tutored by the offstage voice of Obi-Wan Kenobi), she starred in a sketch, "New Girl on Earth," written by Rosie Shuster and Anne Beatts, spoofing the early 1960s surfer movies. Looking great in a gold two-piece bathing suit—with her Leia hair buns exaggerated—she played the game new girl from the galaxy far away in a *Beach Blanket Bingo* world, with Gilda spoofing Annette Funicello and Bill Murray spoofing Frankie Avalon. Belushi, Aykroyd, Jane Curtin, and the then *SNL* member Al Franken all had roles as the irritatingly wholesome Italians-playing-WASPs beach kids. The skit was a hit.

Carrie, says Rosie, "was pretty confident to work with," a surprise, considering she was someone "who I understand had monstrous insecurities about live performing. She got onstage, she stood her ground—and *boom!* She was a pro!"

But Carrie did do something that gave Rosie, who was living with Dan Aykroyd at the time, a bit of pause. "She disappeared into Danny's office for a very, very long period of time—hours. It felt like dog years. I didn't know if it was innocent, but I ended up thinking they were putting a bookmark in something for the future." That future would come in a year and a half.

FIVE

THE FABULOUS LIFE OF THE GIRL IN THE METAL BIKINI

t was a *real* relationship," Carrie has said to many friends, when asked about her years with Paul Simon. It's as if she were saying, I may joke and get sardonic about other things, but this was as real as real gets. The relationship lasted, one way or another, for thirteen years, in Carrie's telling, but she seems to be adding many years of her post-divorce deep dependence on him. Paul could be cold and brooding; still, "there was a fiber between them; they were always strung together," Mark Metcalf noticed. And Carrie's wit also kept him with her. Even when they argued, she would say something hilarious in the middle of a fight, and both of them would break out laughing. "He was always there when she needed him," says her former acting coach Alice Spivak. "She relied on him for a lot of things. Even after they split up, she had a key to his apartment." On their dependence on each other, from the six years from their meeting to their quick marriage and divorce, Richard Dreyfuss says, "The relationship had enough emotional highs and lows to fill books until the end of time."

But the insecurity that had come out with Harrison Ford in terms of her attractiveness was now coming out with Paul in terms of something else: her wit and her intellect. Everyone declared her the smartest person they knew, a world-class quipper. None of this could quell her anxiety.

In the early years of the twenty-first century, she would tell Kerri Kolen, the editor of three of her last books, that when she got together with Paul, "people always saw her as a frivolous young actress—the pretty young thing. And people saw Paul as this soulful, incredibly talented songwriter. She would tell me that that's what [figuratively] killed her." But did her insecurity and sensitivity jibe with reality? Paul has said he knew how special and brilliant and curious she was from the get-go. He would eventually tell *People* magazine, "Anybody as bright as her in the biggest movie of all time when she was nineteen knew that it wouldn't be long before she faced the question of who she was. But she drove herself to learn." Did he show that sincere-sounding appreciation of her *to* her? Or did her insecurity blank it out? One wonders.

Carrie was twenty-two, fifteen years younger than Paul. She might have been regaled as the New Girl in Town, but she felt greatly insecure in Paul's sophisticated world. Being with Paul and his friends, like Lorne Michaels and Steve Martin and his girlfriend, Victoria Tennant, meant she was now around older people of substance and accomplishment. "She was thrown for a loop by Paul; it was a real hardship, trying to prove herself in Paul and Lorne's company!" dramatically asserts Robert Hilburn, the author of *Paul Simon: The Life*, on the basis of interviews he conducted with her around 2011. "She said, 'I was trying to find a way into their world. They were intellectual. *I wasn't ready for them!*'" As she would say to a friend a year before her death, "Suddenly I'm with the people who are best at what they do . . . That was fun and scary to be around that. It was all a surprise."

"I can see Paul wooing Carrie in an extravagant way," Barbara Burns recalls, because Carrie herself was extravagant. Shopping, shopping, shopping! And not casually. Rather, with a car and driver parked outside at choice SoHo boutiques. (Carol Caldwell, Michael O'Donoghue's girlfriend after Anne Beatts, remembers that Carrie would eventually have contests. Sometimes, giving her own money to her friends, she'd say, as they exited the limo for a store, "Who can buy the most things the fastest?! Ready, set, go!" Carol, however, never took money from Carrie.) No one yet knew that this compulsive overbuying was a sign of bipolar disorder; it just seemed a sign of Carrie's wealth, generosity, and endearing enthusiasm. And there was a generosity that went beyond the trivial. "She would give money to bums on the street and tell other people to do so," says a later good friend. "Yes, her tactic was 'Love me, *love me!*' with throwing gifts at people, but it went deeper than that—to true compassion."

But a close friend from the *SNL* crowd contends that this was part of Paul's problem with her. It was Carrie's distinctly "strong independence" that made the relationship hard for Paul, this friend believes. "I'm sure many people" in their crowd "were in awe of her, and many people were jealous of her, and many loved her. But part of what made Carrie unique was that she had so much power and—outward—self-assurance for so long, and at such a young age. A lot of it was from what her parents gave her"—the notoriety. "And money also gives you that. Carrie was young and the wittiest person alive and had her own resources and had her own freedom and her own fame"—a legacy of fame, now augmented by her own sudden stardom and her aplomb with the press.

"Peggy and Shelley weren't famous like Carrie was. Famous as a star and famous from their childhoods," says a friend of Paul's. They were easier for Paul to manage, despite Peggy's no-nonsense toughness with him. "That [autonomy and power] is hard for any man, especially in a woman so young," which makes those women all the more impatient and impulsive and snappy. "And especially for a man who could be moody and insecure. It certainly was, back then, when we were dealing with three revolutions at once. We were in the middle of the sexual revolution, the end of the hippie revolution, and in the feminist revolution." Each one made demands on male-female power dynamics, on lust, on idealism, and on fidelity, sometimes with contradictory implications. It was hard to keep a relationship up, especially in the entertainment world, in that high-energy and high-ideology environment.

Carrie herself said, in retrospect, that "the bad thing about my relationship with Paul was that we were similar animals. Where there should be a flower and a gardener, we were two flowers. In the bright sun. Wilting." To an older confidante she said—exaggerating for effect—"Paul wanted a wife to be home and cook dinner." The confidante continues, "Paul Simon's a genius—no getting around it. You say 'Paul Simon' and it equals 'genius.' And Carrie also came from a very iconic family. There were two egos. She wanted to pursue a career, and he wanted perhaps a wife to be there when he came back." That was one side of it, but of course it was more complicated than that. Says a man who knew Paul very well for years, "With Paul and Carrie there was always a tension. They were *passionately* involved."

Drugs like cocaine were a virtually inescapable part of the young entertainment industry scene on both coasts. If you had money and celebrity, you had more exposure to the illegal but irresistible white powder that could speed up your day (handy when you were on a 24/7 schedule to get a live two-hour evening show written and performed every week), and many people didn't know (or didn't *want* to know) how addictive it was. Some indulged for pleasure, knowing when to stop, but a lot of indulgers found they *couldn't* easily stop. One of Carrie's friends from the *SNL* crowd, who liked her greatly, says this hesitantly: "Carrie was an addict. Paul was not. There are what might be called 'functioning addicts'"—people who indulged considerably but did not have their lives destroyed by drugs—"but Carrie was not a functioning addict. I think she would have *loved* to have been one. And she *tried. She tried!* But she couldn't be. Carrie had lots of different demons. There was an aspect of her that was always trying to figure out how to *not* run away."

"I'm surprised she made it to sixty," says a friend who wasn't a member of *SNL*. "Once she almost died in my apartment."

Carrie, writing about her fictional protagonist, based on herself, would soon describe what it felt like to be in her brain in *Postcards from the Edge*: "She lived in her head like a madwoman locked in a tower, hearing the wind howling through her hair and waiting for someone to come and rescue her from feeling things so deeply that her bones burned."

The friend who introduced Carrie to Percodan—to try to calm the howling—was her close friend Michael O'Donoghue, the head *SNL* writer. Michael had terrible migraines, and he used what was then called a painkiller for his migraines. He shared them with Carrie.

She and Michael were such close friends, and she was so generous, that she never visited him without a present. (She rarely visited *anyone* without a present.) Once, she brought him a big stuffed boar's head that inspired fear and laughter at the parties he frequently threw at his little apartment on East Sixteenth Street. More important, she gave him a gold-and-jade ring that had great sentimental value. Eddie had given it to her, an extremely rare gift from her impecunious father, who was far more a taker than a giver.

Richard Dreyfuss and Carrie shared the bond of their illnesses, too. In their case, it was unnamed and officially unacknowledged for her, but her statement to him that they came "from the same egg" had a meaning they both understood: They knew they shared the bursts of activity and emotional grandiosity, followed by the lows. And they loved the former state. "What we had," he says, "was so scintillating, so exquisitely pleasurable. Your brain feels as vast as the universe; you can make connections other people can't. You're at home in this secret, brilliant, elevated world. It's like Einstein discovering the theory of relativity. Carrie and I both knew how much joy there was to be found in that state." Still, there was another side of that state, and, Carrie has said, it "starts right away in the morning as soon as I wake up . . . I get a feeling like my mind's been having a party all night long and I'm the last person to arrive and now I have to clean up the mess."

Penny Marshall was the co-star with Cindy Williams of *Laverne & Shirley*. She was a young Bronx-raised woman (she proudly never dropped her original accent) who was already a Hollywood success and insider when she met Carrie during these years. Her brother, Garry Marshall, had created not just *Laverne & Shirley* but also *Happy Days* and *Mork & Mindy*. Penny was married to the *All in the Family* star Rob Reiner, also Bronx-born and the son of the comedian, actor, and director Carl Reiner. Together, they were deeply esteemed within the comedic Hollywood in-crowd, which included Carrie's friend and apartment-building mate Richard Dreyfuss and John and Judy Belushi.

Penny was thirteen years older than Carrie and had a daughter, Tracy, from an early first marriage, whom Rob Reiner had adopted. Carrie and Penny—sarcastic, honest, beloved by their friends, and living in the same social world—were a bonding waiting to happen. When Lorne Michaels introduced them in 1979, they became instant best friends.

"There was something *Butch Cassidy and the Sundance Kid* about Penny and Carrie," says Mark Metcalf, who kept up with them in California. "They had a girlfriend connection like I never saw, although they were different. Carrie was tiny; Penny is tall. Penny's much drier and more droll than Carrie." Says Rosie Shuster, "Penny was a worrier; she worried about *Laverne & Shirley*. Carrie wasn't a worrier." Richard Dreyfuss knew both women well. He jokes that he was so close to Penny and Rob Reiner—having lived in their guesthouse for years—that "they told me they waited a year to break up so they wouldn't hurt my feelings." When asked why Penny and Carrie became best friends, he answers, "Because they were both hysterically funny. And hysterically funny means wisdom. One day Penny took up crocheting. I asked her why. She said, 'To keep the hands off my throat.' But Penny was more placid. Carrie was more energetic." Penny (who would die on December 17, 2018) had a tough-seeming exterior; maybe it was that Bronx accent. But inside, says one who knew her, "she was very sweet and kind." And, like her new best friend, Carrie, generous. "She treated her housekeeper to a fully paid-for face-lift birthday present one year." *That* kind of generous.

Penny adored Carrie from the start, and she caught Carrie's keen insecurity about her truncated education. Being a high school dropout, Carrie "thought everyone was smarter than she was, especially Paul," Penny wrote in her memoir, *My Mother Was Nuts*. "In reality, *she* was smarter than everyone." Richard Dreyfuss has said this, too. Penny Marshall again: "[Carrie] was brilliant. Everyone knew it . . . Lorne [knew it] and if you asked him at the right moment, Paul would've agreed, too. Carrie read voraciously. She was funny and clever. She wrote and provided nonstop, hysterical commentary on people, movies, books, and Hollywood."

Carrie was aware of this scintillating nonstop talking of hers, though not consciously aware at the time that it was mania. "I never shut up," she would later say to a friend. "I could be brilliant. I never had to look long for a word, a thought, a connection, a joke, anything." Her wit charmed Paul and kept him there, even if their constant fights had her frequently decamping to her apartment in the Eldorado.

Carrie used her mythic bloodlines to dazzle Penny with funny stories about her parents and her parents' famous friends, though Penny's own high-level Hollywood accomplishments, past and future (she would go on to direct the major movies *Big* and *A League of Their Own*, becoming the first female director to make not just one movie that grossed $100 million but two), and her enmeshment in the inner circle were greater than her new friend's.

Soon after Penny's friendship with Carrie began, Penny and Rob Reiner divorced, and Carrie proved to be the friend to Penny that so many other people also say she was to them: She "helped me through the toughest patches," Penny wrote. "In addition to being available on the phone or in person, she played matchmaker, introducing me to Art Garfunkel." Carrie was in L.A. and having a fight with Paul, so "who better to complain to about Paul Simon than his on-again, off-again partner Art Garfunkel?" Penny said. She dated Garfunkel in the early 1980s. Although "Carrie consumed most of the attention" during the initial three-way meeting, Penny said, "Artie and I hit it off."

Before that fix-up, Artie had been dating another friend of Carrie's. Once the foursome—Carrie, Paul, Carrie's friend, Art—took a trip to the Catskills, singing doo-wop in the car all the way, to the hotel where Eddie Fisher was playing. It was a half-campy excursion—the Catskills resorts had seen their best days two decades earlier—but Carrie really wanted to support her father. As they listened to Eddie sing some classic ballads, including "May I Sing to You," and his rendition of the Leon Russell songs Guy Strobel had mentored him on, "Eddie shouted from the stage, 'My daughter is in the audience! She's with her boyfriend, Paul! Carrie! I keep telling you! *Get Paul's royalties!*' Eddie was shouting it from the stage and it was super embarrassing, oh my God! Carrie *did* have a certain amount of class. She didn't stumble through things, and Eddie just had no class. *None!* But he was also an addict," says Art's date. And there was this: Carrie had an addiction propensity, too. "I think that's why she had so much compassion for him. It was part of her own healing."

This friend believes that "by having compassion for Eddie, Carrie was having compassion for herself."

C arrie was in the two biggest movies of 1980: *The Empire Strikes Back* and *The Blues Brothers*. She spent from March to October 1979 filming them back-to-back—from Norway to London, to Chicago to L.A. and back—and much drama ensued.

Filming of the second *Star Wars* movie, *The Empire Strikes Back*, began on March 5, 1979. Carrie traveled to Finse, Norway, to shoot it and then to Elstree Studios in London. The freezing location in Finse—a rural area with one hotel, a railway station, and a few scattered buildings—which was used as the planet Hoth, made everyone shudder. The area was hammered by a snowstorm and avalanches the day Carrie arrived. But by now the actors were being better compensated than they had been for the first film. "Everybody involved in Lucasfilm got a percentage of the profits," says the *Star Wars* authority Jonathan Rinzler. Lucas chose Irvin Kershner, a veteran director who had done *Eyes of Laura Mars* and TV's *Raid on Entebbe*, to direct the movie (a surprising choice because he wasn't a "young Hollywood hotshot," but Lucas wanted him for that reason). It ended up going significantly over budget.

In the film, Darth Vader is on the warpath. Luke Skywalker, Han Solo, and the Resistance general Princess Leia (in boots and a jumpsuit and a vest this time, and with her hair braided) are being hunted by all the bad guys because the Death Star was destroyed at the end of the first movie. After a battle on the planet Hoth, Luke escapes to Dagobah to train with Master Yoda. Meanwhile, Han and Leia hide from the Empire in a cave on an asteroid. She's less princess than mechanic—working on fixing Han Solo's *Millennium Falcon*. When Han comes to help her, he wraps his arms around her, she flings him off, and witty banter ensues.

"Hey, Your Worship, I'm only trying to help," he says.

"Would you please stop calling me that?" Leia says.

"Sure, Leia."

"You make it so difficult sometimes."

"I do, I really do," he says, then complains, "You could be a little nicer, though. Come on, admit it. Sometimes you think I'm all right."

She says, "Occasionally, maybe, when you aren't acting like a scoundrel."

They snappily flirt; she gives him a hard time.

Eventually, they kiss.

Following another run-in with the Empire, Han and Leia escape with Chewbacca, R2-D2, and C-3PO to the planet Bespin, seeking help from Lando Calrissian, an old friend of Han's. However, Darth Vader has arrived before them, setting a trap to lure Luke into saving his friends. Due to his debts to Jabba the Hutt (a notable villain in the third movie), Han is frozen in carbonite, leading to one of the most quotable movie exchanges. Leia says, as if surprising herself, "I love you." Han coolly says, "I know."

"He improvised his bit," Carrie recalled later, making a sly reference to his withholding personality.

Yet again, Carrie brings dignity to the role of Leia, and even the post-love-confession look on her face—*I could really fall for this man;*

who knew?—is identifiable to women as a marker of self-esteem and bemusement, not weakness.

One of the many young girls utterly fascinated by Princess Leia was a ten-year-old in suburban Pennsylvania named Tina Fey. "Like many women my age, Princess Leia occupies about sixty percent of my brain at any given time," she would later say, when she incorporated Princess Leia clothes and hair into episodes of her subsequent television show *30 Rock*.

When Carrie, Mark, and Harrison got to London for the second part of the shoot, the Rolling Stones called Carrie, who had been renting the home of Eric Idle, of Monty Python fame. The Stones wanted to party! Carrie and Harrison had an early call, but they decided to hang out and drink with the Stones anyway. (Even though Carrie wasn't drinking at the time, she indulged for Mick and Keith's sake.) "We stayed up really late and got to the set about two hours later," she said. "And we weren't hung over, we were still in our cups. And if you watch the movie you can see that: Harrison and I are smiling as we arrived in Cloud City."

Right before *Empire* was set to be filmed, a "trade" Carrie made with her dear friend and drug-mate John Belushi led to the movie she filmed right after *Empire*: Carrie would have a featured role as the Mystery Woman, the sultry machine-gun-toting girlfriend of Jake Blues, in *The Blues Brothers* with Belushi and his partner Dan Aykroyd. The shoot would be an experience combining drama, danger, drug use, and intense, if short-lived, romance.

John Belushi was by now the biggest comic actor in America. *Animal House* was the top-grossing movie in 1978. His iconic bits on *SNL* had given him tremendous bankability, as had his and Aykroyd's now-years-long stint as the Blues Brothers (John as Joliet, aka Jake; Dan as Elwood).

Belushi's reputation as a loudmouth disguised other aspects of his essence, says Judy Belushi. "I think most people wouldn't have thought about him as knowledgeable about politics and history, but he was; he was very up on Watergate, for example." And, far from his full-of-themselves characters, at the peak of his fame, Judy says, when no less than the queen of classic film blasé-hood Lauren Bacall excitedly recognized him at an airport, he was humbled and stunned: Lauren Bacall recognized me?! The *SNL* star Laraine Newman said, "John was typecast as an uncouth, boorish slob with no discipline, so you were constantly impressed to discover he was just the opposite." Not that that was all he was, Laraine says. "He could be so goddamn dogmatic," and he criticized the women writers on the show, prompting charges of sexism. Still, Barbara Burns says, "John could be a real sweetheart." Mary Louise Weller, the actress who co-starred with him in *Animal House,* saw him as a smart, mentoring friend who taught her how to "talk back to the 'suits' [the studio executives]" and who, sadly, had an "illness"— addiction—that was still too little understood. Another female friend from *Animal House* and beyond said he was very supportive of her during a painful breakup—"and," she says with emphasis, he was secretly "sad."

Aykroyd was Belushi's partner in crime and his straight man. With a young political activist turned studio executive, Sean Daniel, in charge of making sure the movie went smoothly, and John Landis directing (both had done duty with *Animal House*) and with Aykroyd and Landis writing the script over a seemingly endless period of time, *The Blues Brothers* as a movie came into existence. Jake and Elwood Blues would pay penance for one of their prison sentences by going on a caper and raising money for a Catholic orphanage. In the process, there would be guest appearances from Aretha Franklin, James Brown, Cab Calloway, and others.

Everybody wanted Carrie for a small but important cameo role, and she said yes. "Princess Leia as the Mystery Woman—how cool was that! We were so excited!" says Sean Daniel. Carrie remembered the casting decision this way: "Danny and John wanted to be monsters in *The Empire Strikes Back,* so I said, 'Okay, then let me be in your movie, too.'" Carrie took the "deal" to George Lucas, who, unfortunately, nixed the casting of the two because "Belushi was such a focus puller," Carrie said.

But Carrie *was* the Mystery Woman: Jake Blues's hyper-vengeful ex-fiancée. She hasn't forgiven Jake for standing her up at the altar with a full wedding party gaping at his betrayal. With a bazooka, remote-control explosives, a flame thrower, and a machine gun—and looking lovely and classy—she attempts to kill Jake and Elwood, campy-dramatically, again and again, including after Jake re-charms her. The filming, expensive and messy, ranged from July to October 1979, mostly in Chicago and environs, and Carrie jumped into the action right after the *Empire* filming. "Carrie was totally committed, a total pro during the shooting," Sean Daniel says. But she was also starting to do about as much cocaine as Belushi was, though her addiction was not as well-known.

"Danny and I decided to break up when he was starting *The Blues Brothers*," Rosie Shuster says of Aykroyd. They figured the long shooting schedule would be a good time to separate from a relationship that was already cooling. Belushi, savvier about the optics of power couples than his blustering naive self would suggest, very much wanted his buddy Aykroyd to date Carrie; she was a "catch" and could hoist Aykroyd to a level of fame commensurate with his own—he wanted them to be a couple, Paul Simon be damned. Carrie has wryly quipped, in a private conversation, "John wanted me to date Danny, so," before filming started, "he invited me to his house with Danny there and then he [John] passed out. That was his"—literal—"idea of a blind date." Carrie was in the midst of one of her many fights with Paul at the time, and she saw the sweetness in Dan that Susan Forristal had seen. As for Dan, he had, people say, a desire to save Carrie.

"My best and my worst experiences with Carrie were both drug related," says Judy Belushi. One night in Chicago, during the shooting of *The Blues Brothers*, Carrie, Judy Belushi, and Penny Marshall shot pool and goofed around in a billiards hall for hours—on acid. It was Carrie's and Penny's first time on acid. (There would be many more, including one when they left Paul's apartment and, according to a probably exaggerating Penny, were so messed up in their privileged way they changed limo drivers "fifteen times.") The pool hall was connected to a bar that was being filmed in the movie. The giggling women took hilarious Polaroids (the selfies of the day) of each other. They thought the cops playing pool were movie extras, but they were actual police officers who, fortunately, whether because they were off duty or merely charmed, did not apprehend the frolicsome young women. When the women got back to their hotel, they ran into their friend Eric Idle in the elevator—Carrie and Penny, zonked on acid, staring at the elevator ceiling. Everyone was too stoned to talk; they could only laugh.

The filming in Chicago and L.A. was bumpy, and a lot of the bumpiness had to do with John's addiction. He often bristled at considering himself in danger, and to some extent Judy resisted, too. "I remember John telling me one time, 'I'm an addict,' in a very dramatic voice," Judy says. "It didn't fit my description of an addict. He came and went with the drugs. He was able to work." Mary Louise Weller recalls, of their *Animal House* time together, that same productivity that made Judy doubt John's identity as an "addict." "We'd shoot the movie all week, and then he'd fly back to New York to do *SNL*—*every* weekend, without fail," Mary Louise says. Were "real" addicts able to do that?

But John's behavior during *The Blues Brothers* was less self-controlled than it had been, and Judy Belushi admits that she didn't want to betray her husband. In looking back on her stubborn innocence or loyalty—or denial—she says, "Sometimes I think today, '*What* were we *thinking?*'! I could have had him committed [to rehab]! I had three different doctors telling me, 'The next time he passes out, call us.' But I thought, 'What if he wakes up in rehab? He won't trust me anymore!'" Sean Daniel wanted John to go to rehab before they started filming. "Who *wants* to go to rehab?" Judy had told Sean, mirroring the defensiveness she felt. Judy is to be admired for being so honest about commonly shared misconceptions and attitudes about addiction in the 1970s.

During the filming, "Danny and Carrie and I and some of the others talked to John and tried to get him into rehab. The whole group was pushing hard to get him there," says Sean Daniel. "But he wouldn't go." In 2009, in an unpublished conversation with the writer Ned Zeman, Carrie said, "John Landis and Sean said, 'If you see John doing drugs you must stop him. He could die!' I didn't know how to do that. I was twenty-one and didn't know anything about addiction, but *I was an addict, too.*"

Indeed, Carrie was so much younger than most of the people she was now friends with that it is reasonable to see that she was caught up in a health peril she couldn't quite comprehend. Still, the calm and unironic way in which she talked about John's addiction during a time—2009—when hers was so well known (through her own prolific writing and talking) is quite un-Carrie-like. She seems to have taken the invitation to be interviewed about the making of the movie in a super-professional, face-value way: not inserting her boisterous personality and already much-self-confessed issues into it.

Perhaps it was a sign of the higher significance of John Belushi over Carrie Fisher, at least in the process of filming *that* movie (which would end up highly profitable), that everything was based on him. Or maybe it was the subtler way Carrie hid her addiction, as a woman and as a sophisticate. But in either case, John was the Addict to Worry About. Period. Sean Daniel and John Landis hired a minder for John—a man who would make sure he stayed away from drugs.

Meanwhile, Carrie and Dan started up the bit of a romance that John had wanted them to have—"well, not really a romance, more an infatuation," Carrie has said.

"I don't think they loved each other. They were both just 'happening' and attractive and"—again the word—"infatuated," says Judy Belushi.

Then came a dramatic moment. One night in Chicago, Dan and Carrie were in the Winnebago that was used as the cast's dining room. Dan was playing the Boy Scout to Carrie's cocaine-abetted heedlessness. He insisted she eat well—including vegetables: Brussels sprouts. She was stoned. She put a *whole* sprout in her mouth and started choking. Dan dashed over, wrapped his arms around her, and performed the Heimlich maneuver. "Danny saved Carrie's life," Sean Daniel says.

The Dan-and-Carrie infatuation deepened into romance. They moved into a penthouse suite at the Astro Tower, whose tacky aluminum look "I knew to apologize for," Aykroyd would later say, because "Carrie had the most refined eye for art and design." He—"a simple Catholic kid from a government family in Hull, Quebec," as he put it—was awed by her wit and her Hollywood pedigree, even though he was a comic star by now. He was knocked out by the fact that when the rambling shoot took them to L.A., "I was embraced in warmly human and Hollywood-glamorous emotional comfort, elegance, and excitement." Debbie cooked for them! And the "tech wizard" Todd Fisher drove him around in his muscle cars with Miguel Ferrer. Dan and Carrie got engaged. "I bought her a sapphire ring," he says. "We went for blood tests." As for Carrie, she recalled the interlude bemusedly and said, "I started saying 'Eh?' instead of 'What?'" like a Canadian.

On acid, Carrie and Dan flew to Lake Tahoe and, through Debbie's connections with Bill Harrah, borrowed a guesthouse on the estate of the casino mogul. In the guesthouse they spent three days "full-on weeping to Christmas classics" that played on TV, Dan said.

But the engagement ended as quickly as it began. "Carrie wanted to give Danny a wardrobe upgrade," says Rosie Shuster. "She wanted him to wear expensive clothes instead of his black motorcycle pants and Harley boots, and Dan bristled at that. That was not him." After a number of scenes of the filming were completed, in October 1979, Dan and Carrie repaired to the Martha's Vineyard house that he was renovating, near the Belushis' own. "It was mid-century and really quite lovely," Judy Belushi says. "But it was in some disrepair. Carrie hated it!"

"It looks like it was abandoned by Fred and Wilma Flintstone," said Carrie.

"A few days later, she asked me to drive her to the airport, and she flew back to New York and Paul," Judy says. But before she flew back, she caused deep worry that was somehow hidden by the group's obsession with John's addiction rather than her own. "She was in very bad shape on the plane" from Chicago to Martha's Vineyard, remembers Judy. "She was very incoherent. And then, at our house, my brother was most concerned about her. He had to carry her limp body from room to room. I guess she was conscious *enough* that he didn't call an ambulance, but he had a strong sense that she was *really* out of it."

Someone else present said, given how stoned Carrie was and had been, "I would have put money on Carrie dying before John did." It was during that spate of days on the Vineyard that John, in a moment alone with Carrie, stared at her and said, "You're like me. We're *not* like them." Meaning he and Carrie were true addicts. He wanted her to know that he knew this and she should know it, too. In 2009, she remembered John's words as if they'd been uttered yesterday, she told Ned Zeman.

Empire and *Blues Brothers* would be released on the same day: June 20, 1980.

Interestingly, before those two huge movies simultaneously hit, the ever-busy Carrie chose to do a Broadway play, *Censored Scenes from King Kong*, with Stephen Collins and Peter Riegert. Its producer was the well-regarded Michael White, an Englishman who had produced *The Rocky Horror Show* and *Monty Python*, and this new play had a buzz about it; it was a campy novelty that *might* be a hit: the two reasons perhaps why Carrie chose to sign on to it. But it turned out to be a dud, closing after five performances, from March 6 to 9. Alma Cuervo, an actress cast late, says Carrie took her under her wing and helped her a great deal during rehearsals: "She was very kind and not at all a diva. We had to learn these really ridiculous numbers with alter egos; Carrie's was Ethel Merman, and mine was Marilyn Monroe. Carrie had one line—'Even with a turkey that you know will close'—and because we *knew* the play would close, she asked the audience to sing the line *with* her. So the whole audience celebrated the fact that the play *was* a turkey!" Debbie joined in the self-deprecatory act with her daughter—standing up from her seat during one sparsely attended performance and saying, "Isn't this the worst play you've ever seen?" and then plopping onto somebody's lap. "Debbie was great; she came backstage and helped us with our makeup, with our lipstick," Alma recalls.

But Debbie was also proprietary. After the opening night's performance, which Carrie's friend the screenwriter Patricia Resnick attended, "we went in a limo back to Carrie's apartment," Patricia says, "and it sticks in my mind that Debbie insisted on taking me through the apartment, room by room, and showing me everything in it that *she* had bought for Carrie: 'I bought this rug; I bought this lamp.'" Having a mother like Debbie was a complex situation. Some people saw her intrusive narcissism; others saw a mother desperate to join in her daughter's fun, as well as to talk her up to influential friends out of motherly concern.

Carrie's parties at the Eldorado were heating up with famous names now, and Alma Cuervo was impressed that evening. "There was James Taylor, playing the piano. And that whole *SNL* crowd—Belushi and Aykroyd. She and Paul seemed so infatuated with one another. She was kidding around"—Carrie's typical joke: "She was afraid to marry Paul because they'd have such short children."

With money now from *Star Wars*, Carrie wanted an outpost in her hometown, so she bought a house next door to her friend Teri Garr's log cabin in Laurel Canyon. It was a tiny house, and Carrie decorated it felicitously: she put a big statue of a foot on the front lawn and had cutouts of Snow White and the Seven Dwarfs on the stairs. When she and Paul were in L.A., she gave parties there, where a gourmet cook was on the premises, teaching everyone cuisine. Sean Daniel's girlfriend, the interior designer Linda Marder, who would later help decorate Carrie's Benedict and Coldwater Canyon homes, loved the parties. The hired chef was "supposed to give us lessons," Teri Garr recalled, "and we'd all watch him cook and try to learn how, but mostly we'd just drink a lot of wine."

Carrie and Teri were very close friends at this point. Through Carrie, Teri met a handsome young doctor named David Kipper, who wooed Teri intensely. At first Teri was delighted to be with a man who was not in the entertainment industry, but Kipper's starstruck ardor became "overwhelming," as Teri put it, and she broke up with him. Teri moved from her log cabin to an apartment in the elegant Sunset Towers, just above the heart of the Sunset Strip.

The Empire Strikes Back would become one of the highest-grossing movies of the year. *Rolling Stone* put Carrie, Mark, and Harrison on the cover in July, Carrie looking fetching between the two men. The magazine reported, "To feed the seemingly insatiable appetite for news about *Star Wars*, Twentieth Century–Fox and Lucasfilm (George's production company) have mounted a promotional onslaught whose scope resembles a rock & roll world tour. Over the last few weeks, the film's stars have been hustled from Los Angeles to New York to Washington to London to Japan and then on to Australia to sit for literally hundreds of newspaper, radio and television interviews. The effort is further supported by a multimillion-dollar ad campaign and a glut of aggressive merchandising schemes that include everything from a soundtrack album to a proposed Yoda doll, the gnomelike Jedi master."

Always happy about hitching a ride on his daughter's fame, Eddie—who was now fifty-two and four years divorced from his fourth wife, Terry Richard—called Carrie to praise her and to tell her that because she was Princess Organa, he was calling himself *King* Organa. Repeating that fact in several interviews, Carrie smiled and conveyed: *Yep, that's my father, a bit of a cheerful rider on my coattails, but that's okay—I'm used to it now.*

Among the many interviews Carrie gave was one to the Canadian TV host Brian Linehan. With her long brown hair in a modified page-boy, photographed from her more flattering left profile, she was lovely and smooth as silk and ingratiating, in all of these interviews frequently smiling flirtatiously, as if to a secret private joke. She spoke of how awkward it was to honestly conduct interviews, which necessarily called for pat responses. "I have to quickly think of an answer, front of mind," she said. "The great relief [is to be able to] say, 'I don't know' or 'I don't remember,'" she said, with a bit of a laugh. She obliged the earnest Linehan's questions with a not quite patronizing sweetness. She said very real things: "I try like the dickens to get out of bed" between projects. And when he asked if she was writing (a great preparer, Linehan knew Carrie had an interest in pursuing the craft), she said she wasn't, because "I've never been able to write anything that's not self-involved." Her movie-release interviews showed a distinctiveness that viewers were beginning to discern. Under that camera-ready appropriateness was someone calmly intent on letting you know who she *really* was.

Carrie was enmeshed again in Paul's Central Park West apartment (and keeping her own, for when they had fights), and the two socialized with their adjacent neighbors, Lorne Michaels and Susan Forristal, who were also given to throwing great parties. "We gave Eric Idle and his wife, Tania, their wedding, and the Stones were there; Mick came with Jerry [Hall]," Susan says. "And Mike Nichols brought along Whoopi Goldberg, whom nobody knew. Whoopi was adorable—'I can't believe I'm at a party with Mick Jagger!'"

Being next-door neighbors with Carrie was complicated for Susan, and very different from the best-friendship-at-first-sight between witty Carrie and funny Penny Marshall. "It wasn't an easy friendship for me, in any way," Susan says. "What the men responded to so well— Carrie's honesty—it was brutal. It wasn't always friendly. Sometimes she wanted to bust you. I was shy. I wasn't intimidated, but coming from Nebraska and Texas," and from a big, traditional Catholic family in which Susan was the oldest of nine children, "I wasn't used to that."

Regarding Carrie's drug taking, Susan says, "We *all* did drugs, including coke, and some did heroin." Although there was much she liked and admired about Carrie, she says, "I know we're not supposed to judge people, but I did feel a little judgmental about it. She would keep a limousine waiting downstairs for hours in case she wanted pizza. It was the drugs that did that." Indeed, Carol Caldwell, Michael O'Donoghue's girlfriend, who would soon become Carrie's close friend, says, "One time when I was staying with Carrie and Paul in New York at his place, he had just gone out. She took me into his closet and pushed aside a panel and tried to listen for the click on his safe, because that's where he kept his stash of cocaine so she couldn't get at it." Hunting after stash is sadly very typical of addicts, and Carrie would later frankly admit her penchant for doing that with neighbors and even with strangers.

Susan continues, "Carrie and Paul fought a lot, and I think it was about drugs." The general atmosphere could be confusing to "Harper, who lived down the street, in the Dakota, with his mother, Peggy. Harper spent a lot of time with us." As a preteen, "he was already very precocious. We always had Christmas Eve at our house, and Paul and Carrie were there, along with Buck Henry and Steve Martin. At one of those parties, Harper was nine years old, and a Frenchwoman came up with two tins of hash brownies. Harper in his little blue Mohawk hair was passed out on the pool table—it was heartbreaking.

"Another night my sister was staying with me, and there was a knock on the back door, and it was Carrie, and she was so fucked up," Susan says. "Carrie crawled into the kitchen, down the hall, and fell asleep under a desk in my office. And my sister and I were like, 'What?' But sometimes that kind of behavior was very funny" and showed Carrie's generosity and taking up for the underdogs, qualities people loved about her. "One day at Christmas my sister said, 'Carrie's doing the weirdest thing. She's wrapping presents with her one-armed assistant. Now that is *pure* Carrie. She hired the girl because she had one arm, and she wanted to be Carrie, the good person. But you don't really have a one-armed person wrapping Christmas gifts. You can barely do it with *two* hands. That was Carrie in a nutshell—so funny, so original. She was always the one to bring everything up, because I had a reputation for being quiet. She challenged you to be honest, and she was aggressive with that. But she was also a bighearted person—one of the biggest. Eddie Fisher—he was such a weirdo! But she welcomed him."

Eddie would be in and out of town, frequently staying at Carrie's, and Carrie came to accept this; he was now less her father than her pal. "One night he came over and was watching TV in the living room and the TV wasn't even on." Susan pauses. "Carrie had a lot of shit to deal with. But it never made her ungenerous. One Christmas she bought me a beautiful Egyptian necklace, with jewels. I felt bad that I'd only bought her a sweater. The stuff she had to deal with"—and there was a lot—"never made her unkind. It never made her unproductive." Indeed, Carrie worked like a demon, ceaselessly, just like Debbie, who had never stopped doing her stage show in nightclubs and had recently opened a dance studio in downtown L.A.

When Carrie moved her father out of her apartment and into an apartment of his own, she paid the full rent on it. Will Trinkle, a real estate developer and gay activist and friend of Paul's manager, Ian Hoblyn, was the landlord. Carrie had become very close to Ian and Will and to their very good friend Julian Ford, the musical director of *SNL*. The three men were in Carrie's age group—early twenties—and being fifteen years younger than Paul, "Carrie would come over to our apartment, looking for a break from Paul—he could be a brooder—or she'd call and say, 'I need to go out! I want to go out with the boys!'" Will says.

"One night she wanted to go to the Saint, but I said, 'Carrie, it's an all-male club; you can't go.' But she pushed and pushed, and I called the club and they said, 'For Carrie Fisher, we'll make an exception. But tell her to wear flat shoes'"—the floor was subway grating—"'and no makeup.'" The night was festive, with Carrie and Julian Ford vamping up a storm to the Bee Gees' "Night Fever" and Diana Ross's "I'm Coming Out." "We were all on the dance floor," Will remembers, "and two stoned queens next to us are yelling, 'Princess Leia! Princess Leia!'"

The good and the bad commingled in 1981. First, the bad: Carrie made a turkey of a film, *Under the Rainbow*, opposite another *SNL* star, Chevy Chase. Set in 1938, on the eve of Hitler's invasion of Germany's neighbors, the story featured her as a woman charged with supervising the Munchkins in the *Wizard of Oz* during an L.A. hotel stay. Chase played a State Department attaché protecting an Austrian duke and duchess from assassination. Mayhem and assassination plots ensue until the story is revealed as a mere dream, and Carrie and Chevy's characters are engaged to be married.

Carrie looked beautiful in the roundly panned movie, but she, always lithe in those days, was *very* skinny; she'd dropped down to ninety-five pounds. The reason: cocaine use—*lots*. And not just that—racing thoughts and wild talking: mania. "*Under the Rainbow* was the one where

I was completely crazy," she later said. "I was super-nuts." One person who knew Carrie during this time blames the excess on others in the movie. "Carrie was trying very hard to stay clean at the time"—she would make these attempts over and over again—"but others got her back on."

Toward the end of the filming of the movie, Carrie overdosed on the set, collapsed, and was rushed to Century City Hospital. The overdose was kept out of the media, and Carrie went to Teri Garr's new apartment at the Sunset Plaza to recuperate. Brian Freilino, whom Debbie had enlisted to monitor Carrie during *Irene* and who'd become Carrie's friend, moved in and was Carrie's minder for several weeks during what was then her secret recovery.

Carrie's "super-nuts" behavior around this time wasn't just the drug use. She was given a diagnosis of bipolar two. Carrie was twenty-four, and the American Psychiatric Association's *Diagnostic and Statistical Manual* (*DSM*) had almost literally just changed the name of the condition from the stigma-producing "manic depression." Bipolar two, of course, was less serious than bipolar one, but bipolar two with mild hypomania could progress, if untreated, to more extreme hypomania, though this fact was imperfectly understood in the psychiatric community at the time.

Carrie rejected the diagnosis—as well as the lithium prescribed for the condition. "I thought they told me I was manic-depressive to make me feel better about being a drug addict," she has said. "'It's what you think. If you could just control yourself . . . You had an indulged childhood . . . You were a child of privilege.' I don't know, that's what I thought. '*You're just a drug addict.*'" She and Richard Dreyfuss, who was diagnosed as manic depressive/bipolar, spoke of their shared mood states, but she was still rejecting the label. However, much later, shortly before her death, she would use the telling words "I *was unable* to accept" the diagnosis, implying that she didn't just dismiss it as clinicians' tactfulness. Whether she rejected the diagnosis because she was too wildly busy and distracted by stardom—and enjoyed getting high and feeling the heady rush of the mania—and really believed the doctors were being tactful, or whether the stigma was off-putting to a twenty-four-year-old (even an ironic one) is hard to know.

"Nineteen eighty and '81 were a transitional period" for the name change, the psychologist Dean Parker says. "Bipolar was a brand-new name." The new name would eventually liberate many people from the stigma of mental illness and enable many more of them to embrace the disease they needed to *not* recoil from in order to have a chance of getting better. But it was a *brand*-new name, and Carrie was not alone. "Rejecting the diagnosis, even with the then freshly anointed name 'bipolar,' is extremely common," says the bipolar authority Dr. James Phelps. "Even today"—thirty-nine years after the *DSM* adopted the less stigmatizing name—"75 to 80 percent of the patients do not want to hear they have this illness. For one thing, it has no 'cure.' For another, recurrence is the norm, unfortunately." So Carrie wasn't the exception; she was the rule.

Carrie continued to *try* to stay off cocaine and Percodan, but it wasn't easy. She was also taking the popular Valium, an anti-anxiety and anti-insomnia drug, and Dalmane, which also fought anxiety. Some she got through medical prescriptions, some from dealers and friends. These medications were all challenging to forgo because they kept her hypomanic to manic episodes in check. She and Brian Freilino took a trip to Africa, and she wrote Alfa-Betty Olsen a postcard: "Lions mate every fifteen minutes. For days. People watch them do it about three times or until their film runs out. It's their rainy season here. We've been robbed, flown in a hot air balloon, been chased by baboons, and put makeup on a Massa warrior's six wives. I gave them great manicures." Then, referring to the dreadful movie she'd just made, "Best of all, no munchkins. Love, the Fishlet."

Two months after *Under the Rainbow* was released, on September 19, 1981, came Simon and Garfunkel's Concert in Central Park, a historic event for the 1960s generation, in which Paul and Artie beautifully reprised the songs that had shaped so many dreams, ideals, and sorrows. Carrie and Penny attended, proudly, with their boyfriends.

Drug taking on or near movie sets was becoming epidemic. How many other actors, like Carrie, were quietly taken to hospitals and then carefully monitored in friends' homes for rehab is impossible to know, but less than a year after Carrie's seizure *The New York Times* featured a major article that began, "The use of illicit drugs in Hollywood has become so pervasive that companies that insure movies have begun to amend their policies to reflect drug-related risks, and some people in the entertainment industry maintain that drug abuse is affecting the content and quality of films and television programs produced here." The article reported that drug dealers appeared regularly on sets, that celebrities were spending a cumulative $1 million a year on cocaine, and that several bound-to-be stars had flamed out or been demoted to parts in B movies.

The casualties were starting to mount.

In January 1982, Carrie began her work on the third *Star Wars* film, *Return of the Jedi*. As she approached a busy Christmas and New Year, she penned a cheerful postcard to her friend Guy Strobel, outlining the four-month shooting schedule. "Merry Christmas, Guy-bone," she wrote, and then noted that the two of them were, alas, "polarized" yet another time—she in Manhattan and he off touring with a play. She happily and proudly reported that she and Paul had an active number of months planned—to Hawaii for a vacation, to Europe for the third *Star Wars* movie, and to Arizona and then Northern California to complete the filming. She then wrote, "Sorry we keep missing each other and I mean that in various and sundry ways." She added two more jaunty sentences and closed with "Merry Christmas and love, Fishie."

In the second *Star Wars* sequel, Luke Skywalker has a confrontation with his father, Darth Vader, and Carrie admits to her lover, Han Solo, that Luke is her twin brother. On the set, Mark Hamill would remember later, Carrie would brandish the works of Nietzsche and

Kierkegaard, while in her dressing room were copies of the *Star* and the *National Enquirer*. Carrie still had the need to prove how smart she was, and—ever questing—she wanted to read the great philosophers.

Return of the Jedi is the film in which Carrie wears—and looks stunning in—the infamous metal bikini. The poster of Carrie sitting on her crossed legs and striped in metal (top, bottom, arms, neck) would become a staple on male dorm room walls. The bikini was inspired by the imagery of the science fiction cartoon artist Frank Frazetta. In many of Frazetta's illustrations, highly muscled women are pictured alone or with macho men. In *The Swordsman of Mars*, a sensual woman in a metal codpiece, metal necklace, metal armbands, and metal headdress is crouching, as if imminent prey, in front of an avenging, sword-wielding macho man in a metal Viking headdress and a flyaway red cape. Yet because of her musculature and her defiant posture, she looks equal to the man who is victimizing her. In Frazetta's image on the cover of Edgar Rice Burroughs's novel *A Princess of Mars*, a woman with metal breastplates, a metal headdress and armbands, and a metal codpiece is leaning defiantly—stomach out—with a sword jutting out behind her.

Richard Marquand, who directed this time, wanted Carrie-as-Leia in the bikini, and an artist followed Frazetta's sketches. The resulting costume was very similar to that of the slave woman in *A Princess of Mars*, and Carrie—in Frazetta's sketch as would be captured in the film—had a clanking chain around her neck, which connected her to Jabba, and a metal neck piece and armbands. Her hair was slicked back and would end in a long single braid.

When Marquand showed her the costume, she thought he was kidding. "It made me very nervous," she later recalled. "I had to sit . . . very, very rigid straight." After all, it was metal. It didn't follow body movements.

The gold bikini is the slave's attire created by Jabba the Hutt, the giant slug and alien gangster. Jabba captures Leia and puts her in the metal bikini with a chain around her neck, while Luke and Han are sentenced to die. Leia sneaks up on Jabba and strangles him to death, continuing to fight, even though she has been injured. Thus, the reasoning behind the metal bikini is as heroic as the bikini is sexy. "Leia goes in to bargain for Han Solo's life. She goes in knowing she was going to get caught but she did it anyway," is how the feminist *Star Wars* fanatic and convention worker Stephanie Wilson puts it. "She had to play this subservient character, in that sexist costume, and she ends up being the total badass killing off the bad guy."

Carrie's instinctive feminism—her understanding of the shortchanging of women in movies—surfaced most when they were rehearsing the key scene, in which she is a hero. "Han and Luke are brought in front of Jabba. They never talk to *Leia* at all." Sarcastically, she said, during the rehearsal, "Don't worry about me—I'll be fine. Seriously!": lines she thought should have been in the scene, to acknowledge her centrality. She was offended: "Like, where am I in all of this? I have to stay with the slug with the big tongue! Nearly naked, which is not a style choice for me."

Carrie, of course, *loved* killing Jabba. Years later she would tell Terry Gross on NPR, "What redeems [wearing the metal bikini] is I get to kill him, which was *so* enjoyable . . . I hated wearing that outfit . . . and I couldn't wait to kill him." Carrie and her bikini graced the cover of *People* and *Rolling Stone*. It was an image that would forever haunt her. "What I didn't realize, back when I was this 25-year-old pinup for geeks," she later wrote, "was that I had signed an invisible contract to stay looking the exact same way for the next 30 to 40 years. Well, clearly I've broken that contract."

The power of the movie—and the franchise—would be enormous. "May the Force be with you" became an internationally known catchphrase, and largely on the basis of the first trilogy (there would be more to come) Lucasfilm would sell the franchise to Disney in 2015 for more than $4 billion.

Two other things transpired for Carrie during 1982, one felicitous, the other tragic. She had a hilarious, *I Love Lucy*–like cameo on *Laverne & Shirley* with Penny Marshall. The two nervously try to be Playboy bunnies, with Hugh Hefner alternating between choosing one or the other of the befuddled, vying friends. Carrie looked fetching in her Bunny outfit, and the repartee between the women—best friends in the sketch as in real life—was funny and touching. They played affectionate and confused rivals, neither wanting to snatch the potential Playboy gig from the other. Carrie sang "My Guy" to Hefner and became "the singing Bunny," trumping Penny. This was a healthy, sexy, comic-actress Carrie at her best.

Then came the tragic. It happened during a break in the *Jedi* shooting. On the night of March 4, 1982, Carrie was back in New York with Paul. Michael O'Donoghue and his girlfriend, Carol Caldwell, were living in L.A. now, while Michael worked on the script of *Easy Rider Two* (which was never produced) with Bert Schneider. Carol, a writer for the edgy monthly *New Times*, as well as for *Rolling Stone* and *Esquire*, was writing screenplays. Carol was friends with Judy Belushi. Judy, currently on Martha's Vineyard, was worried about her husband, who was staying at the Chateau Marmont, working on a script with Don Novello, best known as the *SNL* character Father Guido Sarducci.

Judy Belushi knew that Carol and Michael were "very close" to John, and she put Carol in charge of checking in with John every day. Penelope Spheeris, a documentary filmmaker close to Carol who knew Judy had put Carol in charge of John, called Carol at 6:00 a.m. (9:00 a.m. East Coast time). "Did you talk to John last night?" she asked. When Carol said no, Penelope said, "I think you'd better call over to the Chateau and see if you can speak to him." There was a short list of people whom the hotel operator was authorized to put through to his room, and Carol's name was on it. When she was turned down, "I called Judy," Carol recalls, "and said, 'I can't get through to him.'" The Belushis' assistant called Carol and said, "'Carol, you've got to go over there. They've found him, with a needle in his arm.' We knew John was terrified of needles."

"And then the nightmare began," Carol says. Belushi, who'd been partying the night before with Robin Williams and Robert De Niro, had overdosed by way of a "speedball"—a cocaine-heroin injection, provided by a dealer named Cathy Evelyn Smith.

It was nearing noon in New York when the phone rang in Paul Simon's apartment. Barbara Burns was there with Paul and Carrie. They were about to hop in the sauna. The friend on the phone said, "Turn on TV—*now!*" There was the news: John Belushi was dead. At thirty-three.

"We were so shocked. *Stunned*," Barbara says of her and Paul's and Carrie's reactions. "It was, 'Oh God, how could this happen?' We were young! *John* was young!" They were incredulous. "And then it switched to 'Oh my God, this was *bound* to happen!'" Later would come the funerals— the ornate one at the Cathedral of St. John the Divine and the private Albanian Orthodox one on Martha's Vineyard. But for the moment, sitting in Paul and Carrie's living room, Barbara says, "I looked at Carrie's face and we all saw it—the expression. It was definitely 'There but for the grace of God go I. It could have been me. It *could* have been me.'"

Seven months after John Belushi's death, Carrie's friend Richard Dreyfuss was arrested for driving his Mercedes-Benz into a palm tree in the L.A. canyons. He was drug tested and found to have on his person two vials of cocaine and thirty-one tablets of Percodan. Dreyfuss was now something that Carrie was still rejecting: a manic-depressive; he preferred that term to "bipolar." He and Carrie had talked often of their similar mood swings, and the delight that being "up" gave them both. But she had not acknowledged the disorder he had acknowledged. The cocaine charges against Richard would later be dropped, and he would wax grateful for that. But the fact that he and Carrie were on the same self-medications— cocaine and Percodan—was telling. The bond they had continued.

SIX

"SHE BURNED LIKE A BRIDE"

B y the end of 1982, with the shock of John Belushi's death and with her own serious overdose during the making of *Under the Rainbow*, Carrie decided she wanted to become a serious actress, to appear in something *good*. To her credit, her immense fame as Princess Leia didn't keep her from reaching for a challenging non-Hollywood project. As was often the case, Debbie made the first steps. She knew from her own decades of jostling around that entertainment careers didn't just happen; you had to push them. No matter what agent or manager was shaping Carrie's career, Debbie—achingly aware of her daughter's vulnerabilities and bathed in her own (perhaps overestimated) self-importance as a movie star—would be proactive.

Elizabeth Ashley, the opinionated Louisiana-raised bohemian actress who'd been married to James Farentino and George Peppard, was starring on Broadway in *Agnes of God* as the court-appointed psychiatrist trying to uncover the truth of the death of the infant borne by a young novitiate nun. It was an intense three-woman play: a proprietary mother superior (Geraldine Page); the young nun whose baby has been found strangled and who believes the pregnancy was a virgin birth fathered by God himself (Amanda Plummer); and the tough psychiatrist (Ashley, eventually replaced by Diahann Carroll) investigating the young nun for manslaughter.

Elizabeth Ashley felt she owed Debbie a lot. Debbie had helped her through her divorce with the eleven-years-older and much more powerful George Peppard. Debbie knew Elizabeth felt grateful to her, so when Debbie learned that Amanda Plummer was leaving the production, she went to see Elizabeth.

Elizabeth Ashley recalls, "Debbie said, 'Look, my daughter, Carrie, is going to be auditioning to play Agnes. She really wants to be a serious actress. She went to drama school in London. The competition is going to be fierce. Can you be there? I could just let her know that a friend of mine will be there.'" Elizabeth agreed.

Carrie's audition went well, and the trouper in her prevailed during the hectic process. Carrie was in the "high desert" of Southern California—a place she and Paul loved to go to, not infrequently dropping acid—when the call came in to fly to New York to audition. ("The arc of a love affair / Rainbows in the high desert air," Paul wrote of them in "Hearts and Bones.") She rushed back to New York for the audition, worked with the stage manager, and eleven days later, in January 1983, was performing before the packed audience. "That's show business!" she had said, with justified satisfaction, about the speedy command she had taken. Debbie, fifty, who was also appearing on Broadway in *Woman of the Year* during a break in her nightclub touring schedule, was the proud but agitated mother. "I was terribly nervous because Carrie had been rushed into the part," she told *Playbill*. "She had only ten days to replace Amanda Plummer—which is impossible—but she had a very fine coach who was a real miracle worker, and she came through. She did just fine. I had to go home and take a Valium." Debbie snuck out after Carrie's opening night—so as not to steal the thunder from Carrie, she explained. Carrie was a star now, with considerable experience for a twenty-six-year-old, but Debbie remained flattered by her own fading celebrity, which held now with the over-fifty crowd more than any other. Her worry about Carrie's vulnerability (encompassing everything from the stage fright to the drug use and mania) clearly colored her curiously nervous account to *Playbill*.

Elizabeth Ashley saw Carrie's earnestness. "It was a very physically demanding role and Carrie worked like a *demon*. By the time we got to the full dress rehearsal, she had improved so much since the auditions."

Working with the great Geraldine Page thrilled and intimidated Carrie, she has freely admitted to friends. Most evenings, she would stop by Elizabeth Ashley's dressing room before going to her own, Ashley recalls. "Carrie was desperately ambitious to do well," Elizabeth says. "And I detected her need to ingratiate herself with everyone. She very much wanted to shed the *Star Wars* image and be taken seriously. She was also extremely insecure about her looks. She made jokes about how grateful she was to be in a nun's costume."

It struck Elizabeth that "Carrie's whole existence and identity was totally obsessed with how she related to Debbie. It was so central to her life, both negatively and positively." As many others have said, "She didn't think she was as pretty as Debbie."

In their nightly dressing room talks, Carrie brandished her insecurities about, and her unhappiness with, Paul. "Her relationship was not going well. She'd say, 'Today was a good day. He *actually liked me* today.' Or she'd say, 'Today was a hell day.' Or—she was witty, 'Today was a Sound of Silence day.'

"My response was to say, 'What exactly is the problem?' She would say, 'He just doesn't like me.' He would freeze her out. And she would always say, 'I'm not smart enough.' She would say that he treated her like she was stupid. I heard a lot of 'Maybe I'm not smart enough for him.' And, 'I wish I was smart enough for him.' I never bought that she really believed that he treated her like she was stupid." After all, Carrie was palpably witty, quicksilver-tongued, so obviously smart. "I'd say, 'That's bullshit, Carrie.'"

Elizabeth saw what she thought were Paul's pretensions. Perhaps an artist of his level, of either gender, can be forgiven them, but they bothered the tough-tongued Elizabeth. "One night I went to dinner with Carrie and her little posse-ette—all girls, all short. Carol Kane and others. And Paul. Carrie said something about books and Paul just shut her down, and my ears perked up. Then I heard him say these exact words: 'As an intellectual . . .' *Well!* I could not stop myself! I said"—affecting a recalled angry voice—"'As an intellectual'? You're a tunesmith! You are a great tunesmith, *but you are a tunesmith*! Why the fuck would you ever start a sentence with 'As an intellectual'? And he said, 'We weren't discussing music.' And I said, 'I don't give a fuck! It's beyond me that you would ever start a sentence that way, especially as great a tunesmith as you are.'"

In her interaction with Paul, Selina Cadell had a similar impression: "I met him once at a dinner party. He didn't ask any questions of me; he wasn't interested in me. I said something about England"—Selina's country, after all—"and he disagreed with me violently. He was very keen to make me believe he was right about whatever his point was and I thought, 'Golly; why is he doing that?'"

After a period of weeks, Carrie started missing rehearsals and then missing performances. By March 9, according to *The New York Times*, she had, in less than two months, missed fourteen performances. The thinking was to give the role to the understudy that Geraldine Page liked so much, Maryann Plunkett. Debbie fought this. She said Carrie's absences were a "throat thing," Elizabeth recalls. Elizabeth says she felt sorry for Carrie and that she pleaded Debbie's case with the appropriate powers. "I said to the producer, 'Carrie is sad, and I think the [relationship] is tormenting her.'" Under the guise of throat problems, which certainly might have contained truth, and with an excellent understudy ready to take over the role, Carrie left the show. "She tried. She *really* tried," Elizabeth Ashley says. Given the tremendously hectic schedule of Carrie's previous year, and her history of ending up being intentionally or accidentally irresponsible during productions, it is perhaps not surprising that her stint in the production was short-lived.

In the publicity she did for *Jedi*, which was released on May 25, 1983, Carrie finally struck a balance in talking about the movies. She energetically promoted the tremendously popular franchise with its fan base. But she made benign fun of it to more upscale audiences. Motorcycling through space—actually, against a blue screen—with Han Solo and the large, hairy creature Chewbacca "was one of the most *boring* sequences we had to shoot," and "Jabba the Hutt" was "a cross between Edward G. Robinson and a slug," she told David Letterman's audience. Dressed in chic, simple black—more writer than star—she was messaging, *"Leia isn't me. But, then, you know that,"* to people who understood her sensibility and who would later discover it, in heightened form, in her writing.

It was a challenging life with all of that filming. Carrie would later say that Paul didn't like her being away that much, even though the location work was necessary. They were in one of their many breakup modes for part of this *Jedi*-promoting time, but it was an amicable one, and during the breakup the ever-private Paul, in supplying a rare—and telling—quotation to the story about Carrie and the movie to *People*, explained Carrie's specialness wholeheartedly: "She's gutsy and a real fighter. There is nobody else like Carrie. She's got one of the fastest, funniest minds I've ever known. She is absolutely unique."

For a private and calmly understated man, this outpouring of love and extreme admiration was striking, and that it was made during a breakup interval shows the deep bond between the two. His words are why, people say, he fell in love with her and hung in for so long despite her drug taking and her desire to move to L.A.

It is possible that during this whirlwind time of being (as he would write of them in "Hearts and Bones") "one and one-half wandering Jews," they started to decide to marry.

But first there was an interruption. At some point in mid-1983, Carrie moved back to her Laurel Canyon house. In search of Percodan one night, she drove over to the nearby house that her friend Michael O'Donoghue was sharing with Carol Caldwell. Until that time, Carol didn't really know Carrie very well, though they had been in the company of their mutual friends Judy and the now-late John Belushi and all the other *SNL* folks. Carol and Carrie had met in 1980 at Paul and Artie's small Passover seder, during which Carrie sang an inebriated version of her father's "Oh! My Papa." (She sometimes sang it as "Oh! My *Faux Pas*" and other times as "Oy! My Papa.") Carrie and Carol also had a mutual friend in the tall, enthusiastically brash *Village Voice* style writer and *Mademoiselle* style editor Blair Sabol. Blair was the daughter of a very wealthy Pennsylvania family and a fashion trendsetter: an uptown girl and Finch graduate who in the 1960s helped make downtown clothes chic at Park Avenue parties.

Carol had noticed that Carrie seemed to have "writer lust." They'd first talked about writing at Richard Dreyfuss's apartment when Carrie had learned that Carol wrote for *New Times* and *Esquire*. Carol could tell there was something of this life, this identity, that Carrie wanted for herself and believed she would be good at—something that would set her apart from her parents. But Carrie didn't know how to achieve it. That was partly why Carrie so valued her friendship with Michael O'Donoghue, arriving at his apartment with funny gifts. He had a literary background, and she wanted to engage with that part of him. Gift giving was Carrie's way of saying, "Love me." Carol understood this.

But now they met more intimately at the house in the canyons. Carrie was in a desperate condition.

Carol recalls, "It was around 11:00 p.m., and Carrie was about ten sheets to the wind—extremely vulnerable. She asked Michael if he had any Percodan, and he went to his jar and he shook out four or five into her teeny little paw and then he just took that little fist of hers and opened her mouth and—clump!—pushed them in.

"Well, I was standing there aghast! I'm thinking, 'Ye God, she's gonna die!' So Michael went and got a glass of water, and she's already done for; her eyes are like whirligigs. But she stood there and slugged them back."

Carol was "in shock. I had never seen such a thing." As inured to the hip drug scene as Carol was, Carrie seemed to her to be particularly endangered. "Carrie walked out the door and got into her little Mercedes convertible and drove off with a beauty pageant wave to us—out into the darkness."

Carol says, "I started screaming at Michael: 'Are you out of your mind? This is insane! Why did you give her those pills?' And he said, 'She's got the constitution of a horse. She always does this.'"

Carol was extremely upset. Responding to Michael's blasé attitude, she demanded, "You give me her phone number! I'm gonna go up and stay with her and make sure she's safe."

Carol dialed the number; no one answered. Then Carol insisted Michael give her Debbie's phone number, saying, "'I'm gonna call her!' I didn't care that it was getting toward midnight." Carol coaxed Debbie's number from Michael and left a message on her answering machine. If she had known Carrie's canyon address, Carol says, she would have driven there.

Carol was angry at Michael all evening, knowing their relationship was over. The next morning there was a knock at the door, "and a huge arrangement of otherworldly flowers—birds of paradise—were delivered, with a note that just said, 'Thank you. You are going to be my new best friend.'" The fiat, from Carrie, was striking: so dictatorial and confident. Mark Metcalf had noticed that Carrie could make anyone her sidekick: a stunning skill. Now here it was in action.

"And we did become very close friends," Carol says. She accompanied Carrie to the San Francisco premiere of *Return of the Jedi* and wrote up a witty Q&A with her for *Rolling Stone*, describing how Carrie was turning the pages of Bruno Bettelheim's book *The Uses of Enchantment* and brandishing a quotation about fairy tales and psychodrama.

Carol was twelve years older than Carrie, but, as usual, it didn't matter. Being Carrie Fisher's best friend: "It was very flattering, but at the same time a sort of full-time job."

In short order, Carrie arranged a trip for her and Carol and Blair Sabol to Two Bunch Palms, near Palm Springs, for a spa weekend, complete with acid—all Carrie's treat. Carrie, at the wheel of her Mercedes, drove Carol down the straight line of L.A. to Palm Springs on Highway 10 at about eighty-five to ninety scary miles an hour, changing lanes continually. At the spa, the two met up with Blair, who had flown in, looking impossibly chic. Carrie had recently joined Blair at an Erhard Seminars Training (est) human potential workshop in Hawaii, and they kept repeating the mantra "Make no comparisons! Make no judgments! Delete your need to understand!" Like many during that era, Carrie was very big on Werner Erhard's est and other human potential programs, though not too many people took as many seminars as she did; she exaggeratedly estimated she'd taken "twenty thousand."

The spa weekend was full of massages and saunas and champagne and servants and laughter and gossip—and LSD. Carrie was outrageously profligate with her money on this trip. But she was even more the wild spender on a subsequent, psilocybin-laced trip she took to the same resort with Blair: spending, on that latter trip, $15,000 on memorabilia; buying both of them new outfits at a boutique; and insisting they leave their "old" clothes behind. But that trip, with Blair, was leavened by a stopover at Carrie's grandparents Ray and Maxene's house, just outside Palm Springs, where, despite a lifestyle that was now far better than their hardscrabble life in Texas, commonsensical old-school Ray Reynolds was, according to Blair, going at "his crusty skin cancer with a kitchen knife."

Maxene was a fascinating counter to—*and* mirror of—her sybaritic granddaughter. She and Ray, so suspicious of pretension, had both long been fiercely invested in keeping Debbie from forgetting her roots. Ray, especially, felt this way. Once, very early in her stardom, when a friend of Debbie's had asked Ray which of his daughter's movies he liked best, he'd said, "Why do I have to see her in a movie? I see her in the kitchen every day." Maxene's basic attitude hadn't changed, either, and Carrie would continue to marvel at her toughness, decades later saying, "My grandmother had three looks—glaring suspiciously, glaring hostilely, and glaring with disappointment," which later broke down to "active disappointment, lively disappointment, condescending disappointment." As outwardly unaffected as wildly libertine Carrie might have been by the censure in Maxene, she was likely steeled and inspired by her grandmother. The take-no-prisoners way Carrie lived her life, especially when she got older—seeming to not give a damn about what others thought: that came from Maxene Reynolds.

On the small plane back from Palm Springs to L.A. with Blair, Carrie sang "Fly Me to the Moon" to the other twenty passengers, at least some of whom didn't know who she was, Blair claimed.

Carrie was such a combination of sophistication and vulnerability, generosity and self-destructiveness, several of her close friends would conclude.

And she was a kind of touchingly demanding friend. The middle-of-the-night sad calls she made to Selina Cadell and others—the great unloved-girl neediness that cracked barriers of appropriateness and was startling, given her fame and background—came out differently to Carol Caldwell. When Carol returned from a reporting trip to Nicaragua, Carrie said, "You love Nicaragua more than you love me!"

In late July 1983, Paul and Carrie quietly firmed up their decision to marry. She was twenty-six, he was forty-one, and they had been together, off and on, five and a half years. Maybe taking that determinative step would wash away the angst and fights. Marriage was a way of saying, Now you *have* to make it work.

Carrie was the one who brought up the issue of marriage, Paul mentioned to a mutual friend. But he officially proposed at a Yankees game on August 8, and he called Debbie to ask for Carrie's hand in marriage. However, plans for the wedding were clearly already well under way because it took place at Paul's apartment just eight days after the proposal. (Four years later, on *The Tonight Show*, Carrie and Garry Shandling made fun of the improbable speed of the wedding. Shandling said, "I asked you out. And four days later you married Paul Simon." To which she immediately quipped, "I married Paul to get out of that date with you.") Paul's words in the soon-released "Hearts and Bones" describe the passion that led to the quickly planned wedding: "Two people were married / The act was outrageous / The bride was contagious / She burned like a bride."

The night before the wedding, Eddie spoke to Carrie by phone and was shockingly crude. He said, "You have a great ass. You should be marrying me." She paused and told him, "Thank you," and she later dismissed the encounter (to, of all people, Ted Kennedy, during a social evening in 1985) as something Eddie said because "he was just high and was saying things for conversation's sake." It is hard to know if Carrie was upset by this or had gotten used to her father's relentless inappropriateness. Luckless, feckless Eddie (who *would* attend the wedding) popped in and out of Carrie's life haphazardly and opportunistically. It is to her great credit that she lived a work- and friend-filled life, given the egregious behavior of her father.

Eddie's phone call was not the only upsetting event before the wedding. Carrie had invited Michael O'Donoghue, but he refused to attend. Michael's violent temper tantrums were famous; his friends used to laugh at them because they seemed so exaggerated. But they were also ugly. Michael waited outside Paul's building, and just as Carrie was entering, he dramatically thrust right in her face the jade-and-gold friendship ring that Carrie had given him. It was a payback, some say, for Carol Caldwell's breakup with him in part for supplying Percodan to Carrie. His furious friendship-ending gesture "really hurt

Carrie's feelings," Carol says. Carrie respected Michael's wit and intelligence, and she loved him.

Brushing aside the unpleasantness on her wedding day, "Carrie looked beautiful in a white satin crepe dress" with those 1980s big sleeves and a delicate headband, Susan Forristal recalls, "and pearls." Carrie's bridesmaids were her childhood babysitter turned loyal friend Connie Freiberg and Penny Marshall, Carol Caldwell, and Blair Sabol.

Lorne Michaels was Paul's best man. A rabbi officiated the double-ring ceremony in Paul's living room. Debbie and Eddie were both there, the first time they'd been together since their divorce. Debbie did not seem happy to see her long-ago ex-husband, and she refused to pose in a picture with him. "Debbie was bossing everyone around," but merrily, remembers Susan Forristal with affection.

The wedding—with a photograph of the couple—made the front page of the New York *Daily News*, and with the prominent Peggy Siegal handling PR, it received serious, excited media attention. The guest list guaranteed it: George Lucas, Mike Nichols, Randy Newman, Robin Williams, Art Garfunkel, and Teri Garr, for starters. At the wedding party, Susan Forristal remembers that David Bowie "flirted with me and tried to kiss me and when I wouldn't he never talked to me again." Billy Joel arrived with his wife, Christie Brinkley, and with a huge jukebox—tied with a blue bow tie—filled with 1950s records.

Carrie and Paul's immediate honeymoon was a "working honeymoon"; they were off the next day to Houston, where Paul and Art were scheduled to perform at a concert, which was ultimately canceled because of a hurricane. (The pair had officially stopped being Simon and Garfunkel in 1970 but had reunited a number of times since, and the great success of the Concert in Central Park and the television rights that came from it sealed their decision to occasionally reprise their duo.) Carrie and Paul stayed in L.A. for a few weeks, and Carrie's dear friend Joan Hackett gave them a late wedding reception. Joan, now forty-nine, was weak from ovarian cancer, and the reunion was emotional for Carrie. The day after the reception Joan entered the hospital and vainly kept up her fight. She died on October 8. "Carrie was devastated," says Richard Dreyfuss.

Grief gave way. Two weeks after Joan's death, Carrie and Paul had their proper honeymoon. Paul and Artie were staging a concert in Israel, and Mo Ostin, president of Warner Bros. Records, gave Paul and Carrie a present of a boat trip down the Nile and a stay in King Cheops's tomb. Carrie and Paul invited fourteen people along, including Penny Marshall, Carol Caldwell, Craig and Melissa North from England, and Susan Forristal and Lorne Michaels. Before the trip, Carrie called Carol, who was in L.A., and said, "You've gotta run to my dealer's house and pick up the acid that I was talking to you about"—special liquid Owsley LSD, favored by the Grateful Dead. Carrie told Carol it was secreted in a Murine eyedrop bottle in the dealer's medicine cabinet. Carol raced up to Carrie's dealer's house on Lookout Mountain and retrieved the Murine bottle. Flying to New York and from there to Egypt, Carol hid the Murine bottle in her electric hair rollers case, feeling that was a safe place—"Did they even *have* electricity where we were going in Egypt?"

The plan was to take the acid in King Cheops's tomb. "How else were we going to commune with the ancient Pharaohs?" Carol figured that Carrie thought.

At the customs booth at the Cairo airport, Carol was slightly nervous, but she quelled her worries by thinking, "Who the hell would unzip an electric-rollers bag?" Well, her customs agent did. Not only that; it was 105 degrees and the agent had painful-looking red eyes, the precise kind of eyes that could benefit from Murine. "The Murine bottle comes tumbling out," Carol recalls, "and the customs agent picks it up and is looking at me, sweetly! And I'm looking at him with his eyes so bloodshot from the heat." He looked at the Murine bottle *longingly*—at least that's what paranoid Carol thought. She waited an uncomfortable few seconds as he rolled the presumed eye balm around in his hand. "Fortunately, he just put the container back in the rollers bag and zipped it up," Carol says. She was *immensely* relieved.

Carol then joined Carrie and Paul and their friends and the Egyptologists, who were there as guides as they traveled up the Nile. "Here were these three straight Muslim guys, our guides, and Carrie, being Carrie, she had all these little fairy outfits with glitter on them for us to wear in King Cheops's tomb while taking acid." The trip was a rollicking success.

Afterward, a few of the honeymoon party went to Venice. "Carrie had a seizure there in her hotel room," says Carol, who was with her. "She had likely taken too much of something, but you never knew what she had taken."

Once back at 88 Central Park West, the two next-door-neighbor couples settled into a relationship in which Lorne and Paul, "who had always been extremely competitive best friends, were now competitive about us, their *wives*," says Susan Forristal. "Lorne was always talking to me about Carrie and how great she was and how smart and funny she was. And Paul would say to Carrie that *I* was the perfect wife, a beauty; I was this and that. So they kind of set up a competition with each other" in a way that denigrated their respective wives for their own benefit. "We knew that was happening," Susan says. Somewhat amused, largely annoyed, the two women talked about it, bonding over the men's silliness.

Paul's *Hearts and Bones* was released in November. The album did not do well commercially but was later critically praised. The title song, clearly about Carrie, described their frequent separations and wound licking and would "speculate on who had been damaged the most." Paul also seemed to express her sadness over him, with her asking, "Why won't you love me for who I am?"

Fitting for the power couple they were, both Carrie and Paul had professional breakthroughs of sorts in early 1984. Through Lorne, who was taking a break from *SNL* to produce something called *The New Show*, Paul was introduced to *The New Show*'s now out-of-work bandleader, a

Seattle-reared young female musician of Norwegian background named Heidi Berg. Heidi was quietly obsessed with a little-known style of South African accordion music, which she had discovered one day quite by accident on the car radio and which sounded like the squeeze boxes of her family's Scandinavian background. She shared a homemade tape, *Accordion Jive Hits, Vol. II*, with Paul. The compelling sound grabbed Paul and led him to travel to South Africa. (Initially, the trip was controversial. Apartheid was still the rule of law until the early 1990s, and Paul later told people that Harry Belafonte was very disappointed at his going there at that verboten time.) There Paul found the choral group—Ladysmith Black Mambazo—that would be the key to his next and by far most successful and career-reviving album, the unique, irresistible one that put him back on the map: *Graceland*.

At about the same time, Carrie had, as *The New York Times* put it, her "first breakout performance since *Star Wars*": in the Sidney Lumet–directed *Garbo Talks*. After the devastatingly bad *Under the Rainbow*, Broadway's laughed-at *Censored Scenes from King Kong*, and the unfortunately short stay in *Agnes of God*, it seemed important for Carrie to do well in a movie directed by a name director, even if in a supporting role. In *Garbo Talks*, Carrie played the daughter-in-law of a woman who was the ultimate tough liberal activist Jewish mother, Estelle Rolfe. Portrayed by Anne Bancroft (who was nominated for a Golden Globe for that role), Estelle, learning she has a terminal illness, insists on fulfilling her lifelong dream: to meet Greta Garbo. Ron Silver played Carrie's husband, Estelle's overly dependent son. The acting coach Alice Spivak, who was coaching Diahann Carroll to take over from Elizabeth Ashley in *Agnes of God*, also had a role in the film.

Once they discovered they'd both been involved in *Agnes*, "Carrie glommed on to me—I was happily surprised," Alice Spivak says, with humility and affection. Carrie had thoughts about shedding her then-current acting coach, Mira Rostova, an expensive diva who had coached Montgomery Clift and Marlon Brando, and she might well have felt relief with the down-to-earth Spivak.

"Do you want me to drive you home? Do you want to go get facials?" Carrie asked Alice, after work on the Brooklyn Heights set of *Garbo Talks* that day. From then on, it was instant Carrie friendship: wit and generosity and oversharing and self-absorbed but very amusing talk. "Carrie had a sweetness that is hard to put into words," Alice says. "And she was completely unaware of her writing brilliance during those days." But the *desire* to write that Carol Caldwell and others had seen was there in Carrie. One day, at her Eldorado apartment, Carrie showed Alice some of her girlhood poetry, including a piece she wrote at seventeen: "Hollywood Children." "You were like a female Salinger," Alice said. Carrie said, "You *think* so?" with a genuine surprise.

Like Marilyn Fried, Alice became a kind of mother figure to Carrie. And in that motherly role, Alice worried about her. One time Carrie called and said, "Can you come over?" Alice said, "Yes. Is there anything you need?" Carrie said, "Can you bring me some heroin?" Alice knew it was partly a joke. But the craving Carrie expressed had sounded real.

Meanwhile, in late winter or early spring 1984, Carrie suffered a severe crisis, and she suffered it alone. She became pregnant, something she very much wanted. But it was an ectopic pregnancy; the egg attached itself to the fallopian tube, not the uterus. Such pregnancies are painful and dangerous.

Carrie was in the hospital "for a little over two weeks," says a woman who acted like a therapist with her and spoke to her daily. She not only lost the baby—this is inevitable in such pregnancies—but was very ill after the surgery. "It was personal; it was private. And it was devastating to her. *Devastating.*"

Alice Spivak went through the crisis with Carrie, too. "Paul was very cold to her during this time. It was a terrible time for her. He seemed distracted and not thinking of her. She considered what she'd had as a 'near-death experience.' She said that Paul was not only unmoved by [what she went through]; he actually appeared to be *angry* with her about it." A third person says, "She lost a baby, and it was rough and it was weird. Paul did not deal with it very well." Paul's assistant Ian Hoblyn often filled in at the hospital.

Says Alice Spivak, "This is when Carrie knew the marriage to Paul was over." They had been married less than nine months; Carrie was twenty-seven.

In May 1984, Debbie was about to marry her third husband, Richard Hamlett, a wealthy, handsome, very tall, white-haired real estate developer based in Roanoke, Virginia. Hamlett had proposed to Debbie shortly after they met, and although she had let some time go by before she said yes, she wanted to be married again. She was fifty-two.

As Debbie had been worried about Carrie's vulnerabilities and addiction, and her ectopic pregnancy, Carrie was worried about her mother's bad judgment in men, which had left Debbie working like a dog against their financial irresponsibilities and deceptions.

Carrie's friend Will Trinkle was from Roanoke, and his father was a real estate developer there. One night in early May, at intermission during a night at the Metropolitan Opera, Carrie took Will aside and said, "My mother is going to marry a man from Roanoke, named Richard Hamlett, in a couple of weeks. Do you know anything about him?" Will answered, "He's not liked in the area," and recalls, "Carrie grabbed my arm and said, 'Can you stop it?'" Will felt for Carrie and appreciated how she worried about Debbie.

By now recovered from her ectopic pregnancy, Carrie was in London on May 23, two nights before Debbie's wedding to Hamlett. She was to fly to New York the next day, but she was ambivalent about this new marriage of her mother's. According to an account that Debbie would write in her first memoir (and that Carrie would repeat during the stage run of *Wishful Drinking*), when she was not on the appointed plane, Debbie worried. Todd worried, too, and offered to fly a private plane to London to rescue Carrie.

Debbie called Carrie's hotel several times asking to be connected to her room. The room phone rang and rang. When she called and identified

herself as Debbie Reynolds, the snooty operator didn't believe her, so she
finally said, "Would you go to the room if *Ava Gardner* came to the hotel
and went with you?" The hotel clerk didn't say no, and Debbie called her
friend Ava, who lived in London. Debbie knew that Ava would be awake
at that late hour, drinking champagne and watching TV.

"I'll sure as hell take care of it" was Ava's response.

Good to her word, Ava rushed to Carrie's hotel. The hotel manager immediately opened Carrie's room for the imperious diva (who
was really a tough rural southern girl at heart), and Ava found Carrie
passed out on the floor. Ava called a doctor, who diagnosed Carrie as
not quite overdosed but not far from it. Ava remained with Carrie until
she recovered from this latest incident.

Carrie then flew back to L.A. Debbie married Richard Hamlett on
May 25, 1984; Todd walked her down the aisle. Within months, Hamlett had a health scare—there was a hole in his heart—which left Debbie
worried for him and susceptible to his needs. When he asked to borrow
money from her retirement fund for his investments, she said yes.

By July, Paul and Carrie were officially separated. They would soon
divorce. But it would not be the end of their relationship, nor did
many of Carrie's friends expect it to be, because they had already en-
dured so many separations and reunitings. Still, Selina Cadell, who
always saw the vulnerable in Carrie, remembers, "She was very hurt
and upset when the marriage ended. He needed more attention. She
was hurt that she'd made an error. Men would fall for her charm and
her wit, and then they wouldn't want to have it all the time, because it
took up a lot of space."

Carrie wanted to go home; home was Beverly Hills. In the spring
of 1984, she bought a lovely Cape Cod house in Benedict Canyon, the
more western of the two canyons—Benedict and Coldwater—that
shot off from the streets just behind and north of the Beverly Hills

Hotel. It was on a rusticated street near Mulholland Drive called Oak Pass. Linda Marder helped Carrie decorate it, but the vintage folk art and whimsical Disney touches Carrie loved were all her own. ("How many children live here?" Jack Nicholson reportedly asked when he entered.) There was also a giant dollhouse in Carrie's bedroom, and the immense porcelain foot was moved from outside the Laurel Canyon house, which she rented out, and it now kept company on the front lawn with a large ceramic cow. Carrie moved in her distinctive lodge-pole bed, plus a Muller Frères lamp she bought for $25,000 and would take from Paul's apartment every time they broke up. The walls were dotted with fanciful paintings of clothed animals by her favorite artist, Donald Roller Wilson.

Carrie almost immediately created a party haven. "Come out for my Fourth of July party!" she said to Alice Spivak in May 1984. "Stay as long as you want. I've set up an 'Alice Room' for you." Spivak grate-fully agreed. The minute she alighted from the taxi in front of Car-rie's new house, the party was under way. Inside and milling about the wraparound porch and the backyard were Sean Penn, Candice Bergen, George Lucas, Jack Nicholson, Albert Brooks, David Geffen, Anjelica Huston, and Timothy Leary.

But as the summer went on, Carrie did enough cocaine to concern her friends, including her houseguest Spivak. Spivak recalls that Carrie would stay out very late with new drug partners, including the rock, disco, and funk star Rick James, who was moving toward the peak of his fame. Friends would stop by and put healthy food in her refrigera-tor because they worried.

There was so much to justifiably worry about with Carrie, yet with it all—the debilitating addiction, the unacknowledged bipolar disor-der, the recent (though secret) ectopic pregnancy—Carrie insisted on keeping up her career. With an admirable degree of workaholism and discipline, she did so.

In September 1984, Carrie flew to Washington, D.C., to play a small role in the farcical caper *The Man with One Red Shoe*, in which her friend Tom Hanks starred as a distracted concert violinist who gets set up as the false target of a CIA sting, masterminded by a corrupt CIA agent. Some scenes were filmed in an ivy-covered house on a Georgetown street "that was comfortable to hang out in," recalls a woman involved in the movie. "Carrie was warm and hilarious, chatty and down to earth. She wanted to go shopping. When I suggested antique stores, she said, 'No. *Thrift* shops.' Which are more hip. She had a male friend—a convivial guy—with her, and she seemed very much at ease." No drug problems seemed apparent.

Carrie talked about her family. "Her brother, Todd, and his wife, Donna, had become intense Christians, and it was driving Carrie up the wall," the woman recalls. "She was rolling her eyes like *crazy*. But she was so funny about it. And she came to terms with it." Donna, Stan Freberg's daughter and Donavan Freberg's sister, had started Todd down the path, by way of her close friend Debby Boone. Debby and her husband, Gabry Ferrer, had continued in Debby's parents' intense religiosity, and Todd enthusiastically followed suit. Donna and Todd, and the musician Henry Cutrona, had founded an improvised church for Hollywood peers who wanted to be Christian. It was called the Hiding Place (named for a verse from the Bible's Psalms: "You are my hiding place; / you preserve me from trouble"), and Todd had been ordained a minister. The church was a success and changed locations to accommodate its growth, from a Beverly Hills theater to a space near the grand Mormon Temple on Pico and San Vicente. What Carrie had been looking for in est and other human-potential-movement workshops Todd had found in the Christianity of their mother and maternal grandparents, and other young people in Hollywood had found it as well. Everyone had his or her own way of divining the meaning of life and coping with challenges.

The Man with One Red Shoe, which would be released in July 1985, was, though an enjoyable experience, a box-office flop—as had been *Garbo Talks*. It was time for Carrie to be in a *successful* quality movie.

A few months after filming *The Man with One Red Shoe*, in the fall of 1984, Woody Allen was casting *Hannah and Her Sisters*. The film was a female-centric Upper West Side story in three acts, with Mia Farrow as the anchoring sister, Hannah, whose husband, Elliot (Michael Caine), is attracted to Hannah's sister Lee (Barbara Hershey). Hannah never learns of the affair, and her marriage to Elliot continues. Hannah's sister Holly (Dianne Wiest) starts a catering business with a fellow out-of-work actress, April. April is the role that Carrie got. Holly and April compete for the affection of the architect David, played by Sam Waterston.

The movie's themes of intrafamily romance and infidelity may be seen as prescient in light of the issues that would later enmesh Mia Farrow and Woody Allen, after he was discovered to have had an affair with Mia's daughter Soon-Yi, who would soon become his wife. But at the time, Hannah's issues seemed ordinary: snapshots of the complex, self-absorbed sociology of the Upper West Side, where bad behavior was implicitly excused as "neurotic" rather than immoral.

Woody approached Carrie's agent and offered her the role. Woody was a fan; Carrie was thrilled. She had met him when she was fifteen. As she later told the Canadian talk show host Brian Linehan, "I had the nerve to go up to him in an unbelievable beaded dress at Joan Hackett's New Year's party. I said, 'I like you more than my own hair color,' and he said, 'That's a real compliment.'"

Once she was cast, Carrie hired Alice Spivak to be with her—to coach her and be supportive. Carrie's first day of scenes was on December 6, 1984 (the movie was not released until February 1986), when everyone assembled in Mia Farrow's sprawling Central Park West apartment, which also served as the staging area for the film crew. Mia's mother, Maureen O'Sullivan, was holding court, and Carrie made jokes with Woody and the others.

In the role of April—and looking lovely, with tousled, chin-length hair—Carrie had some sweet scenes: party catering with Dianne Wiest and winning their rivalry for Sam Waterston. Carrie's most memorable moment in the movie, beloved by many fans, came when she sang the tender, romantic "The Way You Look Tonight." Carrie's singing voice was always the secret she protected, ran from, and wanted to deny because of her parents. But beautiful it was, especially when employed on that angelic song. (And for someone of such epic sarcasm, her favorite classics, both to sing and to hear, had an earnest poignance— "Skylark" and "Happy Days Are Here Again" being two.) After her mother's death, Billie Lourd would say April in *Hannah and Her Sisters* was the favorite of her mother's roles.

According to what Carrie told Brian Linehan, only one scene she shot—conversing about architecture with Sam Waterston—was cut from the film. She also said that there were challenging late-scheduled reshoots; one time, Carrie, ever the traveler, flew home from a trip to India for a last-minute reshoot and woke up with food poisoning but adopted a "show must go on" attitude. But Alice Spivak, albeit adoring Carrie, has a different memory of events. Carrie's part in the movie is slight, possibly because "she was too drugged." Rather than merely one scene cut, "Woody cut a *lot* of her scenes out; he couldn't trust that she would be there" to complete them, Alice opines. Because of Carrie's respect for Woody, this upset her deeply, says a man who was a confidant of Carrie's years later. Carrie, he said, spoke frequently of how she felt she had failed with a man whom she deeply admired. "She felt she couldn't do anything right with Woody or for him, and it really bothered her." He told her that she gesticulated like an old Jewish lady: "You're coming in like my aunt Velma." Carrie might have discerned that her reputation for substance abuse had preceded her. Or perhaps she was sensitive that her acting was inadequate, something she would soon frequently mention to others.

No! counters Mia Farrow. Woody admired much in Carrie. "Woody thought she was whip smart!" insists Mia. "Woody would come home at night and speak of Carrie being *so* smart. And he is *not* easily impressed by anyone's intellect. So it was high praise coming from him. And it was a discovery," she says emphatically. "We didn't know she was so smart back then"—in 1984, before she became an author. "Yes, there was buzz that she did drugs. But it didn't get in the way of me liking and admiring her."

Mia didn't have any scenes with Carrie, but "since my apartment was the base, I saw her more frequently than I ever saw Carrie before. She was adorable and sweet and cool. Somebody you would love to hang out with. And we had the shared Beverly Hills childhood; I knew her mom through my marriage to Frank Sinatra, and my mom was friends with her mom." During the *Hannah* shoot, "I introduced her to my kids as Princess Leia to rock the boat a little. She was trying to give them a little treat in that way. They stared at her as if 'How is this possible that *she* is Princess Leia?'" But they were not going to argue, so the kids stared mutely.

There was, however, one frightening experience. "I was coming back to the apartment after lunch," Mia says. "I might have had a kid with me. [Mia had eight children then.] Carrie and I were in the elevator together, and Carrie just suddenly fell to the floor. She *collapsed.* We were the only two adults in the elevator. It happened between the ground floor and my floor, and there were *lots* of floors between those two! Carrie fell down, and I knelt down and tried to cradle her, and then, when we got to my floor, I had to let go of her and try to catch the elevator door when it opened so it didn't close before I could get her out! I tried to get her out of the elevator; thank God the crew saw us, saw me struggling with her. They came and lifted her up and carried her to the apartment. And"—as with the incident at the Belushis' Martha's Vineyard house—"*fortunately,* she came to" so an ambulance did not have to be called.

As Carrie's *SNL* friend had put it, "She was always trying *to not run away.*" Her efforts to work, despite her addiction, were mighty.

Half a year later came the frightening event that inspired her to write her first book and to forge a new identity as an author.

It was the early spring of 1985. Carol Caldwell was renting Carrie's Laurel Canyon cabin while Carrie occupied her Oak Pass home, often with a slew of friends as guests. Carrie had recently come back from a February and March trip to India. Carol was living a clean life; she was practicing yoga and meditation and had "sort of backed away from Carrie because it was just too much—the drugs and the craziness." But one morning Carrie called Carol and "sounded woozy and blurry—'I think I've taken too many tranquilizers,'" Carrie said.

So Carol jumped in the car and headed over to Oak Pass, where Carrie was "stumbling around" amid friends. Carol had a frank talk with Carrie's cook Gloria Crayton and Gloria's sister, Mary French, Carrie's much-loved, inherited-from-Debbie housekeeper, cook, and helper. They were worried about Carrie, too.

Carol decided to go back to the Laurel Canyon cottage, straighten it up, and return to Oak Pass with an extra set of clothes in case she needed to spend the night. By the time she returned, Carrie was "on the floor; she was obviously in trouble. She was conscious, but she was a mess."

Carol called Dr. David Kipper, Teri Garr's recent boyfriend and Carrie's friend. Kipper was the right person to summon; he was on his way to making his name as an addiction specialist. When Carol described Carrie's worrisome condition, Kipper said, in blunt terms, "Get her in the car and drive her to Cedars and I'll meet you at the curb. Keep slapping her; don't let her sleep." For some reason, despite the warm weather, Carrie was wearing "a fox fur, which she wore as if it were a bathrobe, and she was dripping with diamonds," Carol recalls. Given the heavy clothes as well as the fact that Carrie was passed out, Carol needed assistance transporting her. With the help of two friends who were in the house—a male writer and his fashion-model girlfriend—Carol trundled a passed-out Carrie into the front passenger seat of her car. The other couple went into the backseat "and made out the whole way," Carol says.

Carol sped to Cedars and met David Kipper at the appointed place.

David had a blanket to disguise Carrie as they carried her out of the car, and the writer and model who had been in the backseat drove the car back to Oak Pass. "David and I whisked an unconscious Carrie down to a special room they had for pumping stomachs," Carol says. "He said, 'You're going to assist me in this procedure, because if we have someone who's one of the hospital staff, they will sell the story and it will be in the *Enquirer* in the morning.'"

"I said, 'But, David! I don't know how to pump a stomach!' He said, 'Just do what I tell you.'" Carol did. She pumped and pumped and pumped. "I don't remember what time we got there, but it wasn't over until about three in the morning. It took hours and hours. You *can't even think* of time when this is happening. David's putting the tube down her throat or her nose and I'm holding on to Carrie and she's babbling and terrified," slipping in and out of consciousness. "It was just pitiful to watch and frightening to be a part of.

"At one point there was a lull in the vomiting." This seemed to alarm David; knowing what Carrie had ingested would invaluably help the process. He asked, "Who was up there at her house who might know anything about what sort of drugs she was taking?"

Carol went to the pay phone—"there weren't cell phones then"—and called the Oak Pass house and spoke to a woman she knew who happened to be a houseguest there with her husband. When the woman's husband heard the question—"What drugs was she taking?"—he, a successful creative, shouted to his wife, "Get off the phone! Don't say anything! I don't want anyone using your name or my name!" The man didn't want his reputation associated with a drug-overdose story, apparently even if it meant withholding information that could make a life-or-death difference to Carrie, at whose home he was luxuriating and whose largesse he was enjoying.

David Kipper told Carol to take off Carrie's jewels and fur and return them to Oak Pass. He was going to get her out of the secret room at Cedars and into the Century City Hospital drug rehab floor.

And that is what he did. But before being moved, when Carrie came to and understood what had happened—there had been other emergency treatments, but this was more extreme—she realized, "Getting my stomach pumped was my bottom," as she later put it to the writer Nikki Finke. Her previous overdoses had not included this emergency necessity. "So I'm lying there and I'm thinking, 'I don't like this. I don't want to do drugs anymore.'"

Carrie called her mother figure Marilyn Fried, "and she told me she was in the hospital," Marilyn says, "and the papers might report it and make it sound like an overdose, but that it really wasn't. She didn't want to worry me." But Kipper's stealth paid off. The papers missed the incident.

In Carol's telling, Debbie, to whom Carol delivered Carrie's diamonds and fur, didn't want to talk about her daughter's overdose. Debbie did not thank Carol. Todd was similarly circumspect. For these two, Carrie's issues were family business only. "The only person who was nice"—grateful and sympathetic—was Todd's wife, Donna.

Carol was left reeling from the experience. She says, "I kept thinking, 'Well, Carrie will call me when she gets to where she can, and we'll talk about what happened.' But that never transpired. We didn't have any sort of exchange until maybe six weeks later. I was over at Penny's and Carrie was there, upstairs, and Penny told Carrie she had to come down and make peace with me or speak to me about the circumstances. So Carrie came downstairs and she went into this spiel: 'You *don't know* what it was like to grow up with Debbie and Eddie!' I turned around and said I was pissed and that I'd heard that excuse a hundred times and other people had, too. '*Get over it!* We're sick of it! You cannot dump everything on Debbie and Eddie—you're a grown woman!' I said. Carrie started screaming at me, and I started screaming at her, and it was a screeching cat fight."

The friendship was, for the most part, over. Later, Carol says, "I realized what happened: people in that position are so humiliated that someone saw them in that circumstance, they have to remove the person from their lives. Buck Henry explained it to me. He'd done the same thing for one of his friends, and that friend never spoke to him again."

But Carrie would speak, loudly, in a different way. She would use that incident, with names changed, as the starting point for the book *Postcards from the Edge*. It was a demarcation point. As one journalist, Matthew Gilbert of *The Boston Globe*, put it, Carrie became, "when pen comes to paper, a master of the rare and lofty art of point-of-view. She is . . . a gabby analysand reeling off insights and witticisms about her Hollywood life like a defector from behind the celluloid curtain.

"She is a sensibility."

SEVEN

A WRITER WHO ACTS

ʃhe was very sweet at the hospital—and really, really thin," observed someone who saw Carrie at Century City Hospital New Beginnings rehab in July 1985, right after she had completed her treatment there. Carrie seemed to observers to be very dedicated to recovery: subdued, vulnerable, tiny, and curled up in a chair, grateful for a program liaison to take her to AA. At the AA meetings she attended—first in Santa Monica, then on Rodeo Drive—Carrie seemed, to someone who saw her there, "pretty scared by the overdose, and she was taking recovery seriously."

As her recovery proceeded, she went back to her trademark sociability and charisma. She went shopping for clothes. People noticed she had bad taste in that department: "Carrie had a brilliant eye for decor and terrible taste in clothes." (Carrie would later agree with this.) "She had so much personality, I don't think she cared so much how she dressed," a friend says. And she returned to throwing great parties: among other things, hosting a square dance at Calamigos Star C ranch in the canyons of Malibu. "Nobody was more fun or funnier. She was the absolute funniest talker in the world; she was hilarious," says an attendee. "Making jokes about her parents, indulging in wild and witty wordplay—there was no one like her."

Carrie's Oak Pass house became a flocking point. J. D. Souther was there; Carrie might well have had a fling with the noted songwriter for the Eagles, who had dated Linda Ronstadt and Stevie Nicks. Souther's friends Don Henley and Glenn Frey also hung around. (Carrie did a goofy Q&A with Henley for *Interview* magazine.) She befriended Graham Nash and might have dated him, too. "She was adorable—an absolute dude magnet," a friend says. And she was a taker-in of young people. Harper Simon, now thirteen and somewhat estranged from his parents, stayed with Carrie, who adored him. He ended up living with her for a very long time and going on a trip to Dubai with her. Harper's girlfriend, the young actress (and now accomplished writer) Seven McDonald, also stayed with Carrie, and she received much valuable motherly nurturance from her. "Carrie was someone who would go the distance for you, who would fucking *love* you, and find your next boyfriend and dress you up for a party," Seven says. "Carrie was a safe place in my life. She was older and so much more accomplished, and I would sit on her bed and learn from her and she would *never* judge me."

Carrie's friend the writer Bruce Wagner, who lived with Seven's mother, the actress Robin Menken, would become and remain one of Carrie's best friends. A dark-sensibilitied and eccentric questioner, he was a devotee of Carlos Castaneda's Yaqui warrior spiritualism and a Jewish Buddhist. After a childhood in the Midwest, he had moved with his family to Beverly Hills. The city affected him greatly, and he saw perverse glamour in it, perhaps in the way that only one who is originally an outsider can. He had dropped out of Beverly High to work at a bookstore and drive limousines, and he began writing first screenplays and then deeply ironic New Hollywood noir stories and novels about perfidy and humiliation and mythic, twisted families with secrets, privately published in limited edition. He joined the circle of Carrie's best friends: Griffin Dunne, Penny Marshall, Gavin de Becker,

Charlie Wessler, and May Quigley, who had studied at the Stella Adler Studio and had resettled in the canyon house her parents had raised her in, near Carrie's own.

Few women, or men, seemed to possess the charisma of Carrie Fisher or the ability to handle so many intimacies so intensely, much less a houseful of rotating guests. "She was fun, and smart, and there was always good food at her house," says a friend. According to others who were frequently at Oak Pass, David Geffen was around; the actor and comedian Albert Brooks was around. Beverly D'Angelo, the actress who was making her name with Chevy Chase in *National Lampoon's Vacation*, became a close friend, soon to be one of Carrie's several *best* friends, the two sharing much bawdy girl talk. ("Oh my God!" says a close friend of both women. "Carrie and Beverly gossiped all the time. About who was fucking who! They were hilarious together!")

Carrie was so conversationally charismatic that, according to a friend, at one party given by a friend of the record producer Richard Perry, "Carrie and Tina Turner completely monopolized the conversation. They talked in such a fascinating way, about everything from music to sex to food, that nobody could get in more than five words."

Close friends who knew her very well during the months out of Century City rehab have said, "Carrie was pure sober. No drugs, not even an aspirin—for *eleven* months. This was the happiest, most serene, sanest, most generous, most totally sober, most loving, most peaceful period in Carrie's life. And she was funny!" It was a sobriety for which she fought very hard. And it was a great tribute to Carrie that she conquered the urge to indulge in any drugs at all.

During this time, she made two movies. She also ruminated about the book that would become her strikingly well-received debut, *Postcards from the Edge*.

Her first mission was to get back in the game, after having had a reputation for being unreliable because of her vulnerabilities. Carol Caldwell—feeling compassion for Carrie despite the distance that now existed between them—helped her acquire her first post-rehab movie role. After Carrie had had a few months in AA, Carol went to their mutual friend the director Penelope Spheeris, who had been very close with Michael O'Donoghue, the late John Belushi, and Lorne Michaels. Penelope had a second-rate cop movie—*Hollywood Vice Squad*—to cast. She admired Carrie, and she related to her. "Like me, Carrie was able to take negative things, like her parents' public divorce and her own drug issues, and translate them into something uplifting," Penelope says. Penelope's own story was hard to beat. "My father was murdered when I was seven, and my mother married seven more times and we lived in trailer parks. All the adults in my life were alcoholic and physically and emotionally abusive." Would life-weathered Penelope give life-weathered Carrie a second chance? Yes!

"When Carrie got out of rehab," she says, "Carol Caldwell came to me and said, 'You know, Penelope, Carrie would really appreciate it if you would cast her in this movie you're making because she can't get bonded.'" Bonding is insurance coverage for actors: a must before they can be hired. The movie was a comedy takeoff on *Miami Vice*. Carrie would play a neophyte cop.

Penelope had to fight the bonding company—hard. It refused to insure Carrie because of her overdose, and it also knew that her drug problems had caused her seizure during *Under the Rainbow*. "One of the producers kept saying, 'Come on, Penelope, use somebody else!' But I wanted to stick with Carrie, who didn't want to do *that* movie, either, but she wanted to work. I was pretty adamant. Finally, the bonding company required that if I insisted on hiring Carrie, I sign a document saying that if the production was shut down for any amount of time, the cost would come out of my *own* salary." That was a large, generous risk. But "I agreed to that. I trusted Carrie," Penelope says.

Alice Spivak was cast as Carrie's mother—a gratuitously added bit part "to get Carrie to the set on time," Alice says. "I was essentially part of the insurance."

Penelope Spheeris's faith in Carrie paid off. During the August 1985 shooting, "Carrie performed very well in the picture," says Penelope. "She was very professional. She was on the straight and narrow all the way through. And she improvised some great lines. She's a writer and an improviser and an entertainer, and she was really good in that movie. But I have to tell you: I was nervous the whole time during the shooting. I didn't know if she would show up. But she made it through with shining colors."

Carrie was drug tested daily. "After the movie, we were friends," Penelope says. When Carrie's sober eleven months turned into a non-sober period, "we partied together through the cocaine years. And I did a *lot* of cocaine; everybody did," Penelope freely admits, demonstrating the wildly ironic fact that what was punitive for Carrie was very much the norm for others, even those for whom Carrie had recently worked and who had to have her sobriety monitored during work hours. Still, during the filming of the movie, Carrie was sober.

Then something turned. "I don't remember the exact moment where Carrie was not nice," says Penelope, who eventually scored a hit with 1992's *Wayne's World*. "But it happened. She became kind of insulting to me. She made me feel bad when we were together. It felt toxic; that was not a word we used then, but it fits. I remember going to Carol Caldwell and saying, 'Why is this happening?' Carol said the best reason she could come up with is that that period [of begging for the role and having to be drug tested] reminded Carrie of her inadequacies and vulnerabilities and of the overdose. I said, 'That's *not my* fault! I *helped* her!'" Carol helped Penelope realize the truth she herself had learned: when someone is saved from a humiliating situation or a dire ordeal, the need to banish it from memory sometimes, unfortunately, includes the need to shun the person who helped. The last time Penelope saw Carrie, at a party a few years before she died, Carrie was "sort of politically polite, but it didn't heal things," Penelope says. "I was so baffled when she wasn't nice to me. I had done her a good turn!"

Bipolar disorder is the name of a medical syndrome. But in some ways, bipolarity also captures the essence of a person. Suddenly Carrie could turn cool. But she could also be hugely embracing. "She'd go on

a trip and buy thirty dresses," recalls Alice Spivak, "and throw them all
on the floor and say, 'Take anything you want.'" Seven McDonald felt
deeply mothered by Carrie, as did Harper Simon. Years later, when Carrie received an award from Women in Film and Video, Beverly D'Angelo
raved, "She really illuminates parts of the human soul, translates them
into characters, situations, metaphors that make her own challenges less
challenging."

Just after finishing *Hollywood Vice Squad*, during this period of sobriety shortly before sitting down to write *Postcards*, Carrie made *Liberty*, a fictionalized TV movie account of the creation of the Statue of
Liberty, written by the eminent columnist Pete Hamill. Carrie played
Emma Lazarus in the film, shot in Baltimore. Richard Sarafian Jr., a
filmmaker and the son of the film's director (who had worked closely
with Robert Altman and was friends with Sean Connery), was on the
set every day. Richard junior's brother Damon, who worked on the film
as a technician, was so handsome that "Carrie hit on him like no other
girl ever hit on anyone," Richard says. "It was funny as hell! Carrie and
Dana Delany were *really* on him: putting notes under his door. All bets
are off on movie sets; it's like a vacation." Damon ended up marrying
the wardrobe girl, who redoubled her earlier romantic hold on him
after seeing the avarice of Carrie and Dana toward her man. But mainly,
Richard remembers Carrie's humor. "No one was funnier! She was
making fun of Princess Leia, and she was so fricking smartly opinionated on all the BS of Hollywood."

While shooting *Liberty*, Carrie was fixed up on a date with Senator
Chris Dodd of Connecticut by Thom Mount, the former president
of Universal Pictures. The date began with the senator driving Carrie
around and pointing out the major buildings in Washington—"even the
U.S. Mint." Carrie felt slightly cowed by her lack of knowledge of the
government. She recalled that the meal that evening was shared with
Ted Kennedy, who drank copiously, and a young woman Kennedy was

dating. Carrie, still sober, was subdued. As she reported it, "Suddenly, Senator Kennedy, seated directly across from me, looked at me with his alert, aristocratic eyes and asked me a most surprising question: 'So do you think you'll be having sex with Chris at the end of your date?'" Dodd's face flushed; Carrie's riposte was pure Carrie. She doubted it, she said, because she was recently sober and "I'd have to be truly loaded to just fall into bed with someone I've only met *very* recently." Pause. "Even if that someone is a Democrat." Dodd later affirmed that they saw each other several times and called the relationship "a courtship." To which public comment Carrie just as publicly answered, "Is that what they call sleeping together a few times?"

The wittily stated pride in her sobriety that Carrie expressed to Ted Kennedy carried over to a "big sobriety anniversary party" Carrie and her friend Patricia Resnick threw for each other in 1986. Carrie had been off substances for almost a full year; Patricia, for two years. Carrie was proud of herself. "[I was] Joan of Narc, patron saint of the addict," she would later say. For some in their crowd, AA was a permanent part of life, and one-day-at-a-time sobriety was a gratefully honored if hard-fought-for "forever." For Carrie, it would turn out to be not so simple, though she often wanted it to be.

During this period, and because of the near-death impetus to it, Carrie underwent something significant: at some point at the middle or end of 1985, she was diagnosed, once again, with bipolar two. This is the form of bipolar disorder that involves less intense periods of mania—hypomania—as well as some spurts of mania, alternating with periods of depression. After having rejected the diagnosis—and a treatment, lithium—at twenty-four, "only when I was 28—when I overdosed and finally got sober . . . was I able to see nothing else could explain away my behavior," she has said. She even named her two moods. Rollicking Roy was Carrie in the ecstatic, grandiosity-laced manic state, and Sediment Pam was the depressed Carrie, who "sits on the shore and sobs."

The diagnosis made her freer about, and more accepting of, the mania

("I *was* too much; I *went* too fast") that she had *always* understood in herself. She accepted the condition, but in Carrie style—with the unofficial caveat that she didn't have to follow treatment in an orthodox fashion.

The typical "cocktail of meds" in those days was "probably a mood stabilizer, an antidepressant, and sometimes they'll throw in Klonopin, or clonazepam, which prevents panic attacks," says Dr. Dean Parker. Carrie would rarely be a strict adherent to the medications prescribed to her both because of her desire to remain creative (a state that hypomania does seem to induce or enhance, and that medication can dull) and because the medications could have onerous side effects (exhaustion, irritability, and weight gain) or could stop working even after they *had* worked for a while. She would alternately defy and celebrate the diagnosis for years to come, and she would be I'll-get-there-first frank about both her dutifulness and her rebellion.

This was something she and Richard Dreyfuss encountered and talked about again and again. "Carrie and I had a secret code," Richard says. "If we told on ourselves"—in writing or to friends—"before others did, then no one could get to us."

Carrie actually had a dual diagnosis (now more properly called a "co-occurring disorder"): bipolarity *and* drug addiction. When addiction is acted on, this co-occurrence can bring with it "a sky-high risk" of self-harm, says the bipolar patient and authority Marya Hornbacher, author of *Madness: A Bipolar Life*: "It's higher than schizophrenia and substance abuse. If you inherited both," as Carrie did, "it's a perfect storm." It's also a very common perfect storm. In 2000, the National Institute of Mental Health determined that about 60 percent of people diagnosed with bipolar disorder also had substance dependence, partly because of the urge to self-medicate and partly because intense pleasure seeking—through psychedelics and cocaine—is part of mania.

While there are many statistics about bipolar disorder and addiction, one stands out: children of addicts may be eight times more prone to inherit their parents' addiction than children of nonaddicts. Carrie was the daughter of an addict, Eddie Fisher, and she has told friends the obvious: that her appetite for drugs was precisely like his. She also believed her manic depression was inherited from him. "He shot speed for 13 years and then he was a pill addict. And so was I," she has said. Indeed, one day shortly after Carrie's nearly yearlong period of sobriety, Alice Spivak was with Carrie at Paul Simon's apartment. Eddie was there; Paul was not. Alice saw Carrie and her father repair to the bathroom and come out, with the clear indication that they had done cocaine together. As with Eddie's inappropriate comments, Carrie is owed credit for being so prolific in so many creative endeavors despite the sheer challenge their behavior constituted.

Even before the bipolar diagnosis, Carrie was starting the process of using her overdose experience as the beginning of a book. She would soon say to a friend that she'd stopped thinking of herself as an actress who writes and started thinking of herself as a writer who acts. It was an important metamorphosis.

Paul Slansky, an *Esquire* and *New Times* writer, had befriended— and loved—Carrie for several years. "It was impossible to spend five minutes with Carrie Fisher without knowing that you would never meet anyone else like her; we became instant friends," he wrote after her death. He recommended her for a short *Esquire* Q&A, and at some point in early 1985, before she had her overdose, they did an interview that appeared in the May 1985 issue—just when Carrie was in rehab— titled "The Unparalleled Wisdom of 28-Year-Old Carrie Fisher."

In it she called herself "America's Niece" and made the now-famous remark that when she's asked what it's like to be Debbie Reynolds's daughter, she wants to answer, "You mean compared to . . . when I [was an] accountant's kid and a car salesman's kid?" She labeled her family "blue-blooded white trash," briefly answered questions about Paul Simon and John Belushi, and made what we would come to know as typical Carrie remarks: "I feel like I'm the doctor and the patient, but a lot of time the doctor isn't in," and said her favorite bumper sticker was "LOVE IS THE LIBERACE MUSEUM."

As a result of the offbeat charm and wit in the very short piece, Carrie's friend Blair Sabol easily persuaded the literary agent Al Lowman to represent Carrie and Slansky for a book of funny essays about Hollywood by Carrie, to be called *Money, Dearest*. The title came from Carrie. "You're a much better writer than I am, Carrie," Blair, who'd written columns for years, said to her. Carrie thanked Blair and said, "I'm the *worst* actress." The project was initially offered to Crown. The mandate: a series of essays along the lines of "[Fran] Lebowitz West," referring to the black-suit-clad, unsmiling, chain-smoking uber-dark wit of New York, author of *Metropolitan Life* and other books.

At first Carrie took possession of the idea. "I like it. It's a clever title," she said in an interview. "I thought of *Money, Dearest,* as Beverly Hills specifically," quipping that her mother had thought of writing a book about a "celebrity horror daughter." Carrie said, "I'd die if I wrote a tell-all—a scathing exposé." In this interview in early 1986— with her fan, the Canadian host Brian Linehan—Carrie looked, as she still looked, lovely: long-haired, thin, pretty enough to stanch any angry competition she had ever felt with her mother. She wielded that uniquely fine-tuned demeanor—twinkly-eyed and ingratiating but also elegant and blasé (featuring affectionate boredom with *Star Wars*)— that was becoming her brand. Viewers would never know she had suffered a near-death overdose a year earlier. Still, "I always behaved like I had a lived-in quality," she put it aptly.

But soon the idea of the essay series with the Beverly Hills angle and her proffered title fizzled. Carrie didn't like the "snide" factor. After re-reading a Dorothy Parker story, "Just a Little One," about an alcoholic (Parker considered herself "not a writer with a drinking problem but a drinker with a writing problem"), Carrie replaced the snarky-essays idea with the idea of a novel. Lowman sold it to the editor Pat Soliman at Simon & Schuster (S&S) in mid-1985. Carrie engaged her good friend Slansky to work with her on it. She called him her "editor," not co-writer.

The autobiographical novel was pinioned on her drug overdose, moving through passages written in the voice of a dislikable, male wannabe screenwriter and voracious druggie whom Carrie either met in rehab or shrewdly invented. Then, after the theatrics of that character were concluded, the novel turned to its main character, Carrie's alter ego: Suzanne Vale, a complex, bon-mot-spewing actress and overdose survivor with a mother not unlike Debbie—at times *very* like Debbie. To wit: "'Hello, dear . . . This is your mother, Doris.' As opposed to my brother, Doris, or my uncle, Doris?" The foregoing repartee would take on a life of its own, because later Debbie unwaveringly called Carrie most mornings, introducing herself that formal way. Suzanne Vale is navigating the Hollywood of exclusive clubs like Helena's: the Hollywood of young adult ennui (women in their thirties "should agree that we won't get out of bed until we decide what to do with the second half of our lives"), shrinks, scripts, drugs, and deals, bad parts in beggars-can't-be-choosers movies, failed love affairs, and good friendships. Finally—half uncomfortably for one with such an acute and self-prized self-destructiveness—she has settled into a romance with a decent guy.

Carrie opened the book with the line "Maybe I shouldn't have given the guy who pumped my stomach my phone number, but who cares?" She ended it with a letter to that same lifesaving doctor, concluding with witty melancholy: "That night in the emergency room, do you recall if I threw up something I needed? . . . I distinctly feel as though I'm missing something." Pause. "But then, I always have."

Working with her at the Oak Pass house in early 1986, Slansky functioned as what he calls Carrie's "book whisperer." "She would write—in longhand, on yellow legal pads in large loopy letters, or tape a stream of consciousness monologue," and Paul would edit the typed pages. When the book was published, a controversy arose: Did Paul Slansky, not Carrie, write it? In the very first edition of the book, as the author and *Los Angeles Times* book reviewer Carolyn See noted prominently in her review, Slansky's name, credited with "Edited by," was directly under hers, a highly unusual move. Even Larry King brought the rumor up with Carrie on his TV show: Did Slansky write the book? "That's sexist" and *untrue*, Carrie answered. "Ask Paul."

A woman who was very close to Carrie's writing process adamantly puts the rumors to rest. They were started, this person says, by the "crazy claims by [the now-deceased science fiction writer] Harlan Ellison, who decided that Carrie just couldn't have written it. But I know for a fact that Carrie wrote every word herself." For his part, Slansky has staunchly backed up the fact that Carrie wrote the words herself, with him serving as an active editor.

Carrie used her real post-rehab experiences in the book. She transformed her desperation work on the Penelope Spheeris low-budget undercover-cop movie *Hollywood Vice Squad* into her character Suzanne Vale's desperation work on a low-budget undercover-cop film called *The Kitchen Sink*. As in real life, she takes the role because she thought that given her drug history she'd never work again.

Readers would come to know Carrie, the glib and the profound in their own lively mix. They would get the cynical social critic: "You can't find any true closeness in Hollywood because everybody does fake closeness so well." And the standard-issue neurotic: "My problem is, I only know how to need needy people . . . Somebody . . . could be wearing a sign, 'I have no problems, you can believe me,' and I wouldn't even see them." The soon-to-be-very-famous oversharer: "But deep down— and you don't get too far deep down with me, because I've thrust all the deep down right up to the surface." The sociologist: "I guess that's how guys are thoughtful in the eighties—they accompany girls to their abortions." In the book, the "industry" is on display: the woebegone, lowly second-tier status that television work, as opposed to film work, was perceived to have in the 1980s (humorous in today's HBO, Showtime, Amazon, Hulu, and Netflix retrospect) is a running motif. The effect of Eddie Fisher's abandonment is turned into stage banter: "I told [a male friend] about my father leaving when I was very young so I knew how to pine for men, but not how to love them. So he said, 'You probably would have been perfect for somebody in World War Two.'" She expressed many women's paradoxical yearnings: "She had finally decided she wanted stimulating that very subtly became calming—a holocaust that became a haven." She infused her grandmother Maxene's tough pragmatism into Hollywood Suzanne's complication, as if preaching to herself: "Just pick someone and make it work . . . I've stayed with your grandfather now for fifty-odd years. I don't like him but I picked him." In Maxene's generation, "We make a choice and we stick with it and I think you could learn something from that."

There's her owning of her stubborn pathology. A man says, "'I like to feel like I could perform surgery at any given moment.' 'That's interesting,' said Suzanne. 'My goal was to feel I could go *into* surgery at any given moment.'" Some of this is Carrie-shtick, but it's winning and smart and not hollow. And it alternates with enough relatable social terror, such as the anxiety of entering Hollywood parties: "Suzanne walked stoically up the imposing driveway, like a condemned man about to face a firing squad without cigarette or blindfold, to the huge, secluded stone mansion." There's more of her comical description of her ennui: "My life is like a lone, forgotten Q-Tip in the second-to-last drawer." And her distinctively metaphored self-deprecation: "What kind of wimpy, pathetic guy would be willing to crawl through the moat of my personality and live in my house, with my stuff?" There's more about her depression: "My mood is lifting, like a small, heavy plane." There's typical female understanding of a self-forced interest in the non-cad: "Was Jesse a good man? she asked herself. He probably was, because he bored her to death sometimes."

The book ends with Suzanne Vale being driven to the hospital by the decent Jesse for treatment after burning her hand while making waffles. "I should open up a house account here," she says of the venue she was taken to after her overdose. Jesse admits, "They should at least give you a quantity discount." Suzanne Vale amuses us while her angst feels genuine. We envy her blasé worldliness, but the pain that is its price saves us from being jealous of her.

The book's debut was helped by felicitous rave blurbs from Carrie's friends. "Carrie's book is savagely funny and savagely revealing. It makes *Moby Dick* look like a big, fat, dumb book," said Steve Martin. Candice Bergen said, "This is a remarkable first novel. In fact, it is a remarkable second novel."

After the book was finished and shipped off to be published, Carrie, in May 1987, flew to Israel to make the movie *Appointment with Death*, based on the Agatha Christie novel of the same name. She played the daughter of a blackmailing heiress, portrayed by Lauren Bacall, in the whodunit, which also featured John Gielgud, Piper Laurie, and Hayley Mills. Todd—now divorced from Donna Freberg—and his new girlfriend, the model and actress Rene Russo, came along. Todd had met the stunning Rene at his church, the Hiding Place. They were so serious during the Holy Land trip with Carrie that they tried to marry, according to Todd.

Carrie's good friend Bruce Wagner was along as well. The opposite of sunny, Christian, and emotionally uncomplicated Todd, "Bruce is dark and brilliantly funny," says a mutual friend. Wagner might be said to have taken over Michael O'Donoghue's role in Carrie's life—the sardonic, decadent male best friend—but with far more longevity. Traveling through Israel, Bruce, provocatively, wore a kaffiyeh, the native Arab headdress, in solidarity with the children of Palestine. Bruce's highly literary stories-as-novel volume about current Hollywood, *Force Majeure*, in which the protagonist is a failed screenwriter turned limo driver, was creating buzz as a privately published volume, limning, among other things, the unique humiliations abounding in the industry.

There was excitement at Simon & Schuster during the copyediting of *Postcards*, gearing up to its August 1987 publication. "It was such a unique book," says Susan Kamil, who was the editor toward the book's completion (and today is publisher of Random House and Dial Press).

"The intelligence, the transparency—the voice was the voice of a real person. It was the beginning of Carrie Fisher being a centrifugal force," she says. "The combination of celebrity and honesty was so *new*." Indeed, it would not be until years later that female Hollywood insiders wrote tartly about the industry: Julia Phillips's *You'll Never Eat Lunch in This Town Again* came out in 1991; Lynda Obst's *Hello, He Lied*, in 1996; Nancy Griffin and Kim Masters's *Hit and Run*, in 1996. And, for that matter, Peter Biskind's *Easy Riders, Raging Bulls* wasn't published until 1998.

"Her comebacks and her wit were machine-gun fast," Kamil continues. "Unlike many celebrities in Hollywood, she gravitated to the more intellectual people, the brain-driven. And I remember her tremendous generosity. She told me she had a friend, Bruce Wagner—the brilliant Bruce Wagner!—and she told me about his privately published book *Force Majeure*." Carrie gave the book to Susan. "We"—S&S—"ended up publishing it," Susan says. In its major-publishing-house version, it quickly garnered comparisons to Nathanael West and F. Scott Fitzgerald. (Carrie herself blurbed it as the "literary offspring" that would come if "Jackie Collins were seduced by Dostoevsky on the floor of the William Morris mailroom.") The highly praised publication led to a string of Wagner's similarly deeply sardonic, outstandingly reviewed contemporary Hollywood noir accounts: *I'm Losing You, Still Holding* (which a *New York* magazine editor called a weird, coprolalic amalgam of Buddhism and *Us Weekly*), *The Chrysanthemum Palace*, and others. Wagner has many times expressed his gratitude to Carrie, not just for the introduction to S&S but also for her enormous friendship. "She's tremendously forgiving," Bruce has privately said. "I have not been there for her in many ways that she's been there for me, not by choice but out of my own personal weakness," he added.

The rave reviews for *Postcards* were kicked off by the novelist, memoirist, and third-generation Los Angeles native Carolyn See, who provided it with one of the first of many happily stunned reviews. See seemed to be thinking out loud as she expressed her intrigue with and lack of preparation for Carrie the writer:

Everyone knows Carrie Fisher for her portrait of Princess Leia in the film "Star Wars," and all those other movies. And everyone knows her royal Hollywood lineage: the daughter of Eddie Fisher and actress Debbie Reynolds. And no doubt lots of readers will buy "Postcards From the Edge" because of those facts, and all the promotional fallout that comes from them.

But a couple of things come to mind when you get about 50 pages into "Postcards From the Edge." You wonder, thinking back, why Carrie Fisher—why she didn't *grab your mind* as you watched the screen, the way her mother did. And it occurs to you, Carrie Fisher's heart might not have been in it. You deduce this fact because her heart appears to be in this novel and in the writing process. This book is so much better than you think it's going to be! It's intelligent, original, focused, insightful, very interesting to read.

In another paragraph she wrote, "This is not an inspirational novel, but something on the order of a tough look at reality; *a 'serious' piece of work.*"

The Washington Post called *Postcards* "a cult classic . . . a wonderfully funny, brash, and biting novel, the most startling literary debut since Jay McInerney's *Bright Lights, Big City.*" *Time* compared Carrie's Suzanne Vale to Holden Caulfield. The high-barred *Kirkus Reviews* had issues with it (she "slips into a meandering, 'poor me' account of Suzanne's spoiled yet troubled adjustment to post-detox life") but ultimately called the novel "dryly comic . . . often exhilarating." From the *San Jose Mercury News*: "surprising, hilarious, breathtaking, a wry and witty commentary on life in the fast lanes of Freewayland." Between Carolyn See's "serious," *The Washington Post*'s "startling," the *San Jose Mercury News*'s "surprising," *Publishers Weekly*'s "real talent," and the bestselling author Tom Robbins's note of "surprise" at how good it was, there was a sense of a newly revealed identity, once hidden and now excitedly discovered, and that it was *real*. There would come comparisons to Erica Jong, Nora Ephron, and Joan Didion, and to Bret Easton Ellis, Hunter S. Thompson, her role model Dorothy Parker, David Sedaris, Augusten Burroughs, and Martin Amis.

The book launch took place in New York, with a party at the S&S executive Joni Evans's apartment. During a pre-party interview with *The New York Times'* Michael Gross, a merry, antic Carrie "bounced into the bathroom to fuss with her hair for the fourth time in ten minutes" and did not fail to give great, honest Carrie quotations—about the allure of drugs and her friend Belushi, about skipping the snide for the wryly confessional. It was Eddie's fifty-ninth birthday, and he was attending the party night. Ever the father-helping daughter, Carrie had bought him a present: a jacket and pants. Gross left the interview "thinking she was hysterically funny and I left there thinking I had just met somebody extraordinary," Gross says.

Postcards eventually became a bestseller, and feature interviews with Carrie brought her distinctive personality and wit to a public that had formerly thought of her merely as the *Star Wars* heroine. "She is an interviewer's delight: Everything is out on the table. No secrets. The whole shebang," Stephanie Mansfield excitedly told her *Washington Post* readers. There's Carrie's quirky taste in food. French food "is not food. It's like a picture of food," declared Carrie, who always had a yen for Mexican. Mansfield called Carrie what her friends and cognoscenti have known—"small and smart and saucy . . . a girl's girl. You want to go shopping with her. You want to double-date with her . . . even though her new book . . . is all about how she . . . [got] her stomach pumped."

"Most children wait for their parents to die before writing such a book," Mansfield noted. "Boy, when they die," Carrie lobbed back, "I'm gonna come out with a sitcom."

When they get to the Mexican restaurant and two tables are offered and rejected until a third is chosen, she quips to the waiter, "This is the most moving, moving experience."

Mansfield wrote, "She worries that therapy is her only serious relationship . . . About a year ago, after therapy by men, she found a woman shrink." To which Carrie riposted, "Next, I'm going to go for an 11-year-old child." *Who else talked like that?* Her earlier print interviews had a hint of who Carrie was, but *now* her unique personality was in full force. And here came her soon-to-be-landmark honesty about her drug taking. What had she been on? "Everything. Ecstasy. MDA. Percodan. It's hard to get. You have to lie to doctors." Again: *Who else was that damn honest?* She spoke of attending a Paris fashion show. "I thought, oh, man, it didn't take the edge off." Pause. "It took one edge off and put another one on."

Carrie embarked on an eight-city tour for *Postcards*'s publication, and Gary Springer—son of the well-known publicist John Springer (who had had Debbie and Richard Burton among his many clients)—accompanied her as a publicist/minder. "She brought her Bumble and Bumble hairdresser with her because she felt the only way she could feel different at every event was to have a different hairstyle," Springer recalls. Because of the daily washing and setting, she had T-shirts printed BALD BY FRISCO and distributed them to her team. But in the behind-the-scenes portion of the tour, Carrie's vulnerability was very much in evidence. Carrie had so much stage fright before every appearance that Springer would spend "the entire day or morning before the event in the hotel bathroom with her. I was sitting on the edge of the tub while she was on the floor, wrapped around the toilet: throwing up. She was *so* nervous. But then she would go out to the event and she was absolutely delightful—buoyant and energetic, smiling and bubbly. And she wanted every event and presentation to be different than the previous day's. And they were."

Carrie's friend Mike Nichols optioned *Postcards*. He wanted Carrie to write the script, something that she relished but that also made her "a little nervous," says Patricia Resnick. Because Resnick was an experienced screenwriter (and remains an in-demand TV writer), "Carrie asked me to come over and help her. She said, 'Oh my God, I have to *write* this thing!' And she said, in terms of getting advice, 'I'm just talking to you and Buck Henry.' She asked me some basic things about writing. And then, well, either Buck and I are the best teachers in the world, or she didn't need our instruction or *any* instruction. Because she just hit it out of the park."

Meanwhile, Carrie cemented her wise-best-friend role, something she had perfected in real life, by playing Meg Ryan's best friend in *When Harry Met Sally.* This would be one of her best-loved non–*Star Wars* movies and the one in which she played her biggest role. Conceived in 1984, filmed in late 1988, and released in 1989, it was a kind of family affair: Carrie's friend Nora Ephron wrote and co-produced it, and Carrie's best friend Penny Marshall's ex-husband Rob Reiner directed it. Carrie played Marie, the best friend of Meg Ryan's pretty, airy journalist Sally, who has a snappish animosity-cute relationship with Harry (Billy Crystal), and he for her—disguising their mutual attraction. After dating a married man for years, Marie marries Harry's best friend, Jess (Bruno Kirby). The traditional wedding scene is Carrie at her most earnest. Her character is both vulnerable and savvy. She's vulnerable after she has been talking on the phone to Sally (while, in split screen, Jess has been talking to Harry), and she turns to her husband in bed and essentially says she is so glad to be married and desperate not to be abandoned. And she's savvy when, sitting at lunch in Central Park with Sally, who has just broken up with a boyfriend, she whips out a Rolodex of men, single and married and in between, and proffers several selections for the principled Sally, who says she is still in a "mourning period" after her latest breakup. Marie knows Manhattan dating-game rules: She bends, rather than throws away, the Rolodex card of a married man because he might not be married for long. She then pulls out another card while counseling Sally not to wait. "And if you don't grab him, someone else will," she warns, in a much-quoted line, "you'll have to spend the rest of your life knowing that somebody else is married to your husband." It is wittily done, upscale but conventional Manhattan repartee, something for which Ephron was noted. Under her zaniness, Carrie shared that privileged, power-couple-conscious spirit.

Carrie—her hair now cut stylishly but unglamorously short—was the perfect sensible-but-sometimes-snarky best friend in the movie, and this became her after-Leia default casting. ("People come up and ask me where things are in supermarkets; I have a look," she said, as she had said before.) Acting in movies would soon become, she would say, something she did "for companionship and for money"—demarcating that from her more important work: writing.

At night, after a day's filming, Carrie would have Chinese takeout at the apartment of her friend and disco-dancing pal Will Trinkle, and she'd share the day's on-set tales with him, Will's lover, and their close friend Julian Ford. Later, however, alone or with an unknown compatriot, "I would be snorting heroin," she later volunteered to Diane Sawyer on national TV, her blunt tone indicating she knew full well how shocking that would sound. Meanwhile, Debbie was off on a national tour of the theatrical version of her *Unsinkable Molly Brown*, with her fellow former Nazarene singer-actor friend Ron Raines playing opposite her and grateful, he recalls, for her supportiveness and generosity.

The same year that *When Harry Met Sally* was released, Carrie made a new lifelong friend, Nina Jacobson. Carrie had written a screenplay called *The Other Woman*, about a divorced woman who, along with her two daughters, greatly dislikes her ex-husband's new, young wife—until the woman gets cancer and wants the girls to make amends. It became a TV movie for Universal. There at Universal, she met Nina, then a development executive. Today—and for years now—Nina has been one of the most successful, and outspoken, women in Hollywood: a leading, vocal gay feminist, and now one of the most powerful and quality independent producers in the business, having partnered with her friend Ryan Murphy on the multi-award-winning *The People v. O. J. Simpson*, after having been the force behind the hugely successful Jennifer Lawrence franchise, *The Hunger Games* (her Katniss Everdeen a kind of modern version of Leia), which proved a young woman could be a blockbuster screen heroine. (Most recently, she had a massive hit in *Crazy Rich Asians*.) When Nina met Carrie, though, she was just starting out.

She was nine years younger than Carrie, but her attitude, concealed in the work setting at first, was like Carrie's—tough, funny, kick-ass, ribald, confident.

They fell into their bond in an offhand way. For Carrie, Nina was someone she sensed she wanted to cultivate. "We'd have long meetings and brainstorm," Nina told a journalist in an unpublished 2004 conversation about the beginning of their friendship. "She used to hang out in my office and talk about ideas—and she'd eavesdrop on my phone conversations." That Carrie Fisher would do something at once nosy, entitled, and charmingly gauche was weird and flattering and lovable. "When we first got to know each other, she wanted to know about my life, but she was also willing to share about her life. She's a curious, interested person. When a person is willing to share that much of herself, you feel that it's only right that you should do the same, and she's the kind of person who wouldn't understand why you wouldn't."

Nina, at that point and soon after, had a *lot* of her personal life to share with Carrie: Nina had long been in a kind of closet, and she had just found out, to her relief, that her studio colleagues realized that she wasn't straight, as she would later put it. (In 1989 and 1990, most gay Hollywood executives kept their sexual orientation secret.) In a couple of years, Nina would fall in love with a woman, Jen Bleakley, who would become her life partner and eventually her wife.

Shortly before *When Harry Met Sally* was released, Carrie played another sensible, short-brown-haired, pretty-enough middle-class woman in the mediocre slapstick comedy *The 'Burbs*. She was teamed again with her friend Tom Hanks, who, along with their fictional neighbor Bruce Dern, played a suburban man who imagines their new next-door neighbors are ghoulish Satanists. She was, again, the voice of reason and maturity, but this time with far less sophistication than her Ephron movie character. In the film, she is dressed in a housewife's frilly long bathrobe and mall-bought sundresses rather than Calvin Klein jackets. The director of *The Blues Brothers*, John Landis, had recommended her for the role, and even though the director, Joe Dante, found her extremely funny off-screen, her largely passive and reactive character, Carol Peterson, ever chiding her husband to stop spying on the neighbors, constituted a waste of her talent.

Fortunately, it was the *When Harry Met Sally* role—and her personal reputation for arch hauteur and naughtiness—that stuck. Industry producers and executives now shouted in unison, "Carrie Fisher!" whenever anyone in the room asked who would be perfect for the role of a tough, modern film or TV heroine. So, shortly after *When Harry Met Sally* was released, when the young TV producer Wendy Kout, in her first time out as a series showrunner, conceived the role of Hannah, a snappy writer at the fictional *Chicago Monthly* magazine, in a series called *Anything but Love*, "everybody at the network, NBC, *everybody* shouted Carrie's name," Wendy recalls.

Wendy had idolized Carrie from afar, saying, "She was my generation's Dorothy Parker." The late 1980s was a watershed moment for realistic media women as characters on TV series. Female producers who had, as girls, been enamored of Mary Richards's spunky but dignified competence wanted to create next-age, more liberated versions— ambitious women who *didn't* call their bosses "*Mister* Grant."

"Diane English," the showrunner of the wildly popular *Murphy Brown*, "and I came up in the industry at the same time," says Wendy, who has continued as a producer and a playwright. "We were trying, through the characters we were creating for TV, to fight the next stage of the good fight."

Carrie agreed to take a meeting with Wendy. Wendy was thrilled.

"I went to the meeting thinking I actually had a shot at getting her," Wendy says, with a laugh. Instead, the first thing out of Carrie's mouth was "I'll never do a television series." The snobbery of theatrical movie people against the "lower" medium of TV had been half parodied throughout *Postcards*; now Carrie was echoing it. (Jamie Lee Curtis would eventually get the role, and *Anything but Love* would run through 1992.) But there was more Carrie wanted to say to the besotted yet now crestfallen young showrunner. And she did.

"She had a big smile on her face, but her eyes were old," Wendy

remembers. "She had seen so much of life already—you could just tell."
When Wendy asked her why she took the meeting if she knew she'd
say no, Carrie answered, "I had nothing better to do." The two women
could do nothing but laugh at that honesty.

After that ice breaking came the Talk. Wendy sat there for half an
hour and sought advice from Carrie. This new show, on which Wendy
had John Ritter as a co–executive producer, was a step up in power and
authority for Wendy. She asked Carrie, Should she be afraid of what that
would do to her? Carrie immediately answered, with a laugh: "Money and
power don't change you. They *reveal* you." It was, first of all, striking that
Carrie had a riposte so ready. And then there was its mysterious sagacity.

That "resonated so deeply with me," Wendy says, "and it's never
stopped resonating. It meant 'Money and power are not evil and corrup-
tive; they open the door to show your character.' Carrie was a human
tuning fork. I had expected her wit, but not her wisdom. It's one thing to
have an acerbic tongue, but this was something else. This was deeper.
You don't encounter that every day. But I encountered it with her.

"We talked and laughed about men and love." Wendy can't remember the details, but "it just felt like an instant connection—*boom!* Like
we were sisters. She wasn't like, 'We're on a different level; I'm higher
than you, but I'm bequeathing you this meeting'; she had none of that
Hollywood elitism shit. She had an open heart and an open mind. Carrie
is not a sentimental person—I didn't expect that. But she is kind. That's a
good combination." Astringency *and* compassion. "Our talk was as real
as two women can get. She wished me well. And then I never saw her
again. But she affected me, deeply, permanently, with that half hour."

Carrie's next novel, *Surrender the Pink* (meaning "surrender your
virginity—and your heart, your core," as one of her editors put it),
was written about a woman not unlike her and a man not unlike Paul
Simon. (Although Carrie has said that there were aspects of Richard
Dreyfuss, Don Henley, and the producer Dan Melnick in there, too.)

Patricia Soliman was out of S&S now, and Carrie was working with the renowned editor Michael Korda, but she felt Michael was too old for her sensibility, so a young female editor, who had grown up in Beverly Hills and shared Carrie's cultural references, Trish Lande, took over. In the book, the Paul-based character is a thirty-four-year-old playwright named Rudy Gendler—self-assured, Manhattan brisk—and Carrie is a twenty-year-old script doctor named Dinah Kaufman. She feels inadequate to him; she falls in love, they break up fast, and while fending off a nice-guy screenwriter, she repairs to the Hamptons to—desperately—spy on Rudy and his new, supposedly perfect girlfriend.

The difficulty of modern love between not-quite-liberated sophisticates is a theme in the book, and Carrie-isms abound. She takes a swipe at Debbie—"Dinah's mother brought her up to be a virgin, as though it were a high-paying job." And, this being about love gone awry, she writes, in somewhat heavy-breathing prose, about Eddie—the earlier, idealized version of her father, who was far from the actual version. "Whenever she saw him on his once-a-year visits, she'd put on her best behavior so he'd love her. Because she hardly ever saw him, he grew daily in her mind, a paternal tumor in her imagination. She loved—she worshipped—the father she made up in her mind."

One sees clear hints of the Carrie-Paul relationship in the book. There is Dinah complaining that Rudy is "sometimes . . . cold . . . he's selfish . . . I'm high-strung, demanding, he's quiet." They plumb each other's personalities. "You're a very ballsy girl," he says. "You're not afraid of . . . the things that you're afraid of. You keep coming at it. You're nervy." "I don't feel so nervy around you; I feel girly," she says. He says, "You once said I was pompous. Yelled it, even." She says, "I doubt that I yelled it. I don't think you're pompous. I think you're incredibly confident."

She finds herself falling for him in a disoriented, defensive way. "She'd panic in the face of his cool when confronted with his frostiness. She'd hurt him back. She couldn't be caught caring more, waiting for him to want her."

They get to the nub of what is troubling their relationship: sexism.

"I realized from being with you I don't want somebody with an intense career," he says, in a sentiment that sounds dated even in the late 1980s. And: "It just doesn't work when two people are ambitiously pursuing their careers . . . A woman has to have a less intense job." Of course, there was much more to the Paul and Carrie relationship—from her drug use to her enormous, exciting, but challenging intensity ("I didn't give Paul the peace he needed," she would later say to a friend)—and she didn't shy away from expressing it. She admitted, in an interview, that she wasn't the most typical female companion. "If you're going out with me you'll go hungry, but you won't go bored," she said. "Two yangs don't make a right. Paul and I were both yangs." She knew that friendships and conversation mattered to her more than the typical customs of a love affair or marriage. As she said to another reporter, "I like to talk and I like exchanges and I like the contact made through communication . . . and my veal piccata is suffering because of that. So anybody that I'd be with, you'd see them starved and overstimulated and their shirts are wrinkled. I'm just another kind of companion."

At *Surrender*'s end, although Dinah and Rudy are broken up, they can't quite let go. "The thing they were together couldn't entirely come apart," she writes. "It existed out there somewhere, a distant, undeniable fact . . . [and] now mutated and took new forms . . . Nothing is ever really over. Just over there."

And that was true of Carrie and Paul—more so than most people know. Even in 1989, five years after their divorce, she was slipping out to see him clandestinely. Says Trish Lande, "My only experience of the relationship was her racing out to secretly meet him," once in New York. "It was *super*-secretive." The surprising thing is that Paul was already with Edie Brickell by then; they'd met on the set of *SNL* in November 1988, and it was a love-at-first-sight moment.

"When Carrie would see Paul during the work on this book, I wasn't to tell *anyone*," Trish says. "No one was to say *anything*. I did see her sort of being willing to be available to him at his whim, which was a weird way to see her because it was uncharacteristic" of tough, feminist Carrie and of the way she had come to characterize herself and Paul as two equal forces. "She just couldn't seem to get him out of her system," Trish surmises.

"But it is also probably worth remembering that this was when she was very much in the grip of her bipolar episodes," Trish says, "and she was not medicated. She would occasionally take medication, but she didn't like what happened to her creativity and so mostly she didn't take it.

"There was one time that I remember where Carrie and I were at a restaurant in Rockefeller Center, and Carrie always liked to sit cross-legged on the chair, but she started rocking back and forth and speaking very fast and I wasn't sure what to do. That was the most lost I ever saw her. I was a little afraid for her." Trish also saw another expression of Carrie's manic episodes: overbuying. When Trish was staying at her house while working on their next book, Carrie "once bought twenty-five Victorian nightgowns and then she'd offer them to you"—to all her friends. "I would always say, 'No thank you,' but not everybody did." Some happily took the nightgowns.

It must be said that the "exquisite" creative state that she and Richard Dreyfuss saw in mania was something that even the most respected authorities in the field acknowledge as compelling. Though it may certainly seem like it, it is *not* a selfish act of irresponsibility to want to go off your meds or reduce your meds (something that 50 percent of people with bipolar disorder do at some point); it is a normal temptation. The allure of the ecstasy-stoking aspects of the manic state can be so appealing it can feel worth the pain. Dr. Kay Redfield Jamison, a psychiatry professor and co-director of the Mood Disorders Center at Johns Hopkins, herself diagnosed with bipolar disorder, and considered the most esteemed and compassionate authority on the subject, has freely admitted, "When you're high, it's tremendous." And she has said, "I have often asked myself whether, given the choice, I would choose to have manic-depressive illness . . . Strangely enough I think I would choose to have it. It's complicated. Depression is awful beyond words or sounds or images . . . So why would I want anything to do with this illness?

Because I honestly believe that as a result of it I have felt more things, more deeply; had more experiences, more intensely; . . . worn death 'as close as dungarees,' appreciated it—and life—more; seen the finest and the most terrible in people." Jamison resisted acknowledgment of her illness for a long time—an anguished process she recounted in her tour de force memoir *An Unquiet Mind*—and resisted medication, eventually finding salvation in lithium. Still, she appreciated that "I have run faster, thought faster, and loved faster than most I know. And I think much of this is related to my illness—the intensity it gives to things."

From conversations she had with Richard Dreyfuss and from the way she lived her life, it is clear that Carrie felt this, too. Not that Richard didn't counsel his friend sternly on the subject of staying on her meds, even if he sometimes disobeyed his own edict. He knew the danger of going off them. "My friends would say, 'Okay, I guess it's time for us to get out the circus cables and pull Richard down by the ankles,' 'cause I was out of it," he recalls. "I was all manic, all 'up.' There was no 'down' for me until I was forty." Especially after his 1982 car crash, he warned Carrie, "Stay on your meds! Stay on your fucking meds! It cost you a lot to get here [to a stage of stability]." He spoke with the authority of someone who, as he puts it, "had been publicly disgraced. I had fallen from heights and climbed back."

On at least one occasion, Richard says, "Carrie called me and said, 'I need to talk to you. Just stay on the phone.' I knew she'd been off her meds and she had gotten back on and she was waiting for them to take effect. She wanted me to stay on the phone with her until she was calm," which could take a very long time. (Carrie paid Richard back for his help, especially when "my first marriage ended and I was feeling like a bug and full of guilt and I needed someone to hear me say how awful I felt," he says. "Carrie did. I stayed at her house and she gave me advice.")

Surrender the Pink got some excellent reviews. The *Chicago Tribune*'s reviewer declared that Carrie should be "filed between Martin Amis and P. G. Wodehouse." But not all were positive, and the book failed to earn the sales of its predecessor. It was a book about modern romance, not deeper themes. Carrie's next book, *Delusions of Grandma*, actually plumbed such themes as death, family connections, and a search for intimacy.

Carrie was finishing the final edit of *Surrender* while writing the screenplay for *Postcards*, thrilled that Mike Nichols was mentoring her with it. "She gave enormous credit and love to Mike Nichols for what he taught her about writing for the screen," Trish Lande says. Splitting her time between L.A. and New York, she stayed at David Geffen's Fifth Avenue apartment to write the *Postcards* screenplay, and "one day," Trish recalls, "we're working on the galleys of *Surrender the Pink* at Geffen's apartment and Carrie wasn't feeling well, and in came Meryl Streep," who was playing Suzanne Vale in the movie version of *Postcards*, "bringing Carrie chicken soup." This was the start of a close long-term friendship between Carrie and Meryl.

"Between the book and the screenplay, it was also the beginning of Carrie's real identity as a writer," Trish says. As someone who now thought of herself as a writer, Carrie cultivated a friendship with Meg Wolitzer. Meg, then on the rise, is now considered, thirteen books in, one of the foremost novelists of her generation. Later Carrie would be cast in the film version of Meg's novel *This Is My Life*, directed by Nora Ephron.

"I saw her in New York for a period of time," Meg says. "We would hang out sometimes and have lunch. I remember once walking along Central Park West with her, both of us singing a medley of Sondheim songs. It was like being part of a free-form traveling cabaret. Another time, at lunch in a restaurant, the waiter came over, dropped the menus on the table, and stood there as if he was about to recite the specials but then in a quiet voice began to intone, 'A long time ago, in a galaxy far away.' I had a sense, from that, of the singular strangeness of Carrie's life. She was an actress and a writer, but she was also, to many people, a vivid fictional character.

"For Christmas, Carrie gave me a bunch of gifts—I know she gave everyone gifts—including a giant stuffed-dog telephone. The mouth moved when the person on the other end spoke. Someone might call me and say something ordinary or funny or upsetting, and it would all come out through a dog's mouth. That mix of high and low, dead serious and irreverent but always truly expressive, reminds me of what it was like to know her.

"When we'd talk at her place, we might be hanging out on her bed; that was what she did. There was a very comfortable teenage feeling about it that I really liked. She was so smart. And she was interested in writers. She particularly liked witty writers and always asked for recommendations." Carrie broached the idea of working with Meg to do a new adaptation of *The Heiress*, the movie based on *Washington Square*, by Henry James. In the pitch meeting, Meg was impressed by Carrie's predictably "beautiful" speaking: "I felt like a Roz Chast character" in comparison. Conversely, Meg's creative writing teaching was something "Carrie really wanted for herself; she took it seriously. She always wanted to read things I loved. I gave her one of my favorite novels, *Mrs. Bridge*, by Evan S. Connell, and she gave me some pages she had written. She really wanted my opinion of them."

Trish Lande visited Oak Pass to work with Carrie on her third book, *Delusions of Grandma*, in 1990 and then 1991. *Delusions* was, among other things, a paean to Maxene, whose memorable lines (like "colder than a well-digger's butt") so influenced her. It also introduced a version of a most significant man in her life and included a story line of nursing a dying friend. "We did a ton of changes on it," Trish says. It eventually "became a whole different book" when Carrie became pregnant. "She definitely had clear ideas, though she was never stubborn. She wrote, and I worked on a typewriter. No computers then!"

For her editor guests, especially the female ones, life at Carrie's was like a sorority house on Friday night, and it often included a new custom, which made Carrie an icon for thirty years: her legendary joint October birthday parties with Penny Marshall. A more exclusive, A-list-filled, in-demand party in Hollywood—or anywhere—didn't exist than the Carrie-Penny parties. Most of the early ones were held at Penny's Franklin Canyon house. "I can't believe my sister is giving the most sought-after party in town," Garry Marshall said to the *SNL* writer Marilyn Suzanne Miller, as Miller recalls it. Nina Jacobson said that when she and her girlfriend, Jen, first started attending them, "we felt bad for not being famous," because the guests were, by Nina's estimation, "85 percent incredibly famous people. We were wondering what we were doing there."

"I was there for two of the parties," Trish says. "Honestly! I came home from the first one and started to make a list of who was there and realized it would be easier to make a list of who *wasn't* there. I was introduced to Francis Ford Coppola, Tom Hanks, George Lucas, everyone you can imagine. But it was very comfortable and unpretentious." At every single one of these parties, Carrie's housekeeper Gloria Crayton and her sister, Mary, served their famous fried chicken, macaroni and cheese, and monkey bread. Says another guest, "It amused the hell out of me to see these people"—the party guests—"who didn't weigh more than an ounce, who tortured restaurants all year long [for healthy, low-cal food] and there they were, bellied up, eating like they'd never had food before."

Carrie did her girlfriend thing before the party. "I don't know what to wear! I feel so fat!" Trish Lande worried on the phone from New York before she arrived. Carrie immediately said, "Take a water pill. Get some Control panty hose. And get over it." Once Trish got to L.A., "Carrie made an appointment for me with the facialist and the waxing pro to the stars."

As for the parties themselves, Carrie had a unique mission, which she expressed to *The Baltimore Sun* and to the New York *Daily News*'s Sherryl Connelly: "I want to be a good writer, but I want more to be a better friend. I want to keep up with a well-kept group." Literary ambition, emotional giving, and social strategizing: all at once. It was a tripartite goal, and it would *work* for her. It made her who she was.

What the *Vanity Fair* Oscars parties would soon be—star jammed,

ABOVE LEFT Hollywood's sweethearts and their newborn bundle of joy.
(Kobal / Shutterstock)

ABOVE Even as a five-year-old, Carrie was emotionally intense.
(© David Sutton / mptvimages.com)

LEFT Witty and adorable at sixteen, Carrie had already broken the hearts of many boys at Beverly High.
(© Gunther / mptvimages.com)

Gamine Carrie, living in New York, had a distinctive persona, which included her clothes. (Shutterstock)

RIGHT Carrie enjoyed horsing around with Warren Beatty on the set of her debut movie, *Shampoo*. (mptvimages.com)

Princess Leia and Luke Skywalker share a pensive moment in the first *Star Wars*.

(Photo by John Jay / mptvimages.com)

Carrie and John Belushi knew they shared much: friendship, laughter, and, sadly, addiction.

(mptvimages.com)

This iconic image of Carrie, from *Return of the Jedi*, would grace thousands of boys' dorm rooms, but would haunt Carrie later in her life. (© Mario Casilli / mptvimages.com)

Carrie and Paul Simon having happy times together with her bestie Penny Marshall and his musical partner Art Garfunkel.

(Alan Davidson / Shutterstock)

Carrie and Paul's August 1983 wedding was, among other things, an effort by both to beat down the difficulties in their relationship. (mptvimages.com)

Carrie had sufficiently relaxed with her once intimidating costar Harrison Ford seven years and two subsequent *Star Wars* movies after their secret romance.

(© Gary Lewis / mptvimages.com)

When she wasn't portraying Princess Leia, Carrie often played the role of the leading lady's savvy best friend, as she did in *When Harry Met Sally*. During filming, she befriended her costar Meg Ryan. (mptvimages.com)

In the movie version of *Postcards from the Edge*, Carrie's new friend Meryl Streep played the character based on Carrie, and Debbie's old friend Shirley MacLaine played the character based on Debbie. (mptvimages.com)

Even though Carrie and Bryan Lourd split up, they remained happy, amicable coparents to their daughter, Billie. Among the others at the screening the three are attending is Carrie's friend Tracey Ullman.

(Berliner Studio / BEI / Shutterstock)

Carrie wrote *These Old Broads* to celebrate gamy older women stars. In the process, she watched Elizabeth Taylor officially apologize to Debbie for stealing Eddie Fisher away decades earlier.

(BEI / Shutterstock)

Carrie might have called paid appearances at autograph shows "celebrity lap dances," but, admitting she needed the money, she participated in them. At this one in Los Angeles, fans waited almost four hours to meet her.

(© Glenn Weiner / mptvimages.com)

BELOW In the early aughts, Debbie and Carrie—here at a celebrity fashion show—had long gotten over their earlier tensions and wounds. Carrie referred to her mother as "my husband." (Jim Smeal / BEI / Shutterstock)

ABOVE At fifty-eight, Carrie—who hadn't let up as an author, an actor, a mental health advocate, or a friend—gave an award to her buddy Graham Norton in London, and her hilarious speech led her to be cast in the hit series *Catastrophe*.

(Nils Jorgensen / Shutterstock)

(Left to right) Todd Fisher, Debbie Reynolds, Carrie, and Billie Lourd, when Debbie won a long-overdue SAG Lifetime Achievement Award in January 2015. Carrie couldn't have been more proud. (Broadimage / Shutterstock)

Looking crisp and author-ly, Carrie signed copies of her latest bestseller, *The Princess Diarist*, in New York, with her constant companion Gary by her side. She would have a month left to live. (MediaPunch / Shutterstock)

Among the numerous well-known mourners at Carrie and Debbie's joint funeral was her longtime co-party-host, an ailing Penny Marshall, here assisted while walking. She herself would die almost exactly two years after Carrie's death. (Reed Saxon / AP / Shutterstock)

exclusive, and coveted—Carrie and Penny's joint birthday parties were the accidental template for. They were closed to the media, and they were cozy and friendly. In those pre-internet days, one's invitation—and there were never more than two hundred invitees—came through a confidential phone call or, inch by inch, through a fax machine. If you didn't get the magic call or fax, no way could you come. (Although, Penny has said, one year David Bowie and Iman *did* successfully crash.) The guest list was such that celebrities got quietly excited over fellow celebrities. At one party, early on, a friend says, "When I saw Barbra Streisand walk in, I had to walk out and hyperventilate." (In fact it is said that Barbra wanted to hire Carrie's housekeepers, Gloria and Mary, to serve the same southern fare at her parties, but Carrie wouldn't let Barbra do so.)

"It was a very manicured guest list," says one close friend of Carrie's who regularly attended. "And were there drugs? Yes, sometimes there were drugs." Mick Jagger could be counted on to attend if in town, as well as just about every star actor and singer and producer and director. Shaquille O'Neal, too. "At one party the Traveling Wilburys—George Harrison, Bob Dylan, Tom Petty, Roy Orbison—all sauntered in together, wearing sunglasses," reports a friend of Carrie's who went to almost every party but singled out this mélange of legends as the epitome of hip.

Although these evening parties were for pleasure rather than networking, networking inevitably occurred. Albert Brooks says, "Because I met Meryl Streep at a party at Carrie's house and I had just written *Defending Your Life*, I said to her, 'You wouldn't be interested in playing the lead in my movie, would you?'" She was and did.

Elizabeth Taylor and Carrie had long since made peace (as had Debbie and Elizabeth); Elizabeth was often an attendee. Says Bruce Vilanch, "I remember at one party, where there was Jeff Goldblum and Geena Davis, and maybe Timothy Leary, and Carrie said, 'Excuse me, I have to go and feed Elizabeth.' Carrie would give her special treatment. She would trot over to fix Elizabeth a plate and clear a special area where she would dine. Carrie talked about it as if it were her duty."

Another guest remembers this: During one party, "Elizabeth was talking with her hands, and she noticed everyone staring at her huge ring from Richard Burton, the one that went almost straight to her knuckle. So," in a showy gesture to all the gawkers, "she popped her finger in her mouth and theatrically took the ring off with her teeth." Another time, Carrie telephoned a friend in advance of the party and said, "You *have* to come! Elizabeth is coming in her wheelchair, and Eddie is coming in *his* wheelchair. And Debbie"—no wheelchair! sweet justice—"will be at the door greeting them!" When the guest arrived, the friend recalls, "that is exactly what happened. Debbie Reynolds— the queen of the world—still standing!"

Hollywood people were often bored enough with themselves that *other* celebrities became the true stars of the party. At the 1995 party, the year of the O. J. Simpson trial, Tom Hanks was whispering excitedly about the presence of the all-the-rage duo in their midst: the O.J. prosecutors Marcia Clark and Chris Darden.

Nineteen ninety was a good year for Carrie. Aside from her starting work on *Delusions of Grandma*, the movie of *Postcards from the Edge* was released. Carrie had learned a lot from working with Mike Nichols, who raved to Joan Juliet Buck in *Vanity Fair* that Carrie was "a born screenwriter, with tremendous wit and finesse and imagination—and," he joked, "small enough so that if there's a physical altercation, I can handle her." (The blessed-by-Nichols screenwriter credibility would give Carrie a very lucrative second career as a script doctor, a dialogue expert whom producers hired to spice up sagging screenplays.)

Mike Nichols had briefly wanted to change the name of the screen version of *Postcards from the Edge* to *Hollywood and Vine*; Carrie talked him out of it. But in adapting her book to film form, Carrie herself made a big change. She transformed the core of the story from that of a hip actress in Hollywood dealing with post-overdose life to a mother-daughter showdown/odd-couple tale. The plot now hinged on the fact that post-overdose Suzanne has to live with her diva of a mother,

Doris, in order to be insurance bonded for a schlocky film she's making. When Suzanne returns from rehab to Doris's house and a little welcome-home party is staged, the movie bursts into song, with Doris singing "I'm Still Here." She *can't help* but try stealing the show, any more than Debbie couldn't help it when she had arrived at Teri Garr's apartment after Carrie's *Under the Rainbow* overdose and, as one friend recalls, in the midst of Carrie's friends worrying about Carrie, had asked her daughter's doting friends, "What about *me*?"

Self-absorbed but practical old-school Hollywood mother meets self-absorbed drug-era Hollywood daughter. "The movie is a comedy of manners about their contrasting styles of melodramatic narcissism," one reviewer put it. There are other story lines woven throughout. There's the man who saves her life (Dennis Quaid in Carol Caldwell's role, spiced up as a caddish suitor); he tells Suzanne she's "the realest person I've ever met in the abstract." He has an on-the-side girlfriend, played by Annette Bening. ("Annette was going with Ed Begley Jr. then; from him to Warren [Beatty]—what a leap!" Carrie asided to a friend, in irresistible girl-gossip fashion.) There's the schlocky cop movie's annoying director (Rob Reiner as Penelope Spheeris). And Carrie's dear friend Richard Dreyfuss plays the Dr. David Kipper role. And, importantly, there's Suzanne, battling the temptation to do drugs. But it is the mother-daughter knot—the competition—that is center stage of the film version of *Postcards from the Edge*.

"Remember at my seventeenth birthday, when you lifted your skirt up and you weren't wearing any underwear?" Suzanne yells at Doris. (This actually happened.) And, more piercingly, "You want me to do well." Pause. "Just not better [than you]."

Carrie told interviewers she was grateful that Debbie was such a good sport about being turned into the negative character. "I feel the argument weighed heavier against the mother in the movie" due to the editing and performances, Carrie said. "And I feel enormously guilty." (Actually, according to a close friend of Debbie's, her longtime acting mentor Lillian Burns Sidney insisted on vetting an early version of the script on Debbie's behalf. Lillian thought that the original version was too hard on Debbie, and Lillian—and, implicitly, Debbie—got the requested softening of the Debbie character.) Carrie continued, "My mother is so fantastic that she can sit and watch that movie and say, 'Honey. Give yourself a break, or let me give you the one that you can't get. Do not feel bad about this. I don't. It's a great movie.' I don't need a better mother than that." Writing a movie in which your mother is a negative character, and having your mother *like* the movie, can be a great perspective shifter for a once-resentful daughter. Carrie's gratitude to her mother was real.

During conversations about turning the book into a screenplay, Carrie spoke to friends like the writer she had become, complaining that her book had no plot and that she had to reconstruct a new concept for the movie. She also expressed surprise that Mike Nichols was able to get Meryl Streep to play her character. Even though she had become friends with Meryl (and would be for the rest of her life), she was honest: "Meryl was Mike's idea. I left that all to Mike. I never thought we'd be able to get the best actress." Even Richard Dreyfuss says, with an are-you-kidding laugh, that agreeing to play Dr. Frankenthal had nothing to do with it being Carrie's project—and life—and "everything" to do with being asked to be in a Meryl Streep movie by Mike Nichols. Hollywood is Hollywood, even among the closest of friends. "Carrie and Meryl were friends, but to me Meryl was simply the greatest actress," he says. Even after all those years of starring roles, "I felt like an outsider next to Meryl," a humble position that Carrie, who always expected to be in the white-hot center of celebrity, never assumed. "I felt like an outsider next to a lot of people for years," he continues. "I'll always be grateful to Carrie Fisher for dragging me past that part of myself, for saying"—in so many words—"'You're as good as all of these people; come have fun.'"

Shirley MacLaine's performance was praised; she had worked hard on it, even, to Debbie's puzzlement at the weirdness of it, insisting on visiting her friend Debbie and "studying" her. But Meryl Streep's was the performance that was wildly applauded. "Meryl Streep has finally done it!" raved Owen Gleiberman in *Entertainment Weekly*. "The mistress of quick-study accents takes a break from virtuosity and gives a warm, funny, loosey-goosey performance. For the first time in years she lives a role instead of 'acting' it—and, in doing so, she becomes more of an actress than ever." Hal Hinson of *The Washington Post* wrote, "Meryl Streep gives the most fully articulated comic performance of her career, the one she's always hinted at and made us hope for." The movie did well critically and commercially, and won Streep one of her many Best Actress Oscar nominations, and its performers and songwriters were nominated for nine awards, including, for Carrie, a BAFTA for Best Screenplay. (There was another player whom Carrie wanted an award for: Gloria Crayton. Carrie's housekeeper and cook had a bit role in the film, and during award-nomination season Carrie took out ads in *Variety* and *The Hollywood Reporter* touting an Oscar nomination for Gloria. She had T-shirts made up with the ad on their fronts—OSCAR NOMINATION FOR GLORIA!—and had them widely worn, including by Streep and Dreyfuss.)

While Carrie and Debbie were enjoying their moments in the sun, Eddie Fisher was spending four weeks at the Betty Ford Clinic, trying to beat his cocaine and speed addiction. When he completed the course—he would go on to relapse—he gave a baleful interview to the *Los Angeles Times*, saying he had been addicted for fifty-three years and regretted having been a neglectful father to his four grown children. He was now living in San Francisco and dating a wealthy Chinese American businesswoman named Betty Lin. He wanted a relationship with his children but didn't quite know how to achieve it. Eventually, with fits and starts, Carrie would help him bridge the gap. Imperfect as he was, she loved her father.

Carrie's cachet as a script doctor took off. Though there were excellent script doctors who were not well known as film eminences (such as the film producer Kevin Smith), many of the top ones were also famous as writers and directors: Aaron Sorkin, Quentin Tarantino, Terrence Malick, Tom Stoppard. It was an elite crew that Carrie was joining.

On one of her first big assignments, polishing Tinkerbell's lines in Steven Spielberg's *Hook*, she met the man who would become one of her closest friends, Bruce Cohen. The eventual producer of *Milk*, *American Beauty*, and *Silver Linings Playbook* was a young first assistant director to Spielberg on his Peter Pan movie (starring Robin Williams as Peter Pan, Dustin Hoffman as Captain Hook, and Julia Roberts as Tinkerbell) when Spielberg brought him over to Carrie's in the spring of 1990. "Come over to my house and I'll write," she said.

"You kind of needed to be there," Bruce says, for Carrie to get her creative juices flowing. He sat in her bedroom while she made Tinkerbell's words deeper and more significant. "We did that a couple of Saturdays. Carrie ended up doing more than Tinkerbell. Carrie had this beautiful voice—this subtle, nuanced, brilliant way of looking at the world." One soulful, cryptic Neverland exchange between two characters that Carrie slipped into the script was etched into Cohen's memory as he, a passionate, sensitive gay man, found himself captivated with Carrie.

Tinkerbell: "You know that place between sleep and awake? That place where you still remember dreaming?"

Peter Pan nods.

Tinkerbell: "That's where I'll always love you."

Peter Pan: "That's where I'll be waiting."

One of Carrie's most important script-doctoring assignments came a year later, in 1991: spiffing up her friend Whoopi Goldberg's dialogue in *Sister Act*. In the movie, Whoopi plays a Reno lounge singer who hides from the Mob in a convent and turns the convent sisters into a kick-ass chorus. In addition to enhancing the script, Carrie's emotional intelligence saved the movie when two important people locked horns.

Carrie had met Whoopi years earlier, when the then-unknown

comic actress was agog at Lorne Michaels and Susan Forristal's party. Now Whoopi was a full-on star, with a strong sense of self. During a key moment in perfecting the *Sister Act* script, Whoopi got into a furious fight with the Disney Studios chairman, Jeffrey Katzenberg. Katzenberg wanted to audition only black actors as her character's love interest. Whoopi wanted to include white actors as well; she was dating Ted Danson at the time and had a background in the multiracial pre–Summer of Love San Francisco. Whoopi called Carrie, and, car phone to car phone, the two women—whizzing down their respective West L.A. avenues—discussed Whoopi's anger at Katzenberg, which was threatening to derail the movie.

Carrie calmed Whoopi down with shrewd reasoning: "You're having a pissing contest with a guy who actually has a dick. I don't particularly advise people to take my advice"—though they often *did*—"but I would avoid [fighting the head of the studio]." Instead, she had a better idea. "Send Jeffrey a hatchet and say, 'Please bury this on both of our behalfs.'" Whoopi thought it over and agreed with her friend. The hatchet and note were sent. Shortly afterward, Katzenberg expressed his humble thanks for the gesture with a "you won" gift: two very large brass balls.

That's one of the reasons people loved Carrie Fisher: she was witty, raunchy, creative, and effective in solving problems.

That same year, 1992, she also, in an unlikely-seeming assignment, fixed the script of Mel Gibson's *Lethal Weapon 3*. And ever the workhorse, she accepted a role in another mediocre movie: *Drop Dead Fred*. She played, again, the pretty girl star's best friend. This time, the pretty girl was Phoebe Cates. But now Carrie was as much a writer as an actor and not shy about her chops. "The moment we met, when Carrie was sitting in the makeup chair, she demanded, 'Here are the lines I'm going to say for the scene! *Not* the ones *you* wrote!'" says Tony Fingleton, the movie's producer. "She handed us a yellow legal pad. I read it and said, 'This is better than what we've got—let's go with it.'"

In the movie, Marsha Mason played Cates's character's mother.

Carrie improved her lines, too. "Carrie came up with funnier lines for me than were in the script," says Marsha. "And the other writers thought her improvements were terrific. To wield that sort of fierceness in the face of authority when you don't have any quote-unquote real power in the pecking order of the movie: I was very impressed. She had this pretty, childlike face, so to have this ribald, ballsy energy: the opposites were fantastic. I loved her smartness, her edginess. I was extraordinarily naive when I became a public person. Carrie was the opposite: seasoned, prepared. She understood the Hollywood scene that I didn't know, and the difference showed.

"But as much as I was almost intimidated by her brashness and strength and intelligence, I sensed that we were similar." They had something peculiarly specific in common: They were freshly over long relationships with highly talented, dominating, creative Jewish men fifteen years older than they, both with the last name Simon and four-letter first names that ended with *l*. Marsha had been divorced from Neil for several years but was just getting over him. Carrie and Paul had only really ended their relationship when she flew out to L.A. for the filming of *Postcards*. "We discussed how challenging it was to be married to brilliant older men who were very controlling. She said her relationship with Paul had cost her emotionally, as had mine with Neil. It had fed into her dependencies, as mine had. I loved Neil, but I just couldn't handle all the controlling. I was still very wounded. She was wounded by Paul—or maybe by something else. Her woundedness was there, very clearly."

In Carrie's next major relationship, the man would *not* be controlling; he would be nurturing; not moody, but, rather, gentlemanly and sunny. Not fifteen years older and more famous, but four years younger and, at the outset, not nearly as well known. He would be, people would say, the love of her life.

EIGHT

"WHEN I LOVE, I LOVE FOR MILES"

At some point in the early 1990s, Kevin Huvane and Bryan Lourd started joining the group that socialized at Carrie's house on Oak Pass. Kevin and Bryan were two of the famous Young Turks at Creative Artists Agency (CAA), rising stars in the mega-agency then under the directorship of Michael Ovitz. The two had struck up a friendship when they were both junior agents at William Morris, Huvane in New York and Lourd in L.A. They couldn't have been more different. Bryan Lourd was a gentlemanly Protestant from a small town, New Iberia, in Louisiana, who'd always loved show business without ever knowing what an agent was. Kevin Huvane was a tough Irish Catholic from the Bronx whose father worked for a bus company. But their lack of aversion to hard work was a valuable trait they shared. Huvane spent his youthful summers holding down the midnight to 8:00 a.m. shift as an elevator operator for a Manhattan hotel; Lourd has said the best advice he ever got, and which he faithfully took, was from his grandfather: "When you get a job, be the first one there in the morning and the last one out at night." Indeed, when he acquired his entry-level job at William

Morris in L.A., Lourd began his days at 6:30 a.m. doing menial tasks that included washing out coffee mugs used the night before. His background and entry into the entertainment industry could not have been further from Carrie's.

In 1984, just when Carrie was divorcing Paul Simon, Lourd, whom she did not yet know, was considered the "king" of the William Morris mailroom and was about to be promoted to agent. Around that same time, Huvane and Lourd formed a bicoastal alliance that served them well. By 1989, the two were considered "signing machines." When Michael Ovitz brought them over to CAA, they were so close they called themselves a "pen and pencil set."

Tall, blond, and attractive, with impeccable manners, as an agent Lourd was skilled in knowing how to cater to and serve celebrities. In this way, he couldn't have been more different from Paul Simon. A friend of Carrie's says that when, later, in 1995, the charming and gentlemanly Bryan took over from Ovitz as one of the five managing directors of CAA, "you could have knocked me over with a feather. He was the last person I would have predicted would be the next Mike Ovitz. I would not have pictured him as having that level of 'killer' in him."

Still, says an entertainment writer who knew Lourd and Carrie well, "he was probably the most strategic agent in Hollywood—and smart and funny and low-key. And hilarious."

And he was, as Trish Lande puts it, "so kind and protective—a patient, solicitous southern gentleman; a lovely, lovely person." In other words, just the kind of soother someone like Carrie Fisher needed. Carrie had often made references, not as ironically as one might expect, to dreams of "pies cooling on the window sill." She wanted a life to quiet her demons with a solid husband and a happy, normal childhood for her dreamed-of future child—a life she never knew. This is what she would soon get from Bryan Lourd. "Bryan and Billie"—the daughter they would eventually have—"were," virtually all her friends say, "*by far* the best things in her life." Carrie said, in the unpublished part of an interview with the *Los Angeles Times* writer Mimi Avins in

2004, "I'd never been with anyone like Bryan. He was so attentive. He was the first man who ever took care of me."

"With Bryan, as things developed, I thought they would be together forever," says their entertainment writer friend. Lourd understood Carrie's vulnerabilities, and "he wanted to rescue Carrie," opines Carrie's friend the photographer Michael Childers, who, with his partner, the director John Schlesinger, had long been giving the kinds of extraordinary parties in their Hollywood Hills home that Carrie and Penny were now famous for. ("Who would come to our parties?" Childers rhetorically asks. "Warren Beatty, Jack Nicholson, Anjelica Huston, David Hockney, Christopher Isherwood, Ray Bradbury.")

Still, at the beginning of Lourd's relationship with Carrie, around 1991, another observer says, "I wouldn't say she was clearly in love with Bryan. I would use the words 'content with him.'" The entertainment writer friend of Lourd's agrees and elaborates: "I loved their romance and wanted them to get married and have babies. But Carrie wasn't a hundred percent sure about him. She teased him that he wasn't quite 'gigantic' enough a person for her. Bryan wasn't yet the super agent that he is now . . . And at the beginning, when Carrie 'discovered' him, like many women of a certain age, you at first want your man in the power couple to be more powerful than you. That's what she had with Paul Simon. But the relationship with Paul wasn't happy. I kept telling her, 'Carrie, Bryan's going to be a *superstar.*'" (Lourd would become a managing director of CAA only after his split from Carrie. His current clients include George Clooney, Tom Cruise, Robert Downey Jr., Jimmy Fallon, Madonna, Oliver Stone, Robert De Niro, Brad Pitt, Reese Witherspoon, and Oprah Winfrey.)

In her 1994 novel, *Delusions of Grandma* (despite its title, Carrie's most poetic and soulful), her character, the screenplay polisher Cora Sharpe, wants to explain to her new and solicitous lawyer boyfriend, Ray—a character who seems based on Bryan—why she resists him, perhaps echoing or exaggerating those initial feelings about Bryan that their mutual friend described: "She wanted to say, 'I know I have too many friends. I know I'm selfish, that I pay too little attention . . . I know I'm a snob.'" But if any of those, indeed, were Carrie's feelings toward Bryan at the outset, his patience, solicitousness, and charm won her over. The novel, whether true or partly true, shows the push-pull of this process.

And in real life, Carrie's relationship with Bryan, another friend says, moved the needle of his career. "Though other people had discovered Bryan as a great talent agent in New York—as a star—his merely being with Carrie helped him. The power dynamic was mutually beneficial in the beginning."

Shortly after Bryan moved into Oak Pass with her, *SNL*'s music director Julian Ford—Carrie's dear friend and disco dancing partner in New York—became extremely ill in the last stages of AIDS. Originally, Julian had wanted to go home to Australia to die, but it soon became clear that such a plane trip would be too long and exhausting for the fragile man. Their mutual friend Will Trinkle had to be in Virginia on business, "so Carrie called me and said, 'Will! I'll send Julian out here on a plane!'" Will says. "This was in the days when nobody would touch anybody with AIDS. But Carrie did. Julian probably weighed ninety pounds, and he was incontinent. Carrie flew him out on one of those MGM Grand planes they had back then, which celebrities used, and she had him stay at her house." He stayed with her there for weeks.

Carrie nursed Julian through the last stages of his illness—before and after which she quietly wrote checks to the American Foundation for AIDS Research and the Lambda Legal Defense and Education Fund. As Julian's strength was slipping away, Will spoke to him daily on Carrie's home phone. One day Carrie was to meet Madonna at the Four Seasons Hotel and do a Q&A with her there for *Rolling Stone*. Carrie was late for the appointment because, as she told Madonna truthfully, "a friend of mine with AIDS is staying with me, and he developed a fever," later writing of Julian in the interview's introduction, "My friend had been extremely courageous, fighting an unbelievable battle." Madonna, whose allegiance to gay men was second to no one's, understood completely.

Shortly after Julian developed the fever, something worse happened. As Carrie would later recall it, "Julian threw up what must have been about a pint of bright red blood into a stark white bowl. Then, in response to my 9-1-1 call—or, rather, shriek—four men arrived at my home wearing what appeared to be space suits" (AIDS was little understood then) and moved him to a hospital. Carrie paid the bill. And, along with Julian's sister, she stayed with him as he slipped in and out of consciousness.

"Finally, at two in the morning one night I get a call from Carrie, who was sitting next to Julian's hospital bed," says Will Trinkle. "'Julian wants to tell you how much he loves you,' she says." Carrie sat with Julian most of that night. He whispered many things, including that he did *not* want extra measures taken to keep him alive. Of this he was certain.

"The next day at six in the morning Carrie called me again," Will says. She obviously had not slept. "I was Julian's medical power of attorney, and she said, 'Don't go anywhere until you give me his living will! Does he have one? We need that now because they're going to hook him up to the tubes.'"

The following four hours was a relay race on both coasts. Will says, "I had to reach Julian's attorney in New York on the phone—I was in Virginia—and get his living will and fax it to Carrie in the hospital nurses' station." Faxing back then was done on sticky thermal paper. Running between Julian's bed and the nurses' station, Carrie kept saying, "It didn't come through clearly! It didn't come through!" Will would fax it again and again, both of them racing with the clock. After the fifth faxing, "I got it!" Carrie said, and she ran through the hospital halls to give it to the doctor.

"She was hands-on Carrie," Will emphasizes. "Not a celebrity who let other people do things for her. She loved Julian, and it meant a lot to her to honor his wishes. That was Carrie. She was truly selfless. If she had ten dollars, she'd give you twenty."

Carrie sat with her dear friend as he took his last breath. In *Delusions of Grandma*, she writes movingly of Julian's dying (she renames him William) and its effect on her relationship with the Bryan-like character, Ray. After Cora has said "I love you" and goodbye to William, Carrie writes about the way Cora and her boyfriend are affected:

A sort of hush fell over them for the rest of the day. They were gentle with each other, tender even. They looked out of questioning, frightened eyes, gripped hands fiercely in an effort to stay near, to keep each other from being plucked from the earth randomly . . . Loving through the various points of no return and back again.

And:

Coming together out of need instead of want—in deed instead of common speak—had been a fierce and glorious thing. But it was the hardest act in the world to follow. How could they make the leap from death to marriage and a good life, from dark blue to virgin white?

Carrie learned she was pregnant with Bryan's child at the end of 1991. She and Bryan were, friends say, happily and mutually in love ("They were cooking with gas," says a frequent houseguest) when their daughter, Billie, was born on July 17, 1992. A birth announcement was sent to friends: A picture of the naked, round-faced infant was framed in an artistic card bordered by a troupe of dancing boys and girls on top and an orchestra of kittens on the bottom. Inside this tastefully produced announcement, Carrie referred to the seven-pound, six-ounce baby that had "summered in my stomach" as an "infant omelette" produced by scrambling "sperm and eggs."

Carrie sold Oak Pass and bought a bigger house, 1700 Coldwater

Canyon, on almost three acres, for $2.6 million. It was an elegantly vamped-up adobe hunting lodge that had been built in the late 1920s for Robert Armstrong, the star of *King Kong*. It had next belonged to the legendary Hollywood costume designer Edith Head and had previously been inhabited by Bette Davis. Carrie took out a large loan to finance the upgrade. She decorated it with folk art, fine art, Indian rugs, and much whimsy. Stained glass prevailed; she'd been collecting it in England for years, and one of its craftsmen became her close friend. There was her collection of Donald Roller Wilson paintings. She moved in the gargantuan lodgepole bed upon which she wrote and entertained. There was a piano in the bathroom—all Carrie houses had to have idiosyncrasy—as well as a Steinway in the living room. The porch was enlivened by pots of cacti, and the huge porcelain sculpture of a foot, which had welcomed visitors to the Oak Pass house, and, before that, at Laurel Canyon, was also transported here.

A friend says this "was a blissful moment" between Carrie and Bryan. To finish *Delusions*, Carrie rented a house in Santa Barbara, where she retreated with Billie and a baby nurse and a writing coach. Bryan came up on the weekends. Everyone says he was, from day one to present, a remarkable father.

And then came a *non*-blissful moment. One day, in late 1993, Bryan came to Carrie with news: he was gay. He would always be a devoted father to Billie, but he was moving out to be with a man, Scott Bankston, who had been a lover of the super-agent Sandy Gallin. (Today Bryan Lourd is married to the restaurateur Bruce Bozzi.)

Says the entertainment writer who thought the couple would be together forever: "Bryan and Carrie loved each other! I was shocked when he came out as gay—*stunned*! I almost fell off the couch when I heard. Some people said they weren't shocked, but I didn't believe them, and I thought I had good gaydar." Says a male gay friend of Carrie's, "I didn't see it coming for a long time, though I definitely had my suspicions at the end, but I wasn't going to say anything. Bryan grew up in a solidly middle-class family. As a man, it's hard to come out, especially back then, if you grew up in that kind of family."

Susan Forristal remembers being with the actress Jennifer Grey at a party given by the designer Lyndall Hobbs before Bryan and Carrie got together. "Jennifer had come to the party with Bryan. And he was handsome, charming, genteel, southern. But she said, 'He doesn't seem interested in me.' He didn't have a girlfriend. Jennifer and I just looked at each other. The implicit question being, was he gay?"

The world has changed so much in a fairly short time that it's hard to recall that coming out as gay then, even in the liberal entertainment industry, wasn't professionally without penalty. It had only been in the previous year, 1992, that David Geffen and Jann Wenner both came out. That same year, two female performers—k.d. lang and Melissa Etheridge—came out as well. Ellen DeGeneres wouldn't come out until five years later. An older, very sophisticated gay man who knew both Bryan and Carrie separately says, with narrowed eyes, of his own intuitions about Bryan, "Come *on.* I *always* knew"; he sensed it. As for Todd Fisher, he says Carrie broke down in tears when she told him that Bryan was leaving her for a man.

When Carrie began writing *Delusions of Grandma* in 1990, the premise of the book was a wacky scheme cooked up by the script doctor Cora to free Cora's grandfather from his nursing home. But by the time the book was published in 1994, the novel had shifted to being about Cora's relationship with Ray, who "pursued her like some great, almost unattainable idea, wooing her with everything in him that was winning, creeping ever closer to uncovering her willingness." And it became a book about his pain, and anger, at her ambivalence toward him. "'I can't be in this relationship,' he announced almost listlessly . . . 'I don't want to work on it, I don't want to talk about it. I just want to go.'" This snaps Cora awake. Ray represents nurturance to her. "She first remembered seeing him in her kitchen. Consequently she connected him powerfully with nourishment, with food." So different is he from diffident Rudy in *Surrender*. The characterizations of the two men—Ray/Bryan and Rudy/Paul—are almost polar opposites.

Delusions opens with a paean to the mystery of pregnancy, which feels miraculous to Cora, who considers the notion "that babies were the result of sex" to be excessively prosaic. Rather, conception must be "like tornadoes and tide pools and pearls found in oysters," she writes. This is Carrie the romantic.

The opening chapter features tender letters she writes to her unborn baby daughter, "Esme," charmingly signed "Mom Sequitur." There are lines of pure Carrie wordplay, such as "I hope to write you all sorts of pithy, succinct advice to move through the world easily—not without a care in the world, but a care so far away in the world, perhaps, it has another area and zip code. (By the way, I never used the word 'perhaps' before I was pregnant. Perhaps it's a hormonal thing.)" They are intimate, piquant, and confiding. But more than that, they evoke Carrie's intimacy, so essential in her friendships. There's the proffering of that "pithy advice." Then what *seems* like a tossed-off thought ("I never used the word 'perhaps' before") is actually, when you examine it, a sentiment—*I have doubt now*, which potentially opens a dialogue about what the newness of "perhaps" means in her life.

The novel keeps circling back to the stubborn nature of romantic taste. ("She went out on a couple of other dates, one with a fairly accomplished musician and the other with a successful physician. But the spirituality of the first and the squareness of the second bothered her.") And how a decent man's patient, abiding acceptance of Cora/Carrie is both comforting *and* confusing: "The longer she waited to run into something she couldn't put up with in Ray, the more she didn't . . . His power over her was that he never seemed to attempt to have power over her. He didn't insist, demand, or persuade." Ray is not a pursuer who relishes a challenge but, instead, a man who feels insulted about being loved minimally, distractedly, by default. "You don't want to marry me in a good way," he says, hurt. "'We don't love each other the same,' he said flatly. Upset." This jolts her, makes her nervous. "'Ray, don't leave!' she says," with the sudden regret of one who knows she may be pushing away a good man because of ambivalence she should outgrow. But soon she concedes she's too complex to settle for simple love and, indeed, that "perfect contentment can rarely be recognized. Maybe in Tibet, maybe in toddlers." Ray moves out of Cora's house.

In the novel, when the AIDS-afflicted William arrives at Cora's house, Ray moves back in, and while Cora takes care of William, Ray takes care of Cora, and "when you get that close to death, everything living gets a little more lively . . . Everyone vibrated and hummed, and she and Ray started pulling at each other's clothes a little harder again." What Richard Dreyfuss had described as "this secret, brilliant, elevated universe" of bipolar hypomania—Carrie's description, via *Hook*'s Tinkerbell, of the magical place "between sleep and awake"—seems to have been heightened through the intense times Carrie/Cora was living.

Ray has another round of feeling ignored, this time with petulance. "I guess I have to have AIDS or go through some unbelievable depression to get you to pay some sympathetic attention to me," he says. "That or be a powerful celebrity." He moves out, this time for good. It is ironic that the first book that introduces a character based on the love of her life, the man whose loss will send her emotionally reeling, presents him as a devalued courtier, someone she most appreciates when he is angrily wounded.

"The book started out being a love letter to Bryan," says one who watched her craft the early drafts in longhand in the "red room" she loved so much, an old den with a fireplace and music piped in. "But eventually it became a very different book."

In the book, Cora finds out she is pregnant by Ray. After she has had the baby (which Cora names Lily, not Esme) in the company of her friend Bud—and with caregiving from her mother—Ray comes to see her in an ambiguous way, and they will take it from there. In her final note to Esme, she muses about the Italian artist Morandi, who died in 1964, and she touches on the dance of the same name—an acrobatic dance. Giorgio Morandi the painter was heralded for his message that there is much that is profound in life's tiniest things. Cora says Morandi "made the spaces much more important than the objects . . . the No more important than the Yes." The last line of her book is a wish that "the negative space" be so far away that "the No of it just couldn't be heard."

The *Vanity Fair* writer Leslie Bennetts later wrote that tactfully avoiding "the question of [the Bryan character's] vacillating sexual preferences . . . showed extraordinary forbearance on Fisher's part." Still, that avoidance "made the whole story somewhat incomprehensible, since the reader couldn't quite figure out why these two nice people who had just had a beautiful baby daughter were breaking up."

In her next novel, *The Best Awful*, not published until early 2004, Carrie *would* start with honesty on the subject. Changing the identity of *Delusions'* Cora Sharpe to *Postcards'* Suzanne Vale, she would announce having married a gay man. (This time, she called him a film executive named Leland. "Three-picture deal for your thoughts" is his opening flirtation.) She would do so in the book's first *line*: "Suzanne Vale had a problem, and it was the one she least liked thinking about: She'd had a child with someone who forgot to tell her he was gay."

But after such flippancy, she shows us Suzanne's tragic, late-understood dependence—the opposite of Cora's taking this same man for granted: "Leland had cared for her and she'd somehow not seen it working its subtle charm on her. She didn't realize she needed tending like some exotic fragile flower . . . *Who knew she'd come to count on the net he'd always put beneath her not infrequent falls? No one had ever attended to her needs in this way. How could she have missed it happening?*" (Emphasis added.)

Thus began a powerfully unhappy time for Carrie. Says a friend who knew her well then, "Her most depressed moment was when Bryan Lourd left her." After those early months of ambivalence, wondering if Bryan was important enough for her, "she was in love with him and he left her for a man." Was it *that* awful? "Are you kidding!

Yes!" the friend says emphatically. "And it didn't help that she had people around her who whipped her into a frenzy about it." One of them—"a mentor, a person with enormous impact"—was particularly vociferous. "I came to those people and said, 'You can't do that!'" the friend says. "I wanted to calm Carrie down. She was experiencing her biggest catastrophe. She wasn't suicidal, but she took to bed."

Selina Cadell was still taking calls from Carrie "at inappropriate"—cross-Atlantic—"times in the middle of the night. I'd go, 'Car-rie . . . ?' and she'd go, 'Can we talk?' I always talked to her because I knew she needed help, and sometimes you didn't know what it was, but she fell in love with people deeply, and she was longing to put that love that she had all stored up *somewhere*, and it had now all gone to Bryan. She believed that Bryan could give her the stable, loving life she always wanted."

Carrie herself said, in *Shockaholic*, "When I love, I love for miles and miles. A love so big it should either be outlawed or it should have a capital and its own currency."

Many people said this to Carrie: But didn't the fact that Bryan is gay make it *easier*? Less *personally* insulting? Carrie would vociferously deny this. His leaving her, for whatever reason, was a personal wound. A rejection of *her*. It was a pain she would never get over.

"People ask if it lessens the blow that he left me for a man because it's a rejection of my gender and so isn't personal," she said. "But I don't care what people say—I was humiliated and betrayed, and I believed I'd somehow messed up. I don't know if I made him gay but"—emphasis added—"*I'd failed*, and that's all that really counts."

A friend says, "That 'I failed' part? It was Debbie and Eddie and Liz all over again! Carrie was Debbie!"

Despite the gravity of her pain, Carrie was able to go on a limited book tour when *Delusions* was published in early spring 1994. But it was a mixed bag. With one interviewer, Sherryl Connelly, writing for the New York *Daily News*, Carrie could not resist being destructively indiscreet. Connelly had interviewed Carrie for *Surrender* and had found her "a little snooty and condescending, probably because I was from a tabloid," Connelly surmised. (Connelly gave this interview to this author six months before she died in September 2017.) "But this was a whole different Carrie." They sat on a couch in Carrie's publicist's office, and Carrie "was funny and engaged and she bolted upright and said, 'Let's get rid of this interview and just gossip!'" Carrie asked Connelly about her own divorce, and then she stunned Connelly by volunteering, "Well, *my* husband"—though never married, Carrie considered Bryan her husband—"left me for . . ." and, to Sherryl's surprise, Carrie proffered a man's name. "She was absolutely dead serious," Connelly said. "And I'm wondering to myself, 'How is it that I *didn't even know* that Bryan Lourd was gay?'"

Connelly had no intention of printing the gossip, but as she walked out of the office, "I get as far as the elevator, and Carrie *races* down the hall and drops to her knees and literally grabs my knees with her hands—and she's got a *tight* hold! She's looking up at me, all wide-eyed, saying, '*Please* don't use that! You *can't* use that!' I was trying to extract myself—I smiled, I laughed. I *wasn't* going to use it. But the whole incident was jarring. Then Carrie's publicist comes running out of the office, yelling, 'Carrie! What did you do?! What did you say?! Please let me know!'"

Plugging the book a month later on *The Charlie Rose Show*, Carrie could not have seemed more relaxed, engaged, and captivating. She started out by saying, in her typical way of making her hometown a quirky oddity, that there was a "law—it's a *Hollywood* law," not a New York law, she stressed, that once a woman reached thirty-five, she had to write a book, then have a baby, then write a screenplay, and then repeat the cycle all over again. Acknowledging that she was no longer with the father of her baby daughter, she said that her relationships were damaged by the fact that she was so invested in her friendships that the men often felt left out. This was true; her friendships were enormous. And, as often, she spoke of how important she thought a "good conversation" was. Charlie Rose, seeming to adore her (she flirted with him right back, proposing they have a "trial marriage"), tried to make her admit her books were autobiographical: "*Come on, that's your life!*" She cleverly got herself half off the hook. She talked about her lucrative career as a script doctor, refusing to describe the outsized income, saying that making a lot of money for so little work was "disrespectful because people are dying in places and can use this money for better things." She spoke of how much friendships mattered to her; she was a "loyal, alert, fierce, vulnerable friend. I can go the distance with people." "Vulnerable?" Charlie asked. "Unfortunately, yes," she answered, and then continued: "But through my weakness you will find my strength." Few of her friends would likely disagree with that telling adage.

She went on to tell Charlie Rose that, yes, she had done drugs—she seemed entirely clear-eyed in the interview—because "I had no coping skills" and "I'm a very good learner," meaning a learner from her father's addiction. She distinguished herself from Dorothy Parker by saying that Parker was "an angry drunk and I am *not* an angry doper." She kidded—or didn't kid—that she had bought the Coldwater Canyon house "because it looked so great on acid. I thought, 'This will be a great place to have parties.'" (It was!) She said—her charm took the edge off her grandiosity—she was "exactly like Coleridge" in terms of soothing emotional demons through addiction: his addiction was to opium. She said she had been off drugs for ten years but had slipped when her dentist gave her Percocet. This might not have been entirely true. But for someone who already had an A plus for ballsy candor, it was an excusable half white lie for a book-plugging TV interview. "I'm very powerful about my weaknesses," she told Rose. "I can do what I do wrong better than anyone." *I can do wrong better than anyone.* This was Carrie Fisher at her best: provocative, braggingly self-deprecating (a neat trick), honest enough. With a dash of forgivable self-importance. (And looking lovely.) It was a stellar performance. No one would have known how anguished she was.

Delusions did not do as well commercially as *Postcards*, but it was a national bestseller, and it earned some of the kind of praise Carrie was now used to getting for her books. The *Los Angeles Times* called it "an amazing achievement: a snappy, wise-cracking novel." Not all reviews were as positive; the *Hartford Courant*, for example, found it too "chock full of puns" and "strained." Oddly, the sharp emotions of death and love were lost for many reviewers amid Carrie's familiar witticisms. But the *Los Angeles Times* review *also* called it "wrenching, poignant and wise"—understanding the depth beneath the puns.

Just as Carrie was going through the pain of Bryan's leaving, Debbie was in the midst of an ugly divorce from her third husband, Richard Hamlett, who had—as Harry Karl had done before—left her bankrupt. Years earlier Carrie had asked Will Trinkle if he could somehow "stop" her mother's marriage to Hamlett. Now Hamlett had apparently deceived Debbie in myriad ways during the years she had been looking to turn her collection of vintage MGM movie costumes into a proper museum. Debbie had finally purchased a hotel, the Paddlewheel, in Las Vegas and, with Todd as her CEO and partner, turned it into the Debbie Reynolds Hotel and Casino.

"I wept when I first went into the lobby," Carrie said of her mother's new acquisition when she visited shortly after Billie was born. "This mastodon in the desert—it looked like a sound-stage, black and dusty. She would be waving at these black caverns of space and saying, 'This is going to be Bogart's Bar!' and 'This is where the show room will be!' What I understood was that she wanted me to be excited for her, which is like saying she wanted me to be tall for her."

The hotel would eventually fail, and on its way to its 1998 bankruptcy Debbie asserted that Hamlett had been robbing her blind, as Harry Karl had. Hamlett also appeared to have a mistress; he might have had a child with the woman. Debbie filed for divorce in 1994. When, two years later, the divorce was finalized, she tried to get back the money she said he owed her, but her efforts were fruitless and expensive.

When Carrie would sit down to write *The Best Awful*, she would have Suzanne Vale's mother, Doris, say, "You're just like me, dear. We can't pick men," with Doris described explicitly as a "famous fifties movie star whose three failed marriages had left her publicly humiliated, bankrupted, and bankrupted again." Then Doris would perkily add a line that Carrie would repeat as one of Debbie's landmark quips: "Anyway, think of it this way: We've had every kind of man in this family. We've had horse thieves and alcoholics and one-man bands and singers—but this is our first homosexual!"

Actually, Debbie and Carrie were growing closer out of mutual necessity. When her Las Vegas hotel dream was on the shakiest of ground, mother called daughter and said, "I'm out of money!" Carrie sent her mother a big check, even though she was having trouble herself, sustaining the expense of the Coldwater Canyon house. "I had already borrowed so much money for this house," Carrie told Leslie Bennetts, "that I loaned [Debbie] some of it," adding wryly that she thought she could use that anecdote in one of her books. (She didn't.) Debbie would eventually move into the house adjacent to Carrie's; the dual residences would be called the Compound.

Carrie now talked about her mother's terrible choices in husbands with psychological acuity and thoughtful measure rather than sarcasm or bitterness. "There's something that happens with regard to a powerful woman and friendly, congenial men who fasten themselves onto a larger body of light. It's corrupting. In the beginning they like the reflected glory, but they end up hating you because you're asked too many times if Mr. Reynolds would like another drink. They might start out with good intentions, wanting to protect Debbie and prevent her from being hurt again, but they end up doing it themselves." After some angry years of her twenties and thirties, railing at and avoiding her mother, here was a meaningful connection from—and to—Carrie.

Carrie made two other gestures of help and homage to her mother during these several *Best Awful* writing years. The first was imploring her friend Albert Brooks to cast Debbie as the domineering mother in *Mother*, the film Brooks wrote, and would direct and star in, about a man who comes home to live with his mother after his marriage has collapsed. "I had really wanted Doris Day for the role," Brooks says, and although he tried hard to get the singer-actress, Day declined. In the same way that Debbie had long pushed Carrie to others, "Carrie kept saying, 'What about my mother?'"

Debbie was startled and wary that she had to *audition* for the role. The last time she'd been asked to audition, at least a decade earlier and for a sitcom, she had been treated insultingly. But, pro that she was, she auditioned and got the part. It would be her first major role in twenty years.

In the wake of the debacle brought about by her divorce from Hamlett, Debbie had been working hard to keep her debt-riddled Debbie Reynolds Hotel and Casino solvent. Keeping the hotel afloat meant she had to perform six nights a week. She was turning sixty-four and exhausting herself, something she was all too used to doing. Shortly before filming on *Mother* began, Debbie was hospitalized for a week with severe stress. Nevertheless, she rallied. Brooks was empathetic and did not pressure her, and she was able to start filming *Mother* on time. The film—released at the very end of 1996—was a critical and commercial success. It earned Brooks esteem as a writer, director, and actor, and—importantly—it earned Debbie a Golden Globe nomination for her much-praised performance.

Two years after *Mother*'s release, several things happened: The indomitable Maxene Reynolds—the force for tough common sense, the keeper of the Depression-era El Paso flame—died. And Debbie officially moved into the house next to Carrie's at 1700 Coldwater.

It was a good time for Carrie to be close to Debbie. In 1999, Eddie published his second memoir. *Been There, Done That* was quite brutal toward Debbie. (His earlier memoir, *Eddie: My Life, My Loves*, had been bland.) The extent to which Eddie had disliked Debbie during their short marriage was brandished cavalierly, and, particularly angering Carrie, he called Debbie a lesbian. Carrie, who had coddled her father (and would go back to doing so), was so incensed that as she later said in a much-replayed statement, "I'm having my DNA fumigated!"

Two years later, in what was seen as a love letter to her mother, Carrie wrote a TV movie in tribute to Debbie, and to Elizabeth Taylor as well. *These Old Broads* was the story of four studio-system queens reuniting after an old movie of theirs has been revived. Its wider story was how difficult it was for women to age gracefully in Hollywood. Along with Debbie and Elizabeth Taylor, it starred Shirley MacLaine and Joan Collins.

The movie's director, Matthew Diamond, remembers, "It was great fun—and meaningful. In one scene, Debbie and Elizabeth have a kind of rapprochement as characters, and I felt that echoed the rapprochement they must have gone through earlier as mutual exes of Eddie. The scene was staged very simply with Debbie sitting on Elizabeth's bed, as a tête-à-tête. They spoke honestly and were incredibly forthcoming in their emotions. Having watched every take, I felt—and we all suspected—that with *this* scene there was enormous meaning ricocheting between their real lives and the characters they were playing. At the very least, I felt that they knew how to use what they had lived."

Diamond continues, "In the beginning there was a certain kind of wariness [between the actresses], mainly because they had never really acted together every day before. But by the end of filming, they were so madly in love with each other I couldn't get them off the set." Diamond could sense the resonance of their personal history and experiences in their interactions with each other and in the movie. "I felt that they knew how to use what they used."

In *Shockaholic*, her 2011 memoir, Carrie wrote that in private on the set one day Elizabeth Taylor formally apologized to Debbie (for "taking" Eddie from her) and that "I saw my mom following Elizabeth

out of the [*These Old Broads*] trailer that day with tears in her eyes."
Debbie had, of course, forgiven Elizabeth years earlier. (There are, indeed, no shortage of Debbie-and-Elizabeth healing stories, but all of
them make good copy.)

As for Carrie and Elizabeth themselves, they had forged a friendship in 1998. After Elizabeth had sent Carrie an almost form-letter
thank-you for Carrie showing up at Elizabeth's AIDS benefit, Carrie,
feeling rebuffed, called Elizabeth's assistant and got herself invited to
Elizabeth's house for an afternoon party. At that party, for some quizzical reason sparked by Carrie, it was determined that Elizabeth should
push a clothed Carrie into the swimming pool. Elizabeth complied.
The curious baptism—which logically made no sense (shouldn't Carrie
have pushed Elizabeth into the pool?)—was the beginning of a friendship that Carrie has described as full of "love."

Still, at least according to Matthew Diamond and Carrie, Elizabeth's
late-life personal apology to Debbie on the set of *These Old Broads*
seemed particularly significant. The filming was capped off by an invitation from Elizabeth for them all to come over and watch the film
together at her house.

Seven months after *These Old Broads* aired on TV, Debbie and
Elizabeth were both in New York, on September 10, 2001, for Michael
Jackson's performance at Madison Square Garden. The next morning,
September 11, Debbie awoke in her downtown hotel smelling smoke.
She fled uptown and joined Elizabeth in her suite at the Pierre hotel.
There, together—like everyone else in the city—they struggled to make
sense of the incomprehensible. How egregiously insignificant was a long-
ago dustup over a feckless man!

Being a good mother to Billie mattered desperately to Carrie. She had
been raised by nannies, and of course Billie had them, too. ("Not
much had changed," her alter ego Suzanne Vale noted in *The Best
Awful*, "except the uniforms were gone. The nannies were still . . . the

organizers of all the things that make up a child of Hollywood's life.")
Says a confidante, "Carrie wanted to make up for what Debbie didn't
do—like cook and bake." Which Carrie did, quite successfully. She was
always offering friends her proudly homemade chocolate soufflé and
her risotto "like a Jewish mother," one said. "What—you *aren't* going to
eat this?" she would say, placing one or another treat in front of a guest.

"Later," when Bryan was fast becoming a powerful and wealthy
agent, "Carrie was very concerned with keeping Billie down to earth,"
says Betsy Rapoport, one of her *Best Awful* editors. "Because Bryan was
going on yachts with Barry Diller, Carrie really wanted Billie grounded.
She was encouraging Billie to take French"—Carrie was a near-fluent
French speaker—"and she was very interested in also making sure that
Billie had a wide-ranging intellectual upbringing. She was just *so proud*
of Billie! Carrie talked about how much she loved her and what an
amazement it was to have her."

Carrie could be a stern taskmaster when she needed to be. In a
magazine interview, Billie recalled that once, when she was nine, "I got
in trouble in school for stealing something out of someone's backpack,
and she picked me up [from school] and she sat me down in the car.
And she turned to me and said, 'Are you going to grow up to be an
asshole?' And I started crying." The blunt words stayed with her. "I
always think that now: I don't want to grow up to be an asshole!" Meryl
Streep has said, "Carrie always talked to Billie like an adult."

Many have said that Billie was Carrie's lifeline, but Carrie also understood that a steadier life likely lay with the other parent. In *The Best
Awful*, using the names of the characters based on Billie and Bryan,
she would write that Honey's "dad became her hero, her sure thing in
a sea of uncertainty . . . He provided her a safe harbor, something she
could rely on and flourish in." Then, with delicate wisdom, she wrote,
"Maybe her dad made her mother possible."

Carrie writes lovingly of the wise Honey, and in her stirring appreciation of Leland's soothing southern parents you can hear Carrie's
appreciation of her ex-husband and what he gave to their daughter:

"Honey loved visiting this homey, slowed-down world of her extended family. Loved this place . . . of unlocked doors and potluck dinners and drive-ins. The reassuring feel of the relative reclined in the La-Z-Boy chair, dozing or watching TV till the early call of 'Supper's on!'" Of course, as Suzanne Vale quickly noted, her own mother and grandparents had come from such a place, too—Maxene and Ray most certainly had been steeped in it—"but show business had blunted her mother's accent away, even some of her mother's mother's . . . Hollywood had taken all that remained of Suzanne's extended family . . . The end result was that Leland supplied the mother lode of family . . . It wasn't surprising which [parent] Honey drew more stability from."

This is wistful, humble, generous—and sad: a peacemaking with her own vibrant but, for practical purposes, less conventionally punctilious parenting, within which Carrie would always find crevices of guilt, especially when she "slipped" with her medication. Years later, Tony Taccone, the director of Carrie's one-woman show, *Wishful Drinking*, would understand, he says, that "Carrie really, really, *really* loved her daughter," those excessive modifiers indicating her deep desperation. And as Carrie herself has said, she wanted to be "worthy" of her daughter's love. ("I aspire 2 deserve you," she would tweet in 2016.)

During some of the worst of this period, and certainly later, Carrie would, a female friend says, "be very, *very* agitated about what Billie might think of her" when she was not taking her meds. Her friends' hearts bled for her during these intervals. There is little more touching than a mother's feeling fearful that her flaws, despite her magic and her love, will involuntarily darken the sun of a child's respect for her. But Carrie seemed to know that the pies cooling on the windowsill—what she'd dreamed of—might very well be in a home for her daughter.

In a home of a man she loved. But a home other than her own.

NINE

"I AM MENTALLY ILL, I CAN SAY THAT"

sobriety and treatment for her bipolar disorder had never mattered more to Carrie than it did now, when, separated from Bryan, she was co-parenting Billie. She tried very hard to master sobriety and get her mental illness under control.

Carrie had traveled the circuit of different AA chapters—using meetings as social gatherings as much as routes to a cure, some say. In West L.A., AA was so ubiquitous—*and* so social—that when Carrie was having her house photographed for *Architectural Digest*, the photographer happily said he knew her from meetings. But now she wanted a sponsor and a group that would *really* help her. Shortly after the overdose that had inspired *Postcards*, Carrie had met an older gay actor from Louisiana who had a master's degree in psychology, a genial fellow named Bill LaVallee, at an Artists and Sobriety meeting. She and Bill had immediately bonded—"she raced across the room and flew into my arms," he says. "We became a kind of AA husband and wife because we talked about the program with each other so much and we were both people without borders; anything we did, we said out loud."

LaVallee was her AA sponsor briefly and her confidant. She would call Bill "in the middle of the night," he says, "her voice *plaintive* when she said, 'I can't be alone.' It was hard for her to ask for help. But you could always tell she wanted it; she sounded like a child. 'Would you like me to come over?' I'd ask her. 'Yes, please,' she'd say. So gentle. Even though she could make great fun of herself, at these times she was so vulnerable."

Bill would drive to her house and sleep in her bed, next to her, platonically. Carrie was emotionally needy, but she also felt, because of her snoring, which could be intense, that sleep apnea would endanger her. So she often had men platonically spend the night in her bed. One night, Bill says, "Richard Dreyfuss and I were strewn all over her bed—nothing sexual. We hear these three claps and it's Debbie: 'Time to go home, boys!' We put on our clothes and went home. We both felt very puzzled because Carrie didn't open her mouth to protest her mother."

Carrie paid Bill LaVallee back many times over for his nurturance. When his car broke down, she sent a car and driver and kept the driver with him for days. She used her influence to get him into subsidized senior housing, where he still resides. She bought him furniture. She helped close members of his family.

But the biggest role they played together was both getting into the Pacific Group, which was part of her post-motherhood effort at conquering her addictions. The Pacific Group, which met in Brentwood, was where elite hard-core substance abuse cases congregated. "It's a group of people," LaVallee says, "who simply could not get sober anywhere else. The people there devote themselves to public service. You get busy. You make commitments. You follow directions. You get a good sponsor. You change your whole psychological makeup." That's the ideal, anyway. "For a long time, I would pick Carrie up on Wednesday night, and we would go to the meeting together."

The Pacific Group was run by an eminence of AA, Clancy Imislund, who for decades helped countless men and women get sober. He was in his seventies at the time, and he's now over ninety years old. He also took over and breathed new life into a charity for Skid Row addicts called the Midnight Mission, which Carrie eventually adopted as one of her several pet philanthropies, contributing to it generously. (Carrie was the first of the Mission's annual special awardees for her supportiveness.)

Imislund's history was mythic. A native of Wisconsin, he'd begun drinking in the navy during World War II; his alcoholism deepened for years, until he found himself on L.A.'s Skid Row. He walked seventy-one blocks in the rain to "surrender" to a downtown rehabilitation center. After he'd been sober for five years, his wife took him back and he rebuilt his life, becoming a TV executive and speaking about addiction, widely and effectively. He is known as a charismatic, if near megalomaniacal, curmudgeon.

Imislund had for a long time been strongly against alcoholics taking any medication for any additional problems, whether depression, bipolar disorder, or schizophrenia. For years, that fiat was a catch-22 for people with a dual diagnosis—co-occurring condition—and those people, like the lawyer and author Terri Cheney (*Manic: A Memoir*), felt, even as recently as ten or fifteen years ago, deprived of the services of some AA groups because of these original hard-and-fast rules.

"A lot of times, people like Carrie and me were frowned upon" for going to AA meetings while "we were on meds for other psychological issues," Bill LaVallee, who had had suicidal ideations, says. Imislund eventually made exceptions for them and for some others, joining the leaders of the more enlightened chapters by doing so. The move in favor of stricture loosening had actually started way back in 1976, when Jennifer Jones's daughter Mary Selznick, twenty-two, had, per strict AA rules, withdrawn from her antidepressants—and her depression had deepened. Finally, Mary had gone to the roof of a tall building in Westwood and jumped to her death. (Her mother, a friend of Carrie's and Debbie's, had attempted suicide nine years earlier.) Another person with depression who was an AA member hanged himself, LaVallee recalls.

After those two tragedies, many AA chapters began to change. Yet resistance was strong, including from Imislund's group. Eventually, with a new understanding of co-occurring disorders (also called dual diagnosis), Imislund and other AA leader holdouts relented and accepted members who were on medications for related problems. It is said that when another AA purist complained to Imislund about his lapse in purity, Imislund had snapped (LaVallee paraphrases), "Okay, the minute I get them off their pills [which had ameliorated their other disorders], I'm gonna send them over to *you* with all their baggage. And they can sit in *your* office while they withdraw." Translation, with sarcasm: Enjoy the ordeal of quieting these people's demons.

Clancy became Bill LaVallee's sponsor. Carrie sat next to Bill in meetings led by Clancy, and, Bill says, "one day she said, 'I want him to be *my* sponsor. Would you ask him for me?' I said, 'No, Carrie. You have to ask him yourself.' First she kind of glared at me; she had given me an order and I'd said no. But it wasn't ego that made her resist asking him herself, I don't think. It was fear. She was afraid she was going to be hurt. Then those eyes just got so big. She was"—irrationally—"afraid he would turn her down." Of course Clancy said yes to her, and he remained her sponsor until the end of her life. Imislund was the first person she mentioned in the acknowledgments to *The Best Awful*— thanking him for, among other things, "a sane life." She also pointedly thanked him in her subsequent books.

Carrie's generosity of spirit seemed to deepen over the years as she fought off her demons and made her peace with her very different parents. When she'd told Charlie Rose she was an excellent friend, she wasn't overstating. When Bill LaVallee's sister Judy, who had Down syndrome, visited L.A., "Carrie had Judy over and cooked for her and treated her like a queen," Bill says. She threw Bill a birthday party—as

she had for countless friends—this one with a Marilyn Monroe imper-
sonator, who cooed to Bill as if he were JFK.

Carrie fought to get a promotion for a mutual friend of hers and
Bill's, a woman named Maggie, who worked at a major network.
"Carrie kept telling her bosses, 'She deserves more money!'" Bill says.
For her part, Maggie says, "I wouldn't be where I am today without
Carrie's encouragement and enduring friendship. Carrie's death felt
like someone carved my heart out of my chest and left it beating on
the sidewalk."

When the hairstylist Roy Teeluck relocated from England to L.A.
with his family to take over the Beverly Hills Frédéric Fekkai salon,
"Carrie was an instant friend," Roy says. "Our daughters were the same
age, and Carrie never missed an opportunity to reach out and invite us
to a Halloween party—and *all* her parties. That's how I met most of the
people I know" and through whom he made his reputation as a hairstylist in Hollywood. "She was so generous." Carrie wanted to write
a remake of *Shampoo*, with a hairdresser clearly based on the dashing
Roy as its hero; that would have really caused his already-ascendant
career to take off. "We were like Frick and Frack," says Roy. And he,
like the similarly straight Richard Dreyfuss and the gay Bill LaVallee,
was often, at her request, her platonic bedmate.

When Jim Hart, a poet and Carly Simon's second husband, had an
addiction—and sexual-identity—issue (not unlike Bryan, he came
out as gay in the middle of his marriage) and was leaving after a brief
stay at McLean Hospital in Massachusetts and flying to L.A. to check
into the Betty Ford Clinic, Carrie called him at his Boston hotel room.
"I *so* understand what you're going through! You're *not* going to be alone
[in your recovery]," she said. Jim remembers her empathy with gratitude
to this day. She had offered to have a car meet him at LAX, and though
his change of flight made that moot, her supportiveness was paramount.

Before she even knew the O.J. prosecutor Marcia Clark, Carrie saw the pain that the divorced—and, thus, essentially single—mother was going through as the entire country watched. When, one day, Marcia had child-care problems and was forced to share them with TV-viewing America, pleading with Judge Lance Ito for a half day off, Carrie recognized the sexist trap Marcia was in. She felt for Marcia's public humiliation. "I got shit from Ito! I thought I was gonna get slammed by the public with 'She can't handle it as a prosecutor! Women can't do this job!'" Marcia says of that harrowing moment. The next morning Marcia walked into court to find a "huge basket of flowers from Carrie, with a note that was so empathic and right on it made me think, 'Oh my God, *thank* God! This is what I needed!'"

Perhaps most Carrie-like, when Carrie's friend Heather Ross was told by a Hollywood producer that she would "never make a movie in my town" if she resisted his advances, Carrie sent that producer a Tiffany-gift-wrapped box containing . . . a cow's tongue. The attached note read, "If you ever touch my darling Heather or any other woman again, the next delivery will be something of yours in a much smaller box!"

"Carrie was a wonderful, wonderful person," says the L.A. superior court judge Scott Gordon of the woman he met when she was an active board member of his Victory Against Violence, shortly after the O.J. trial made domestic violence an important issue to face. Gordon's family and Carrie and Billie went to Disneyland together, "and she was a mom, not a star. My son was peppering her with questions about *Star Wars*, and she was phenomenally patient with him and just wanted to make sure the kids were having fun. She's a remarkable person." Dignified, low-key male judges are not known to rave. But this one did.

Carrie's house remained "the center of the fame universe. Bernardo Bertolucci. Dave Stewart of the Eurhythmics came and played three or four songs from their new album," recalls Frank Coraci, who had Carrie polish the script of *The Wedding Singer*, the Adam Sandler hit he directed. Coraci remembers sitting on her bed every weekday for months in 1996—"pinching myself that I, a guy from Queens, was close friends with Princess Leia." The two listened to the Beatles—"she wanted to hear their song 'Julia' because the character she was writing for, played by Drew Barrymore, was named Julia. We held hands and sang that song. We watched *Roman Holiday* again and again." Carrie used old movies—especially on Turner Classic Movies—to try to relax, but she would much later admit that, given her often-present mania, "I relax badly"; TCM and old movies were ploys.

Carrie took six months to do not a mere polish but a careful re-write on the film. Her self-imposed mandate for *The Wedding Singer* was to add "heart and strength and dimension" to the voice of Barrymore's Julia, and she did that, Frank says. She also added dimension to the other characters. Carrie now had an answer when asked about the secret sauce she used as a script doctor: "Make the women smarter—and the love scenes better."

She also gave Frank personal advice. "I had fallen in love with some-one at the time, and part of what got into the movie was something Carrie said to me: 'It's not how you feel about someone; it's how they make you feel about yourself when you're with them.' It pointed a way. It meant 'You can be infatuated, but the person might not be good for you.' It was one of the most truthful things I heard, and I've applied it to my life. Carrie was also single and dating at the time, so we would compare notes. She showed me you could be strong and intelligent and extremely loving: the first two didn't have to be opposite the third."

As she had been with Frank Coraci, Carrie was an unofficial thera-pist to many friends and, during this span of years, possibly to none more so than a young British military man turned aspiring musician and pop singer named James Blunt, whom she met in 2002 when he was twenty-eight. Blunt considered her his "American mother."

Blunt had gone to boarding school and then enlisted in the Brit-ish army, getting a trial by fire in war-torn Kosovo. "He'd never been to therapy, and I've had enough for both of us, so we started talking quite deeply about his time in the army and the kind of impact it had," Carrie said. "I was kind of his shrink/landlady" for the five months he stayed there in 2003. "We became very, very good friends by the end" of his stay. Blunt was new at devoting himself solely to music, and he was passionate about his new calling. He would practice on Carrie's bathroom piano. Blunt has said, "Carrie fed me soup, showed me old movies, and put a cardboard figure of her in *Star Wars* outside my room to protect me." Carrie played his music to all her friends; she was champion and publicist.

It was during this time that Carrie made several other important new friendships. One was with Salman Rushdie. Rushdie was the kind of literary eminence in whose company Carrie wanted to be, especially while she was finding her own way as a writer. "Carrie loved London," Rushdie says he soon learned. "She came as often as she could, trolling around in antique and junk stores on Portobello Road." She was "this ridiculously generous person who's a genius at gifts," he says. Once, when Rushdie was staying at a house Carrie had rented in London, he complimented two watercolors on the wall; the next day she shipped them to him. Another time, she felt he *had* to have a large, hand-carved African mask; *that* arrived at his door.

The two had significant connections. Both had spoken out with bold, even fearless honesty about controversial subjects. Carrie had talked about her own—and others'—addictions. In Rushdie's far graver case, he had satirized the Prophet Muhammad in *The Satanic Verses*, which had earned him a ten-year-long fatwa, an order of execution from Iran's spiritual leader. Yet, despite the fatwa, he spoke out for freedom of speech.

They shared painful relationships with their substance-abusing and abusive fathers. Rushdie's father, Anis Ahmed Rushdie, a Cambridge-educated lawyer, was a violent alcoholic who terrified Salman's mother and whom Salman had to flee, "putting oceans between us." Salman and Carrie wrestled with depression and wrote their way through it.

The ayatollah's fatwa and Rushdie's terror and initial need for hiding had made him deeply depressed; he was just emerging from a very bad time, while Carrie was just entering one of her most challenging mental and emotional periods.

A mutual friend of theirs, Ruby Wax—an American comedian who lived in Britain—had them on her late-night conversational television show together and then arranged a dinner for them in London in mid-1997. "I think Ruby was trying to set us up," Rushdie says. "She didn't know I was married and about to have a child. So I arrived in the restaurant, the River Café in London, and I had my cell phone in my hand and I said, right away, 'Look, if that phone rings, I'm leaving; that means I'm having a baby!'" Rushdie laughs. "That sort of destroyed any romantic expectations. But Carrie and I immediately found each other funny. She became one of the most important people in my life. Like many people who give the appearance of being open, there are very few people Carrie trusted and talked to very frankly, and I was fortunate to be one of them."

Rushdie saw Carrie's prickly points. "She was still," after all the years, "sensitive about the comparisons to Debbie." When Rushdie saw a video of Carrie singing "Bridge over Troubled Water," he said precisely what so many had said, for decades: "That's not an easy song to sing! You have an amazing voice—why don't you use it?" She answered, as she had before, "'That's my mother's thing.' She didn't want to be treading on Debbie's toes in any way." Still, "she and Debbie were like Laurel and Hardy," with Debbie—as has become well known—calling every morning and formally identifying herself: "This is your mother, *Debbie*." Rushdie is amused that "Debbie had no clue who I was and was completely uninterested" in his dramatic saga as a death-threatened author.

Salman Rushdie credits Carrie for giving him "*all* my Los Angeles friends. She opened the door for me in that city. She gave me a way to *be* there. She threw a series of dinners at her crazy house just for me to meet people. I met her good friend Bruce Wagner. When my friend Helen Fielding was living in L.A., she became very close to Carrie." The friendship between the *Postcards from the Edge* writer and the writer of *Bridget Jones's Diary* would be enduring. "I met people writing for shows like *The Simpsons*. The funniest people in America were at her dinner parties—the most ridiculous, comic people in the world! If you weren't funny, you couldn't come." There was comic one-upmanship. "And, shamefully, I threw my hat in the ring."

Carrie might have been trying to curb her demons, but as others have noted, she would go on and off her medications for her creativity's sake, and sometimes the mania got away with her, Rushdie recalls. "You would walk into her house, and she would start talking and not stop for an hour and a half, complaining or joking about whatsoever. I remember one day she was ranting and literally ninety minutes later she held her breath and said, 'How are you?'" Rushdie felt her pain. "She would talk very openly about it," but there seemed more under the surface.

"Mostly it was a private friendship, and she helped me in many ways," including offering romance advice. At one point early in the twenty-first century, when Rushdie and Padma Lakshmi were dating but not yet married, Carrie felt that her friend Meg Ryan would be a better match for him. But Carrie's fix-up failed. According to Rushdie, although he liked Meg at first, he thought Carrie's *When Harry Met Sally* co-star was too besotted with the Indian maharishis Rushdie looked down upon.

The mania Rushdie saw in Carrie—the nonstop talking—was something that increased during the time she was beginning to write *The Best Awful*, which started to be about her 1993 breakup from Bryan (now named Leland) but ended up being about her 1997 psychotic break and much more, and which would be published at the end of 2003. The book would contain landmark lines. Suzanne asserts that Leland has suggested her partaking of such drugs as codeine has something to do with his being gay. "Oh, I'm sorry," she says. "I hadn't read that part of the [codeine warning] label! I thought it said 'heavy machinery,' not 'homosexuality.' Here I could have been driving one of those big farmyard tractors all along!"

The Best Awful is full of zesty wordplay about human nature and darkness. "You've totally taken all the charm and romance out of self-pity for me," complains Suzanne's best friend, Lucy, who bears a decided resemblance to Carrie's good friend Beverly D'Angelo, then very pregnant with twins fathered by Al Pacino. And the novel is full of gambits that one suspects are stand-ins for similar hijinks. Suzanne manically shears off her hair, gets a tattoo, and high-steps it to Mexico on opioids. ("You *could* wind up at a tattoo parlor with Carrie if you visited her on a certain day," says Bill LaVallee.) Early in the book, Carrie lays down the gauntlet of her/Suzanne's mania, announcing that Leland has accused her of "refus[ing] to take her bipolar medication" and complaining that she would "talk talk talk . . . *talk* all the time."

Like Salman Rushdie, her other new close friend Bruce Cohen—an intense, sensitive, West Virginia–raised Yale graduate who was then just emerging as an extremely successful movie producer—saw the mania, the incessant talking. Bruce was entranced by the endless talking for its brilliance, although he worried about the pathology it hinted at. "During one night that I particularly treasure, I was on the phone and she talked for twelve hours," Bruce says. "I was in my house in L.A. She was in her house. If I understood she would go that long, I would have driven over; I lived ten minutes away. The journeys she would take you on! I felt like I was manic *with* her! I got high from the phone call."

Bruce says this with the knowledge of, and respect for, her condition. He produced the multiply awarded *Silver Linings Playbook*, about a young bipolar man, played by Bradley Cooper, who returns from an institution to live with his parents. Bruce, like Richard Dreyfuss—and like Carrie, most of all—understood the magic and poetry of mania.

"Every single moment you were with her was fascinating—sometimes frightening, sometimes horrifying, but never dull. She often had no schedule or organization, and there wasn't anything ever planned. You'd show up at her house, and you might as well not have any plans. You wouldn't know how long you would be there or what's happening," Bruce says. Yet the sadness and difficulty were palpable. "I think her apparent willingness to talk about everything and anything and her deepest, darkest secrets publicly in film and television and on-stage and with you in all-night phone calls—I think it actually covered a morbid truth, which was there was a lot that she kept to herself. And I have a sad feeling that the daily, hour-by-hour existence with that brain chemistry and that disease was way more painful and difficult and heartbreaking than she wanted people to know.

"I almost wish the expression 'One of a kind' didn't exist," he says, "because it applied to Carrie in a deeper way than it applied to others. Some combination of her brain as it would have been anyway was combined with the mental illness and mania and the drugs and her upbringing and her life experience, and it all created this outpouring of creativity unlike anything else. All you had to do was look at her house. It was the most magical house"—full of whimsy and folk art and stained glass and Indian rugs; rare antiques and elegant lamps; Howard Finster and Donald Roller Wilson paintings; 1930s club chairs and Pro-zac floor tiles in the kitchen. "Up front she was this incredibly joyous, brilliant person. But there was a lot of despair and pain and hardship. I got the deepest, darkest truths of her life, but they were curated to the extent that she wanted to share them."

And there was this as well: "She was an incredible listener," Bruce continues. "When something would be wrong, she would drop every-thing and be there for you. My time with her was so rich and full, but it was only a fraction of her time. She had so many friends. If I ever wanted to know what she was doing for more than six hours a week, I couldn't know." Others of her many friends had that time. "And it was a total meritocracy: Can I connect with your brain? It wasn't money or status; it could be anyone on the street. With some people, you have five good memories. With Carrie, I had *forty*."

Among them, one Thanksgiving, "it was Carrie and myself and my husband, Gabe, and Harper Simon and Mick Jagger and Jerry Hall's daughter Lizzie, and Sean Lennon and Yoko Ono and maybe a couple of others." Carrie was very close to Sean Lennon, through Sean's closeness with Carrie's virtual son, Harper Simon. Both young men stayed at her house, and it was through Sean that Carrie met Yoko. The Thanksgiving "was *sensational*, as you can imagine: totally all-American and very subversive at the same time. Carrie's home was wild and artistic and crazy, but it was also homey, and once you walk in there, you never want to leave. Especially *that* night."

Bruce was amused that Debbie had bought the turkeys they would feast upon not at a gourmet market but at a "fast-food chicken joint. Yoko was quiet but warm and funny and quite engaging and lovely. And it somehow came up that Yoko and Debbie were the same age. Which was a mindblower because Debbie was the archetype icon of the '50s— the Goody Two-Shoes, the American dream—and Yoko was the archetype of the '60s, Miss Counterculture. So everyone thought that was crazy, including Yoko and Debbie."

Being a friend of Carrie's came with a bonus: access to Debbie's rare collection of costumes and movie memorabilia. Bruce remembers that when Kathy Najimy was hosting a *Sound of Music* night at the Hollywood Bowl one July 4, Debbie declared, "I have the original curtain dresses!" which Julie Andrews's Maria made for the von Trapp children. Billie and her friends wore the dresses that evening, and Debbie brought along the guitar that Julie Andrews had strummed in the movie. At another party, for Bruce's birthday, Debbie arrived with Dorothy's ruby-red *Wizard of Oz* slippers, and Carrie gave her Princess Leia hologram speech. *"This is our most desperate hour. Help me, Obi-Wan Kenobi, you're my only hope."* Bruce says, "She *loved* giving that speech. It was one of the great contradictions of her life: she would bitch and moan about how Princess Leia had stolen her identity, but at the same time she took very seriously her responsibility for the character. She knew how many people took it seriously." At Bruce's birthday, "she held my hand when she gave the speech, as if it was a love sonnet for me."

But Carrie talking on the phone for eight to twelve hours—there was no contradiction there. This was the sign of serious mania. Bruce knew it. Richard Dreyfuss forcefully told Carrie, "Get back on your meds! Get back on your meds!" Other longtime friends were concerned, Albert Brooks among them. "You could joke with Carrie about [her condition], and I remember driving to Palm Springs with her and laughing with her, and it could be so easy. But you knew the pain was real, and you wished you could fix it. Whatever the demons were, they weren't going to be exorcised by chatting. I didn't see her on a daily basis, but you could tell she was getting crazy, getting overdosed. You knew she was looking for some kind of peace, and you were worried she could die. I would call Connie [Freiberg], who kept an eye on her, once in a while and ask, 'Is Carrie okay?'"

One night Carrie asked Bill LaVallee to spend the night with her. LaVallee says, "I woke up in the middle of the night, and she wasn't in bed. We were in the back bedroom, and I went in and found her on the floor in one of the bathrooms. And I panicked, so I ran up and talked to [the young woman who was Carrie's assistant at the time]. And we came down and both went into the bathroom, and then she ran and got Debbie."

They took Carrie to the hospital. "And at the end of the next day when everybody was leaving, when Debbie had her back turned, Carrie mouthed at me, '*Please stay with me.*' I could read her lips. I said, 'Okay.'" He sat in a chair near her bed until the next morning, when Debbie called and chastised him for being there. Debbie was wildly protective of Carrie. A longtime friend of Debbie's says, "Debbie thought almost all of Carrie's assistants"—like the woman with her that evening—"were drug dealers." Not at all true, say many who have known Carrie's assistants well, but Debbie's maternal worries are certainly understandable. "If I could, I would suffer for her," Debbie had once written, and her desperate desire to save her daughter manifested itself in many ways.

It's not that Carrie didn't try to curb her problems, but the dearth of good—lastingly good—medications made it a challenge. Once Richard Dreyfuss found a bipolar medication that worked, and he excitedly called Carrie about it. But almost immediately it was off the market. Richard wrote to the manufacturer, who wrote back to him saying he was glad that the drug had worked for Richard and for the relatively few other patients who had praised it, but there wasn't enough of a market to keep producing it.

Carrie made a new, immediately close friend, the singer-songwriter Rufus Wainwright. He was, in a way, the folk music royalty counterpart to Carrie; his mother was the folksinger Kate McGarrigle, and his father was the folksinger Loudon Wainwright III, and their breakup was legendary to folk fans. Rufus was the brother of the singer Martha Wainwright. More, he was close friends with Leonard Cohen's daughter, Lorca (with whom he would eventually have a child). Leonard Cohen was one of Carrie's—and many other people's—idols, and she had used his words as a capstone to *The Best Awful*.

Seventeen years younger than Carrie, Rufus was "out" as gay early, proudly, and defiantly, and like Carrie, he had struggled with an extreme addiction problem. In 2002, Rufus's addiction to crystal meth was so intense he was temporarily blinded. His friendship with Carrie was meaningful and personal, and when he fell in love with Jörn Weisbrodt, a tall, handsome, German-born musical director of Toronto's Luminato concert series, Carrie was delighted. Some of Carrie's friends and their significant others tended to be competitive with one another; such was her charisma. When, for example, it was casually mentioned to Jörn that Carrie was friends with Salman Rushdie, Jörn made clear in a phone conversation that Carrie's friendship with Rufus was *much* closer than hers with Rushdie was. Among some of the most accomplished sophisticates, Carrie had managed to create a high-school-like popularity pecking order with herself at the center.

But at least one friend chose to pull out of Carrie's midst. After their robust friendship in London and New York and points beyond in the mid to late 1970s through the mid-1980s, and despite her enormous sympathy for Carrie, Selina Cadell now gently but "consciously" cut off her friendship with Carrie. "I didn't need a drug addict in my life, though I loved her," she says. "And I was too far away" geographically and pursuing a successful career as an actress in Britain, requiring sleep, not phone calls in the middle of the night. These calls from Carrie now were "not the calls I had received from her before, when she was very vulnerable and needy; those I *would* have taken. Now she would call me because she was on drugs. Ted Pugh confirmed this for me—I was so naive I didn't know it right away—but everybody else knew it. And Carrie herself would have been the first person to admit it."

Carrie struggled to stay the course. The queen of conversation, she got her own talk show, *Conversations from the Edge*, from 2002 to 2004, on Oprah's Oxygen network. Sitting in her living room, with a fire lit behind her, often wearing her trademark black with her legs curled up under her in a chair, she interviewed fellow celebrities, some of whom had interviewed *her*: Diane Sawyer, Diane Keaton, Ben Affleck, Robin Williams, Melanie Griffith, George Lucas. This time she played the relatively quiet questioner. She uttered a quip here and there, but she was generally reserved. One reviewer said her interviews showed "a great deal of compassion and camaraderie," and they did. She was like a taming older sister to Courtney Love, who, in other situations, played the arrogant wild child yet not only was comfortable with Carrie but also seemed impelled, in Carrie's presence, to spill out information with girlish openness. And in a different context—driving down the street and running into her, each of them in their respective cars—she befriended a low-key, dignified young actress named Sarah Paulson whose renown would grow quietly and steadily over the years and who would eventually win *five* major awards for her portrayal of Marcia Clark in 2016's *The People v. O. J. Simpson* (co-produced by Carrie's friend Nina Jacobson). But at first Sarah was lonely and confused, and Carrie's counsel to her was classically blunt and helpful. "You've *got* to find the funny, Paulson," Carrie said one day.

She dated. For a few months, she went out with L.A.'s famous helicopter-pilot newsman Bob Tur, who had given riveting moment-to-moment coverage of the O. J. Simpson freeway chase. Nine years after that dramatic moment, Tur would come out as transgender—something highly unusual at the time. He was transitioning to a female identity, Hanna Zoey Tur, and she has kept that identity ever since. Far more unusual, at the time, than having a husband who came out as gay was having a boyfriend who later changed genders, but Carrie said of Tur, "I sincerely wish her the best," adding, "I only dated him for a few months. Maybe if we dated longer, I would've been reassigned as a man and we'd still be together."

She met one of her most consequential new friends on a plane to, of all places, a dude ranch in Nevada. She was seated next to a young man with whom she bonded immediately. In his late thirties, he was natty, verbose, gay, electrifying, and, given that she was so taken by him, surprisingly (Carrie being a die-hard Democrat), a Republican. His name was Greg Stevens. "You're a captive audience when you're with Carrie on a plane," Bruce Cohen says. "She can tell right away which people can keep up with her intellectually and creatively and imaginatively; she has [using the same word Rushdie used] a pure meritocracy with that." Despite the political difference, "she knew she and Greg were kindred spirits."

Greg had grown up in San Clemente and had worked, as a very young man, for the administrations of Gerald Ford, Ronald Reagan, and George H. W. Bush. He'd acted as a "fixer" (employed by the law firm of the recently notorious Trump-linked arrested duo Paul Manafort and Roger Stone) and had then become an adventurer, traveling the world. He withstood illness in Africa, ducked bullets in the Middle East, and managed to survive intrigue in South America, East Asia, and the former Soviet Union.

Greg Stevens was a raconteur and a drug addict. He was connected to a small contingent of Hollywood Republicans with lobbying firms (Bo Derek, meet Haley Barbour, for example). He was a wheeler-dealer, but he had personal angst: members of his conservative family had trouble not only with his addiction but also with his homosexuality. Greg was, as Bruce puts it, "a force of nature." Carrie would later say, "He fell into my life as if he had always been there." Through Carrie, Bruce and Greg "collided into each other," Bruce says, "and Greg and I ended up being boyfriends for a couple of months."

This was the year, 2000, that Bruce Cohen's biggest movie, *American Beauty*, swept the Oscars, winning Best Picture, Director, and Actor (for Kevin Spacey). Bruce and Carrie attended a Democratic Party fundraiser at the Beverly Hilton; Greg was still Bruce's boyfriend, but he was out of town. When Hillary Clinton was introduced to Carrie, the First Lady gushed, "Oh my God, I'm such a huge fan of yours!" Hillary asked how Carrie and Bruce knew each other. Carrie, without missing a beat, replied, "We've been sleeping with the same man." Hillary, also without missing a beat: "How very twenty-first century of you!"

Greg Stevens's drug addiction proved too much for Bruce Cohen, and they broke up, but they remained friends through Carrie.

In *The Best Awful*, published in 2004 and relating what happened in 1997, Carrie describes what transpired quite closely to what she would later state was the real version. "Suzanne hadn't gone back on all her medications" and had rejected the diagnosis that she had "mental illness." Suzanne enumerates the psychiatrists she visited over the years, the first one saying she had "breezy bipolar two instead of the more challenging bipolar one." She resists the categorization and then says that the (*Postcards*-inspiring) overdose made "the subject return with a vengeance or two." Suzanne now devotes herself (again, all true) to a year of sobriety, but then the "outbursts" return, their "unmanageable upsets" accompanied by "those glorious times as well—times too wonderful to stop for sustenance or sleep, too glorious to blaspheme with ordinary tangibles like words."

The psychotic break she slightly fictionalized in *The Best Awful* went like this: It was summer 1997 and Carrie was "still trying to act as if I wasn't hurt by [Billie's] father who had left me for a man," she told a writer for *bp Magazine*. "I got unbelievably depressed. My daughter was going to camp, and I would get out of bed every day—this swamp—and go pick her up. It was the most complicated thing in the world," rising from bed.

"It must have been very unpleasant for [Billie]," Carrie continued. "I went to a doctor who gave me these new medications that sounded as if they came from Venus—they had no vowels in them—and something very bad happened . . . The medications collided, and I became very, very ill.

"I collapsed, I stopped breathing, and I was taken to a hospital," where she was given "a medication vacation" and sent home. She couldn't sleep for six days straight. "My mind was open and some bad thing oozed out . . . I thought if I fell asleep I would die . . . I kept talking and talking and talking."

She was sent back to the hospital—ironically, to the Thalians Mental Health Center at Cedars-Sinai, the center named for the very organization her mother had co-founded in the 1950s and to which Debbie remained an eminence. "Something was breaking," Carrie told Diane Sawyer in December 2000, while she was still writing the novel that contained a version of this scene. When she was asked by the hospital to sign a form, "I signed with my left hand: '*Shame*.' It was horrible, terrible, terrifying." Watching TV in the hospital, she thought the person featured on CNN—the criminal Andrew Cunanan, hunted for the murder of Gianni Versace—was *her*.

Bryan Lourd came to the hospital to see Carrie as soon as he could. "And I said to him"—pointing to an imaginary Carrie across the room—"'She's in the chair and she's letting me out for a second, and I have to tell you something: *I can't take care of Billie*. I really need you to help me. I can't do this anymore . . . *You must listen to me!'* . . . And I was hallucinating, I could see futuristic cities out the window.

"Losing your mind is a terrible thing." Carrie revealed all of this in her Diane Sawyer interview, in which she acknowledged to the world, "I am mentally ill. I can say that."

Carrie continued, to Sawyer and the viewers: after that outburst, the doctors told Bryan, "You should make plans for your daughter because we don't know if she'll ever come back. I mean, she will but we don't know in what kind of shape."

Carrie needed long-term care and was soon transferred to the Silver Hill Hospital in Connecticut, where she completed an initial thirty-day inpatient program.

Diane Sawyer ended by cheerfully saying, "Thanks to doctors and six different medications taken daily, she's back." But Carrie would soon be upped to seven different medications, and she would end up having five months of outpatient treatment after her month at Silver Hill.

Diane Sawyer asked Carrie if people were sympathetic to her story. Carrie replied, "I used to think people's hair was heavier on one side [of their head] because they would say"—in a dramatically sympathetic voice—"'How *are* you?'" To which Diane quoted another now-famous Carrie line: "I have a visa for happiness, but for sadness I have a lifetime pass." Playing the cheerful naïf, which she did so well as a foil while interviewing, Diane asked, "Happily ever after?" Carrie stared at Diane solemnly and said, "No. Such. Animal."

It was a harrowing public confession and a truly remarkable interview. To cement her commitment to speaking out on the subject, she agreed to be *Psychology Today*'s November 2001 cover story: "The Fisher Queen: Her Battle with Bipolar Disorder." To break the solemnity, at Carrie and Penny's first party after the Sawyer airing, Carrie rented an ambulance and a gurney that had a life-sized cutout of Princess Leia hooked up to an IV on it and had IV hookups with colored water as the centerpiece of every table. "She plucks out that thing that would destroy the rest of us. Then she makes fun of it—I'm sure it saves her," Meryl Streep said in the same article.

Then Carrie went back to finishing the very overdue book. She had three consecutive Simon & Schuster editors on *The Best Awful*. All were women; all stayed in her house. They also enjoyed the Carrie-Penny parties that included, as guests, recalls the first editor, Sydny Miner, "Warren Beatty, Parker Posey, Amanda Peet, Courtney Love, and [the Sony executive] Amy Pascal at the height of her power. But it was all low-key." Sydny received the *Best Awful* typescript after Carrie had written and rewritten it on the legal pads. "Carrie was a perfectionist. She worked and reworked everything. She was very honest about her struggle. Her challenges and my challenges were making the story linear. Talking about the hard stuff"—the drugs, the breakdown—*"wasn't* an issue"; the structure was. Carrie was on her medications and was often cooking. "She was obsessed with making risotto," Sydny says. "She got angry if I didn't eat it. So I ate." Billie was living with her; mother and daughter were close. And her door of course was always open to the endless parade of friends.

The next editor was Betsy Rapoport, who became very close to Carrie. "I flew out from New York and—benignly—kicked out the minor TV stars who were staying with her," Betsy says. "I said, 'We really need to focus on the book. We're right on deadline.' Carrie sent them home. I don't know if we'll ever know how many people Carrie was den mother to"—James Blunt, Harper Simon, dozens of fluctuating others—"but there were *a lot* of them.

"I would say to Carrie, 'I need a scene that has to accomplish this—these characters have to be in it.' She would grab her legal pad and scamper up to the pool and hours later come down and it was 90 percent there. We would work late into the night. When we decided we had worked hard enough, we would give ourselves the treat of watching TV." One night they watched Barbara Walters interview Angelina Jolie about her newly adopted Cambodian child and her UN activism. Betsy and Carrie started out skeptical—"we were settling in for a night of mockery" about the gorgeous actress who'd carried Billy Bob Thornton's blood in a vial hanging from her neck and had kissed her brother passionately at the Oscars—but "ended up looking at one another, like, *Isn't this an amazing woman?*'"

Betsy found Carrie "incredibly witty, absolutely brilliant, and she raved about Billie; she *gushed* about Billie." Betsy and Carrie stayed in touch even after Betsy's work on the book was done.

The book's final editor was Kerri Kolen, a young Simon & Schuster assistant to the editor in chief, David Rosenthal; Rosenthal was crazy about Carrie and oversaw almost every one of her books. Kerri was sent out to tie things up. Carrie took to Kerri right away. "Carrie was not always the easiest to get along with, but she was also great fun," Kerri says. "She decides she likes you or she doesn't, and once she gets that idea, she kind of holds on to it. You don't get a lot from her if she's not comfortable." Carrie was comfortable with Kerri.

"People use the term 'Oh, she's gifted' about all kinds of people," Kerri says. "But Carrie was in the true sense a comic genius. She wasn't a writer who has a thought, writes it down, and then keeps editing that thought until it's a really great line." Rather, "her original thought *was* the great line. Those gems would spill out of her. I would tape them and write them down and then string it all together.

"Sometimes Carrie would get inspiration in the middle of the night." At the end of *The Best Awful* and especially on the next two books, "She would wake up [and say], 'I have to write about this in my book.' Even if she didn't say it, I would know this was happening because I would hear the soda can opening." Carrie was a Diet Coke addict. "The next minute I could smell the cigarette smoke. Then I would open my eyes and she would be sitting on my bed. It's a little creepy actually," Kerri says affectionately, "to wake up and find some-one sitting on your bed. I'd say, 'Hi . . . ?' She'd say, 'I just thought of something so brilliant! Are you ready?' I'd say, 'I'm not, but I *can* be ready. Hold that thought.' I'd write it down.

"We worked around the clock. I transcribed all the time because we were working in real time. She was always writing in the notebook and would hand me random things that she'd just written. She would throw something in there, and I would turn her great passages into a [workable draft] and then hand them back to her. We would go back and forth until we both really loved it." After Kerri's being out in L.A. for a week at a time, "David would say, 'Come back with the book.' Well, I'd come back with a *draft* of the book." It was intense, but it was worth it.

The Best Awful received rave reviews and became a *New York Times* bestseller. *The Washington Post* hailed its "bravado, intelligence, wit and iffy medication. Suzanne Vale (or Carrie Fisher) uses every weapon in our fragile human arsenal to fight against the numb horror of madness." The *Los Angeles Times* praised its "intelligence and humor—sometimes wicked, sometimes winningly self-deprecating," surprisingly hitting the nail on the head by praising its "no-nonsense quality." As "funny," "tartly funny," and "trademark-snappy" as it was (said *The New York Times*, *Time*, and *Entertainment Weekly*, respectively), the *Los Angeles Times* caught its marching orders with that "no-nonsense" remark: it was a book about bipolar disorder and parenting, attempts at discipline, lack of "discipline," love of a child, getting over the rejection of a man, and living with mental illness. No nonsense—like it or not.

The message of the autobiographical novel was crucially important. At Carrie's book signings "people were always coming up to her, wanting to share their own [mental health] experiences, and she dropped everything to hear them," says Bruce Cohen. "She knew that she had power for good, that she was saying things about her life that people don't want to say. 'If my reach-out through my story has affected someone, I owe it to them to hear a piece of them back.'"

The Best Awful marked the beginning of Carrie Fisher's life as an advocate for proud truthfulness and lack of shame about the challenges of mental illness. She spoke about bipolar disorder in interviews. "The manic depressive's battle is you don't know where you're going to land, and you don't know how long it could take to get back if you land in the bad place. That's why I call it the best awful," she said to Mimi Avins of the *Los Angeles Times*. "It gets great! And then very rapidly it gets to the point where you don't make sense. I've gotten to where I don't track. It's derailment. That's embarrassing to someone whose identity is rooted in being articulate. It is fun when you're in your 20s. You feel you can house this energy. Maybe it's sort of OK in your 30s, but it's starting to be not right. And when you get off the tracks it's not right at any age."

It is important to remember that Carrie Fisher acknowledged her mental illness on network TV in 2000, before virtually any other celebrity had the nerve to make a similar acknowledgment. The only one who had done so before was the former child actress Patty Duke, who paved the way eight years earlier, in 1992, with the book *A Brilliant Madness: Living with Manic-Depressive Illness*, describing her life with the disorder.

But Carrie's speaking out on Diane Sawyer's highly viewed TV special had broader impact than Duke's disclosure. Carrie was an icon—as Princess Leia—and a favorite hip actress to her generational peer group.

It would be four years before Jane Pauley wrote about her bipolar diagnosis, twelve years before Catherine Zeta-Jones opened up about hers, fifteen before Demi Lovato admitted that she had been diagnosed, and eighteen before Mariah Carey was able to admit that she, too, had received that diagnosis years earlier, a diagnosis she did not want to believe, even though breakdowns in 2001 and 2016 had indicated to fans that something was wrong. Britney Spears, who also experienced a very public breakdown in 2007, waited until 2013 to reveal the diagnosis.

Carrie's early opening of the conversation about bipolar disorder and her insistence on continuing to talk about it—and to cheerlead others, right until her death—occurred a whole eighteen years before the designer Kate Spade tragically died by hanging herself instead of allowing herself to be hospitalized because, some said, she feared the illness's stigma would hurt her brand. Several months before Spade's suicide, the Hollywood producer Jill Messick, who helped bring the great Amy Poehler–Tina Fey movies to life and who had two teenage children, committed suicide, too. Although the ostensible reason for that tragedy was her unfair tarring by the Harvey Weinstein scandal, Messick's recent years of debilitating bipolar disorder were a factor. Though her family did not hide the fact of her mental illness, it was overwhelmed by the conversation about Weinstein.

Simply put: Carrie Fisher was a dogged paver of the way for honesty on and emphasis of a subject that for too long has remained shame inducing in women. And there had been shame: in 1996 Carrie's friend Margot Kidder was found walking in the bushes of an L.A. neighborhood, in a state of mental distress. But curiosity and mockery, not sympathy and respect, were visited upon Margot, who was later deemed to be bipolar. The quite remarkable deviance from "good behavior" in celebrity women is given startlingly stronger disdain and less leeway than the same behavior in men. The overdose deaths of Heath Ledger, Philip Seymour Hoffman, and Tom Petty and the suicide of Robin Williams: none of these were accompanied by the condescension and tsk-tsking that accompany far less dramatic lapses from "normalcy" and propriety by women. Anthony Bourdain's tragic and publicly unexpected suicide (preceded by his candor about drug use) invited not one negative word against him. Reactions to Kate Spade's suicide focused on the impact on her daughter. (Bourdain's daughter was roughly the same age as Spade's.)

Interestingly, Carrie's fierce honesty and intense likability made her, in a very different way, the female analogue to Bourdain and in that regard a first for women. The extraordinary loyalty to her and the adoration of her by her discerning friends, despite the disease of addiction that in others would be at least slightly judged as "bad behavior," also made her a female analogue to the *New York Times* media columnist David Carr, who died in 2015. Carr had been an acknowledged crack addict in his early career, including during the raising of his young twin daughters. But no one who knew him could offer anything but breathless praise. This does not often happen to women—and, in this sense, Carrie was a barrier breaker. But it would not be easy.

everal months after *The Best Awful* was published, on June 2, 2004, Carrie and Debbie flew to Indianapolis for a talk at the Murat Theatre, arranged by a lecture bureau that had a mother-daughter series; Joan Rivers and her daughter, Melissa Rosenberg, and Naomi and Wynonna Judd were also booked. Debbie had told the organizer in her pre-interview about her many travails. When the organizer booked Debbie and Carrie, he saw "the helicopter mom in Debbie." Carrie might have been helping support Debbie, but "Debbie was putting a bubble around Carrie so she wasn't in situations where Debbie didn't have control over her."

The lecture bureau's advance team picked the two up at the airport on the day of the SRO-booked event, and as someone in the retinue recalls, "Carrie came out of the car and—how do I put this gently?—she was in a *very* bad state. She looked disheveled. Debbie said, 'Let's get her up to the room right away! She needs to rest!'" explaining, as they were on their way to the hotel, "'Carrie doesn't have her meds. She *needs* her meds.' It was a really bad scene, and Debbie was taking control of the situation; her motherliness was coming out." The lecture bureau staff feared it would be "an evening from hell" if the two of them took the stage together. "We were madly thinking of contingency planning: Could Debbie 'adopt' a 'daughter' from the audience and make a game out of it?" But somehow Debbie dealt with Carrie as she had, years earlier, at the London Palladium.

The bureau rep remembers, "Amazingly, Carrie hit the stage that night, and like a true professional she 'delivered.'" It is not known if she found her meds in her luggage or if she simply forced herself beyond her mania. "She pulled it together out of what seemed like intense will. The two of them had a connection with the audience." Still, "when the evening was over, they looked at each other and said, 'We're never doing *this* again.'" The lecture series staff was impressed by "the symbiotic relationship Debbie had with Carrie and the professionalism in Carrie, her determination to outwit her illness," one staffer says.

It would be thus. As Carrie would say in an interview to other people diagnosed with bipolar disorder, "You can outlast anything. It's complicated. It's a job, but it's doable. One of the greatest things that happened for me was that psychotic episode. Having survived it, I now know the difference between a problem and an inconvenience. Bipolar disorder can be a great teacher. It's a challenge, but it can set you up to be able to do almost anything else in your life." And, "if you feel like your child or friend or spouse is showing signs of this illness, if you can get them in touch with somebody else they can talk to and share their experience with and not just feel like they're being told they're 'wrong' or 'bad' or 'stupid,' then they can relate somehow."

A greater challenge for Carrie would come in eight months. Bipolar disorder plus a propensity to addiction—dual diagnosis/co-occurring disorder—was a constant siege. As one of the staffers at the Indianapolis lecture event recalls, "Debbie said to me," with pride, "'Can you believe? Three failed marriages and I'm still here?! I keep getting knocked down, but I keep getting up!' And I thought, '*So does your daughter. I saw her get up.*'" Or, as Carrie's close friend Gavin de Becker once put it, "Carrie is funny, wise—*and beaten down by every aspect of life.* But she continues to get up and share her insights." And, as her equally close friend Bruce Wagner said, "Carrie is a warrior."

TEN

THE WARRIOR IN
THE WAR ZONE

For the denizens of the industry, Oscars night is New Year's Eve plus Mardi Gras. Each year, Carrie was either at the Awards itself or at home, hosting everyone she knew to all watch it together. At the 1989 ceremony, she was a presenter, and in a very funny skit she and Martin Short came out, each from the opposite side of the stage, wearing the same black sheath and beaded jacket. It was a witty moment. Carrie waxed deadpan, fake-upset, to which Short complained: Why was she kvetching? She had so many dresses and he had only four!

Carrie walked to another lectern; Short clomped behind her, then finally agreed to leave and change clothes. "But the shoes stay!"

Carrie's longtime pal Bruce Vilanch had just started as head writer for the show that year, but the skit was Carrie and Martin Short's own idea. By the late 1990s, Bruce decided Carrie should not only help write the show but also be chief wrangler for it "because she knew everybody and everybody loved her." She was one of the only people, for example, who could talk Courtney Love—who was then very "hot" for playing Mrs. Larry Flynt in *The People vs. Larry Flynt*—out of reading an X-rated poem on the stage. "Carrie got Courtney to allow us to rewrite it so it wasn't quite as erotic as Courtney wanted it to be." Carrie "wrangled almost everybody for that show" and subsequent ones, says Vilanch. Not many people still smoked in the early years of the twenty-first century, and because the writers' room was "almost an afterthought—a security room near the fuse boxes," when Carrie would light up there the smoke set off the alarm system, annoying the producer. So Carrie and Russell Crowe ("the last of the smokers," as Vilanch recalls) were shunted onto a loading dock to puff away. Vilanch then put Carrie in the greenroom—everyone gets nervous in the greenroom—to cheer the presenters up as no one but she could do.

Just before the 2004 Oscars (which were held on February 27, 2005), Carrie's dear friend Greg Stevens came to stay at her house. He had just gotten back from a trip to Bosnia, arriving in L.A. on Friday, February 25, and he got to Carrie's house around midnight. He was very tired, but he and Carrie stayed up and talked on her bed for a bit and watched *Mrs. Miniver* on TV. Greg went to bed next to her. Her brother, Todd, has reported that they snorted OxyContin, an opioid, together. When they put their heads down, Carrie put a pillow between herself and Greg. Then she woke him up, and they talked for a while, and then both fell asleep again.

Bruce Cohen and his boyfriend, Gabe, came over the next morning, Saturday, February 26, for brunch. After brunch, they were all—Bruce, Gabe, Carrie, and Greg—to go off to have tango lessons. But none of that happened.

"Carrie came running out of the bedroom," Bruce recalls, "and said, 'Something's wrong with Greg!'

"I was the one who found out he was dead," Bruce says. Greg and Bruce had of course recently been lovers. Bruce walked into the bedroom where his ex-boyfriend lay. "He was cold and stiff and dead." It was horrific. "I called 911 and they said to me, 'Mr. Cohen, here's what you're going to do.' They kind of yelled at me, which was good;

I needed the slapping. They told me to deliver CPR for half an hour." He did, but it was fruitless. "And that was Greg's death," Bruce says, summing up the sudden horror. "It was incredibly traumatic to Carrie. And it sent her on a downward spiral."

Carrie felt Greg's death was her fault. "From the first moment, I blamed myself," she said. "I thought I had put the pillow on his face. I was in shock for months." The reason she feared she had killed him was that "it happened on my watch and I had failed to save him."

Greg Stevens's final autopsy, issued in April 2005, reported the death of the forty-two-year-old as caused by cocaine and oxycodone use and also referred to two forms of heart disease, previously undiagnosed. It was clear that although the drugs he took were powerful, without the heart conditions he would not have succumbed. But for a long time Carrie continued to blame herself.

It didn't help that immediately after Greg's death the newspapers carried the story, calling the death a straightforward "overdose" (the word was not used in the autopsy report), with no qualifiers. Tabloids suggested that Carrie was unfit to have custody of her daughter. It was wrenching. Carrie told friends that her head was frozen for seven weeks and that her hair had turned white at the temples.

Carrie's second-to-last *Best Awful* editor, Betsy Rapoport, was in touch with her during these weeks. "I watched the tabloids after that," she says. "There was zero truth in" the sensationalistic way the tabloids covered the story. "The headlines were blaring that she would lose custody of Billie. Oh my God! It was the most stressful thing for her!"

Yet in the middle of her angst, Carrie asked Betsy, via email, if she could send a present to Betsy's cancer-ill mother. Carrie wrote, "I'm lucky to have you in my life. And I have your mother to thank for that. Please thank her for me. I love to hear about people being courageous and, more than that, humorous in the face of something that, among other things, terrifies so many of us. It sounds as though your mother is finding whatever good she can in what most would experience as a purely awful situation. A misery. A frightening march to the ultimate change." Carrie asked for Betsy's mother's address because "she has given me such a gift by giving me the treasure of you, I'd like to hurl a token her way, if that's alright with you."

After praising Betsy's mother's courage, Carrie segued to the death of Greg Stevens. "I find myself thinking of Greg now and then—not like losing a friend is anywhere NEAR like losing a mother—but I find myself thinking of him, and that's when I think he's probably thinking of me . . . All these people we weren't finished talking to, that we will never be finished talking to until we see them again someday and pick up where we left off. OR we can talk to them as we go along . . . like talking to ourselves but so much better."

What Betsy didn't realize was that, despite these wistful words, Carrie was so distressed that she had developed post-traumatic stress disorder and started doubling down on OxyContin, the very drug she had imbibed with Greg. Todd accompanied Carrie to a discreet rehab clinic in England, as he wrote in *My Girls*, and didn't leave her side while she was being weaned off the drug, soon turning so "very small, withdrawn, depressed, frightened, trying desperately to understand" why she had been spared Greg's fate.

As soon as she recovered, she wrote to Betsy, "You know how"— in *The Best Awful*—"we wrote about how I was always losing things, until I finally lost a DOG—well, now I've gone and lost a person!" She had lost people close to her before—Griffin Dunne's sister Dominique, John Belushi, Joan Hackett, Julian Ford, Michael O'Donoghue, who'd died in 1994, her grandmother Maxene, and others—but *this* death somehow hit a singular nerve. Even three years later, when she was being directed in her one-woman show *Wishful Drinking* at the Berkeley Repertory Theatre, the two accounts she wrote but found too painful to tell in detail onstage were about her psychotic break and about Greg's death. "She wrote out the stories," *Wishful*'s director, Tony Taccone, says. "They were very, very dark stories, and she wrote them out in a way that was unbelievably moving and scary and brilliant. And I said to her, 'Put these in the show and the show will be amazing.' And she looked at me and said, 'I can't do it.'"

The experience and the lesson it taught her seemed to lead Carrie, an atheist, to turn to an offbeat form of spirituality. "But I HAVEN'T lost [Greg]," she insisted to Betsy. "I think he's with all my stuff. Wearing the earrings and the necklace I lost in Acapulco, reading the TV pilots I was supposed to read as reference that disappeared one day, the T shirts, the pens, the cord for the computer, the diamond from the ring Paul gave me: Greg's playing with them all."

As she was putting her life together, Carrie received the Women of Vision Award from the Washington, D.C., chapter of Women in Film and Video. Says Susan Lovett, who was the branch's president, "I nominated Carrie not because she was an iconic actress and writer but because I wanted to honor a script doctor. She was the top script doctor in Hollywood. It was wonderful to choose to go beyond being a celebrity and be *a craftsman*."

The ceremony took place in Washington on April 13, 2005. Carrie and Debbie were in the audience while Richard Dreyfuss gave a hosanna-filled introduction. "If Carrie and I could have been lovers, we would have completed some kind of Hindu prayer wheel, and the world would completely have ended, so you should be grateful," he said. "We were so overwhelmed by this extraordinary inner commentary that made us laugh *so* much. And, God, she's gonna look up and make me laugh." The camera panned to a wryly smiling Carrie. "So I just had to settle for adoring her . . . She has made me more honest. She has made me see the grandness in her secretless-ness. She is disturbing because of how brilliantly she describes her own disturbance. Her friendship is the only friendship that saves me, and I often try to ruin it by not returning phone calls or staying away, or some insensitivity that is none of your business. I do this because the loss of Carrie's friendship would be so devastating to me that I find myself wanting to end the suspense. I would hate it if she didn't love me."

Then came video tributes by Bruce Cohen ("She's one of the great minds on the planet today"), Beverly D'Angelo ("She's my idol"), George Lucas ("I was looking for somebody who was very young but very commanding"), and Debbie ("I became Princess Leia's mother instead of Debbie Reynolds").

Finally, Carrie took the stage. She started with a laugh line: "I'm Carrie and I'm an alcoholic." It set at ease an audience who might have thought she *might be* tipsy. ("We were told she was on medication," Susan Lovett says of Carrie's affect.) After that, another laugh line: "Now I can't live up to that." Then she got down to business: "Everybody here had a husband except the last woman. She had an *ex*-husband. I had one of those and then I had one who was gay. He forgot to tell me. You know how it goes in Hollywood; things slip your mind.

"But there are too many husbands in Washington!" she wailed, suggesting that she'd hoped to find a single man here. She thanked the honoring organization. "That was very nice of you to give to me, Women in Film. I thought it was for my body, and I was very excited. I thought I should get it that time I wore the metal bikini . . . and I'd like to get an award posthumously for my good body." She thanked "my mother, who *is* my husband. And I have some other husbands." Carrie mentioned Bruce Cohen and Richard and spoke of the passing of Greg. "And thank you, and for all of you women who got this award and *have* husbands." She raised the award high.

The audience drank it in; Carrie never disappointed. Afterward, she autographed *Star Wars* merchandise to help raise money for Women in Film scholarships.

Carrie signed on for the voice of snarky but commonsensical Angela, boss of Seth MacFarlane's oddball Peter Griffin at the Pawtucket Brewery, in the popular animated TV series *Family Guy*. Says *Family*

Guy's showrunner Steve Callaghan, "Peter the character was all about hijinks and shenanigans, so he wanted a female boss who wouldn't take his crap. When it came to thinking, 'Who would be a perfect Angela?' Seth said, '*Carrie Fisher!*' Happily, she said yes." She shot her first episode on the show's season 4; it aired in late 2005.

The animated series had advantages for Carrie. She didn't have to show her face or the weight she had been gaining, due in part to the side effects of her medications. She was thoroughly professional as Angela: the snappy, cheerful, but sometimes eye-rolling boss. "Everybody loved working with Carrie," says Callaghan. "She was always funny. One day she was sitting outside the booth, waiting to go on, and she had all these old movie magazines, and *Life* magazines, from the '50s. She was reading articles about her parents that made mention of her, and she seemed to take great delight in them. She was turning pages, and," as cast and crew leaned closer in, "she was giving her own narration of their lives, giving it her comic play-by-play in a funny almost monologue. It was hysterical. It made us grateful to have Hollywood royalty working on our little cartoon. It was like watching a one-woman show."

Actually, the reviewing of the old magazines *was* part of a one-woman show in the works. Carrie was intent on turning the "If my life wasn't funny it would just be true, and that is unacceptable" aspect of her life—meaning *most of* her life—into a theater piece. She would title it *Wishful Drinking*: brilliantly, because drinking was one of her few *non*-addictions.

She was close friends with David Geffen, whose foundation had funded the old Westwood Playhouse's renovation and transformed it into the Geffen Playhouse. She came into the Playhouse one day in early 2006 and made a casual pitch for her show to the theater's artistic director, Randall Arney, its producing director, Gil Cates, and members of their team. Carrie's *whole life* had been a one-woman show—her notorious hilarity and irony, her unique conversations and manic dialogue, her advice to friends, her interviews both print and TV, her books and talk show appearances and hostings. She was now going to mine it all: the nutty Hollywood royalty childhood that kept multiplying in glamour, decadence, and idiosyncrasy and that followed her (with the help of her *always* calling attention to it) wherever she went—to the *Star Wars* merchandise. Added to that: her two very different serious relationships, her manic depression and addiction, and the curse of that ubiquitous poster image of her super-svelte younger self while she now struggled with her weight like any fifty-year-old who enjoyed southern and Mexican food and had to be on an assortment of weight-inflating medications.

One-man or one-woman shows had a happy history as theater pieces. Spalding Gray had brought the convention into the current age in the 1970s with his series of pieces about his life for the Wooster Group. Anna Deavere Smith (*Notes From the Field*) and Lily Tomlin (*The Search for Signs of Intelligent Life in the Universe*) and *Elaine Stritch at Liberty* had made the genre comfortable for women.

Arney and his team watched Carrie's pitch, and, he said, "even before the meeting started, she told us stories and we were crying, we were laughing so hard. Gil Cates green-lighted it right away. Now all Carrie had to do was write it."

Carrie found a partner in the talented young playwright Joshua Ravetch, and they got to work. The finished script was approved and announced in early June.

Her eight-week performance at the Geffen—from November 2006 to February 2007, with Ravetch directing—was sold out. As Randall Arney put it, "Her appeal crossed all boundaries: men loved her, women *absolutely* love her, from young to old." Charles McNulty of the *Los Angeles Times* called the still-unpolished but rambunctious show a "Beverly Hills yard sale" of wild stories "that would defy credulity were it not for the very credible presence of the narrator."

It was Carrie's life. During this and the subsequent, more polished version, there were bons mots galore as she spoke of Debbie and Eddie ("I was born in Burbank, California, to simple folk—people of the land"), which got a big laugh, because *Photoplay* and *Modern Screen* magazines were plastered all over the stage's backdrop. And there was Elizabeth and Eddie after Mike Todd's death. ("So my father flew to Elizabeth's side, slowly making his way forward to her front"—riotous laughter—"and ultimately he consoled her with his penis.") There were jokes about *Star Wars* and its crazy merchandising. ("They made a *Star Wars* Mr. Potato Head line with a Princess Tater.") And there were jokes—enormously identifiable to women—about old images of your body dogging your present and the pain that it entails: "Recently I googled myself. Somebody said, 'WTF—whatever happened to Carrie Fisher? She used to be so hot. Now she looks like Elton John.' This hurt all seven of my feelings." (Sometimes she said "seven"; sometimes she said "three.")

She talked about the songs Paul wrote for her, quoting the lines about her "cold coffee eyes" and conceding, "I am a bitch!" and about how Bryan "forgot" to tell her he was gay; how her mother had married someone (Hamlett) four years younger and from the South, which were, indeed, the same as her coordinates with Bryan. She admitted her extreme addiction, of course. Piercing honesty, by Carrie, enabled every audience member to exhale, as if their own lesser secrets were being exonerated by her greater, humorously embraced "misdeed." She made faint-praise irony of the fact that "after writing all my life, I now get awards *all* the time for being mentally ill." She made her family seem full of great material for her daughter, who, she reported, said she wanted to grow up to be a singer or a writer. "You have tons of material. Your mother is manic-depressive; your father is gay; your grandmother tap-dances and your grandfather eats hearing aids." "It was a triumph for her," says Sean Daniel, who saw the Geffen version and had kept up his friendship with Carrie intermittently since *The Blues Brothers*. "It was pure Carrie—hilarious and wise."

During the Geffen engagement, Carrie made a featured appearance on *30 Rock* that cemented her as a heroine for the younger hip comediennes—the third generation of *SNL* after Carrie's own *SNL* friends. Tina Fey, Amy Poehler, Maya Rudolph, and other comic actresses like Amy Schumer and the next-gen ruler Lena Dunham had come to view Carrie as an older sister. Tina had used her girl-crush on Princess Leia on the show, with her character Liz Lemon dressing as Princess Leia to get out of jury duty. But Tina's bigger admiration was for Carrie's "honest writing and razor-sharp wit," which she called "a gift" to herself and to her feminist comic peers.

The *30 Rock* episode in which Carrie had the cameo was called "Rosemary's Baby." Carrie played Liz Lemon's fictional feminist heroine, a once-prominent and admirably controversial TV writer named Rosemary Howard, who has seen better days. Liz meets Rosemary at a book signing and says, "I grew up wanting to *be* you!" She excitedly invites Rosemary to guest write on one of the shows she produces, *The Girlie Show*. Rosemary has some edgy ideas—too edgy for Liz and for the show. But it's when Liz ends up in Rosemary's cramped, window-gated apartment in "Little Chechnya"—with the F train rumbling inches away—that she realizes Rosemary might have been her heroine long ago but that time is way past over. Liz is threatened by Rosemary's depressing life and her onetime heroine's presumption that she has remained Liz's role model.

Rosemary gets unattractively possessive and guilt inducing with Liz: "You can't abandon me, Liz. You *are* me!" Then: "You wouldn't have a job if it wasn't for me! . . . I didn't have any kids—*you're* my kid!" Rosemary shouts, as Liz makes an awkward effort to get going. Finally, in homage to Princess Leia, Rosemary yells, "Help me, Liz Lemon! You're my only hope!" Liz makes a mad dash out of the apartment.

The appearance won Carrie an Emmy nomination, her first.

Carrie pointed up older women's neediness in a moving, chilling way. The point of the *30 Rock* piece was that tough-mouthed women who don't stay young looking and thin and on zeitgeist point are not only doomed in the entertainment industry (this we were expected to know) but are also scary and unattractive to *feminist* women. It was button pushing for Fey and Fisher to make that leap, daring the women in the audience to ponder that their true fears might collide with their politically correct and sisterly self-congratulation.

But, really, with *Wishful Drinking*, Carrie was going 180 degrees in the other direction: creating, through self-deprecation, the most beloved and durable and multiply platformed of her self-depictions. Carrie might have *played* a poignant, repellent Rosemary, pushing away even supportive women, but Carrie herself was the opposite of Rosemary. Women, especially, would metaphorically run *to* her dark depths, not *away* from her and them. The character Carrie would create in *Wishful* had a sophistication ("They say religion is the opiate of the masses? Well, I've taken masses of opiates"), a generosity, and a self-confident humor that could absorb the Liz Lemons, the Tina Feys, and their peers unthreateningly—as friends and fans. She tiptoed up to desperation's edges and then firebombed the path and the destination. Perhaps it took the subtly known reputation of Carrie Fisher—the impressive fact that she was the center of in-group Hollywood—to help effect that enviable impression.

While the original version of *Wishful* was having its sold-out Geffen Playhouse run, Tony Taccone, the artistic director of the Berkeley Repertory Theatre and a respected theater presence who had partnered with Tony Kushner on six projects, including *Angels in America*, visited Carrie in L.A. He wanted to broach the subject of rewriting and deepening the piece for his own theater—and others. At about the same time, Kerri Kolen, who had been the last Simon & Schuster editor on *The Best Awful*, flew out to Carrie's house and explored the idea of turning the script, in the current or enriched form, into a book.

Wishful Drinking would be Carrie's late-career, endearment-enshrining, long-running signature piece. With *Postcards*, fans were surprised and delighted by the flinty humor of the-woman-otherwise-known-as-Princess-Leia. With *The Best Awful*, she'd come out as an early, brave, and daringly funny advocate for destigmatizing bipolar disorder. But with *Wishful Drinking*, Carrie moved up a notch: she became a representative of perplexed and sophisticated modern womanhood; a soothing ally in the world of craziness, self-sabotage, and disappointment; your funniest and most honest best friend. She had found a way to make no one not love this work, this life of hers. It helped that she was no longer the sexy, darling, younger Carrie—skinny and shapely, suave-voiced. In fact, the transformation from Carrie of the early 1980s to Carrie of the early years of the twenty-first century was so extreme it was almost as if she were a different person.

She had ballooned up to 180 pounds—the first 20 pounds, by 2004, from the medications, the rest from a combination of the medications and eating habits that those who cared about her described as "pretty awful." Her face was puffed and fillered; she was hardly alone in this in Hollywood or any elite circles, and her close friendship with Michael Jackson's friend and dermatologist "the Botox King," Dr. Arnold Klein, led to no dearth of procedures. But the change in her face also showed the effects of emotional and physical self-abuse. Her voice was deeper and . . . different: no faux-minor-English accent, no silky, suave, confident archness. That voice that went down like ice cream on *The David Letterman Show* in 1983 was gone. Now she had a cranky, almost-rural, but tell-it-like-it-is quality, as if willed to her by her late grandmother Maxene. Yet the new voice made her more life worn; quips were softened by a touch of audible pain.

By the time the play would open on Broadway on October 4, 2009, after two years of performance elsewhere, the patter and Carrie's empathic touch with the audience were so finely tuned that, as the *New York Times* critic Ben Brantley wrote, calling this an "achievement," "Ms. Fisher, daughter of the movie star Debbie Reynolds and the crooner Eddie Fisher, cannot be said to have had an Everywoman's life. Yet 'Wishful Drinking' makes you believe, for a couple of hours, that Carrie Fisher is you."

When Tony Taccone first visited Carrie at her house, she had asked him, "'What do you think?' and I said it needed to be overhauled entirely," Taccone recalls. "I said, 'Carrie, you can act in a more impassioned and nuanced way and the piece would be much improved.' Carrie said, 'Ha! Have you seen *Star Wars*? I'm not much of an actress.' She had a bemused relationship with her *Star Wars* persona. She often commented to me on what a weird thing it was, being Princess Leia. But she was very grateful to the character because it gave her eternal fame that allowed her to do other stuff."

Starting the revised play with Carrie standing in front of a revolving set of all the ridiculous *Star Wars* merchandise—the shampoo, the sex doll, the soap bar, the Pez dispenser—Taccone had her hit that point right away in her new raspy voice: "If someone offers to make you into a Pez dispenser, *do it*!" (Later in the evening, she reprised that exhortation with "If Paul Simon offers to write a song about you—*do it*!") Taccone put her in pajamas (later, black leggings and a big top or a three-quarter-length coat) to emphasize the slumber party intimacy of her disquisition.

"She wasn't trying to be anything other than what she was. That's what we worked on" when Carrie flew up to Berkeley: to turn the glib self-absorption into depth and identifiability. The *Times'* Brantley said, "She has the gift, possessed by only the smartest and most charming of narcissists, of making you think that it's somehow all about you when of course it's all about her."

Carrie lived in a hotel in San Francisco and then a house in Claremont and, after that, a house in the Berkeley Hills. (She told a friend, "I would have moved to Berkeley in a heartbeat! Hollywood is no place to raise a child!") "The result" of their collaboration, which included two years of tinkering, Tony says, is "she ended up being so authentic. When you were in an audience, you were *with* her. She said to me, 'When I'm on, there's nobody better,' and it was true. She could be not just phenomenally entertaining but, with that rapier wit, fantastically smart."

Through the performance "she became a symbol," Taccone says, "for a lot of people suffering from bipolar disorder and so much else. She wasn't afraid to say, 'This is me! All of us: Wake up!'"

That *Wishful Drinking* was a record-breaking hit at the Berkeley Rep was quite an achievement, considering the tumult during its creation. "You really didn't 'direct' Carrie Fisher," Tony says. "You were a witness to what was happening. We put her in an environment that was smart and welcoming, so that lifted the performance." But "she argued a lot with Tony," says a friend of Carrie's. "She'd come off the stage and ask [negatively], 'How do you think that scene went?'"

Most dangerously, Carrie's mania went into overdrive at the beginning of the run. Either she had gone off her medications, or whatever meds she was taking had sabotaged her, badly. Taccone says that while mania "may have been really entertaining to talk about onstage, it was *not* fun to be around. It was like a manic eat-up-the-world-and-eat-up-everybody-in-it. She was truly captivating and so wicked smart you thought this person was *gonna* take over the world. But when she was off her game, it was '*Oh my God!*' I actually fired myself—for one day. I was, 'I'm done with this! I don't need this in my life!' Then I calmed down and thought, 'Well, I've done all this work. Somebody else will take the credit if I quit, so why don't I suck it up?' So I ended up 'coming back'—I rehired myself.

"It was just too difficult at times to get her to actually do the real words. She was caught up in the drama of her life. During those periods, if you weren't in her entourage and willing to be like an acolyte to her, she wanted no part of you. I'm just too old to be somebody's acolyte, so that caused some friction between us."

At the beginning of the Berkeley run, Carrie was sometimes too revved up to eat; she only imbibed liquids. She would order chicken for dinner but simply sip the chicken broth, unable to cut and chew real food. When the theater staff realized what was going on, she was given liquid vitamin infusions for nutrition. Someone who worked as a theater employee on the production with her at the time recalls, "She seemed to be *all* mania—*no* depression." "When she would go into one of her manic episodes, it was pretty terrifying," Tony says. "She was just kind of on fire. Irrational. A bit crazed. I remember going to her hotel room, and she had written in lipstick all over the bathroom mirror. I'm thinking, 'Oh, great! A psychotic experience right here! How am I gonna protect myself?' But then the storm would pass." Taccone isn't effusive with compliments, so when he says this it carries weight: "Carrie was on her way to becoming a kind of current-day Mark Twain—one of the most significant storytellers we have in America."

George Lucas came to see the Berkeley performance, which pleased Carrie. ("George Lucas ruined my life" was one of her laugh lines, segueing into the metal bikini and the Leia sex toy.) Both of her parents came as well. "When her mother came, Carrie was nervous," Tony says. "She loved Debbie and had a very complicated relationship to her." As others had said, "Her mom was like her husband. And she didn't want to hurt her. But Carrie exposed her mom's past"—with Eddie and with Harry Karl—"so that was a delicate thing. But Debbie seemed impervious to it—'Yes, dear. Whatever.' It was easier when Eddie showed up. He was super old and frail" and had lived a life of decadence and disorder. He didn't seem to mind that Carrie said he dated all of Chinatown and had had so many face-lifts he looked as Asian as his recent girlfriends and wives.

Kerri Kolen flew up to Berkeley to see one of the shows Eddie attended. "It was so moving," Kerri says. "You could tell these two people deeply loved each other. She kept saying, 'My father is coming! Did I tell you? My father is coming!' Like a little kid. That's who she was. They had that amazing moment where she called him onstage at the end of the show. They sang a bar or two together." Eddie was in a wheelchair, singing "If I Loved You," "but he stood up. She started to get nervous, but she saw that it was so important to him to do so. He was so proud" to be standing onstage with her, "and *she* felt proud to give him that moment.

"She kept saying, 'Wasn't that amazing?' He came backstage. He chose his words carefully" to compliment his daughter. "He said, 'You breathe rare air.' Now we're all practically crying. She said, 'Rare air: that's a good line.'"

Yes, they'd had a bumpy, complex, highly unorthodox relationship, but, Kerri says, "I believe in my heart that she in *her* heart really did forgive him at the end." She began to see Eddie a lot in the Bay Area, which was now his home. "It was clear the shape that he was in. He did not have a lot of time. She became very sensitive about that. Toward the end"—in 2008, 2009, and going into 2010—"you could see it was the end for him. It was important for her that, however his life ended, she not have regrets. That she did not write him off. She started spending time with him. To see them together—they would touch each other. It was real."

"There hadn't been a note he couldn't hit, a girl he couldn't hit on, an audience he couldn't charm or bring to their feet cheering," Carrie would later write about her father. "He'd done everything . . . to excess." As, to a large extent, had she.

At some point toward the end of the Berkeley Rep run, "Carrie lost custody of her daughter when she started using drugs again" and the fact was revealed to Bryan, someone close to the theater says. "Bryan got custody of Billie." The loss of her daughter "*wrecked* her."

The custody loss—temporary though it would turn out to be—was an unsurpassable blow. "Billie! Oh my God, she was the center of Carrie's universe! I don't think she had the wherewithal to be the super mom she would have liked to be [at the time], but the connection was there—deeply, *deeply* there," says one confidante. Tony Taccone says, "Carrie's love of her daughter was her tether. She trusted her love for her daughter—she knew *that* was true—and that gave her her sense of well-being about herself." As Carrie herself put it, several years later, in *Shockaholic*, "For the first time in my life I really felt that I understood the word 'heartbroken.'" She wrote about the contrast of being onstage, making fun of her life to the great amusement and entertainment of others, and then coming offstage and thinking, "pretty much 24-7 . . . 'My daughter hates me . . . I just knew she hated me, because she had every right to hate me. *I* hated me." Putting her "feelings into words and praying they wouldn't be able to get out again" had "always been my salvation," she wrote. This time, although the Berkeley audiences loved the show, that salvation didn't work. "Carrie was *very* agitated about what [she imagined] Billie thought of her—*very, very* agitated," says a friend.

During the period of temporarily lost custody and afterward, Bryan Lourd's mother came to live with him to help care for Billie.

Carrie had said that writing with lipstick on her dressing room mirror was therapeutic. But when she wrote, "I'm not depressed, I'm defeated" multiple times, it seemed a clear call for help. Caring close friends sent Carrie "long descriptions—almost a booklet"—of electroconvulsive therapy (ECT), the once-maligned treatment formerly called shock treatment. The information detailed "who this works for, the benefits and side effects, and the potential negative side effects," recalls a friend.

It's also a fact that at the time—just about a decade ago—there were fewer effective treatments for bipolar depression and mania than there are now. But it is also true that, for some people, ECT is the best—and even the only—effective treatment.

Kitty Dukakis, the now-eighty-two-year-old wife of the onetime Democratic presidential candidate Michael Dukakis, had experienced extreme, unabated depression from the early 1980s. It intensified when her husband lost the election in 1988. She spent her days drinking and sleeping, and her husband often, heartbreakingly, found her at day's end comatose in a pool of her own vomit.

ECT changed all that. At first Kitty was as resistant to it as many others had been, thinking it a gruesome relic of a bygone age. But having hit bottom—as Carrie did—she reluctantly tried it in 2001. After her first treatment, she wrote in her 2006 book, *Shock: The Healing Power of Electroconvulsive Therapy*, "I felt alive." The weight of depression had lifted so sharply that she suggested to her husband, when he picked her up at the hospital, that they go out to dinner, a social pleasantry that her depression had long kept her from considering. Michael Dukakis was happily stunned, he said, because "I had left this wife of mine at the hospital a basket case just the night before."

From that day forward, Kitty and her husband had become evangelists for the treatment, and they led support groups for ECT patients and those considering the procedure. Michael Dukakis describes his wife's prior decade and a half of severe depression as "brutal." He says, "Given Kitty's experience, I can't support the notion that you try everything else before you try ECT." Kitty herself said, to an FDA panel in 2011, "It is not an exaggeration to say that I doubt very much that I would not be alive today without ECT. The treatment has been a miracle in my life . . . I feel so strongly about the importance of ECT as a treatment for severe depression and other mental and emotional illnesses that I have spoken to grand round meetings in hospitals in close to 30 states."

Finally, Carrie conceded to her friends' exhortations. She agreed to have ECT.

I t is fairly amazing that Carrie's high-pitched mania, her difficulties with Tony (who would be her enduring director during the entire run of the show, beyond Berkeley), her heartbreaking temporary loss of custody of Billie, and her juggling with the decision about ECT— an unsurmountable-seeming cluster of crises—did not keep the show from being a huge hit. Not only did it sell out every performance in Berkeley, but as it was beginning its multi-city hop, it garnered reviews that guaranteed a long and successful post–Berkeley Rep life. *Entertainment Weekly* called it "drolly hysterical." The *San Francisco Chronicle* said, "Fisher knows how to write wickedly comedic material and, better still, how to deliver it." *The Wall Street Journal* decreed, "Addiction, mental illness, movie-star parents, bad marriages, really bad hair . . . You got it: Princess Leia has recycled her nightmarish life yet again . . . [She's] drop-dead funny about a string of personal crises so horrific that the only alternative to laughing at them is slashing your wrists in sympathy."

Although she had initially declined to use the original, dark, and sad material she had written about her psychotic break and about Greg Stevens's death in her bed—material that Taccone thought was her strongest and most plaintive but that she judged too painful—she ended up making light jokes about the former, and after dealing with it in different ways, she decided to dare the audience to ask her questions about Greg's death. As Ben Brantley would later put it, with that provocative but clever approach "you don't think she's trivializing a tragedy. What she is doing, most cannily, is letting you see the Carrie Fisher Defense System in action." Eventually, she and Taccone worked out how to deal with the psychotic break: by giving the audience a "test" to see if they, too, were bipolar. Taccone took the storyteller and helped her turn the audience into those friends who, in her real life, sat on her bed with her.

Regional runs were scheduled: Santa Fe, San Jose, Seattle, Boston, Hartford, Washington, D.C., Houston, and, farther off, in 2010, a whole month in Australia. This was a lot of traveling and work for someone who was struggling, but Carrie undertook it. Her intimacy with her audience and her likability glistened. As she strode around the various stages and picked people from the audience to participate in bits with her, all the snappy candor she'd evinced until this moment was now shorn of hauteur. She was not a celebrity star but your menschy best friend. She would kiss her audience members. Ironically, one of her front-row fans at the Bushnell theater in Hartford, Connecticut, was a Yale-trained psychologist, Kathleen Cairns, who was using the new "collaborative care" method—now considered the gold standard of bipolar treatment by many authorities. It involved the patient, her doctors, and her family all working intensely together. "Carrie's show was fabulous," Cairns says. "She was so funny and engaging and very open about herself and her life. At the end there was a standing ovation, and she reached toward me and—for some magical, unknown reason—we held hands and I reached my head up and she kissed my cheek."

During the patches of time off in the summer, Carrie returned home to Coldwater Canyon, where Kerri Kolen would spend a week at a time with her, the two working to turn *Wishful* into a book. It would be published in December 2008. "The script of the one-woman show were the bones of the book," Kerri says.

The resulting book was brief and breezy and conversational, re-counting the stories she hit on onstage: her parents and their scandal; Greg's death; the crazy quilt of interlocking relatives; her weird, too-luxurious life with her stepfather Harry Karl; performing with her overly pretty mother; attending Central in London; *Star Wars*; Paul, drugs, Bryan, Billie.

But most significant was the Author's Note at the end:

One of the things that baffles me (and there are quite a few) is how there can be so much lingering stigma with regards to mental illness, specifically bipolar disorder. In my opinion, liv-ing with manic depression takes a tremendous amount of balls. Not unlike a tour of duty in Afghanistan (though the bombs and bullets, in this case, come from the inside). At times, being bipo-lar can be an all-consuming challenge, requiring a lot of stamina and even more courage, so if you're living with this illness and functioning at all, it's something to be proud of, not ashamed of. They should issue medals along with the steady stream of medications one has to ingest.

Carrie meant this. At the *Star Wars* conventions and autograph shows she had begun, in her forties, to routinely attend (collecting a fee, as is the practice), she changed her talking points. David Zentz, a nuclear plant operator and an enormous fan of the franchise, had met Carrie at many such shows. "Don't you have enough autographs from me?" she once asked, recognizing his face. "No," he answered, dead seriously. "Thirty-eight isn't enough."

Carrie was honest about doing what Harrison Ford (now a huge star as Indiana Jones) refused to do: appearing at these autograph shows and Comic-Cons. On the one hand, she disparaged her participation in these "celebrity lap dances." But she admitted that she was financially overextended (her house "was mortgaged to the skies, and not . . . friendly ones") and couldn't afford not to participate.

Shortly after the book version of *Wishful* was published, David Zentz attended a San Diego panel that she was on. Her talk was now morphing from Jedi-land (a theme she had been expected to probe) to her own demons, shared by others in the audience. "She talked about her substance abuse and depression issues," Zentz says. "There was a girl with a copy of *Wishful Drinking* who had depression and abuse problems, and Carrie talked to her for a long time. The event was supposed to be over by 7:00 or 8:00 p.m., but Carrie stayed until 11:00 to talk to them all."

Wishful's shortcomings as a book were noted in *The New York Times* by Charles McGrath. It's "pretty slight, padded out with big type, extra space between the lines . . . and it displays at times an almost antic need to entertain. The . . . jokes—the puns, the wisecracks, the deadpan one-liners—come rattling along at the rate of one every other sentence or two . . . Her book is sometimes like a smile so forced it must hurt."

But it didn't matter. Both its brevity and Carrie's hectic humor were things her fans loved. Beverly Hills! Debbie and Eddie and Liz! Movie magazine covers! "They couldn't get enough of it!" Kerri Kolen says.

Kerri was also impressed with Carrie's compassion and generosity, not merely to friends but also to so many fellow sufferers of addiction and pain: "When I was there [staying at Carrie's house], Brooke Mueller was there, Charlie Sheen's wife." Mueller lived with serious drug addiction, including repeated relapses, after she became a mother to twin boys. "Brooke was like, 'I'm at Carrie's house slash rehab,'" is how Kerri remembers Brooke describing it. "It was a sort of gentle rehab," says Kerri. "Which says a lot, positively, about Carrie." Yet this willingness to take in people with serious addictions also left Carrie open, and not everything *was* gentle, at all. For, whether or not Brooke Mueller was part of this, Carrie had, unwisely, formed a kind of partnership with the radical addiction therapist Warren Boyd, who had already worked with Carrie's friend and neighbor Courtney Love. Boyd had been a heroin addict and had pleaded guilty in 1991 to armed robbery. But that was almost twenty years in the past. For a number of years, he had been taking on the hardest Hollywood cases—not just Courtney, whom he accompanied to court when she faced a misdemeanor drug charge, but also Robert Downey Jr. And, for alcohol, Mel Gibson, from whom Boyd is said to have received referrals to other celebrities. Boyd was with a deeply drugged Whitney Houston, trying hard to help her, shortly before she drowned in her bathtub, before the February 2012 Academy Awards. Boyd's life was fictionalized in a TV series that he co-produced, called *The Cleaner*, starring Benjamin Bratt. But were his methods ethical and safe? That was a very open question.

Sometimes Boyd's patients were people whom Carrie did not know, yet like Brooke Mueller they lived in Carrie's guesthouse. Boyd compensated Carrie for putting these strangers up: sometimes as much as $10,000 a week. Many people worried that Boyd was using Carrie's celebrity for his own purposes and that Carrie's generosity in having a house open to fellow addicts (and her interest in helping them) left her vulnerable to exploitation.

Meanwhile, after the launch of the book version of *Wishful*, Carrie and Tony Taccone took the play to Seattle, then to Boston. Seattle is where Todd Haimes flew to see the show and to meet Carrie in April 2009. Haimes was the artistic director of New York's Roundabout Theatre Company. By now the show had been perfected by Carrie and Tony, and the rave reviews had continued through its regional runs.

Still, Haimes was initially hesitant to bring the show to the Roundabout, which had just been officially renamed from Studio 54 but was often still referred to by its previous classic name. "I can't exactly remember what it was that made me schlep up to Seattle to see a one-woman show by Carrie Fisher," he says. "I mean, it wasn't like a one-woman show by *Meryl Streep*"; Carrie wasn't *that* big a deal, he'd been thinking. "But when I saw the show, I was totally taken by it.

It was hilarious, and it's so rare to see somebody bare their soul on the stage, especially when their soul is so interesting."

Love the show as he did, Haimes was a bit frightened of Carrie. Her notoriety had preceded her. "I was a little scared about the fact that she might be—well, a little *nuts*," says Haimes. "I remember going backstage in Seattle and being polite, and she threw glitter all over me." This was Carrie's "glitter bombing" period. It might have been her way of saying, "Let's be a little crazy, despite the anguish I am talking about." "Every time I hugged her, I came away with glitter," Haimes says. At first this seemed suspiciously eccentric. "But," in time, "I thought she was unbelievably professional and engaging: eccentric in a *kind* way."

Three months after Haimes's meeting with Carrie in Seattle— at around the time the show was opening in San Jose, in late July 2009—Carrie had the first of her ECT sessions. The session began with anesthesia, then the careful attachment of wires to the sides of her skull for the small spurt of electric currents that would pass through her brain, intentionally triggering a short seizure. She started with an intense regimen—three times a week for three weeks. Then it was decreased to once every six weeks. "Once she started, she almost began to crave it," says a friend. Later she would say she wished she had started it earlier. At around the same time—on July 25, 2009—her friend Michael Jackson died of a lethal dose of the anesthetic propofol, medically administered by his doctor, Conrad Murray, who was later convicted of involuntary manslaughter for that act. Carrie was close to Michael through her friend and dermatologist Dr. Arnie Klein (the supposed "real" father of Jackson's children), through their mutual dentist, Evan Chandler, and through Elizabeth Taylor. The death was as shocking as it might also have been predictable. Carrie later said, "I could swear that I could see things more clearly once he'd passed. Clearly and completely different, at least for a while."

With admirable fortitude, Carrie continued doing the play shortly after the first of the ECT treatments began, despite the pain of Jackson's death adding to the impact. (Over its run of several years in numerous cities, she would never miss or cancel a single performance.) "Indeed," Tony says, "at one point her favorite thing to do *was* ECT. I'm directing her in a show, and the only known symptom is short-term memory loss. Memory loss while memorizing your lines? It was terrifying for me. But you had to take the good with the bad when you worked with Carrie."

Haimes brought the show to the Roundabout in October 2009, with Tony still directing. Carrie strolled around a homey stage, with its big couch, narrating the celebrity genealogical board that connected all her disparate relatives, with drolly authoritative aplomb and an instructional pointer. The female-skewed audiences loved it; this was Carrie's part-time home: New York! So did the critics. That they might have already known these stories—how many times could you tell Debbie-and-Eddie-and-Liz?—*helped*, not hurt, the cause. She was a favorite neighbor, repeating her best anecdotes because you'd begged her to, and if you hadn't begged her to: well, you liked them anyway. The now very heavyset Princess Leia, making fun of her vivid but catastrophic decades, let every woman in the audience off the hook for worrying like hell, in their bedroom mirrors, about going to their thirtieth high school reunion overweight and with a messier life than their classmates. In fact, they could have kissed Carrie for opening that door for them to this relief through, as Ben Brantley put it, her "extremely funny, subliminally sad full-frontal confession."

Many of Carrie's old friends attended, including the still somewhat love-struck Guy Strobel, who left sunflowers and a note in her dressing room. (She never responded to his request that she get in touch with him, alas.) Good friends—like Salman Rushdie—reveled in how, as he puts it, "she turned stories that we'd heard while sitting around drinking Coke into a show that kept a thousand people riveted for a couple of hours. You could see what 'star power' was." When Rushdie brought his teenage son, Milan, to the show, Carrie plucked him from the audience (with his father's consent) to give him the Princess Leia sex doll. Ron Raines, who had toured with Debbie in *The Unsinkable Molly Brown*, saw it and loved it and called Debbie to say so. "Debbie cried"—Carrie so often made her cry. Debbie had seen the show in Berkeley, of course, "but she didn't want to see it here, because she didn't want to steal Carrie's thunder," Ron says. Between mothers and daughters, certain sensitivities were eternal.

Marsha Mason came to see the play and noticed, as many had, the toll the years had taken since their time in *Drop Dead Fred*. "She was heavy"—Marsha wasn't judging, just surprised. "Whatever medication she was on, it seemed important. She said she was having a wonderful time with the play, even though some of it was terrifying. I wouldn't want anybody to have to struggle as hard as she had to."

Robin Williams came backstage one night, and, says a theater person who was there, "he was talking about how beautiful and wonderful it was that she was able to be so open and honest." Carrie knew Robin's private turmoil—"and she, in a roundabout way, kind of asked him, 'But isn't this *your* life, too?'" Of course it was. Williams was afflicted by much depression and emotional pain. But "he kind of shook his head and said no. He was so in denial about it, poor guy." Carrie remembered their meeting after the play this way: "He . . . looked lost, kind of, and he said that he didn't think he was bipolar. He took the [bipolar] test that I gave the audience"—as part of her performance—"and [he] got all the answers right, but didn't think [being bipolar] was something that had anything to do with him. I never heard anything so off the mark."

One of the most gratifying compliments came from someone she'd long thought disliked her. Two and a half decades after he directed her in *Hannah and Her Sisters*, Woody Allen saw her show at the Roundabout. Says a friend of Carrie's, "The next day he sent her a hand-delivered letter gushing about how wonderful the show was. When she read it, she burst into tears. She didn't have a good experience in *Hannah*. She felt she couldn't do anything right for him. To finally get that kind of affirmation meant so much. Woody's note fixed a hole from the past."

That Carrie handled the fifteen-week-long Broadway run while enduring ECT treatment was a testament to her dedication. "She would have the sessions on Monday, the show's off day, and on Tuesday she would come in and was a little concerned about her memory," Todd Haimes says, "but it was somehow always okay. I expected a mess, but the mess that she may have been internally"—no one denies this—"*didn't* manifest itself in her personal behavior." Even when she almost missed a show, on one Wednesday—a matinee *and* evening show day, and she made the mistake of going home between the two shows—she was frantically intent on getting back to the theater on time. Unable to find a taxi, she hailed a pedicab, and in that bicyclist-drawn, open-air, wheel-anchored bench she bumped along. There, for everyone to see, was Carrie Fisher, bouncing down the street!

She got to the theater at zero hour and made it onto the stage, and her pedicab rush was much appreciated by Haimes. "I've worked with a lot of talented but difficult people, but she wasn't difficult, which surprised me," says Haimes. "She was kind and incredible and I loved her." Her performance earned her a Drama Desk nomination for Outstanding Solo Performance.

Fenton Bailey and Randy Barbato were two gay filmmakers whose World of Wonder Productions had produced *Inside Deep Throat*, *RuPaul's Drag Race*, and other naughty treats. HBO's Sheila Nevins, an adorer of Carrie, had approached them to make *Wishful* into an HBO special. The men had met Carrie years before, when they were producing a documentary on Edith Head, who had once owned Carrie's current house. "We wrote Carrie, asking if we could come and photograph the house," Fenton says, "and she said, 'Sure.' She was very welcoming and generous. We stayed in touch ever since."

In taking the stage play of *Wishful* and turning it into an HBO special—spiced up by archival footage and interviews with family and friends with its opening and closing frames set to Carrie's favorite song,

the Depression-era classic "Happy Days Are Here Again"—Fenton and
Randy spent a lot of time at Carrie's house. Though it would not air on
HBO until December 2010, they began their visits in the summer. They
saw the mass of guests, as everyone had, especially recently. "People of
renown were there," says Fenton. "She was incredibly generous and maternal to people who experienced the kind of pitfalls she had, whether
addiction or mental health. Her home was like a celebrity halfway house.
She reached out her hand to everyone through that house."

One young woman living in Carrie's guesthouse briefly during that
time, in June 2010, was a patient of Warren Boyd's: an extremely
pretty and extremely troubled would-be actress named Amy Breliant. Like Carrie, the large-eyed, twenty-one-year-old brunette was the
daughter of a wealthy Beverly Hills couple and an alumna of Beverly
High. She had become severely vulnerable in her teens, and she had
fought her blazing addiction—to cocaine, heroin, and speed—for years.
Her parents had enrolled her in rehab programs, and they referred
her to specialists during her entire adolescence. Amy also did good
works—volunteering at a Romanian orphanage, among other things.
She was now under the "interventionist" Warren Boyd's treatment, and
Carrie was compensated by Boyd for boarding Amy in her guesthouse.
Over less than a year, Boyd would eventually be paid $222,000 by
Amy's desperate mother, Gianna Breliant, for a range of services—or
so-called services—that included not just housing and sober companionship but also a writing coach, an acting coach, and a fitness instructor.

Carrie wanted to help Amy. According to what was seen and at-
tested to (in a legal deposition) by a woman named Jade Charnick, who
was the Boyd-hired daily "sober companion" for Amy (at $300 a day),
Carrie would sometimes come to the guesthouse where Amy was staying. Just as Joan Hackett had done for her years earlier, Carrie would
encourage Amy to write in her journal. Sometimes she invited Amy
into the main house, and they watched TV together; Carrie did that

with everyone. She seemed to feel that Amy was smart and beautiful and tragic and had the potential to turn her struggle into an in-
spiring story. She told Amy she'd help her get a book published. One
wrinkle in the scenario was that Carrie's assistant at the time, Garret
Edington, was bringing marijuana to Amy, with Boyd's permission. As
a radical interventionist, Boyd had his own rules; for many desperate
clients, they had amounted to success, and he was touted for them.
For more by-the-book addiction specialists, they were just plain wrong.
Marijuana was not legal in California in 2010, but Boyd prescribed it
for Amy to lessen her more serious addictions.

Carrie got along famously with Fenton and Randy, and they cooked up
a project together they all planned to do after *Wishful* on HBO: a
history of madness. Fenton says, "It came from her idea. She said, 'Follow me to one of my ETC sessions.' She was incredibly knowledgeable
about mental illness, so we were going to do a world-class documentary
about lunatic asylums and all these strange, barbaric historical treatments. She was very keen to do it."

Randy and Fenton knew that Carrie felt very heavy when she was
doing *Wishful* at the Roundabout, "but she was surrounded by a posse
of gay men so it didn't matter so much," they surmised. Still, being
heavy bothered her more than they knew. Richard Dreyfuss had also
gained weight on medication, and he and Carrie talked about this a
lot. "Weight gain was more painful to talk about than bipolarity itself," Richard says. Almost all the "mainstay treatments" for bipolar
disorder cause weight gain, which "is a tragedy," Dr. James Phelps says.
Another irony of timing: "One medication, lamotrigine, is one of the
few that doesn't cause weight gain. But it came along relatively late in
Carrie's time"—it wasn't approved by the FDA until 2003—"and isn't
anti-manic enough to have been a monotherapy [single treatment] for
her, most likely."

"I'll lose it! I'll lose [the weight]!" Carrie would vow to Richard, as if making the promise to her fellow bipolar and dear friend would ensure that the hard work would get done.

At the tail end of 2010, Carrie took a step to solve her weight problem: she signed on as a Jenny Craig paid spokesperson and made a goal of losing fifty pounds. It was good, she said, to have her Jenny Craig spokesman to "whine to . . . because I'm a big, childish, fifty-four-year-old cheat [at eating]." Her joking put-down of herself hid the earnest discomfort she'd expressed to Richard and the pain that would make her, as Salman Rushdie says, "almost agoraphobic" toward the end of her life. The project resulted in a—temporary—loss of thirty pounds in eighteen weeks, with the next twenty pounds' loss much more "daunting."

Just before Carrie embarked on the diet project, she had a profoundly emotional encounter. In early September 2010, Eddie Fisher was at death's door. Carrie knew it. She broke from all else she was doing to ask Randy and Fenton to fly with her up to Berkeley, where Eddie still lived in a house that Carrie might well have been paying for. She *had* to say goodbye to him in person. Fenton and Randy said yes, of course. "There was a sense," Randy says, "that she needed to get to him fast," so they immediately flew her up to San Francisco with their crew. "Carrie was very vulnerable that weekend," Randy says. "There was something different to her. She always traveled with so many books. But this time she was too nervous to read."

Eddie was a severely broken man, fairly hideous looking, the result of two strokes, the beginning of dementia, and decades of dissolute living. He'd been wheelchair-bound for years.

Fenton, Randy, their camera crew, and Carrie drove to Berkeley to see Eddie. "She sat on his bed and fed him marijuana and ice cream. She became, before our eyes, a little girl looking for her father," says Fenton. Yes, the cameras were rolling, so there was *some* affectation— these were show-business folks! But not much; through the sheer awful shape he was in, reality won: he was dying.

"Was I always funny?" Carrie asked Eddie, tenderly and worriedly.

Then she half answered her own question: "You know what? I used to be funny *for you.* I thought if I was really funny, you would want to be around me all the time." Her personality, she was as much as saying, came from her desperate need for him to love her. "I wanted to be your best girl. And that's tough competition."

"I'm *crazy* about you," Eddie answered, dreamily. Then, answering the implicit question, he said, "I *love* you."

"See," she said. "It finally paid off." In that moment, at least, she imagined that all her years of wit had been acquired for him and him alone.

"It was a magical moment," Randy says of the father-daughter scene. "For all the issues she had had with him over the years, she was still a little girl and he was still her dad. And she had won his love. You could see her feeling it.

"When the crew turned the cameras off, we left very, very quietly. We knew what we had seen."

Eddie died soon after on September 22, 2010. One day before his death, another death occurred without Carrie knowing it. Amy Breliant, the young actress who, three months earlier, had lived for a brief while in the guesthouse on Carrie's property, was found dead of a heroin overdose in a house she was sharing with a friend in Studio City. This was another "sober house" that the radical interventionist Warren Boyd had arranged.

The unconventionality and, some would say, apparent dereliction in Boyd's expensive supervisory treatment of Amy for seven months (at one point, Amy—obsessed with Boyd—called him "Dad") were targets for Amy's understandably heartbroken and angry mother, Gianna Breliant. The allegation that Carrie had received $10,000 a week from Boyd to house Amy, during that brief time three months earlier, was also concerning to Gianna.

A month after her father's death, Carrie took *Wishful* on a long, winding tour of Australia, from mid-October to mid-November. They loved her in Sydney in mid-October; in Melbourne, in Canberra, in Adelaide, and in Perth. ("Her acid tongue, cynicism and frankness made for a hilarious night packed with dark comedy," one reviewer wrote.)

Shortly before she embarked on the tour, she gave a deeply thoughtful interview to *WebMD*, admitting she was an "overweight oversharer" who didn't like watching herself in snippets of the upcoming HBO presentation of *Wishful* because of her heft. And she did seem to notice that since she "came out" as bipolar, "now it seems that every show I watch, there's *someone* bipolar in it." She spoke of her symptoms, "mostly mania," as the worried staff at the Berkeley Rep had noticed, but also something called "*agitated* depression: I could get really impatient; I was going much faster than everything else around me, and it drove me crazy. You feel out of step with the world." The ECT, she said, had helped this. She was still encountering a social "stigma" against ECT, "but it's getting better." (Some of the destigmatization had to do with her talking frankly about it.) She said, philosophically, that she'd "gotten to an age"—fifty-four—"where I enjoy my life. I've spent enough time struggling with it, and at this point it's living on one side of the magnifying glass. I stay on the side of making big things appear small." And she spoke of the healing done to her by the love received from—and given to—Billie. Now that her painful custody loss was over and she shared parenting with Bryan, she was striving for, and achieving, some equanimity. She was also at peace with Debbie's mothering now, and in a different kind of peace with her relationship with her late father.

"My mother, she loved us and demonstrated that. Whereas my father may have loved us, but he didn't demonstrate it. What I've learned over a lifetime is that love is an *action*. So I grew up feeling loved on one side and not on the other, which did not make me the most confident of people. Billie has been shown love on both sides and it's an amazing difference."

Even through difficult times, it was clear to all that Billie loved her mother, whom she called Momby. (Billie called Debbie Abadaba.) As Tony Taccone recalls, when Billie would come to visit Carrie, it "was like literally the roof blew off the house and the heavens opened up and the light shone down."

With *Wishful Drinking* for two and a half years, Carrie had been papering the world with her High Irony Essence. But underneath, a different Carrie was coming into consciousness. Now that the one-woman show's run had tapered down considerably, Carrie and Kerri Kolen produced a new memoir, *Shockaholic*. The book was ostensibly occasioned by the fact that because her ECT was causing memory loss, Carrie had best write it all down before she forgot it. But though it started with mockery of her self-absorption ("No wonder she's mentally ill. She's got herself on her mind ten, fifteen, twenty hours a day . . . And the thing is, *Who's asking?*"), it largely showed a less flippant Carrie—a sensible, realistic, and *judgmental* woman. Some of her insights, in fact, contained precisely the kind of common sense that her worried friends had privately wanted to use *on her*. And they contained the dignified judgment that privately made her such a valued friend.

The arduousness of writing a book on ECT might have contributed to its gravity. Carrie's treatments left her depleted. "It was hard to get anything out of her from an energy or fun standpoint [when she would return from the treatments]," says Kerri Kolen. "After the therapy Carrie would go dark for some time; I would never talk to her. And there was very little interaction with the other people who would come to the house. I think it made her feel better in certain ways"—less manic—"but she also hated it. It really made her feel a little empty. It's unsettling to lose your memory." Carrie would relay this unhappiness to an old close friend from her New York partying years. "You're lucky I remember who you are," she said about the ECT that she would soon stop. When the friend asked how she was, Carrie said, "I'm on, I'm off."

This was a weary Carrie, far different from the tiny, sexy, game girl who blew thousands of dollars on psychedelic luxury at spas.

"The thing with that illness"—bipolar disorder—"is *it's very hard*," says Kerri. Starting and stopping and restarting her medication, Carrie "vacillated, in an exaggerated fashion, from being despondent or melancholy about something—to thinking it was hilarious. That's very much on the page. She could go from sentimental and weepy to snapping out of it. She would make a joke: 'Of course I'm a person of extremes—I'm bipolar.'"

In writing *Shockaholic*, "It was intimate—we would lay in her bed side by side," Kerri says. "She would turn her eyes up and talk. When she had something really emotional to say, she couldn't look me directly in the eye."

What she talked to Kerri about, and what went into the book, showed a different side of Carrie from the quipper. This was Carrie the sensible confidante her friends valued.

She passed judgment on our culture's weight obsession, especially for women. She decried the self-starving culture that leaves "a breed of women in Hollywood . . . looking very tense and very mad. Who wouldn't be enraged about having to ensure you're looking an age you haven't been in a generation?"

Of her friend Michael Jackson's death, she not only expressed predictable outrage that Dr. Conrad Murray "swapped his reputation in exchange for shekels and the ability to say, 'I'm Michael Jackson's doctor'" but was honest enough to say that privileged Michael "died because he could get people . . . to give him something he had no business having," she said. "No one but a ridiculously wealthy celebrity could have persuaded a doctor to go against his principles, to risk losing his license." No small number of people who had fretted that Carrie had obtained drugs that led to her seizures and overdoses could read these lines and not see a kind of rebuke of her *own* behavior.

When she spoke of things Michael, her mind traveled back to 1993 when her own dentist, Dr. Evan Chandler, had sued Jackson for

$22 million for allegedly molesting Chandler's son Jordan. Carrie was profoundly disgusted that Chandler had bragged about his son's attractiveness to Jackson (her "skin [was] crawling") and then had turned around and used his own son as big-cash bait. Carrie thought Jackson innocent and Chandler repugnant—for encouraging the overnights and now publicly exploiting his son as a "victim." (The Chandlers eventually received $15 million from Jackson's estate. In 2009, Evan Chandler killed himself.) Carrie's own father had made inappropriate comments to her and did drugs with her. Gavin de Becker—whose own childhood had been full of adults doing very bad things—had said that Carrie's compromised life, past and present, had given him, in his work with endangered people, the gift of real-time experience. Now Carrie was giving her readers that gift: becoming a moral arbiter not despite but *with the benefit of* her own rare understanding of imperfect behavior.

Her most surprising umbrage was reserved for Ted Kennedy. For years, she had told the story of her 1985 date with Chris Dodd and made jokes about Kennedy asking her if she thought the evening would end in her having sex with Dodd. Now she said that Kennedy's question itself was "completely not okay" and added smarmy details of what he had said, with the others at the table hearing it all. "Why ask someone a shocking, taunting question like that unless it was your intent to make that someone look and feel like a fool?" a serious Carrie asked the reader.

In *Shockaholic*, she also spoke of her father's death, saying that her absence when he actually drew his very last breath had turned that moment into "just another missed opportunity with Eddie" to "gaze at him with tender, anxious eyes" before his own eyes closed forever. "I've helped people die," she wrote, adding, so characteristically, "Not that they couldn't do it without me." Then, earnest again: "[But] there's something in that final, fatal situation that I understand completely . . . And I find relief in the . . . acceptance of the unspoken urgency in this arrangement."

Shockaholic was released on November 1, 2011, and its reviews were positive, as her books' reviews tended to be. Many reviewers kept to the same kind of praise as for many of her prior books, calling it "witty, ramshackle and outrageous" (*The Washington Post*), "wicked, relentless, and playful" (*San Francisco Chronicle*), and "hilarious" (*Marie Claire*). The Cleveland *Plain Dealer* likened her to S. J. Perelman and (particularly meaningful to her) Woody Allen. It was the Louisville *Courier-Journal* that picked up the book's gravity, its "pathos."

Carrie of course did book signings for *Shockaholic* and for *Wishful Drinking*, sometimes together, while continuing her occasional performances of *Wishful*. Working this relentlessly was "so *good* for her," she told a confidante. "It made her unable to fall into her bad habits."

During one of her book tour visits, in September 2012, she gave an interview to Houston's PBS host Ernie Manouse. It was typical of how relaxed and approachable she seemed now. She talked about how her script-doctor work, which she'd recently suspended, had been purely "in the service of the director," and she kidded about how she'd wandered into it for free at first—"Steven [Spielberg] didn't pay me; he just let me use his car." She mused about how "extremely insecure" she had been at nineteen—about her looks, her lack of a high school diploma, *everything*. About selling her likeness to *Star Wars*, she quipped, "I own my shoulders but the rest is George Lucas's." She made it clear that Eddie leaving her mother was so long ago it didn't affect her anymore: the memoirist being honest about the effect of the passage of time on even those memories that were most pivotal and painful—not to mention good copy. She asserted a bond with her audience and displayed self-acceptance. In our fifties, "we're more alike than not." If you can make peace with your age, then aging, for a woman, "has less power over you," she said. Years later her friend Sharon Horgan would say, "Carrie was so real, it was dangerous." Here was a Carrie so real it was *comforting*.

In a way, her equanimity was surprising. Eight months earlier, she had received news that had left her shattered. During a week of performances of *Wishful Drinking* in Baltimore's Hippodrome in late

January 2012, on the theater's dark night, she appeared as the guest of honor at a benefit at the Towson, Maryland, library. Her long hair sleeked back and neatly gathered into a spreading ponytail, she stood in a dark coat at a lectern and, with her glasses on, read from *Shockaholic*. Afterward, she signed autographs for about a hundred fans. Some had brought their own copies of her books to sign. One person—a *seeming* fan—had come armed with two items: a book to proffer and tucked alongside it, in such a way that none of the other patrons could see, a legal summons. Carrie was being informed—in what was technically known as a minute order—that she was being named a co-defendant in "dependent adult abuse" and as a provider of "unfair business practices" in a developing wrongful-death civil lawsuit that was being filed by Gianna Breliant against Warren Boyd and others. Boyd, the suit alleged, was far more unconventional than most "interventionists."

Four years of telling her story hundreds of times onstage; bearing the pain of temporarily losing Billie; destigmatizing mental illness; completing ECT; and now a legal accusation of being an accessory to a drug death.

Carrie kept signing autographs and books after receiving the summons. There was a room adjacent to where she was signing. As soon as the event was over, she collapsed. One person saw her "rocking back and forth, almost sucking her thumb, almost curling up. Just about as anguished and vulnerable as I have ever seen anyone, ever."

ELEVEN

WORKING THROUGH ANYTHING

ike her mother, Carrie could work through anything. Her friend Tracey Ullman had also made that observation about her. But this legal summons was not just "anything"; this was a world rocker for Carrie. Still, as 2012 advanced, she concentrated on moving forward. She continued to play the voice of Angela on *Family Guy*, now bringing her new baby French bulldog, Gary, to the studio. Carrie had bought him in New York at, as she put it, "a very tragic pet store in the West Village." "Everything was wrong with Gary," she told NPR's Terry Gross affectionately. "His tongue got longer and longer and never [could stay in] his mouth. He follows me everywhere." Because he came to be designated as a comfort dog, she *could* bring him everywhere—to restaurants, onto airplanes—to calm her. And she did. Carrie Fisher and Gary Fisher would be a unit now; he had his own Twitter account. They seemed like twins, lovingly sharing imperfections, joined by their neediness.

The *Family Guy* showrunner Steve Callaghan remembers that "one of our casting directors would feed pieces of beef jerky to Gary. And one of the sweetest things was that Gary would move over to the door and sit outside the glassed-in record booth and watch Carrie record. He was such a dear little companion."

"He would sit like Winston Churchill," Carrie noted.

Before the end of the year, word trickled in that the minute order that Carrie had received in Towson, Maryland, was moving to a next step. On August 23, 2012, attorneys for Gianna Breliant filed an official complaint against Warren Boyd and, among others, Carrie. It would be formally presented to Los Angeles Superior Court on May 7, 2013. Breliant's attorneys, Balisok & Associates, were, in one part of the suit, suing three psychiatrists; in another part, suing one intervention specialist, Boyd, as well as Boyd's company and associates, and "Carrie Fisher, an individual residing in Los Angeles County." The complaint described Amy Breliant as a "dependent adult under the provisions of Welfare & Institutions Code §15610.23," dependent because of her "drug addiction, which restricted her ability to carry out normal activities or to protect herself or her rights. She was at various times throughout the transaction on which this action is based an in-patient in a 24-hour health facility which was required by law to be licensed [this former involved the care of the doctors] and [then] in the care of Boyd, [his associates] Commerce, Schmidt, Fisher and Does 1–30 who acted as care custodians for Amy." Carrie was *not* a care custodian for Amy, but she had been paid by Boyd for the use of her guesthouse; this was the justification for her inclusion in the lawsuit.

Among the claimed "breaches" of the agreement with the original doctors was that they had "failed to provide Amy with appropriate therapy." For Boyd and the others, the charge was that they had assigned Amy to live "in one locale after another with untrained 'sober companions' and without adequate supervision" and that in those locales Amy "was provided with drugs including marijuana and heroin or morphine by Boyd and his agents, and isolated from her parents and family."

It is extremely doubtful that Carrie knew anything near the degree of the unconventionality of the man who had paid her to house his recovering patients in her guesthouse, but several things would prove troublesome. First, it was reported that Carrie's assistant Garret Edington had, by way of Carrie's concerned maid, found a heroin kit, complete with syringes, in Amy's room. A concerned Edington had gone to Boyd, expecting Boyd to confiscate it. Instead, Boyd told a startled Edington to "hide" it "for now."

In the "third amended complaint," Carrie's name, preceded by "Defendant," is the first name on the list. The complaint alleged seven illegal actions: breach of oral and implied contract; fraud (misrepresentation); fraud (concealment); constructive fraud; dependent adult abuse; unfair business practices; and, key here, wrongful death. It was a civil, not a criminal, complaint, to be sure; no one was liable to prison time. Furthermore, only Boyd, not Carrie, was actually charged with wrongful death. But the mere association was frightening. And in it was an allegation that Carrie almost certainly knew nothing about. It asserted that "during the last week of June, 2010, Boyd allowed one Keith Salmon, who was then receiving assistance for alcohol dependence from Boyd, to reside with Amy in the Fisher guesthouse. On information and belief, Mr. Salmon offered to obtain drugs for Amy in return for sex and Amy complied in order [to] obtain drugs which were furnished by Mr. Salmon and other unsupervised clients and caregivers including sober companions hired by Boyd."

Sex for drugs in Carrie's guesthouse? Allegedly authorized by an interventionist whom Carrie presumably trusted? And, according to the charges, with whom she had been in a paid business arrangement?! Sex for drugs is precisely the kind of thing that Carrie would have been adamantly against—and broken off her business relationship with Boyd—had she known about it. Carrie, after all, had threatened a man who had sexually harassed her friend Heather Ross. And she had felt insulted by Ted Kennedy for humiliating her with vulgar, nosy questions. Sexual abuse and manipulation were things Carrie counseled her female friends to resist, several people who knew her say.

On top of these worries came another scare: according to a friend of Carrie's, Debbie suffered a strong adverse reaction to a prescription medication she was taking and had to be hospitalized at Cedars. The bookings of the indefatigable performer (now eighty-one) were canceled for three months, this after she'd already logged forty-two weekends of performances across the country.

On February 26, 2013—three months before the complaint was officially filed in Los Angeles Superior Court, and while Debbie's health was still rocky—Carrie appeared as a "surprise" celebrity guest on a gay-and-lesbian-focused Holland America Caribbean cruise. She later said that two nights before she boarded the ship, she'd had a nightmare about accepting the engagement; she woke up feeling that something was off.

On the boat, Carrie performed in a non-stage area in front of a couch on which two men were seated. A video of the incident shows her beginning to sing the lovely classic "Skylark." Her sonorous rendition of some of the lyric snippets—"to a blossom-covered lane . . . Sad as a gypsy serenading the moon"—is performed casually, as if she were extemporizing for friends. She is wearing a colorful blue print top over black tights; she seems to have gained back some of the weight she'd lost through Jenny Craig. Gary is with her. She is slurring and forgetting words. As she sings, she squats down with napkins in her hand to clean up after Gary, who has urinated and defecated on the rug.

Confused and seeming disoriented, she asks the two guys on the couch what to sing next. "This is your world. We're all extras," one of them says very genially—the implication being "You're Carrie; we love you in all your idiosyncrasy." She proceeds to sing "Bridge over Troubled Water" but stumbles over it.

It was a chaotic performance, and a sad one. This was the first of Carrie's breakdowns (she herself termed it that) to have occurred in the high-social-media age, and the media ran with it. It was widely

reported as "bizarre" and "strange" and as a function of her bipolar disorder. Which it was. Carrie was taken off the ship in Fort Lauderdale
the next day for hospitalization.

There was an edge of cruelty to the viral rush to show the unattractive video. Carrie immediately acknowledged she was worse off
than she even looked. "I was in a very severe manic state, which bordered on psychosis. Clearly delusional. I wasn't clear what was going
on," she told *People*. She was on Seroquel, which is helpful to many
people with bipolar disorder. Yet it had backfired on her. As she had
during her mania in Berkeley, when she'd scribbled on mirrors, "I was
writing on everything. I was writing in books, I would have written on
walls. I literally would bend over and be writing on the ground, and
someone would try to talk to me and I would be unable to respond."

She had attended the ship's AA meetings, but they weren't
enough. "I went completely off the rails," she said. After deboarding
in Fort Lauderdale, she flew to L.A. and checked herself in to UCLA's
Resnick Neuropsychiatric Hospital and then into a residential facility
for a month. "This is not a neat disease," she said of bipolar disorder. As
Carrie had put it on the *Today* show in 2008, "When you're living with
manic depression, it's a war story." The episode on the cruise ship was
one of many unavoidable periodic battles.

Despite her illness, Debbie rushed to her daughter's side. Then,
while Carrie was in inpatient psychiatric care, Debbie rallied. Aside
from her endless nightclub shows, she was looking for one more good
film role—like *Mother*—and she was determined to get it, even though
her doctors, nurses, and minders told her to take it easy. She met with
Steven Soderbergh to play Liberace's mother in his forthcoming HBO
movie, *Behind the Candelabra*, starring Michael Douglas, in what
would be his much-praised role as the campy pianist, and Matt Damon
as Liberace's much younger chauffeur and lover. She was determined
to do the audition *right*. So she'd come to the Four Seasons Hotel to
meet Soderbergh in a "vintage" dowdy outfit, which Liberace's mother,
Frances, would have worn. She spoke in Frances's Polish-German accent.

She won the role. She mustered her health to perform in the film. The biopic aired in May 2013, with Debbie's performance praised.

The year 2014 was a busy one for Carrie. But it started out rocky. In February, the tabloid the *Daily Mail* followed her several times a week from her Coldwater house as she drove to an apartment in Hollywood. As invasive, if not unethical, as trailing a celebrity may be, the result of this trailing was worrisome. Often wearing a long, dark coat, Carrie looked very bedraggled. When she would arrive at the Hollywood apartment, one or another female resident walked down to her car and stayed there a very short time before returning to the apartment. Once in a while, Carrie made the trip up to the apartment herself. The inference was that she was purchasing drugs. In addition, "I saw her several times in the Rite Aid on Canon Drive," says the friend of hers from high school who became a psychologist. "She looked like she was really suffering."

Still, the year picked up after that. After working with a nutritionist and a trainer to trim down, she began shooting *Star Wars: The Force Awakens*, in May in Abu Dhabi. She would be compensated $1.5 million (Harrison Ford was said to have made $25 million) and reunited with Mark and Harrison, their first reunion since 1983. Now she was *General* Leia Organa, not Princess, the promotion long overdue. Her hair was worn in what *The New York Times'* Manohla Dargis called "a tasteful updo."

George Lucas had sold his Lucasfilm to Disney; he didn't need to keep working, and, he noted, the cruelty of the internet was a reason the work lost its pleasure. (Carrie would find this true as well. But she soon learned to fight back, becoming a proficient tweeter.) The new film would be directed by J. J. Abrams, then forty-eight, who had directed and won awards for many TV shows, including the riveting drama *Lost*. He had plunged into movies, most relevantly directing the last two *Star Trek* films. Lucas wanted Abrams to direct *The Force Awakens*.

A new generation of high-level *young* stars had to be added to stock up the movie; after all, Carrie, Mark, and Harrison were in their late fifties to late sixties. Abrams and the executive producer Kathleen Kennedy did not fail to gather a glittering group: unconventionally handsome Adam Driver (of Lena Dunham's *Girls*) as Kylo Ren, General Leia and Han Solo's son. His Kylo Ren—fitted out in glorious metal—would be the bad guy who, in the way that things go with this franchise, is destined not so much to be a *permanent* bad guy, meaning "bad, or evil, or a villain," as Driver put it. Rather, Kylo would be "more three-dimensional. He's more dangerous and unpredictable, and morally justified in doing what he thinks is right." The elegant Kenyan actress Lupita Nyong'o, who had won a Best Supporting Actress Oscar for *12 Years a Slave*, would be Maz, an alien pirate who has lived for a thousand years. Oscar Isaac, so appealing as the brooding Greenwich Village folkie in the award-nominated title role of the Coen brothers' *Inside Llewyn Davis*, was cast as the fighter Poe. The British newcomer Daisy Ridley would be an intrepid scavenger, Rey. John Boyega, a black English actor, would play the reformed storm trooper Finn. And Billie Lourd, with her mother's blessing, had a small role as Connix, a Resistance lieutenant.

Finn defects from Kylo Ren and crash-lands on the planet, meeting Rey; Rey's droid has a revelatory map. Finn and Rey join Han Solo to help the Resistance—Leia's Resistance—receive information to find Luke Skywalker. But Han Solo is killed in the process—by Kylo Ren, his son with Leia. (*Star Wars* was nothing if not rife with such head-spinning plot twists.) Luke and Han are the old souls amid the new blood, and Carrie's Leia seemed wearier. A confidante during this period says that throughout her time on the sets (the filming itself hopscotched from Abu Dhabi in May to Ireland in November, with Harrison's fracturing of a leg holding things up), she was preoccupied. The weight of Gianna Breliant's lawsuit hung over her, and the relapse she'd suffered, so publicly, on the cruise ship remained in her memory bank, as well as on the internet.

Yet in the movie she dazzled. Everyone wanted to see Leia again—as *General* Leia. The stills from the movie, taken by Annie Leibovitz for *Vanity Fair,* show, in Carrie's/Leia's face, a lovely gravity and dignity that her long life of generosity, humor, and difficulty had given her. "Bipolar can be a great teacher," she had said. Her visage and her performance proved that. She had fun with this movie, modeling gutsiness to Daisy Ridley and saying, to another character in a more Carrie-than-Leia fashion, "Not all the senators think I'm insane. Or—maybe they do." (The scene was deleted but popped up later on the internet.)

On August 11, 2014, Robin Williams hanged himself in his Northern California home. Like many, Carrie was shattered, though not entirely surprised. She remembered his denial of his strongly suspected bipolar disorder when they talked after her performance of *Wishful.* Now, speaking of what was wonderful about him, she seemed to be speaking of herself. "He made us all feel like he wished we could [feel]. He brought joy and surprise, and he would take you places you wouldn't even know you wanted to be . . . And that's what made him so generous," said this most intensely generous friend. Now she explicitly mentioned herself: "Like I did, he was driven by that frantic eagerness that you want to explode on [people's] night sky like a miracle. And he *did.*" She could tell, when she last saw him, that "he was struggling. But when you get there it's hard to talk. You are reaching from such a far away place. What do you say? You don't want to be a burden and you don't want to seem like you feel sorry for yourself. It's humiliating."

She painfully understood his dilemma. "Everything would end up on his grid. He'd walk in a room, and all the energy there would impact him . . . Anything would hurt him . . . It's fun to be brilliant, but who are your peers? Who was his peer? *It's incredibly lonely to be that.* And he didn't have a choice. And that's why you take drugs, so you can slow up and smell the roses just to know that they are there, and it's

not all you. Drugs for a lot of people kept them alive. Without them
they would've committed suicide. Not that I think that in any way
drugs are positive. But I can certainly understand what drove his need
for them, his appetite for them." Like Carrie herself, Robin Williams
was the "center of attention" in any room. "He was something you just
don't see, like a comet. I hope he's like a comet and he comes again, but
that would be selfish . . . I'm sorry he punctuated his sentence before it
had run its course. But he packed in five lifetimes before he left."

That passionate, original description—delivered with love to a
friend—was as close to a eulogy for herself as anything Carrie ever
said.

n October 2014, when she was in London during the *Force Awakens*
shoot, Carrie was asked to present the Icon Award at the gay pride Attitude Awards to the popular English talk show host Graham Norton.
Graham was one of her countless close friends.

Carrie's attendance at the event caused flashbulbs to pop. She arrived,
smiling, in a royal-blue coat; a tattoo visible on her ankle; Gary in tow;
her friend and sometime assistant the writer Abe Gurko behind her.
Once she got onstage, her introductory words about her friend Graham
were "rude and irreverent and funny—she managed to at once charm
and insult everyone present!" excitedly noticed one audience member.
This was the young Irish actress and screenwriter Sharon Horgan, who
had just had a wacky and profane sitcom about marriage green-lighted
for British TV. The show was called *Catastrophe*, and Sharon co-wrote
it and would co-star in it with the rising American comedy star Rob
Delaney. She played Sharon Morris, an Irish elementary school teacher,
and Rob played Rob Norris, an American advertising executive (and recovering alcoholic). The two meet at a London bar, and after six days
of voracious sex Sharon discovers she is pregnant. They try to make the
best of a shotgun wedding and a bumpy but sex-filled marriage. Sharon's

middle-class Irish accent, full of puzzled interrogatives, and Rob's dash of doofus confer on them a charming haplessness.

Rob and Sharon were sitting next to each other when they saw Carrie's introduction of Graham Norton, and they had the same epiphany. They had written an unfilled role for Rob's mother, Mia—a "dreadful" woman, as Sharon put it, but someone whom they needed to be dreadful in a distinctive and funny way. When they saw Carrie, "I turned to Rob," Sharon said, "and said, '*That's* Mia! That's your mother!'"

They asked Carrie through her agent; Carrie said yes. "It was a *writers'* show," said Carrie, of her reason for accepting the role. "I loved it! And I *wanted* to play an awful person instead of carrying guns for Harrison all the time!"

Catastrophe, which first aired in January 2015, would be a hit with British audiences, winning a raft of awards, and it also gained traction in America. It is woebegone reality: Rob gets fired via Skype when he relocates his business to London; Sharon has postpartum depression after the birth of their second baby; they talk in innocence, confusion, humor, and vulgarity, like real people. As Mia, Carrie is crotchety and snarky and kooky. She disapproved of her son marrying the teacher he hardly knew, and she made her feelings known. She's a shopaholic and an overstayer and humorously clueless. Sharon's father has dementia; Mia doesn't care.

It took a while for Carrie, Sharon, and Rob to "become pals," said Sharon. "We treated her like everyone else did: an icon, not a real human." And Carrie was oversubscribed and aware of the expectations she had set up. She had wanted to be compelling, and she had achieved that; she was "a magnet," as her former in-law Donavan Freberg put it, adding that sometimes "people who are magnets secretly want to be left alone because everyone wants a piece of them." Carrie knew this, felt this. "She was, she said, Mickey Mouse," Sharon said. "Everybody owned a piece, or felt they had the right to a piece," of her.

When Carrie finally accepted an invitation to Sharon's house, they sat with their dogs and "talked about everything." Carrie's talk was "entertaining and wise and scattershot and full of quips . . . with a dash of subliminal therapy. But . . . there was pain there, and responsibility, and her own demons.

"I asked her when she ever got to have a moment of normal. She pointed at me and then back at herself and said: 'Doing this.'"

*B*ehind the Candelabra had been a triumph, but Debbie's health was flagging, and she was sparring with her minder, Donald Light, re-calls a friend of the two women. He wanted her to take it easy; she dismissed that advice. She fought with him and with her nurses. In her early eighties, she was still waking up every morning as if for a show, and nothing was going to keep her from this.

At some point in late 2014 or early 2015, when Carrie was back in L.A., she was sitting on her bed at the Coldwater house with her close friend Charlie Wessler. Carrie said to Charlie, "Somebody should do a documentary about my mother and me because I don't know how long she'll live." The emotional second half of that statement was im-pactful, and friends of Carrie's knew that it was true; Debbie's 2012 hospitalization had worried Carrie deeply, just as Carrie's 2013 hos-pitalization had dismayed Debbie. Mother and daughter were now a round-robin of hard work and vulnerability, celebration and deep concern.

Charlie Wessler contacted his friends the filmmakers Fisher Ste-vens and Fisher's wife, Alexis Bloom. Alexis says that under no cir-cumstances were they going to do a "Debbie tribute" film; "it had to be real." The filmmakers and Carrie and Debbie and Todd all got together and got along well enough to take first steps.

The HBO documentary, which was called *Bright Lights*, ended up being a love story between mother and daughter, who, despite their obvious generational and lifestyle differences, were so involuntarily alike that when they were taking a walk together, they discovered they were wearing the same shoes.

Most moving was footage of Debbie's receipt of the Screen Actors Guild Lifetime Achievement Award on January 25, 2015. Debbie is being long-overdue honored, and she and Carrie and Todd and Billie travel to the Shrine Auditorium in a limousine. Carrie seems tense and earnest: very proud of and worried for her mother, who had felt ill just before accepting the award.

Carrie introduces Debbie, saying, "Actually, she has been more than a mother to me, not much"—the audience laughs—"but definitely more. She's been an unsolicited stylist, interior decorator, and marriage counselor." Carrie proudly trots out the landmark moments of her mother's career, and when she gets to the fact that Debbie had helped raise more than $30 million, through the Thalians, for mental health, she quips, "Four and a half million of that money is allocated just for me." The audience members—Meryl Streep, Julianne Moore, Jennifer Aniston, Billy Bob Thornton, among them—are ebullient witnesses. It is tremendously moving watching Debbie thank the Guild for honoring her sixty-six years in the business. Her gratitude is palpable, as are the pride and protectiveness Carrie evinces, standing next to her mother, holding the trophy for her as she speaks. After Debbie takes the award in her hands, Carrie breaks down in emotional tears.

Alexis saw the melancholy in Carrie, who would "sometimes brush off sadness with a joke." And in hanging around Debbie's and Carrie's next-door houses, Alexis and Fisher got a sense of the grittiness of their "fierce" mother-daughter love, the rough-and-tumble history behind it. "The idea that love is some linear, unfolding, healthy reward is a sham, and they called that out better than anyone else," Alexis said, essentially encapsulating the long, mottled history of mother and daughter. "Love is pain, as much as it is joy . . . Loving each other not despite your imperfections but because of them." Alexis sensed that "they were intimately familiar with each other's imperfections and by this time in their lives had accepted and embraced those imperfections." As Carrie would put it a year later to NPR's Terry Gross, "I just admire my mother very much. There's very few women from her generation who worked like that, who just kept a career going all her life, and raised children, and had horrible relationships, and lost all her money, and got it back again. She's had an amazing life and she's someone to admire."

"Survivor" is too overused, too hackneyed to apply to these two old pros. And that's a shame, because the word fits Debbie and Carrie better than it fits most of those who flatter themselves with it.

Debbie's worry about Carrie's mental illness is mentioned in the documentary, but more is made of Carrie's worry—and the filmmakers' worry—about Debbie's increasing frailty.

In the documentary, Carrie is watching her mother pack for her "last" nightclub appearance—in Connecticut. "I tried to stop her" from accepting the engagement, Carrie says, but it was impossible. Debbie is cavalier. "Losing your memory brings so many surprises," she says. Carrie *becomes* the mother. "I worry about you. I worry about what the show costs you."

"I want to work until I drop dead," says Debbie. "And then I want to have myself stuffed and they'll put me in museums." How *like* each other the supposedly different women had become: the workaholism, the irony.

Turning serious now, Debbie uses all her life experience, from El Paso to the three bad marriages, to speak words her daughter spent a lifetime absorbing, initially against her will: "The only way you make it through life is to fight. You don't make it there the easy way. If you feel sorry for yourself and let yourself slide back, you will drown." Almost three decades earlier, Carrie had told Carol Caldwell, as an excuse for her overdose, "You *don't know* what it was like to grow up with Debbie and Eddie!" Carrie would not say that now.

The *Force Awakens* was released with all the fanfare that could be expected of the next megahit in the most successful movie franchise in the world. On December 14, it premiered at three major L.A. theaters, with a white tent stretching for many blocks down Hollywood Boulevard to welcome its five thousand viewers. But the more attention paid to it, the more attention was paid to Carrie—much of that, negative.

Even though she had lost weight for the movie, Carrie was fat shamed and age shamed terribly—her fuller-sized image profusely compared with the pretty young girl in the metal bikini. Carrie fought back. At the New York premiere she tried to preempt the flood of social-media dissing by men—"Carrie Fisher is this angry, loud mouth fat woman now" was one of many tweets—by saying that to research the role, she had talked to the younger version of herself, who "was very busy partying and making sure that I look" terrible later.

Of course she would broach the subject humorously—that was who Carrie *was*. But now she went further. In interviews for magazines, on CNN, on ABC, and in tweets, Carrie made her strongest feminist statements, sometimes with humor but now also seriously. "I think it's a stupid conversation—the obsession with [my] weight and aging," she said to Amy Robach on *Good Morning America*. "Youth and beauty are not accomplishments. They're the temporary, happy by-products of time or DNA." She told *Good Housekeeping* that of the thirty-five pounds she was asked to lose before filming, "They don't want to hire all of me—only about three-quarters!"

Now she added a gender layer: "Men don't age better than women; they're just *allowed* to age." And, "I'm a female in Hollywood over the age of, let's say, forty. We could also say fifty. You don't have to ask if you want to work at that age." At the Tribeca Film Festival, she had even said, "There are not a lot of choices for women past twenty-seven."

An uprising against sexism in Hollywood had begun brewing robustly since the previous winter with roots predating that time by a number of years. Several issues were colliding at once: the representation of women on-screen, the paltry number of female directors of big movies, the wage gap, and ageism.

As far back as 2004, the actress Geena Davis, inspired by her role in the feminist movie *Thelma & Louise*, co-founded the foundation See

Jane ("If you can see her, you can be her") to combat the fact that even though women and girls made up 51 percent of the population, males were represented on-screen (even as extras) three to one. Women in Film, partnering with the Sundance Institute and USC's Annenberg School for Communication, had put together a comprehensive study of sexism in filmmaking and found that even as of January 2013, while 30 percent of all filmmakers (directors, writers, producers, cinematographers, and editors) were female, if you looked at the top thirteen hundred highest-grossing movies from 2002 to 2013, men directed them by a whopping ratio of twenty-three to one. The disparity, said the rare female war-movie director and Oscar winner Kathryn Bigelow, was overtly "horrific."

Then came the hacking of Sony Studios' internal emails by North Korea in October 2014. Among other things revealed was the fact that Jennifer Lawrence, the highest-paid actress in America, and her co-star Amy Adams, were both paid a 2 percent smaller cut of the profits (7 percent) of the movie they starred in, *American Hustle*, than that which was paid (9 percent) to each of their three male co-stars: Bradley Cooper, Christian Bale, and Jeremy Renner. Lawrence had just won the Oscar for *Silver Linings Playbook*. At the same time, it was revealed that two Sony senior VPs, a male and a female, doing essentially the same job, had a $1 million pay disparity. Guess who got the extra million? George Clooney said the revelation of the sexist pay gap was the only good thing to come of the Sony hacking.

After the Sony revelations, Hollywood feminism just got jazzier, more righteous, and filled with more glamorous names, all making essential points. Patricia Arquette, upon accepting her Oscar for Best Supporting Actress, made an impassioned plea for gender equity in pay in the industry. Cate Blanchett made the same point in her speech later that night. At the same event, Reese Witherspoon launched an Oscar red-carpet campaign, #AskHerMore, so that fawning mic holders would be shamed past "Who are you wearing?" to ask women about, well, more. Exciting and impressive producing deals, for example.

Witherspoon would eventually become one of many leaders of feminist production in Hollywood.

One of the sharpest, fiercest, and most hilarious attacks on the ageism Carrie decried came from the comic Amy Schumer. For a one-off comic sketch, she gathered together Patricia Arquette, Julia Louis-Dreyfus, and Tina Fey to join her in an imagined ceremony called "Last Fuckable Day." It took dead aim at Hollywood's double standard. In it, an incredulous Louis-Dreyfus tells the other women, "They let me stay fuckable in my *forties*! Did *Us Weekly* have a misprint?" Arquette informs the group, "They're doing a sequel of *Boyhood*. Selena Gomez is playing my role." The skit exploded on the internet.

On the heels of this, thirty-seven-year-old Maggie Gyllenhaal announced that she had been told she was too old to play a fifty-five-year-old man's love interest. And in May, at the Cannes Film Festival, Emily Blunt launched a "Wear flats!" protest when the tin-eared festival organizers ordered women: Manolos or else. Frances McDormand showed her non-lifted, non-Botoxed face as "This is what fifty-seven looks like and I still get roles." Meryl Streep announced that she was funding a screenwriting workshop for women over forty. On and on it went.

In a Carrie Fisher–style moment in October 2015, Jennifer Lawrence wrote an essay in Lena Dunham's newsletter, *Lenny Letter*, in which she acknowledged the lower pay she received relative to her male co-stars in *American Hustle*. She told the readers that she blamed herself and sexism. She wrote, "When the Sony hack happened and I found out how much less I was being paid than the lucky people with dicks, I didn't get mad at Sony. I got mad at myself. I failed as a negotiator because I gave up too early." Why did she give up early? "I would be lying if I didn't say there was an element of wanting to be liked that influenced my decision to close the deal without a real fight. I didn't want to seem to be 'difficult' or 'spoiled' . . . Again, this has nothing to do with my vagina, but I wasn't completely wrong [in that assumption] when another leaked Sony email revealed a producer referring to a fellow lead actress in a negotiation as a 'spoiled brat.'"

In this context, Carrie's anger—and *pain*—at the shaming that was directed at her now was indicative of how even the toughest and most self-confident young women in Hollywood could be derailed.

Tina Fey particularly admired Carrie's *personalization* of the fact that, as Tina would later put it, "women become obsolete in this business when there's no one left that wants to see them naked." The fact that Carrie had weathered the nasty tweets and admitted they'd hurt her feelings was "heartbreaking and also *smart* of Carrie to be like, 'This *hurts*,'" Tina said.

The fat shaming was the worst. Richard Dreyfuss says that when she was melancholic about how pretty she once was, he would say they'd both wasted good years moping when they needn't have. "Don't waste your bad shit on years that were great," he would say to her. Meaning why do we go back in time and think we were unhappy when we were young and comely? "Did she agree with me? Yes! We're all nuts about our weight. It's the most vulnerable subject in the world. I think the reason her bedroom became so popular is because she didn't want to leave it—*she was too embarrassed.*"

Salman Rushdie saw the same vulnerability. "Carrie was very sensitive about her looks," he says. As she turned heavier, "in her later years, if you wanted to see her, you basically had to go to Coldwater Canyon. And if she was persuadable"—willing to leave the house—"the one restaurant she always chose was Trader Vic's in the Beverly Hilton—*awful* food. But, mostly, I would go to her home."

Sometimes she didn't hide her pain at the fat shaming very well at all. When an editor for *The Guardian*, Merope Mills, visited her to persuade her to write an advice column for the paper (Carrie said yes and ended up writing two), Carrie told Merope that she hated the way she looked and then, in front of this woman she'd just met, "suddenly, unexpectedly, she was in tears."

round the same time that Carrie was making both a personal and a feminist point by fighting off the shamers, Debbie was ill and hospitalized. In November 2015—just a month before the *Force Awakens* premiere—while very sick (likely with a stroke), she received the penultimate tribute, the Jean Hersholt Humanitarian Award from the Academy of Motion Picture Arts and Sciences Board of Governors. Neither Carrie nor the infirm Debbie could be there to receive the trophy at the Dolby Theatre ceremony. But what an evening it was! Zooey Deschanel sang "Tammy." Carrie, in a prerecorded video tribute, said she had "no idea how my mother did all the things she did." Jane Fonda praised Debbie "for so much life and energy [she brought to] her classic film roles [and] for the outstanding work she has done outside her day job to improve our city, our country, and the world." Then she made a joke, similar to Carrie's at Debbie's SAG Awards presentation: Debbie was so devoted to mental health "she persuaded her daughter Carrie to pretend that she suffered from mental illness." That drew laughs.

Meryl Streep then took the stage and gave a passionate tribute to Debbie's unceasing work in saving Hollywood's classic costumes and memorabilia from extinction: Debbie had recently been able to auction off part of her costume and memorabilia collection for $25 million, with an additional auction fetching $6 million for Marilyn Monroe's *Seven Year Itch* dress. Billie Lourd, looking lovely in a black-and-white V-necked, long-skirted dress, picked up the award for her grandmother, saying it was "weird" standing there with the trophy in her hand because her grandmother was "the leader of our family." She said that she and Debbie would "cuddle with it later." Finally, a still portrait of the young Debbie at her most beautiful was flashed on the screen while Debbie's real-time words were transmitted over an audio monitor. Especially against that gasp-inducing visual, her weak, shaky voice was heartbreaking. "I'm so sorry that I can't be here. I'm thrilled beyond words." The frailty in her voice underscored both the unintended unfairness of the extended wait *and* the justice in the outpouring of industry appreciation at such a late date.

November 2015 was a month of being reminded of mortality for Carrie. Her good friend Melissa Mathison, Harrison Ford's second wife, died of cancer. (Harrison had been married, for five years now, to Calista Flockhart.) Carrie had recently spoken to Melissa of her thoughts of writing a book about her secret romance with Harrison during the first *Star Wars*. The idea, Carrie said, came from old diaries she had written when she was nineteen, which she had only recently discovered under the floorboards of her bedroom during a home renovation. Melissa thought the idea was fine, and she said she had no emotional investment in the book's being written. After all, she wasn't the cheated-on wife at the time; Harrison's first wife, Mary Marquardt, had been. Carrie started the book, which would be called *The Princess Diarist*.

November was also a month in which Carrie was selected for honoring. She got a call from a young woman named Sarah Chandonnet, the director of community development of the Humanist Hub. The group was formed in 2007 and operates in partnership with the Harvard Community of Humanists, Atheists, and Agnostics. "Good without God" is its motto. It had awarded its first Outstanding Lifetime Achievement Award in Cultural Humanism to Carrie's good friend Salman Rushdie several years earlier and gave another to her friend and *Family Guy* star Seth MacFarlane and a third to her friend the brilliant English comedian, writer, and fellow bipolar Stephen Fry.

Sarah, a recent Harvard Divinity School graduate, had been aware that Carrie was speaking boldly about her bipolar disorder, her addiction, and, to some extent, her atheism. "And when," in the early fall of 2015, "I started seeing the media buildup for the new *Star Wars*," which Carrie was to start shooting in England the next year, "I knew that Carrie was the right person" for the prestigious award. But would the busy celebrity accept?

Sarah acquired Carrie's assistant's contact information through Carrie's friend Stephen Fry, and to Sarah's amazement "Carrie called back right away—the same day—and said, 'Absolutely, yes!' She said, 'I will make time.' We talked about our moms; we'd both had challenging relationships with them. Her mom had a 'time share in my brain'—that's how she put it. 'She's always part of how I'm thinking and what I'm thinking about, for better or worse.'

"But, mainly, Carrie wanted to know about *my* life. We talked as if she'd known me forever. It was like a therapy session for me.

"She was really psyched about coming to Harvard" for the event, scheduled for April 2016. "She said, 'This is the closest thing to a Harvard education that I'm ever going to get.' She immediately followed up with 'Do you know any single professors that you can put in the front row? 'Cause I'm single now and this really seems like the best place to find my next husband.' It sounded like she meant it. I found myself saying, 'My father's single . . .'"

Carrie's comment to Sarah about looking for a husband wasn't mere banter. With *The Guardian*'s Merope Mills, she was even more explicit. She told Merope that she wanted a "British professor who will be able to put up with me, so you can put the word out." She had very specific qualifications: "Good sense of humor, intelligent, not hideously unattractive, and sort of confident without being arrogant." Merope spent a very Carrie-typical day at her house—thinking it would be an hour, ending up texting her husband that it was lasting all afternoon. Carrie fed Merope banana pudding she had made, plied her with wine (while restraining herself), took her shopping, and "plotted endlessly," Merope said, "how we were going to get her a boyfriend. Her desire for companionship and sex were to become a running theme" as the year 2015 ended.

TWELVE

A YEAR FROM HELL,
A YEAR OF FINAL KINDNESS

This whole year was the year from hell," Carrie would tell NPR's Terry Gross in November 2016, a month before she died. It was a chilling unintentional prediction, and Carrie was—at least *explicitly*—mostly referring to the maladies Debbie had begun to suffer in earnest in late 2015 and would suffer well into the coming year. Debbie would endure "two strokes as a result of having an abscess on her spine," Carrie told Terry. She would come down with pneumonia. "Everything that could go wrong [would go] wrong" with Debbie's health. "I asked the nurse, 'Have you ever seen anyone come back from this place?' And the nurse would only say, 'Sometimes.'"

Debbie had nurses on duty in her home, "and she hated them," Carrie said. "So I had to tell her, when she was yelling at the nurses, 'Mom, *not cool!*'" Carrie started spending many mornings at Debbie's house, tending her.

"I couldn't write when this was going on," Carrie said. Yet she *had* to. She was writing her seventh book, *The Princess Diarist*, about her long-ago affair with Harrison during the first *Star Wars*. Her friend

Paul Slansky helped her with it. The diaries on which the book was based made for a startling look at the nineteen-year-old Carrie.

Carrie was taken by her younger self—the earnestness, the insecurity, the self-analysis, and the lack of wisecracks. It was like "this incredible archaeological find," she would say of coming upon lines like "Why am I so accessible? Why do I give myself to people who will always and should always remain strangers?" And the perception that she was "caught in the whirlpool, without an anchor, relaxing into it, calmly going under for one more of many last times." She had also written, "I wish that I could leave myself alone. I wish that I could finally feel that I punished myself enough . . . [that I could] let myself off the hook, drag myself off the rack, where I am both torturer and torturee."

She had not yet encased herself in the armor of irony. And she knew her most distinctive quality: "I confide in everyone. I have no restricted, private self . . . I trust and mistrust anyone." She could be morose and excessively self-abnegating: "I am on my way to becoming a very skilled loser . . . I'm on physical and mental reserves . . . Homemade hysteria . . . Torment to go." But this may be how a very intelligent young woman would react not merely to her unrequited love for a distant and handsome older married co-star but to an unknown condition, bipolar disorder, that was producing "mood swings that," as her friend the fellow bipolar Margot Kidder would later say, "could knock over a building."

Nineteen-year-old Carrie understood that "I am the only one who can come to my rescue. I am the only one who can help me now. But I don't know how to help myself." And, presciently, "Which must mean that I don't want to help myself." Comprehending self-sabotage at so young an age is unusual. In these diaries, she identified not merely her self-destructiveness and her longing but also her future profession: "I need to write. It keeps me focused long enough to complete thoughts."

Her daughter, Billie, so accustomed to her mother's wit and toughness, thought the contents of her mother's girlhood diaries were "so emotional," Carrie said. "No one had seen me like that." She also said, "This is the most personal thing I have written."

And with this book, unlike the others, Carrie had reticence, and she admitted to it. Later, when giving interviews about the book, she would say, "I've spent so many years *not* telling the story of Harrison and me having an affair on the first *Star Wars* movie that it's difficult to know exactly how to tell it now." She had told Harrison that she was writing the book "and that I would give it to him and if he didn't like anything in it I would take it out, and he seemed surprised at that," she said. Then she sent the draft to him "and I never heard from him."

During this busy time of caring for Debbie, Carrie wasn't just writing *The Princess Diarist* but also flying back and forth to London to play Rob's bitchy mother, Mia, to Sharon and Rob's imperfect couple in *Catastrophe*. She was also looking for a house to buy there. And during the longer intervals in L.A., she was script doctoring with Rian Johnson, the new director who was replacing J. J. Abrams on the next *Star Wars* film, *The Last Jedi*, for which she was losing more weight in preparation of filming in Ireland and England. In this film, General Leia Organa would have an even bigger role than she had in *The Force Awakens*, and the new screenwriter-director, Johnson (who had previously directed *The Brothers Bloom* and *Looper*, not huge movies), did the typical Carrie routine: sitting for hours on her bed, he said, "in her insane bedroom with all this crazy modern art around us, TCM on the TV, a constant stream of Coca-Cola, and Gary the dog slobbering at her feet, going over the scripts with her, draft after draft." Carrie supplied a needed lightheartedness to the film. It was Carrie's idea to have General Leia point out to Luke Skywalker, when they reunited, that she'd changed her hairstyle—a laugh line in the movie.

The shooting went from February to July 2016, and Carrie traveled back and forth, mainly to England and Ireland and back to L.A. She slipped in a July appearance at Comic-Con in Florida.

The Humanist Hub Lifestyle Achievement Award in Cultural Humanism was bestowed upon Carrie on the evening of April 18. But half a month earlier, on March 30, something less honorific had transpired: the lawyers for Gianna Breliant officially filed their civil suit motion, *Breliant v. Marmer*, in the Second District, Division Four, California State Court of Appeals. (Stephen S. Marmer was the name of the first of three psychiatrists entrusted with the care of Amy in 2007, before Gianna turned to the "radical interventionist" Warren Boyd.) As part of the proceedings, Carrie was named as one of the defendants in the second suit in the wrongful death of Amy. As had been indicated in the prefilings, Boyd, Boyd's business entity, another "recovery center" and its owner, and another man were also named in the second suit. Carrie was the only female.

A deposition was requested of Carrie. Carrie's attorney, Vicki Greco, had first attempted to get her removed from the lists of accused, saying that she had nothing to do with Amy's death. The judge denied that motion. Then Greco delayed the date of Carrie's deposition due to her extensive travel commitments. All of this was kept confidential. Virtually no one outside Carrie's inner circle knew about the lawsuit at all.

Sarah Chandonnet and her crew were sure to make a big deal of the Humanist Hub awarding, which was being held in the Harvard Memorial Church and which attracted five hundred ticket buyers. "We hired the Harvard Orchestra, so there was a full band of trumpets to play the *Star Wars* theme," Sarah says. She enlisted *Star Wars*–dressed fan-actors to stand around outside the historic church—this was Princess Leia, coming! "It looked like a carnival to me and my colleague the chaplain, Greg." It looked that way to the Harvard students, too. "Storm Troopers, Wookies [*sic*], and Star Wars fans gathered to watch" Carrie enter the church, with Gary at her side, *The Harvard Crimson* reported. "The Harvard Pops Orchestra played the iconic theme music from the epic sci-fi film series as a tribute to Fisher's work."

Actually, at first Carrie—dressed in a dark jacket over a blue T-shirt, her wispy hair tucked behind her ears—went to the wrong venue. Her Uber dropped her off at a fancy building across the narrow street, where Stephen Hawking was being given a formal dinner. "Carrie's security guy called and said, 'I can't find you guys!'" Sarah recalls. "And the guard at the Hawking dinner had no idea who she was. He said, 'Your guest is at our venue, but we're going to hold her downstairs, so please get her.'" Sarah raced across the street from her audience-packed venue and went down to the basement of the building where Hawking's dinner was being held, "and Carrie and Gary were there. And just as I was arriving people were noticing who she was, and I said, 'Let's get you across the street to the right place,' but then somebody said, 'Professor Hawking heard you were here. He's such a big fan of yours! He's eating now, but can you find a time to meet later?'" The meeting didn't happen, but Carrie and Hawking exchanged phone numbers.

Sarah touted Carrie—boldly and familiarly, on the basis of their now weeks of conversations—as a "compassionate, funny, deeply flawed, deeply brave, slightly inappropriate, bighearted bipolar human." Then Carrie came to the lectern, received a standing ovation, gazed at her fans, shuffled her prepared typed notes in her hands, and dramatically threw half of those notes up in the air and spoke from her heart and her gut, referring only occasionally to her remaining notes.

She addressed many topics. First, spirituality and *Star Wars*. (She described the ideology of the Force as influenced by Zoroastrianism, and she recited the whole hologram speech.) Then addiction and bipolar disorder. "I've never been ashamed of my mental illness," she said in an earnest portion. "What is vital is having a community. If you can find some people who have the same thing you do, it can be a lot easier than wandering around," she said. But she was also more Carrie-like. "I like to remind myself that I am a self-medicated, dessert and food obsessive-compulsive, overly talkative . . . with no formal education. I think it's okay to say . . . that Princess Leia is bipolar, too. It seems to relax people." Because Princess Leia had now turned into General Leia, she was asked which appellation she preferred. "*Princess* Leia! Princesses get to *shop*!" Laughter filled the house.

On April 30, Carrie was a guest of *The Guardian* at President Obama's last White House Correspondents' Dinner. (Carrie had dedicated *Shockaholic* to "Billie and Barack.") At evening's end, when she was waiting for the car to take her back to her hotel, Carrie called Debbie, and—as someone overheard—she touchingly ended the conversation with "I love you, Mommy." Two weeks later, Fisher Stevens and Alexis Bloom's documentary on Carrie, *Bright Lights*, debuted at the Cannes Film Festival. It was heralded, and it was scheduled on HBO for March 2017.

In June, the Carrie-written announcement of her *Guardian* column, "Advice from the Dark Side," appeared. She had copiously apologized to Merope Mills for being late with her promised column-proffering write-up. ("I'm a giant asshole. It's official," she had texted. And "I'll try to make it up to u.") Her invitation was charming, encouraging younger people to write to her for advice. Carrie wrote, "I can't help you with your homework, but I can tell you what I did if I've had an experience like yours." Then, before soliciting questions, she said something important: "Hilariously—after all the drug addiction and celebration [perhaps meaning 'celebrity'] marriage and mental illness and divorce and shock treatment and heartbreak and motherhood . . . I've turned out to be . . . a kind of happy person (go figure!). A human who's had her fair share of challenging and unhappy experiences. Over time, I've paid attention, taken notes and forgotten easily half of everything I've gone through. But I'll rifle through the half I recall and lay it at your feet."

A kind of happy person (go figure!). It seems that in mid-2016 Carrie *did* want to be happy. Despite the angst that Sharon Horgan and others had seen in her, there was a kind of reckoning going on in her life, bringing her fulfillment. She was confronting her genuine pain at the fat and looks shaming visited upon her. She was *earning* her role as the feminist heroine she'd already been enthusiastically taken to be. She had a loving relationship with her lovely daughter and a good relationship with her ex. Their co-parenting was a success. She was making two *Star Wars* sequels in a row—padding her financial coffers significantly and now able to upgrade the Coldwater house and to buy another in the London that she loved. She had more devoted friends than anyone in Hollywood—and perhaps beyond. She was creatively afire: *Catastrophe* was not only a hit but fun to shoot, with Sharon and Rob pinching themselves to be working with her. There was a new film, *Wonderwell*, which she had signed for, to start shooting in Italy in the fall. Not only was *The Princess Diarist* gratifying to write, but because the book so heavily relied on her teenage diaries, it was also already half-written. As for her *Guardian* advice column: she loved giving advice! And she felt emotionally healthy enough to look for marriage and to tell near strangers to be on the lookout for appropriate men for her.

In fleshing out *The Princess Diarist*, after the diaries and providing reminiscences of Harrison and Mark and the flush of success, Carrie waxed on about her ambivalence about signing autographs at conventions. Even though she had admitted calling them "celebrity lap dances," she insisted that she was not "cynical" about her fans at those *Star Wars* and Comic-Con shows but, rather, "moved" by them. She fretted about her weight gain, a theme that would continue to the end of her life. "Now the reaction I sometimes get is disappointment, occasionally bordering on resentment, for my having desecrated my body," she wrote. "It's like I've TPed myself, thrown eggs at myself, defaced myself as if I were a rowdy trick-or-treater." It was sad but honest.

She ended the book by writing a pages-long list of the perks and ambivalences and craziness of being Princess Leia, earnestly making the point, in the middle of a theatrical jumble of words, of "how proud I am of her, making sure I'm careful not to do anything that might reflect badly on her or that she might disapprove of."

Still, the most emotional lines in the book were encased in the long acknowledgments: "For my mother—for being too stubborn and thoughtful to die. I love you, but the whole emergency, almost dying thing, wasn't funny. Don't even THINK about doing it again in any form."

Carrie herself was not healthy. A journalist had to reschedule an interview with her twice because she had bronchitis. Her fear of the sleep apnea remained, and she still regularly had people platonically share her bed. Her weight-loss regimen was almost dangerously intense. There was all that traveling! The year included London, Ireland, home again, D.C., Boston, Florida, Cannes, back to L.A., to Colorado, back to London and Italy and London.

And then there was Margot Kidder's warning to her.

At some point after the middle of 2016, Margot "warned Carrie to get off some of those medications" she might have been taking, recalls a close friend of Kidder's. Margot (who would eventually commit suicide in May 2018) and Carrie both knew they had serious bipolar disorder. They also both had dual diagnoses. They had spoken intermittently over the years, but now Margot went out of her way to contact Carrie.

From her home in Montana, she called to "strongly warn Carrie against something she felt she herself had narrowly escaped—'death by shrink': excessive Wellbutrin, Effexor, Adderall," and other drugs, says a friend. It is not clear how Carrie reacted to Margot's impassioned warning or what medications she was taking. Carrie's closest friends were also worried about all the medication she was taking.

In early September, Carrie wrote her first real advice column for *The Guardian*. Even though she had invited young people to write in, this advice seeker was a long-married woman who had recently learned that her husband of over thirty years had been seeing prostitutes since before their marriage. The woman was furious at the revelation. But it had been a long marriage, and he had admitted his wrongdoing. What should she do?

Carrie's response was nuanced and wise, and one could see pieces of her own life in her answer. She empathized with the advice seeker for feeling like a failure, but she also told the woman not to throw away thirty years of her life—more than half of her life—so quickly.

She said that his lying was a major issue not to be ignored; still, in a typically Carrie way, she put some wit and perspective in it, saying, "Everyone always lies about sex." This is pure Carrie: "If you haven't lied about it, it isn't sex. Have you ever faked an orgasm? Some might say that's a kind of well-meaning lie, but it's still lying, no?"

Quite like a marriage counselor, she looked at the situation from multiple angles, noting the importance of shame and the virtue of her forgiveness. She said, "It's the most amazing thing to be able to forgive. And so difficult. But relationships are difficult." Then she split the difference, saying he needed to prove he was finished with hookers and she needed to put a limit on her punishment of him. She said, "I want him to send you a present or get you flowers." And, of course: "If he doesn't, I will. You're a good gal and don't deserve this. I'm proud of you for taking the long road and not the easiest and fastest." She asked the woman to remain in touch with her and to "keep up with the gusto. I'm cheering. Love, Carrie."

That thoughtful, experience-based, measured advice represented what Carrie had become. She often talked of "a good conversation" being one of the most important things in life. *This* was a good conversation.

The column was published on September 9, days after Carrie and Debbie accompanied Fisher and Alexis to the Telluride Film Festival, where *Bright Lights* was being shown. She ran into Bruce Cohen there and told him that because of the time she'd be spending in Europe on her next movie, *Wonderwell*, she and Penny were going to have their usual big birthday party—for Carrie, the big six-oh—a month later than usual, on November 19.

The *Guardian* column comported well with Carrie's role as a wise woman on the set of *The Last Jedi* months earlier. In the new film, General Leia, Resistance leader still, had a larger role, and a new solemnity. In a rich chocolate-colored coat with a high, straight neck piece, her hair slicked back, her face dignified, Carrie presented a soulful, serious creature to be revered. Laura Dern, now in the mix as the purple-haired, hippie-like admiral Amilyn Holdo, adored working with and learning from Carrie. "Being around Carrie was an irreplaceable gift of a lifetime," Laura said. It was Carrie's idea, she said, to have General Leia Organa say, "*You* go; I've said it enough," in handing over the line "May the force be with you" to Admiral Holdo. (When the movie was released, after Carrie's death, viewers loved that touch.) Laura said, "I remember she was like, 'May the Force be with you—*always*.'" Even though Carrie had come up with the line herself, "it got her teary and me teary, because it was like imparting a prayer."

A month earlier, in August, Carrie learned she would now have to be immediately deposed in the Breliant case, but her attorneys succeeded in requiring that the contents of her deposition be sealed. In a dramatic last-minute ruling, Judge Laura A. Matz of the Los Angeles Superior Court's Glendale branch signed an order assuring that a video-taped deposition by Carrie—questions that would be put to Carrie under oath, about her acceptance of $40,000 for housing Warren Boyd's client Amy—would never be heard by the public, nor their contents revealed anywhere except in private court hearings. The deposition would be confidential, the judge said, "to avoid controversy" and "in light of the sensitive nature of the case."

On an August afternoon, with video cameras rolling in a conference room whose location was not revealed, Carrie, with her lawyer present, answered questions put to her by Gianna Breliant's lawyer.

Immediately after the deposition, Vicki Greco released a statement asserting that "Ms. Fisher was not involved in Amy's care or her efforts to remain sober and denies all of the allegations of wrongdoing. We anticipate the court will dismiss the subject lawsuit and render a judgment in our favor."

During this privately fraught time, Carrie spent a day with her old friend Selina Cadell. Selina was in L.A. for work, and serendipitously her twin brother, also an actor, was working on a commercial a few doors from Carrie's house. He saw Carrie and said, "Do you remember my sister Selina?" *Of course* Carrie remembered her once-close friend! "And so we made a date and I came and had lunch with her," Selina says. After years of neither phone calls nor physical contact, Selina was startled by the difference that age and circumstances had wrought on the delicate "American girl" at Central and the tiny-figured darling of the brand-new hip entertainers in Manhattan. "On the one hand, she was Carrie, my friend, whom I had always known, and we picked up where we left off. On the other hand, she looked older." Selina pauses, as if she doesn't want the next words to sound mean, just worried. "Much older. She had taken on the mantle of an old Hollywood dame. Her voice had changed, and her walk had changed."

Carrie talked to Selina about Debbie. "She said, 'I look after my mom now,' and since she was talking to *me*"—who knew more than many others of her previous estrangement from Debbie—"she *did* slightly raise her eyebrows in a quizzical way. Like, 'Ironic, isn't it? Who'd have thought?' But she was so clear that she had made strides around that issue and that Debbie's failing health had pushed Carrie into an empathic new sphere with her mother.

"I was so pleased that we had a hug and talked about our mothers and our daughters. And she talked about Bryan; she had *nothing* bad to say about Bryan. I know she had wanted a life with him. This was going to be her fairy-tale life. And it was a real fairy tale when Billie was born; that is when she was going to get off drugs." Of course, things had not been so simple, but Carrie had climbed back from that crisis, with ECT and so much else. Selina could feel the effort Carrie had made toward that end, fighting her two diseases. Carrie seemed reasonably at peace. In-control "old Hollywood dame" voice or not, she was still needy. The original *love-me!* mistake that Carrie had made—inviting so many Central students and teachers she didn't know to her apartment in London that one nasty male guest callously threw the grand piano out the window—was born of an impulse that hadn't faded, Selina could sense. She had no idea about the Breliant lawsuit, but in a way Warren Boyd was like that nasty guest at that long-ago party. Yes, he had paid Carrie, and not unhandsomely. But he used her celebrity name, and he took advantage of her distracted lack of judgment and her naive desire to help young female addicts who were as desperate as she had been.

On October 24, three days after Carrie's sixtieth birthday and close to the release date for *The Princess Diarist*, Judge Matz refused to remove Carrie from the list of defendants in the wrongful-death lawsuit. Matz wrote that Carrie "did not meet her burden to be found that she cannot be held responsible as a matter of law, for the conduct of Boyd, a joint venture." Judge Matz decreed that the Breliant family's court papers "would support a reasonable inference that defendant [Carrie] engaged in contact [with Boyd] with respect to taking or obtaining funds or assisting in taking or obtaining funds from the dependent adult with intent to defraud."

So, Carrie was set to stand accused in a civil trial—date undetermined. Her lawyers vowed they would continue to push to get her off the lawsuit, a move they felt was fair and just. One of Breliant's lawyers, Stephen G. Larson, argued differently, stating, "We are pleased with the Court's decision ordering Carrie Fisher to stand trial, and we look forward to our day in court and obtaining justice for Amy Breliant." But Larson *did* paint Carrie as having been exploited by Boyd. "As explained in our court documents, Warren Boyd used Carrie Fisher's celebrity status to lend credibility to advance his corrupt drug rehabilitation program."

Carrie issued this statement: "I feel great compassion for any parent's loss of their child in an untimely death. I have a daughter. To lose a child is an unimaginable tragedy and the grief must be devastating. Unfortunately, I am not able to talk about the details of this case because it is ongoing."

That "ongoing" almost certainly added to Debbie's failing health as part of the end-of-2016 "hell" that Carrie would soon tell Terry Gross that she faced. But the people who were with her in October in Italy did not know the circumstances and did not see her pain—at least not directly. She was in Rome for a small but key cameo role in *Wonderwell*, a stylish contemporary movie about fashion, with a touch of glam sci-fi. She played a mysterious, benign hermit-like woman named Hazel who comes upon a troubled twelve-year-old girl, Violet (a teen actress named Kiera Milward), who is jealous of her older sister, Savannah (another teen, Nell Tiger Free), who is on her way to becoming an Italian supermodel managed by a model mogul played by the music star Rita Ora. Violet runs into the mystical good witch Hazel in a forest, and Hazel guides Violet into a supernatural future.

The movie was never released, and there were problems with its schedule. But Carrie—thanks to the executive director Fred Roos, who had championed her years earlier for the role in the first *Star Wars*—was protected from the production delays that hounded the filming. She had a "stop date": her scenes were done in a row with dispatch, and if the production schedule went overtime, she was free to leave. Many of the other players did not have that guarantee in the film, produced by the new producer Orian Williams and directed by the Russian director Vlad Marsavin.

Orian Williams saw Carrie's strength and her world-weariness. "She was smart and witty and wonderful, but you could tell she'd packed a lot into her short years," he says. "Though she had her sixtieth birthday during the filming, I was very surprised by her age. I thought she was somewhere in her late seventies." Orian moves away from his implication that she *looked* old. "It's not that her mind wasn't adept, but she seemed to have a fragile disposition, and she *seemed* 'older,' but not in a bad way. I remember a friend of mine who passed away years ago. A director said of him, 'You could cut him in half and count the [experiential] rings on the trees and you would have a hundred of them.' It was the same with Carrie. There was a sense of life lived that was *way* beyond her years—a lot of rings on the 'tree' of her life."

The actor Vincent Spano, who was playing a glamorous fashion photographer in *Wonderwell*, became quite close to Carrie during the shooting. "She had a joie de vivre that reminded me of my mother," he says. He saw Carrie's professionalism underneath her charisma and wisdom and how both elements affected the cast, especially the teenagers. "The kids in the movie"—and they ranged from twelve to seventeen—"loved her; they *loved* her!" In the same way that Carrie had helped young Daisy Ridley, and had wanted her *Guardian* advice seekers to be young people, she was enormously tutorial toward these novices, in terms of training them in craft *and* life, with humor.

But Vincent also saw how worried Carrie was, first about Harrison Ford's reaction to her soon-to-be published *Princess Diarist* and, second, about her dog Gary's mess making. Without knowing anything about the additional agony of the Breliant matter, he sensed "there was a lot of stress on her with all the travel"—England, Italy, L.A., England, back to Italy—"and it was very unfortunate that we didn't have that much time to get to know each other better because she was the kind of person who, when she liked you, she treated you like an old friend. And we hit it off."

In the time they had together, she talked a lot about Harrison and her new book. Vincent could tell that that early, intense, and unrequited love still exerted a hold on her. "The affair with Harrison—it had really affected her. She was *whooshed* into this thing, and it was bigger than she was. It was one of those life experiences that sweeps you off your feet, and it meant a lot to her."

Carrie shared with Vincent her worry that Ford wouldn't like the fact that she wrote the book. "She was sensitive," he recalls. "She was concerned if he would be okay with it." She had never seemed so doubtful about a book or a subject before.

But if her vulnerability came out around the subject of Harrison, it came out even more around her dog. As with Carrie's chaotic performance on the Holland America cruise ship, Gary seemed the surrogate for her own occasionally out-of-control behavior, and it was very clear that she loved the dog dearly. "She was very dismayed and worried because Gary was pooping and peeing everywhere," Vincent says, adding, *"Her love for that dog was so big!"* In the elegant five-hundred-year-old villa where they stayed, Spano had a room with a roof garden; Carrie did not. Carrie ruefully told him they wouldn't give her a grand room "because to get to one you needed to mount a spiral staircase, and the banister had recently broken, and they worried that I would fall down the stairs." The producers knew she had collapsed on the sets of former pictures and that her history was full of (potentially lawsuit-baiting) difficulties. "She had an 'I'm not gonna let them tell me what to do!' attitude," but she still had a room without a backyard, so she asked Vincent if Gary could use *Vincent's* room's roof garden. She was very grateful when he said yes. She had a uniquely advantageous contract as an actor in the troubled movie, yet she still had to *plead* for a place for her dog to relieve himself.

On October 21—Carrie's sixtieth birthday—there was a huge party on the set. Says Orian Williams, who hosted the party, "There was a ruckus until four in the morning." Carrie tweeted that the party started at 2:00 a.m. and the police were called because of noise at 5:00 a.m.—"always the sign of a successful evening."

But her official big sixtieth bash, with Penny, was now rescheduled to November 19, at which point she would be finished with her *Wonderwell* work and back in L.A. Richard Dreyfuss was starring in a play in Connecticut and couldn't get out of it for that night so, he says, he wrote her back, "Okay, look, it may seem hard but it's really easy. If you change the date of the party, I can make it. Otherwise, I can't." He never heard back from her.

What a party it was! Bruce Cohen remembers there was a glow to it; it's not as if people *expected* it to be Carrie's last party, but "I had wonderful deep catch-up moments with all of the friends. There were a few people"—like Dreyfuss—"who couldn't make it, but almost everyone else was there and we all embraced the momentous occasion: Carrie was sixty! And the Coldwater house never looked more beautiful. Because of the *Star Wars* money, she had the resources to collect even more things. And she had just opened a new wing of her bedroom, which was a physical representation of her brain and her creativity. We all kind of realized, '*Oh, we're all here!*' and were busy little bees, talking to each other—'What's going on?' 'What is your life like?' Carrie and Nina Jacobson and Bruce Wagner and Gavin de Becker and Meg [Ryan] and Meryl and Beverly D'Angelo and Helen [Fielding]." Some events have a mystical prescient significance, and this was one. "We knew Carrie was leaving the next day"—for signings of *The Princess Diarist* in New York City bookstores, and then to London, to film final episodes of the current season of *Catastrophe*. "And being there together with her in the beautiful house ignited some special happiness. Little did we know we'd be there, again, a month later—without her."

This party was different from her previous Carrie-and-Penny parties. Debbie had a big hand in it—sixty was a big year for a daughter!—and she invited a wider array of people, including Carrie's old Brownie and Girl Scout troopmates. Carrie complained about Debbie making such a big deal of the party, and toward the end of the party Carrie and Todd had what he has called a tense conversation. Carrie complained that Debbie was pushing the party down her throat. At the end of a bit of an argument, Todd said Carrie "broke down [in tears] and said, 'We have to be OK with each other. It's the foundation.'" Those were the last words Todd ever heard from his sister.

What would turn out to be Carrie's final *Guardian* advice column was published on November 30. In it Carrie wrote from her heart, and from her decades of experience, about bipolar disorder. If she had opened her house to other sufferers, like Amy Breliant, there was a reason, well aside from the financial compensation she ill-advisedly received from Boyd: *She wanted to help.* She had a great deal of help to offer, and this column proved it.

A young man named Alex wrote to her, admiring her frankness about her diagnosis. He was bipolar, too. He poignantly asked, "Have you found a way to feel at peace when even your brain seesaws constantly? . . . I hope you can give me some insight."

Carrie told him he was lucky to have been diagnosed early and to have accepted that diagnosis. Only her overdose at twenty-eight had forced her to make the same acceptance. She suggested he join a group for affective disorders (depression, bipolar disorder, and so on) and told him she'd had a bit of an epiphany: You didn't have to *want* to go to meetings. She had realized that her "comfort wasn't the most important thing—my getting through to the other side of difficult feelings was."

Then Carrie made her most earnest statement: "We've been given a challenging illness, and there is no other option than to meet these challenges. An opportunity to be heroic. Not," she was quick to qualify, "'I survived living in Mosul during an attack' heroic," but emotionally so. Then she waxed admiring of him, saying, "I've never done what it sounds like you're doing: balancing school, home and work." She told him he was "doing more than I did at your age, and that's courageous." She applauded the fact that he had contacted her. "Now build on that," she exhorted. "As your bipolar sister, I'll be watching. Now get out there and show me and you what you can do."

During this end-of-year time, Carrie was working with Sharon and Rob on the third season of *Catastrophe*, and both her kindness and her melancholy were evident to all. In regard to the latter, one night, "when she was going up to her room after dinner, she was mocking herself for her slow pace, her 'old lady body.'" Orian Williams and Selina Cadell had noticed, startled, the aging that Carrie now saw in herself. "She looked back at me," Sharon recalled, "and said: 'If I'd known back then that I had something worth looking at, I'd have looked after it better. I was in good shape." That regret, long privately expressed to Richard Dreyfuss, was now too top of mind to hide. The internet shaming had deeply affected her. "She was very aware of what people thought and said," Sharon knew. "I didn't like that she felt so hurt by it! I didn't like that she criticized her own looks so much." A few weeks earlier, in mid-November, Carrie had told *Rolling Stone*, "The worst part [of fame] is being criticized [by the internet]. I'm not someone that can sort of just not look." Sure, she tweeted back angrily (often with a string of emojis). But her feelings were hurt permanently, and there was no more hiding that fact. She made an even stronger version of that statement a week later to Kelly McEvers on NPR, lamenting the pervasive "rejection, the criticism: especially now. It used to be that you're your own worst enemy. No longer. The internet is. And they say really, really vicious things about you based in some sort of truth. *So it's painful.*" For any young actress, she warned, "Eventually it's going to dump you. Eventually it's going to say, 'You look old. You look fat. *It's over.*'"

But it wasn't just darkness she expressed; it was also a bit of piety. She acknowledged, the month before to *Rolling Stone*, a change in attitude that might have surprised anyone who knew her only in her brittle twenties and thirties. Debbie's two strokes and plummeting health; her internet tormentors and her pain over them; her more forthright feminism (including passages in *The Princess Diarist* that hailed the early *Ms.* magazine); her continual ride on her bucking bronco of a mental illness and the help she was able to give people: *all* of this might have merged to give her a respect for virtues at which she had long scoffed. What were her new life lessons? she was asked. Carrie told that onetime premier journal of hipness, "Be kind. Don't hurt other people. It's all the sort of Christian ethics stuff I thought was bullshit when I was a kid. It turns out it's *not* bullshit. Tell the truth, be kind." She said it twice in those five sentences, this onetime mean girl: "Be kind."

During one of their last days shooting *Catastrophe*, Carrie could sense Rob was in emotional pain. "I was feeling guilty about being on set pretending to have a hard time managing a [fictional] young family while my real-life wife tended to our three kids under the age of five, one of whom was a newborn," he admitted, shortly after Carrie's death. The next day, Carrie "brought me a tin of biscuits shaped like syringes and thermometers and other medical things and said she was 'prescribing me cookies.'" The extremely inventive gift must have cost a great deal to have been specially made so fast, and the medical theme had a sorrowful subtext: Rob's infant son had been diagnosed with a brain tumor very shortly after his birth. (Little Henry Delaney died in January 2018, after spending most of his very short life in hospitals.) Rob doesn't remember if he actually told Carrie what was wrong or she simply sensed it, but she responded in her patented way: with compassion wrapped in expensive thoughtfulness. The gift was amusing and flattering rather than patronizing or sad.

In late November, *Rolling Stone* asked Carrie, "Are you happier now than you've ever been?" "Well," Carrie answered, "I'm not happy about being older, except what are the options? . . . I've been through a lot, and I could go through more, but I hope I don't have to. But if I did, I'd be able to do it. I'm not going to enjoy dying, but there's not much prep for that."

She was asked, "Do you fear death?" She answered, "No. I fear dying. Anything with pain associated with it, I don't like. I've been there for a couple of people when they were dying. It didn't look like fun. But if I was gonna do it, I'd want someone like me around."

In the interview, she also said, "I trust myself. I trust my instincts. I know what I'm gonna do, what I can do, what I can't do."

Right after her death, there were reports in various tabloids that Carrie had "relapsed" around Thanksgiving. The reports were dismissed as sleazy clickbait—cruel and wrong. Fans were mad and largely disbelieving; friends were defensive or silent. But one friend feels, merely from knowing Carrie, that she simply thought it was her time to live it up—that on some unarticulated level she had seen enough of life. Perhaps she'd simply been careful long enough; her sober periods inevitably gave way to relapse. But she couldn't have thought she was putting her life at risk, because she was planning for the future: in early December, she made a "handshake deal" with the Geffen Playhouse to create a sequel to her massively popular stage show—*Wishful Drinking Strikes Back: From Star Wars to, Uh, Star Wars!* She apparently planned to return to her original co-writer Joshua Ravetch.

On December 17, she appeared as a guest on her friend Graham Norton's morning talk show, to plug *The Princess Diarist* and to shoot the breeze with the man through whom she had met her *Catastrophe* co-stars and friends. Though she was feeling ill the day before, she rallied for the show, and she spoke of how bad she felt that because of her book Harrison would now be asked about his affair with Carrie for the rest of his life. She was *that* uncertain of having done the right thing, that vulnerable about his reaction, and *that* physically shaky.

On December 22—her last night in London—she had a restaurant dinner with Sharon Horgan and Salman Rushdie. Salman was happily up for the date, but Carrie had to persuade Sharon to join them. It was the final day of filming *Catastrophe*, and Sharon tried to beg off, using a hangover as an excuse. Carrie would have none of it: she reminded Sharon that she had once "dragged her ass" out to Sharon's house, outside London, so Sharon *had* to return the favor.

Sharon also used Salman's presence as a reason not to come. She let out a yelp: "I'm not feeling smart enough to talk to him!"

Carrie shot back, "Are you kidding? He's just gonna talk about girls!"

So they met at the restaurant, and, recalls Salman, "Carrie seemed to be in very good spirits." She did not seem particularly vulnerable to him that night, and he was a decent judge of that. "Over time, I saw Carrie in every conceivable position, from very low to very high to out of her head," he says, and that night he saw none of these extremes. He loved the chocolate tits she gave him as a present. (Carrie had taken a side trip to Bruges, Belgium, three days earlier and had posed in front of a store, Chocolatier Dumon; the randy gift likely came from that emporium.)

The threesome chatted like old friends. "See? Isn't he fun? Do you like him?" Carrie asked Sharon, when Salman excused himself for a moment. "Of course I did," Sharon later said. "But what I liked *more* was that she cared enough to make sure that I was having fun. And that was her wont."

Though Carrie had a well-known habit of solipsism, she could curb it. "If she felt she was talking about herself too much, she would say, 'Wait! What about you? We haven't talked about *you!*'" Salman says, "We sat and drank and talked till 11:15 and then she said, 'I have to go. I have a plane to catch in the morning.'"

Carrie hugged Salman goodbye. "I felt cheered by how good she seemed," he says; he had worried about her in the recent past. And she brought Sharon up to her hotel room and gave her a present: "a beautiful little cocktail stick holder she'd bought at a flea market."

Then to sleep. She and Gary had a flight to catch, back to L.A.: United Airlines' morning Flight 935.

Carrie and Gary were seated in first class. The plane took off, arched over the Atlantic Ocean, on the long trip to California.

Then, after the two small incidents of sleep apnea, fifteen minutes from the scheduled landing, Carrie started vomiting uncontrollably and went into severe cardiac arrest. The pilot radioed to emergency services; the plane was given permission to accelerate its speed; the L.A. Fire Department truck met it on the runway, paramedics rushing to Carrie, who was then brought to UCLA Medical Center's intensive care unit.

Todd, Billie (with the support of her boyfriend, the actor Taylor Lautner), and Debbie raced to the hospital. It was first reported by *The New York Times* that Todd had told the Associated Press that Carrie was "receiving excellent care" and in "stable condition." In quickly subsequent statements, he was more measured, saying, "We hope for the best. We certainly do not know her condition, that's why she is in the ICU. I'm sure everyone wants to speculate, but now is not the time for that."

Meanwhile, hearing of this and fearing a worst-case scenario that seemed evident from the changing updates—and from Carrie's own history—Carrie's friends scrambled for news. Salman Rushdie says, "After seeing her in such good shape the night before, I was shocked that this had happened. Helen [Fielding] and Bruce [Wagner] and I were on the phone constantly to try to find out what was going on." Richard Dreyfuss called Ed Begley Jr. "I said, 'I'm in San Diego. If I come up now, can I get in the hospital?' Ed said, 'No. The family is trying to keep people away.' I was so fucking angry at myself" for missing her birthday party because of his play.

Carrie was in the ICU for three and a half days. On Christmas Day, Debbie tweeted, "Carrie is in stable condition. If there is a change, we will share it. For all her fans & friends. I thank you for your prayers & good wishes."

Many suspected that it was only a formality that she was being kept on life support. On the morning of December 27, Bryan Lourd's spokesman Simon Halls solemnly and simply announced Carrie's death. The official cause of death was heart attack; no toxicology report was in the immediate offing. (Says a confidante, "The family didn't want the toxicology report released. The airline almost certainly did," to prove no negligence on its part.)

The death, of course, made war-worthy web and newspaper headlines, just as her original heart attack had, and it generated intense TV coverage and a social-media landslide. Among the early tweets was this from the usually very private Paul Simon: "Yesterday was a horrible day. Carrie was a special, wonderful girl. It's too soon." (Simon was criticized for calling her a "girl," but he had *known* her as a girl.) Mark Hamill tweeted, "No words. Devastated." A little while later, he composed himself and wrote a longer tweet. Harrison Ford released a statement: "Carrie was one of a kind . . . brilliant, original. Funny and emotionally fearless. She lived her life bravely." J. J. Abrams wrote, "You didn't need to meet Carrie Fisher to understand her power. She was just as brilliant, tough and wonderful, incisive and funny as you could imagine. What an unfair thing to lose her. How lucky to have been blessed with her at all."

Among the hundreds of ensuing tweets, from the famous and the ordinary, were these. Billy Dee Williams: "I am deeply saddened by the news of Carrie's passing. She was a dear friend whom I greatly respected and admired. The force is dark today!" Samuel L. Jackson: "The light in the Galaxy is dimmed by the loss of our Princess Leia. May the Force be with her! RIP." Mia Farrow, who had so liked her: "Oh no!! Carrie wasn't done yet." Margaret Cho: "We just lost a great ally for mental health and addiction. Be strong. As she'd want you to be. Rest in paradise." Alyssa Milano: "Thank you, Ms. Fisher, for opening up a world of possibilities, strength and hope for all little girls."

Debbie had braced herself for imminent news of her daughter's fatal overdose for four decades, and their closeness over the last year and a half had been profound. Three months later, Todd would tell the media about his talk with Debbie the night that Carrie died. "She was setting me up for her leaving the planet," is how he put it. Debbie told Todd she wanted her own funeral plans changed, from a low-key cremation to burial with Carrie. "She was, like, asking my permission to go," Todd said. "She literally looked at me and said, 'I want to be with Carrie,' and closed her eyes and went to sleep." Media reports understandably said that Debbie was "distraught" at her daughter's death, but Todd said that when the two of them left the hospital right after one of their last visits with the dying Carrie, *he* was the one who was crying while their mother "truly understood" what had transpired.

On Wednesday, December 28, the day after Carrie's death, the seemingly inevitable happened. At Todd's house, as Debbie was helping Todd plan Carrie's funeral, she collapsed: another stroke—this one fatal.

The entire country reacted to the tragedy of a beloved famous mother dying one day after her beloved famous daughter. That night a cross-country light saber vigil to Carrie was held; incited by social media, thousands of Princess Leia fans lifted their bright vertical sabers in the darkened sky in tribute to their fallen heroine.

"Come to the house on Thursday [the twenty-ninth]," Richard Dreyfuss says Ed Begley Jr. called and told him. A private memorial service was taking place there, for Carrie and Debbie. Carrie's friends—about two hundred people—assembled. "It was so crowded I barely got into the living room, but I sat next to Penny," Richard says. So shocked and saddened that he wouldn't be able to break down and fully cry for another three months, he said to Penny, as he would say for weeks, as a coping mechanism, "'Let's just pretend Carrie's in Australia.' That's when I thought, 'Who *are* we? Who are we without Carrie?' We were really a lot of interesting people, but we were not tied together—*except* by her."

Decades earlier, in *Delusions of Grandma*, she had written of the way the death of a mutual loved one brings together people who wouldn't ordinarily have that bonding: "Without William there was no cause to intensely connect them. Without William they'd be together alone." Richard now felt this; Carrie was their William, several-dozen-fold. As did many others. Bruce Cohen had said virtually the same thing after the post-funeral gathering, seeing Meg Ryan, Meryl Streep, Buck Henry, Beverly D'Angelo, Bruce Wagner, Candice Bergen, and all the rest: "We are all here because of Carrie." Courtney Love attended with her daughter, Frances Bean Cobain; Eric Idle was there. Sarah Paulson was there. Carrie had created a world; not many people can do that. A world including the most accomplished, even snobbish people; almost *no one* can do *that*. Gloria Crayton made the food that had been the staple of all her birthday parties, including the one the month before: fried chicken, collard greens, and corn bread. Billie spoke briefly, as did Stephen Fry, Tracey Ullman, and Meryl Streep. Meryl sang "Happy Days Are Here Again" to close out the occasion. This was Carrie's favorite song.

Media reports of the gathering made it sound like a "celebration" of Carrie and Debbie, but there was clearly a lot of pain and guilt. Says someone who knew Carrie through the worst of her times, "A lot of those people there—*famous* people—felt so guilty," rationally or not, "for not being able to help Carrie over her addiction. For not pushing. Not staging an intervention. For knowing the addiction had never quite left her. As adored as she was, and as full of madcap joy as she was, hers was also a very dark story, and we knew it."

The funeral for Debbie and Carrie was held at Forest Lawn Memorial Park on Friday, December 30. The cemetery—occupying many acres on high hills overlooking Debbie's Burbank—has numerous corridors: patches of lawn squared off by sparkling white marble mausoleums containing neat rectangles of crypts. Under the cloudless sky, it suggests the desertlike Indian land that the Spaniards, under Father Junípero Serra, colonized three and a half centuries earlier. In a city insulted for its sprawl and occasional architectural cheesiness, Forest Lawn and its adjacent sister cemetery, Mount Sinai, have a primal dignity. And their corridors have evocative names, thoughtful names. The Courts of Remembrance was where Debbie and Carrie would be laid to rest.

A hearse carried Debbie's body, clad in her favorite bright red dress. Todd Fisher carried Carrie's cremated ashes in, of all things, a giant Prozac capsule—approximately eight inches tall and eight inches in circumference. This was a prized possession of Carrie's that Todd and Billie decided was precisely what Carrie would have wanted. Carrie had once insisted Mark Hamill heckle her funeral. The grieving, single-file procession of black-clad mourners, most of them celebrities, was the precise opposite of heckling, but Carrie-in-Prozac conveyed her message in a way that only she would have been bold enough to deliver.

Debbie and Carrie were laid together in a handsome burnished-wood casket, with their names and dates alongside each other on the front panel. A cluster of red roses capped the casket, which was placed in a white marble semicircle bearing a statue of two women. All those who had been at the memorial service were there, plus Gwyneth Paltrow and Jamie Lee Curtis. Bryan Lourd looked somber. Billie was with her boyfriend, Taylor Lautner, and their young fellow castmates from the TV show *Scream Queens*, Lea Michele and Emma Roberts. Billie gave a big hug to Sarah Paulson. Carrie's elegant daughter seemed to be taking control with astonishing maturity for a twenty-four-year-old. Having majored in religion and literature at NYU, now back in her hometown as an actress, Billie had read the book *Adult Children of Alcoholics* and had appreciated that her mother was always honest with her. Despite her problems, Carrie had managed to raise a loved, emotionally healthy daughter. Soon after Carrie's death, Taylor Lautner tweeted of Billie, "This girl is one of the strongest, most fearless individuals I've ever met. Beautiful inside and out." The Monday after the funeral Billie would tweet, "There are no words to express how much I miss my Abadaba and my one and only Momby."

The night of the funeral—Friday, December 30—every Broadway theater went dark to honor Carrie and Debbie.

At the record-breaking women's marches all over the country on January 21, 2017, posters of Carrie and posters of Princess Leia were hoisted by countless marchers. It had happened subtly over the years and was finally, just before her death, met with her own prideful ownership: Carrie Fisher was a major—badass, as the approving term now went—feminist hero, with a sweeping reach. Carol Caldwell, living in Nashville for several years now, was surprised—and gratified—to see the images of her onetime best friend being held high by southern girls in their twenties as a major role model in their lives.

On the afternoon of Saturday, March 25, a memorial "show" was held at Forest Lawn for Carrie and Debbie, streamed live on Debbie's website. Todd organized it, saying, "My mother didn't want a memorial. She wanted a party." Some of Carrie's friends were initially skeptical about the corny or excessive aspects, from the formal military color guard that opened the ceremony ("Debbie was a patriot," Todd decreed, while some of Carrie's hip friends rolled their eyes) to the presence of R2-D2 as a speaker on the stage, talking to an empty director's chair marked "Carrie Fisher" and being hugged by Todd. But sentimentality won out. Home movies and film clips were shown, some of Carrie as a child and many of Debbie: singing "Good Morning" and entertaining troops in war zones for fifty years. Debbie's longtime friend and co-Thalians founder, the actress Ruta Lee, sang "I'll Be Seeing You" in her honor; Debbie's many charities were touted; and a group of students from her dance studio did a modernized, hip-hop-studded version of the "Singin' in the Rain" tap dance. The Gay Men's Chorus sang Cyndi Lauper's "True Colors" for both women.

The Carrie-based segments were separate, and touching. James Blunt sang "You're Beautiful," the song he had written at Carrie's house and that Carrie's publicist-like zealotry had lofted to stardom, while a montage of pictures from her life played out on the screen behind him. He also premiered a new song he'd composed for her after her death. Because Carrie had lived for decades with TCM on her bedroom TV screen—all her friends and book editors and film colleagues had talked and worked with her while classic black-and-white films, many made before she was born, were playing soundlessly a few feet away—it was apt that one of the network's hosts, Ben Mankiewicz, gave a speech. He called her what no one disagreed with: "One of the greatest bullshit detectors of all time." The most personal of the Carrie tributes came from an ashen Dan Aykroyd: "We shouldn't be here so soon in our lives." In private, in recent years, he had been tough on Carrie, says someone who'd heard him talk. But her death clearly shocked him. He would publish a tribute to her, calling her "one of the most brilliant and original minds of our eon." Especially moving was the presence of Griffin Dunne and Gavin de Becker, together at the microphone, referring, with the sincerest affection, to themselves and "Charlie [Wessler] and May [Quigley Goodman]," who were in the audience, as the intimate Carrie inner circle, dating back to their youth. Gavin, wiping tears, told a joke about the incident in Paris with Carrie, when he'd filched the bathrobe from the Hotel George V and gotten caught—and she'd been impressed with his chutzpah.

The lingering image on the screen was a childlike painting of the backs of mother and daughter, arms around each other: Carrie in her Princess Leia gown and hair buns, Debbie in her *Singin' in the Rain* raincoat, dropping her opened umbrella onto the ground. Decades of struggle and worry between the two vanished with that painting, so intentionally naive and loving.

Billie Lourd decided not to sell her mother's wildly idiosyncratic house but, rather, to keep it and, she said, eventually move her friends in, as a commune.

The last episode of the third season of *Catastrophe* aired on April 4, 2017, with viewers tweeting weepily about Carrie's performance as the cranky, odd Mia. In it, Mia declares that she has been loving a TV series called "All My Children Are Schizophrenics." It was a line that could only have come from Carrie herself. At the end of the episode, across the screen it read "For Carrie."

On June 19, the internet came alive with the long-delayed results of the Los Angeles County Coroner's office's toxicology report. It had been performed and written up during Carrie's autopsy, shortly after her death. But the announcement of the results was delayed for half a year, which is unusual. (Philip Seymour Hoffman's toxicology report was released twenty-six days after his February 2014 death; Heath Ledger's was delayed only half a day after his January 2008 over-dose.) "There are significant limitations in one's ability to interpret the toxicology results and their contribution to her death," the report opened. The official cause of death was, as it had been stated in late December, "sleep apnea," but now the words "and other undetermined factors" were added to that sentence. The report continued, starting with the already known, "Ms. Fisher suffered what appeared to be a cardiac arrest on the airplane, accompanied by vomiting and with a history of sleep apnea." The coroner's release continued, "Based on the available toxicological information, we cannot establish the significance of multiple substances that were detected in Ms. Fisher's blood and tissue, with regard to the cause of death." And then came the headline-causing news: "Those substances, for which she tested positive, were cocaine, methadone, ethanol and opiates." She had apparently ingested the cocaine within seventy-two hours of her death. She had also been exposed to heroin, but the time and dose of the exposure could not be determined, and there was "remote" exposure to ecstasy: MDMA. It could not be determined if the heroin or the ecstasy had contributed to her death. The report's specificity and nuance were obliterated by the three drugs in the viral headlines: *cocaine, heroin, ecstasy*. In short, Carrie had relapsed.

Decriers of "Hollywood morality" and of the Democratic "elites" blasted the now-long-deceased Carrie on social media, while those who loved her—and her fan base was enormous—defended her with mama-bear intensity. Addiction was a disease, not a sin. Some fans said that the sneering decriers and prim moralists didn't possess half the character Carrie had, drugs or no drugs. The news of the drugs in her system did not shock many of her friends. Their unease—their unjustified but inevitable feelings of guilt—had already been evident at the memorial service. But it saddened some old friends who were no longer in touch with her, who remembered the dangerous intensity of the earlier addiction of the much younger woman and had hoped she had moved on from that. Carol Caldwell cried and said, "It makes me so sad! It's too horrible. *She never had a chance!*"

Todd Fisher calmly said that the news of the drug use did not surprise him. As for Billie Lourd, she issued a statement so forthright there could be no doubt that in the best sense she was her mother's daughter. "My mom battled drug addiction and mental illness her entire life," Billie asserted. "She ultimately died of it. She was purposefully open in all of her work about the social stigmas surrounding these diseases. She talked about the shame that torments people and their families confronted by these diseases. I know my Mom; she'd want her death to encourage people to be open about their struggles. Seek help, fight for government funding for mental health programs. Shame and those social stigmas are the enemies of progress to solutions and ultimately a cure. Love you, Momby."

Billie's words were importantly echoed by the former representative Patrick Kennedy, an advocate for the destigmatization and funding of addiction as well as mental health programs. "If it weren't for Carrie Fisher" and her toxicology report, he said shortly after the report was made public, "we would have just thought she died of sleep apnea. If she weren't an uber, uber celebrity, we wouldn't know what the true overdose rate is. We have found out everything else in this country, but we don't want to know what the true overdose rate is." The report was a blessing, he was saying.

The Last Jedi was released on December 15, 2017, virtually a year after Carrie's death, and it became not just a commercial but a critical hit. Carrie's presence in the movie was much remarked upon. Though Rian Johnson credibly swore that nothing had been altered in the editing of the film since her death, it is hard not to see the scene of General Leia going into a near-death state after she leads the Resistance into a mad dash to escape the First Order, led by her son and rival, Kylo Ren, as eerily and poignantly predictive. During the battle, we see Leia's body first disappear and then spin through space. She is—as she put it in those lines for Tinkerbell that so moved Bruce Cohen—between asleep and awake. When she does awake, she utilizes all her stamina for one final push of Force, through which she is space-borne back to the ship. As one reviewer put it, among the viewers grieving Carrie's death a full year later, "Onscreen, at least, Carrie Fisher has come back from the dead. In my screening, the audience lost their freaking minds at this moment. It was the purest form of cinematic wish-fulfillment I've seen all year."

She wakes up from her time of unconsciousness ready to take command, has a meaningful reunion with her twin, Luke Skywalker, and seems prepared to pass the leadership over to Poe (Oscar Isaac). In the last scene—after she has told Vice Admiral Holdo, "*You* go; I've said it enough"—Leia boards the *Millennium Falcon* with Rey, Daisy Ridley. They're off into the galaxy. At the end of the movie is the dedication, of course: "In loving memory of our princess, Carrie Fisher."

The love for Carrie was echoed in many reviews, including this first line from *New York* magazine's *Vulture* when the movie was released: "We'll just cut right to the chase: Carrie Fisher is a goddess, we miss Carrie Fisher every damn day, and Carrie Fisher was one of the most hilarious humans to ever walk this dysfunctional planet."

The continued mourning and appreciation of Carrie, among friends and fans, proved something she had understood when she wrote of the death of her friend William/Julian in *Delusions of Grandma*: "After death takes someone from you, it gives you something back. It makes smells sharper and the sun brighter and sex more urgent. It's as though you're living for two now. The memory lives inside you, and you feed it. You live for them now that they can't any more . . . Death chose our friend, our loved one, over us. He took the bullet, and we were left standing there with our empty guns."

Meanwhile, Billie Lourd gave permission for the outtake footage of her mother from *The Force Awakens* to be used in what is planned to be the final *Star Wars* film, *The Rise of Skywalker*, until recently called *Episode IX*, which was always intended to be, as Kathleen Kennedy put it, "Leia's film."

Carrie had wanted to be so wildly popular she could "explode on your night sky like fireworks at midnight on New Year's Eve in Hong Kong," and she had achieved that. She was able to emotionally feel, as her friend Richard Dreyfuss said, something "so scintillating, so exquisitely pleasurable, you're at home in this secret, brilliant, elevated universe."

She died just before her brand of raunchily self-styled feminism, a candor she possessed all her life, swept over her town, her industry, America. The girls hoisting the Princess Leia posters at the women's marches were not even born when the first *Star Wars* movie was released, but Carrie had managed to become that rarest thing: a marker, a way pointer, and, as the producer Wendy Kout put it, "a human tuning fork."

She was born into a fantasy world, with a brain and a sensibility that found comfort there, and she fought her way to reality. As Sady Doyle, the author of *Trainwreck: The Women We Love to Hate, Mock, and Fear . . . and Why*, aptly captures it in a website item, "Carrie Fisher could have made things easy on herself . . . But that wasn't Fisher's style. In fact, she refused to fit *any* of the stereotypical and limiting roles that the world tried to force upon her: Hollywood heiress, bimbo in a bikini, drug-addled trainwreck, crazy showbiz reject, washed-up old lady. She managed to reclaim her own narrative by relentlessly confronting the world with the spectacle of her human complexity . . . By peeling back the edifice of her glamour and insisting we meet the messy, funny, flawed woman underneath, Carrie Fisher became her own legend."

Carrie Fisher has been missed far more than she could ever have expected. She has become an icon, both accidental and necessary— a rare woman "famous just for being herself." In an America led by a man who has persistently gotten away with being a liar, her legacy as a startling self-truth teller has made her triply relevant. And, one has to assume, a woman at peace. As she wrote to the mother of her friend Betsy Rapoport as she was dying, "There's a chance that there's peace at the end of the march. Peace and companionship with old friends, waiting eagerly for your arrival. Yes, you will be missed. But the best of those who love you will always carry a part of you inside them—in that way you never die. You exist as a soft smile . . . in the midst of a fond memory."

NOTES

For each chapter, the names of people I spoke to are enumerated at the outset. The vast majority of the conversations are attributed in the text, and they are always attributed in the journalistic present tense—"he says," "she recalls," and so on—thus making restating in the notes unnecessary. (When it is not clear where an anecdote came from, the interviewed source is mentioned in the notes.) When an anecdote recalled by the person or people goes on for several pages—with their attributed quotations interspersed—and is clearly told by them, I do not refer to the anecdote in the notes. All interviews were conducted between February 2017 and November 2018.

Material acquired from sources other than interviews and conversations with the author is included under the list of firsthand sources in each chapter, with specific references given. When tweets are referred to, they are self-referential and not recited.

INTRODUCTION: FAMOUS FOR SIMPLY BEING HERSELF

This chapter draws on interviews and conversations with Salman Rushdie, Carol Caldwell, Albert Brooks, Richard Dreyfuss, Bruce Vilanch, Todd Haimes, Patricia Resnick, Dr. James Phelps, Joanne Doan of *bp Magazine*, Bill LaVallee, Vincent Spano, Orian Williams, and two confidential close friends of Debbie Reynolds's.

3 *a year-round Christmas tree:* "Exclusive Live Look Inside Carrie Fisher's Memorabilia-Filled Home and the Items for Sale," ABC News, June 13, 2017.
3 *The plane was scheduled:* The exact time of scheduled departure and arrival of Flight 935 was verified by an agent of United Airlines, by phone, on March 9, 2019.
3 *"It matches my sweater":* Chris Ariens, "Let's Revisit Amy Robach's Interview with Carrie Fisher," *Adweek*, Dec. 27, 2016.
5 *she started sprinkling the audience:* Bruce Vilanch, Todd Haimes, and others, in interviews with the author.
5 *silly fairy costumes to camp up:* Carol Caldwell, interview with the author.

5 *the tiles in the kitchen were embossed*: Hunter Harris, "In Case You Forgot Carrie Fisher Is the Greatest: Her Urn Is Shaped Like a Giant Prozac Pill," *Vulture*, Jan. 7, 2017.

5 *"ugly children portraits"*: Amanda Buckle, "13 Surprising Facts We Learned in the Carrie Fisher and Debbie Reynolds HBO Documentary," *Mic*, Jan. 7, 2017.

5 *"Don't stand next to me"*: Robert Hilburn, *Paul Simon: The Life* (New York: Simon & Schuster, 2018), 221.

5 *"I didn't know you were a thief"*: Videotape of Carrie and Debbie memorial service streamed live on www.debbiereynolds.com.

5 *"My mother is not a lesbian"*: Carrie Fisher, *Wishful Drinking* (New York: Simon & Schuster, 2008), 67.

6 *"celebrity is just obscurity"*: "Carrie Fisher: I Didn't Want to Be Famous," CNN, Nov. 12, 2009.

6 *"Resentment . . . is like drinking poison"*: Carrie Fisher, *The Best Awful* (New York: Simon & Schuster, 2004), 30.

6 *"If my life wasn't funny"*: Fisher, *Wishful Drinking*, 17.

6 *"I am a very good friend"*: Carrie Fisher, *Charlie Rose*, April 5, 1994.

6 *she'd had dinner with another one of her best friends*: Sharon Horgan, "Carrie Fisher Was So Real It Was Dangerous," *Guardian*, Jan. 3, 2017. All quotations from Horgan are taken from this source.

7 *she'd filmed her part in a glamorous sci-fi movie*: Vincent Spano and Orian Williams, interviews with the author.

8 *she was almost ill enough to cancel a TV show*: Lucy Mapstone, "Graham Norton: Carrie Fisher Nearly Cancelled Her Final Interview with Me," *Independent*, Sept. 28, 2017.

8 *"Don't know how to process it"*: Jessica Roy, "Passengers Aboard Carrie Fisher's Flight Say She 'Wasn't Breathing' Before Landing," *Los Angeles Times*, Dec. 23, 2016. All tweets from Brad Gage and Anna Akana are taken from this source.

8 *The pilot radioed*: Olivia Blair, "Carrie Fisher: Flight Audio 'Describes Actress as Unresponsive After Cardiac Arrest,'" *Independent*, Dec. 24, 2016.

8 *According to a log*: "Medical Incident 12/23/2016," Los Angeles Fire Department, www.lafd.org/alert/medical-incident-12232016.

9 *"It is with a very deep sadness"*: Jess Cagle and Lindsay Kimble, "Iconic *Star Wars* Actress Carrie Fisher Dies at 60: 'She Was Loved by the World and She Will Be Missed Profoundly,'" *People*, Dec. 27, 2016.

9 *"I cried when I heard Carrie Fisher had died"*: Karen Karbo, *In Praise of Difficult Women: Life Lessons from 29 Women Who Dared to Break the Rules* (Washington, D.C.: National Geographic, 2018), 315.

10 *"miss [Carrie] as long as I am able to miss"*: Sheila Nevins, *You Don't Look Your Age . . . and Other Fairy Tales* (New York: Flatiron Books, 2017), 252.

10 *"brought a rare combination of nerve"*: Dave Itzkoff, "Carrie Fisher, Child of Hollywood and 'Star Wars' Royalty, Dies at 60," *New York Times*, Dec. 27, 2016.

10 *"famous and beloved for simply being herself"*: Josh Rottenberg, "Carrie Fisher, Child of Hollywood Who Blazed a Path as 'Star Wars' Heroine, Screenwriter, and Author, Dies at 60," *Los Angeles Times*, Dec. 27, 2016.

12 *"Debbie had been America's sweetheart"*: Confidential source, friend of Debbie Reynolds's.

12   *Reynolds's Facebook message*: Lesley Messer, "Debbie Reynolds Speaks Out After 'Beloved and Amazing' Daughter Carrie Fisher's Death," ABC News, Dec. 27, 2016.

12   *Debbie wanted to be with Carrie*: Brent Lang, "Todd Fisher Opens Up About Deaths of Carrie Fisher and Debbie Reynolds," *Variety*, June 18, 2018.

13   *Debbie had braced herself*: Confidential source, close friend of Debbie Reynolds's.

1. HOLLYWOOD BABY

This chapter draws on interviews and conversations with George Schlatter, Lawrence Schiller, Ron Raines, Dr. James Phelps, Kathleen Cairns, PhD, Julie Fast, Dr. Dean Parker, a confidential friend of Catherine Hickland's, Marilyn Fried, a confidential longtime friend of Debbie Reynolds's, and Elizabeth Ashley.

17   *These were the "Flats"*: Author's personal memories, along with author's book *Dancing at Ciro's* (New York: St. Martin's Press, 2003).

21   *"The baby was born"*: "Eddie Fishers Have Daughter," *New York Times*, Oct. 22, 1956, 25.

22   *"My brother and I slept"*: Debbie Reynolds, *Unsinkable* (New York: William Morrow, 2013), 112. Other details of Debbie's childhood are taken from this source.

24   *he was an early patient of Max Jacobson*: Eddie Fisher, *Been There, Done That*, with David Fisher (New York: St. Martin's Press, 1999), 48–49.

25   *wild buying sprees were a sign*: Information about manic depression, bipolar disorder, addiction, and their relationship to heredity was found in the following: "What You Should Know About Mania vs. Hypomania," *Healthline*, Feb. 15, 2018; "Bipolar Disorder," National Institute of Mental Health, www.nimh.nih.gov/health/statistics/bipolar-disorder.shtml; Daniel J. Smith et al., "Childhood IQ and Risk of Bipolar Disorder in Adulthood: Prospective Birth Cohort Study," *BJPsych Open* 1, no. 1 (June 2015): 74–80; Katherine Taylor, I. Fletcher, and F. Lobban, "Exploring the Links Between the Phenomenology of Creativity and Bipolar Disorder," *Journal of Affective Disorders* 174 (2015): 658–64; Carol A. Prescott and Kenneth S. Kendler, "Genetic and Environmental Contributions to Alcohol Abuse and Dependence in a Population-Based Sample of Male Twins," *American Journal of Psychiatry* 156, no. 1 (1999): 34–40; M. A. Enoch and D. Goldman, "The Genetics of Alcoholism and Alcohol Abuse," *Current Psychiatry Reports* 3, no. 2 (April 2001): 144–51; K. R. Merikangas et al., "Familial Transmission of Substance Use Disorders," *Archives of General Psychiatry* 55, no. 11 (Nov. 1998): 973–79.

25   *about 50 percent of the risk is genetically based*: Maia Szalavitz, "Genetics: No more addictive personality," *Nature* 522 (June 25, 2015): S48–S49.

25   *Debbie would unwaveringly blame*: Anonymous source, good friend of Debbie Reynolds's, in an interview with the author.

25   *Eddie recalled meeting Debbie*: Fisher, *Been There, Done That*, 71. Additional information came from the manuscript copy of Helen Weller (author's mother), "Elizabeth and Eddie's Wedding Day," sourced by a member of the wedding (Gloria Luchenbill) for *Modern Screen*, May 1958.

25   *Debbie, within months, would be named*: *Modern Screen*, March 1954.

26   *With the unflagging energy*: Debbie Reynolds, *Debbie: My Life*, with David Patrick Columbia (New York: William Morrow, 1988), 125.

26 *For his part, Eddie was smitten*: Fisher, *Been There, Done That*, 70.

26 *Debbie remembered first meeting Eddie*: Reynolds, *Debbie*, 125.

26 *They married at the Catskills home*: Fisher, *Been There, Done That*, 86.

27 *It was Eddie who chose the name*: *Modern Screen*, March 1953.

28 *"Is Debbie a good mother?"*: *Modern Screen*, Aug. 1957.

29 *"jumped to the usual conclusion"*: *Modern Screen*, Aug. 1957.

29 *Three months later, Louella Parsons*: *Modern Screen*, Nov. 1957.

30 *Debbie's old MGM classmate*: Personal notes from Gloria Luchenbill to the author's mother.

31 *Mike Todd was en route back to his bride*: Multiple websites, including *Public Domain Footage*, March 27, 2011.

32 *another cover story to Louella Parsons*: *Modern Screen*, Sept. 1958.

32 *Debbie was at Edie Adams's house*: Reynolds, *Debbie*, 186.

33 *"but he never came by to see Carrie and Todd"*: Ibid., 194.

34 *The scandal made headlines for months*: Alice Spivak, interview with the author.

34 *Debbie and Eddie were officially divorced*: Weller, "Elizabeth and Eddie's Wedding Day."

34 Modern Screen *ran another article*: *Modern Screen*, Dec. 1958.

34 *Eddie made a date to see the children*: Reynolds, *Debbie*, 199.

35 *Catherine Hickland, would tell a friend of Carrie's*: Confidential source.

35 *"His leaving affected her terribly"*: Marilyn Fried, interview with the author.

35 *"I knew in my heart"*: Carrie Fisher, *The Princess Diarist* (New York: Blue Rider Press, 2016), 57.

35 *Debbie met Harry through the charity*: Reynolds, *Debbie*, 202.

36 *"For the first time in my life"*: Ibid., 220.

36 *"Uncle Shoe isn't here"*: Elizabeth Ashley, interview with the author.

2. A COMPLICATED CHILDHOOD

This chapter draws on interviews and conversations with Selina Cadell, Donavan Freberg, Lisa Karlan, Lynn Pollack, Lawrence Schiller, George Schlatter, Alice Spivak, Elizabeth Ashley, Nancie Lewis Levey, Barry Schwartz, Jeffrey Sherman, Stephanie Charles, Michael Vilkin, Fredrica (Fredi) Duke, Peter Ames Carlin (author of *Homeward Bound*), five confidential El Rodeo Girl Scout troop members and Beverly High alumnae, a confidential friend of Carrie Fisher's, and a confidential friend of Debbie Reynolds's.

37 *"Did your mother ever put you to bed"*: Selina Cadell, interview with the author.

38 *"a multimillion-dollar mansion"*: Carrie Fisher, *Shockaholic* (New York: Simon & Schuster, 2011), 67.

38 *give her daughter half an adult tranquilizer*: Confidential source in an interview with the author.

38 *once, when Carrie was four*: Debbie Reynolds, *Debbie: My Life*, with David Patrick Columbia (New York: William Morrow, 1988), 344.

38 *"Since Carrie was a child"*: Todd Fisher, *My Girls: A Lifetime with Carrie and Debbie* (New York: William Morrow, 2018), 191.

40 *At ten, Gavin had witnessed*: Gavin de Becker, *The Gift of Fear: Survival Signals That Protect Us from Violence* (New York: Little, Brown, 1997); various published interviews with Gavin de Becker.

41 *"When I was young, I was raised"*: Kevin Sessums, "Carrie Fisher's Crowning Moment," *Daily Beast*, Oct. 25, 2009.

43 *"It looked more like a place"*: Carrie Fisher, *Wishful Drinking* (New York: Simon & Schuster, 2008), 47.

51 *Paul Simon and Art Garfunkel*: Peter Ames Carlin, *Homeward Bound: The Life of Paul Simon* (New York: Henry Holt, 2016); Peter Ames Carlin, interview with the author.

54 *"The first time I touched a piano"*: Videotape of Carrie and Debbie memorial service streamed live on www.debbiereynolds.com.

56 *"I think every time we were together"*: Ibid.

56 *Carrie was wildly attractive*: Joan Juliet Buck, "Carrie Retakes Hollywood," *Vanity Fair*, Aug. 1990.

56 *"I knew with the profound certainty"*: Fisher, *Wishful Drinking*, 50.

57 *"I know I'm not pretty"*: Confidential interview with author.

57 *Debbie's new obsession: collecting*: Hilary Weaver, "Debbie Reynolds Protected and Preserved Hollywood's Most Precious Relics," *Vanity Fair*, Dec. 29, 2016.

58 *She had lost a TV show*: Kyle Smith, "Debbie Reynolds was more than just beauty," *New York Post*, Dec. 29, 2016.

58 *"It was fun" having the casino town*: Chris Chase, "At the Movies: Carrie Fisher Recalls Pains and Joys," *New York Times*, June 3, 1983.

59 *"As a child, you want to fit in"*: *The Arsenio Hall Show*, Oct. 1, 1991.

59 *Lisa Karlan was a popular Beverly junior*: Lisa Karlan, interview with the author.

60 *"the oldest living child"*: *Brian Linehan's City Lights*, summer 1980.

62 *Debbie had taken Carrie and Todd*: Carrie Fisher in conversations with friends relayed to the author.

62 *"I was aware of my mother's bad taste"*: *The Arsenio Hall Show*, Oct. 1, 1991.

62 *"In my weakness there is strength"*: Carrie Fisher, *Charlie Rose*, April 5, 1994.

62 *"We did fight"*: Carrie Fisher to a friend.

62 *"Carrie and I were always buddies"*: Reynolds, *Debbie*, 387.

63 *shortly after New Year's 1971*: Ibid., 332; Irene Lacher, "Princess Carrie: Books: Carrie Fisher Seems to Have Mastered the Art of Turning a Troubled and Glamorous Life into Bestsellers," *Los Angeles Times*, Sept. 7, 1990.

64 *"I was almost forty"*: Reynolds, *Debbie*, 333.

64 *"Debbie pulled Carrie out of Beverly"*: Confidential source, Carrie schoolmate, in an interview with the author.

3. FROM BROADWAY TO BEATTY TO BRITAIN

This chapter draws on interviews and conversations with Lee Grant; Selina Cadell; Alfa-Betty Olsen; Bruce Vilanch; Donavan Freberg; the Central School of Speech and Drama professors and students who knew Carrie (Ian Closier-Hawkins, Lyall Watson, Alan Marston, Clare Rich, Deborah MacLaren, Christopher John, and Barbara "Bardy" Griffiths); Michael Childers; Owen Elliot-Kugell; two confidential friends of Carrie's; and these bipolar authorities: Dr. James Phelps, Dr. Dean Parker, Julie Fast, Marya Hornbacher, Terri Cheney, and Kathleen Cairns.

65 *out-of-town previews of Irene*: Various interviews Carrie gave, including with Brian Linehan on *City Lights*, and from Selina Cadell, Bruce Vilanch, and Alfa-Betty Olsen to the author.

65 *"My mother taught me how to sur-thrive"*: Julie Miller, "Inside Carrie Fisher's Difficult Upbringing with Famous Parents," *Vanity Fair*, Dec. 27, 2016.

66 *Todd was already a gun aficionado*: Various Carrie interviews; Donavan Freberg, interview with the author.

66 *a handsome young dancer named Albert*: Stephanie Mansfield, "Carrie Fisher's Candid Conversations," *Washington Post*, Aug. 13, 1987.

67 *"obsessed" during these years with "homosexual men"*: Carrie Fisher, *The Princess Diarist* (New York: Blue Rider Press, 2016), 121.

69 *"I drank champagne and ended up in a room"*: Carrie Fisher, interview with Suzanne Finstad, unused material for Finstad's biography *Warren Beatty: A Private Man* (New York: Harmony, 2005). Finstad provided the transcript for the author.

70 *"And George suggested that I would be good in* Shampoo": Ibid.

74 *Carrie attempted to get several roles*: Fisher, *Princess Diarist*, 17.

76 *she had just written a letter to her daughter*: Owen Elliot-Kugell, interview with the author.

76 *Carrie experienced almost paralyzing stage fright*: Debbie Reynolds, *Debbie: My Life*, with David Patrick Columbia (New York: William Morrow, 1988), 385.

77 *Central was not the school*: Interviews with Deborah MacLaren, Alan Marston, and others. Details of Carrie's audition at Central School of Speech and Drama and the culture of Central come from these sources.

80 *Mother and daughter had a whopper of a fight*: Reynolds, *Debbie*, 386.

80 *Debbie would tell Oprah Winfrey*: "Watch: Debbie Reynolds and Carrie Fisher's Amazing 'Oprah' Interview from 2011," *Variety*, Dec. 28, 2016.

81 *"I was the youngest student there"*: Brian Linehan's City Lights, summer 1980.

83 *Selina Cadell met Carrie for the first time*: In addition to the many quotations from Cadell to the author here and throughout the book, some details of their meeting at Central come from Cadell's tribute to Carrie, "My Friend, Carrie Fisher: 'You Could Have Lit a Candle with the Twinkle in Her Eyes,'" *Guardian*, Dec. 30, 2016.

85 *"For the first time, I was with people my own age"*: Chris Chase, "At the Movies: Carrie Fisher Recalls Pains and Joys," *New York Times*, June 3, 1983.

86 *It received mixed reviews*: Vincent Canby, "Shampoo," *New York Times*, Feb. 11, 1975; Peter Biskind, *Star: How Warren Beatty Seduced America* (New York: Simon & Schuster, 2010); Nora Sayre, "The Screen: Shampoo," *New York Times*, Feb. 12, 1975.

86 *"Are you a magician?"*: Jerry Parker, "Eddie and Debbie's Baby Grows Up," *Newsday*, May 23, 1975.

87 *Carrie proudly said that Beatty*: Ibid.

87 *the tongue twisters that were a staple*: Carrie Fisher, *Wishful Drinking* (New York: Simon & Schuster, 2008), 75.

87 *Then she heard about an audition in L.A.*: Carrie Fisher, interview with Suzanne Finstad.

88 *Carrie was strongly recommended to Lucas*: Confidential friend of Carrie Fisher's.

4. PRINCESS LEIA BECOMES THE TOAST OF YOUNG NEW YORK

This chapter draws on interviews and conversations with Eve Babitz, Anne Marshall, Marilyn Fried, Donavan Freberg, Fredi Duke, Stephanie Wilson, Jonathan Rinzler, John Kestner, David Zentz, Vincent Spano, Richard Dreyfuss, Rosie Shuster, Barbara

Burns, Susan Forristal, Judy Belushi, Mark Metcalf, Sarah Kernochan, Guy Strobel, Selina Cadell, Jesse Kornbluth, Greg Fleeman, Elizabeth Ashley, Carol Caldwell, four confidential former confidantes and associates of Paul Simon's, Jeff Margolis, and, regarding bipolar disorder, Dr. Dean Parker, Dr. James Phelps, and the bipolar authors and community members Julie Fast, Marya Hornbacher, and Terri Cheney.

Again, all quotations, assertions, anecdotes, and narrative movement implicitly ascribed to the above people are not redundantly cited below. Readers will infer the sources from the attendant attributed quotations. Cited below is only information obtained from other sources.

90 *During the interview with Lucas*: Carrie Fisher, *The Princess Diarist* (New York: Blue Rider Press, 2016), 23.

91 *His name was Harrison Ford*: Eve Babitz and Anne Marshall, interviews with the author.

91 *In their videotaped scene together*: WishItWas1984, "Longer Carrie Fisher Star Wars Audition," YouTube, posted Nov. 26, 2006, www.youtube.com/watch?v =kCXrGuLix7M.

93 *"This isn't a hairdo, it's a hair don't"*: Fisher, *Princess Diarist*, 40.

94 *"Oh, God, I'm acting opposite"*: Joan Juliet Buck, "Carrie Retakes Hollywood," *Vanity Fair*, Aug. 1990.

94 *Harrison, whom she'd perceived*: Fisher, *Princess Diarist*, 71. Other details about Carrie Fisher's relationship with Ford come from this same source.

95 *Griffin Dunne had done her the friendly favor*: Bright Lights: Starring Carrie Fisher and Debbie Reynolds, directed by Alexis Bloom and Fisher Stevens (New York: HBO, 2017).

96 *she worried what he would think*: Vincent Spano, interview with the author.

97 *"We were really attracted to each other"*: David Kamp, "Cover Story: *Star Wars: The Last Jedi*, the Definitive Preview," *Vanity Fair*, Summer 2017; Hadley Freeman, "Star Wars' Mark Hamill—'I Said to Carrie Fisher: I'm a Good Kisser—Next, We're Making Out Like Teenagers!,'" *Guardian*, Dec. 15, 2017; videotape of Carrie and Debbie memorial service streamed live on www.debbiereynolds.com; Mark Hamill, "Mark Hamill's Carrie Fisher Tribute: 'Making Her Laugh Was a Badge of Honor' (Guest Column)," *Hollywood Reporter*, Jan. 2, 2017.

97 *"Wait'll you see it"*: Joan Juliet Buck, "Carrie Retakes Hollywood," *Vanity Fair*, Aug. 1990.

98 *Steven Spielberg saw it and raved*: Jonathan Rinzler, interview with the author.

98 *The special effects and the sound*: Ibid.

98 *"I want to give young people"*: B. Myint, "George Lucas and the Origin Story Behind 'Star Wars,'" *Biography.com*, Dec. 16, 2015.

98 *Star Wars would end up being that much bigger*: Jonathan Rinzler, interview with the author.

99 *Carrie attended the May 25, 1977, grand opening*: Todd Fisher, *My Girls: A Lifetime with Carrie and Debbie* (New York: William Morrow, 2018), 169.

99 *"as everyone this side of solitary confinement knows"*: *Baltimore Sun*, June 29, 1977.

99 *"The girl is not an alcoholic"*: Anna Quindlen, "Carrie Fisher Wonders Where She'll Fit In," *New York Times*, July 14, 1977.

100 *"Leia's nerves as a revolutionary"*: Alyssa Rosenberg, "Princess Leia, Political Icon," *Washington Post*, May 4, 2015.

101 *"things happened very fast"*: Buck, "Carrie Retakes Hollywood."

101 *the thrill of having just worked*: Quindlen, "Carrie Fisher Wonders Where She'll Fit In"; Guy Flatley, "The Crème-Rinsing of Carrie Fisher," *Chicago Tribune*, Aug. 14, 1977; *Brian Linehan's City Lights*, 1978.

102 *there was a "visceral catharsis"*: Quindlen, "Carrie Fisher Wonders Where She'll Fit In."

102 *Carrie once described her*: Horatia Harrod, "Carrie Fisher Interview: The Secrecy Around the New Star Wars Film 'Is Like D-Day,'" *Telegraph*, May 24, 2014.

102 *She would become one of Carrie's closest friends*: Confirmed independently in author interviews with Elizabeth Ashley, Selina Cadell, and Richard Dreyfuss.

102–103 *"I know I'm getting a reputation"*: Flatley, "Crème-Rinsing of Carrie Fisher."

103 *"Move out of the hotel"*: Hamill, "Mark Hamill's Carrie Fisher Tribute."

105 *Dunne introduced Carrie to John Belushi*: Buck, "Carrie Retakes Hollywood."

105 *The show's writers and cast*: Author's earlier articles, and author interviews with Shuster, Belushi, Forristal, Caldwell, Burns, and others.

110 *a Sarah Lawrence teaching assistant*: Don Steinberg, "Help Me, Obi-Wan: Carrie Fisher's Private Philosophy Coach," *New Yorker*, Dec. 11, 2017.

117 *"If I could've ever been a fan"*: "In Bed with Carrie Fisher," *I Mean . . . What?!?*, found on YouTube as "Carrie Fisher: Romancing the Stoned," July 25, 2010, www.youtube .com/watch?v=MWcHMMzPa8M.

117 *"Paul's choice of women was very interesting"*: Four anonymous sources, friends or former friends or colleagues of Paul Simon's; Peter Ames Carlin, interview with the author.

121 *"I have always considered myself street smart"*: Carrie Fisher, Twitter post, Jan. 3, 2016, 7:41 p.m.; previous remarks she made to various people, such as Abe Gurko: "In Bed with Carrie Fisher."

123 *what is now called bipolar disorder*: Information about manic depression and bipolar disorder, here and throughout the book, was found during extensive conversations with Drs. Phelps and Parker, author Julie Fast (*Loving Someone with Bipolar Disorder* and others), Marya Hornbacher (*Manic: A Bipolar Life*), Terri Cheney (*Madness: A Memoir*), and the psychologist Kathleen Cairns. In addition, these sources were utilized: Joel Paris, MD, "The Bipolar Spectrum: A Critical Perspective," *Harvard Review of Psychiatry* 17, no. 3 (2009); Neel Burton, MD, "A Short History of Bipolar Disorder," *Psychology Today*, online June 21, 2012; Rashmi Neimade, PhD, and Mark Dombeck, PhD, "Historical and Contemporary Understandings of Bipolar Disorder," *MentalHealth.net*; *The Secret Life of the Manic Depressive*, directed by Ross Wilson (Glasgow: IWC Media, 2006); Nassir Ghaemi, MD, "Bipolar Imperialism or Freedom?," *Psychology Today*, May 28, 2009; Joanna Moncrieff, "The Medicalisation of 'Ups and Downs': The Marketing of the New Bipolar Disorder," *Transcultural Psychiatry*, April 7, 2014; Frederick K. Goodwin and Kay Redfield Jamison, *Manic-Depressive Illness: Bipolar Disorders and Recurrent Depression* (New York: Oxford University Press, 2007).

125 *"I will tell myself nine stories"*: Irene Lacher, "Princess Carrie: Books: Carrie Fisher Seems to Have Mastered the Art of Turning a Troubled and Glamorous Life into Bestsellers," *Los Angeles Times*, Sept. 7, 1990.

5. THE FABULOUS LIFE OF THE GIRL IN THE METAL BIKINI

This chapter draws on interviews and conversations with Richard Dreyfuss, Susan Forristal, four former confidantes and associates of Paul Simon's, Carol Caldwell, Barbara Burns, Alice Spivak, Mark Metcalf, Guy Strobel, Kerri Kolen, Rosie Shuster, Robert Hilburn, Dr. James Phelps, Dr. Dean Parker, Jonathan Rinzler, Stephanie Wilson, Alma Cuervo, Patricia Resnick, Mary Louise Weller, Katherine Wilson, Sean Daniel, Linda Marder, Will Trinkle, Alfa-Betty Olsen, Penelope Spheeris, several confidential friends of Carrie Fisher's and Paul Simon's, and a confidential friend of Penny Marshall's.

130 *"Anybody as bright as her"*: *People*, May 30, 1983.

132 *"the bad thing about my relationship with Paul"*: Suelain Moy, "Paul Simon and Carrie Fisher's Anniversary," *Entertainment Weekly*, Aug. 13, 1993.

133 *"She lived in her head"*: Carrie Fisher, *Postcards from the Edge* (New York: Simon & Schuster, 1987), 171.

133 *She and Michael were such close friends*: Carol Caldwell, interview with the author.

133 *"starts right away in the morning"*: Nikki Finke, "Carrie Fisher: Over the Edge and Back in Her First Novel," *Los Angeles Times*, July 31, 1987.

135 *"thought everyone was smarter than she was"*: Penny Marshall, *My Mother Was Nuts* (Boston: New Harvest/Houghton Mifflin Harcourt, 2012), 150.

135 *"helped me through the toughest patches"*: Ibid., 152

138 *"Like many women my age"*: Zach Johnson, "Tina Fey Remembers Carrie Fisher's 'Honest Writing' and 'Razor-Sharp Wit,'" *E! News*, Dec. 28, 2016.

139 *Everybody wanted Carrie for a small but important cameo*: Ned Zeman, "Soul Men: The Making of *The Blues Brothers*," *Vanity Fair*, Jan. 2013.

140 *shot pool and goofed around*: Judy Belushi, interview with the author.

140 *they changed limo drivers "fifteen times"*: Marshall, *My Mother Was Nuts*, 160.

141 *in an unpublished conversation*: Ned Zeman interview with Carrie Fisher for his *Vanity Fair* story, supplied by Zeman to the author.

142 *She put a whole sprout in her mouth*: Sean Daniel, interview with the author; Tracy Swartz, "How Carrie Fisher and Dan Aykroyd's Love Blossomed in Chicago," *Chicago Tribune*, Jan. 25, 2017; Dan Aykroyd, "Dan Aykroyd's Tribute to Carrie Fisher," *Empire*, March 6, 2017.

142 *"I knew to apologize for"*: Aykroyd, "Dan Aykroyd's Tribute to Carrie Fisher."

143 *"I started saying 'Eh?'"*: *Brian Linehan's City Lights*, summer 1980.

143 *"It looks like it was abandoned"*: Swartz, "How Carrie Fisher and Dan Aykroyd's Love Blossomed in Chicago."

145 *she bought a house next door*: Carol Caldwell, interview with the author; Teri Garr, *Speedbumps: Flooring It Through Hollywood* (New York: Hudson Street Press, 2005).

146 *"To feed the seemingly insatiable appetite"*: Timothy White, "'Star Wars': Slaves to the 'Empire,'" *Rolling Stone*, July 1980.

146 *"I have to quickly think of an answer"*: *Brian Linehan's City Lights*, summer 1980.

149 *"Under the Rainbow was the one"*: Diane Sawyer, *Primetime*, Dec. 21, 2000.

150 *Carrie overdosed on the set*: Ibid.

150 *Carrie went to Teri Garr's new apartment*: Author interview with a confidante of Teri Garr's.

150 *She was given a diagnosis of bipolar two*: Carrie Fisher in many interviews, including one with Diane Sawyer, *Primetime*, Dec. 21, 2000.

150   *"I was unable to accept"*: Carrie Fisher, "Ask Carrie Fisher: I'm Bipolar—How Do You Feel at Peace with Mental Illness?," *Guardian*, Nov. 30, 2016.

151   *She was also taking the popular Valium*: Carrie Fisher in various interviews, including Stephanie Mansfield, "Carrie Fisher's Candid Conversations," *Washington Post*, Aug. 13, 1987.

151   *"Lions mate every fifteen minutes"*: Carrie Fisher in postcard to Alfa-Betty Olsen, given to author.

152   *"The use of illicit drugs in Hollywood"*: Robert Lindsey, "Pervasive Use of Cocaine Is Reported in Hollywood," *New York Times*, Oct. 31, 1982.

152   *"Merry Christmas, Guy-bone"*: Carrie Fisher in postcard to Guy Strobel, shared with author.

152   *Carrie would brandish the works*: Christopher Borrelli, "Mark Hamill Pays Emotional Tribute to Carrie Fisher at 'Star Wars' Gathering," *Chicago Tribune*, April 14, 2017.

153   *the science fiction cartoon artist Frank Frazetta*: Author conversation with Jonathan Rinzler, as well as various websites.

154   *"What redeems [wearing the metal bikini]"*: Terry Gross, *Fresh Air*, NPR, Nov. 2016.

154   *"What I didn't realize"*: Carrie Fisher in *Wishful Drinking* stage show and many interviews.

154   *Lucasfilm would sell the franchise to Disney*: Jonathan Rinzler, interview with the author.

156   *John Belushi was dead*: Reported by Carol Caldwell, Penelope Spheeris, Judy Belushi, Barbara Burns, and many articles and websites.

156   *Richard Dreyfuss was arrested*: Richard Dreyfuss, interview with the author.

6. "SHE BURNED LIKE A BRIDE"

Author interviews and conversations with Elizabeth Ashley, Selina Cadell, Carol Caldwell, Blair Sabol, Stephanie Wilson, Susan Forristal, Marilyn Suzanne Miller, Alice Spivak, a confidential friend of Carrie's, a confidential friend of Debbie's, three confidential friends of Paul's, Will Trinkle, a confidential acquaintance of Carrie's, Mia Farrow, and Richard Dreyfuss.

158   *Carrie was in the "high desert"*: Brian Linehan's *City Lights*, 1983.

158   *"I was terribly nervous"*: Bruce Feld, "When Debbie Reynolds and Carrie Fisher Simultaneously Starred on Broadway," *Playbill*, March 1983.

160   *By March 9, according to* The New York Times: Leslie Bennetts, "Stage Absenteeism Said to Be Rising," *New York Times*, March 9, 1983.

161   *Motorcycling through space*: Carrie Fisher on *Late Night with David Letterman*, 1983, 1987.

161   *"She's gutsy and a real fighter"*: *People*, May 30, 1983.

161   *But first there was an interruption*: Carol Caldwell, interview with the author.

163   *wrote up a witty Q&A*: Carol Caldwell, "Carrie Fisher: A Few Words on Princess Leia, Fame, and Feminism," *Rolling Stone*, July 21, 1983.

164   *Carrie arranged a trip*: Carol Caldwell and Blair Sabol, interviews with the author; Blair Sabol, "No Holds Barred: Palm Springs Pilgrimage," *New York Social Diary*, March 24, 2017.

164   *"his crusty skin cancer with a kitchen knife"*: Sabol, "No Holds Barred."

165 *"Why do I have to see her in a movie?"*: A close friend of Debbie Reynolds's, interview with the author.

165 *"My grandmother had three looks"*: Carrie Fisher, *The Princess Diarist* (New York: Blue Rider Press, 2016), 11.

166 *Carrie and Garry Shandling made fun*: *Tonight Show*, undated 1987, featured in *The Zen Diaries of Garry Shandling*, directed by Judd Apatow (New York: HBO, 2018).

166 *Eddie spoke to Carrie*: Carrie Fisher, *Shockaholic* (New York: Simon & Schuster, 2012), 49.

166 *They snorted cocaine together*: Alice Spivak, interview with the author. Carrie Fisher also mentioned it to friends, reported to the author.

166 *he dramatically thrust right in her face*: Susan Forristal, Marilyn Suzanne Miller, and Carol Caldwell, interviews with the author.

167 *Carrie and Paul's immediate honeymoon*: Peter Ames Carlin, *Homeward Bound: The Life of Paul Simon* (New York: Henry Holt, 2016); Hilburn, *Paul Simon*.

167 *Joan Hackett gave them a late wedding reception*: Joyce Purnick, "Joan Hackett; Actress Won 1982 Oscar Nomination," *New York Times*, Oct. 10, 1983.

168 *a boat trip down the Nile*: Carol Caldwell, interview with the author.

169 *Paul was introduced to* The New Show*'s now out-of-work bandleader*: Assorted clips; Carlin, *Homeward Bound*.

172 *Carrie was in London on May 23*: Ibid.; Carrie Fisher, *Wishful Drinking* (New York: Simon & Schuster, 2008), 135.

173 *she bought a lovely Cape Cod house*: Linda Marder, Carol Caldwell (Jack Nicholson comment), and Alice Spivak, interviews with the author; Nancy Collins, "Inside Carrie Fisher's House in Beverly Hills," *Architectural Digest*, Sept. 29, 2016.

176 *"I had the nerve to go up to him"*: *Brian Linehan's City Lights*, 1986.

179 *"sounded woozy and blurry"*: Carol Caldwell, interview with the author. (Note: David Kipper was called and interviewed by the author. He spoke at length about his work as an addiction specialist but cautioned that he could not talk about patients, past or present.)

182 *"when pen comes to paper"*: Matthew Gilbert, "Carrie Fisher Talked Very Candidly About Her Mother, Debbie Reynolds," *Boston Globe*, Sept. 14, 1990.

7. A WRITER WHO ACTS

Author conversations and interviews with confidential source who saw Carrie at rehab. And with Carol Caldwell, Penelope Spheeris, Richard Dreyfuss, Alice Spivak, Seven McDonald, Michael Childers, Mark Metcalf, two confidential friends of Carrie's, a confidential friend of Debbie's, Richard Sarafian Jr., Blair Sabol, Dr. James Phelps, Dr. Dean Parker, Marya Hornbacher, Julie Fast, Terri Cheney, Susan Kamil, Michael Gross, Bill Gross, Gary Springer, Wendy Kout, Trish Lande, Patricia Resnick, Will Trinkle, Meg Wolitzer, Marilyn Suzanne Miller, Bruce Cohen, Albert Brooks, Bruce Vilanch, Ron Raines, Tony Fingleton, and Marsha Mason.

183 *"She was very sweet at the hospital"*: A confidential observer, interview with the author.

184 *Carrie's Oak Pass house became a flocking point*: Anonymous friend of Carrie Fisher's, interview with the author.

188 *"She really illuminates parts of the human soul"*: Beverly D'Angelo, tape-recorded tribute at Women in Film and Video awards ceremony, April 13, 2005, on video provided by Women in Film and Video, Washington, D.C., chapter.

188 *Carrie was fixed up on a date*: Carrie Fisher, *Shockaholic* (New York: Simon & Schuster, 2011), 38; numerous interviews such as the Reliable Source, "Carrie Fisher on Her Blind Date with Chris Dodd," *Washington Post*, Nov. 10, 2011.

189 *"big sobriety anniversary party"*: Patricia Resnick, interview with the author.

189 *"[I was] Joan of Narc"*: Irene Lacher, "Princess Carrie: Books: Carrie Fisher Seems to Have Mastered the Art of Turning a Troubled and Glamorous Life into Bestsellers," *Los Angeles Times*, Sept. 7, 1990.

189 *she was diagnosed, once again, with bipolar two*: Many interviews and statements, including "Ask Carrie Fisher: I'm Bipolar—How Do You Feel at Peace with Mental Illness?," *Guardian*, Nov. 30, 2016.

189 *She even named her two moods*: Numerous interviews, including one with Diane Sawyer, *Primetime*, Dec. 21, 2000.

190 *Carrie actually had a dual diagnosis*: Information about mental illness and its relation to creativity and intelligence, here and throughout the book, was found during interviews with Dr. Parker and Dr. Phelps. In addition, these sources were utilized: Stephen M. Strakowski et al., "The Impact of Substance Abuse on the Course of Bipolar Disorder," *Biological Psychiatry* 48, no. 6 (2000): 477–85; Erica Cirino, "Bipolar Disorder and Creativity," *Healthline*, Feb. 7, 2018; Robert A. Power et al., "Polygenic Risk Scores for Schizophrenia and Bipolar Disorder Predict Creativity," *Nature Neuroscience*, June 8, 2015, 953–55; Donald W. Goodwin, "Alcoholism and Heredity: A Review and Hypothesis," *Archives of General Psychiatry* 36, no. 1 (1979): 57–61; Donald W. Goodwin, "Alcoholism and Genetics: The Sins of the Fathers," *Archives of General Psychiatry* 42, no. 2 (1985): 171–74; C. Robert Cloninger, Michael Bohman, and Sören Sigvardsson, "Inheritance of Alcohol Abuse: Cross-Fostering Analysis of Adopted Men," *Archives of General Psychiatry* 38, no. 8 (1981): 861–68.

191 *"He shot speed for 13 years"*: "Carrie Fisher Says Her Dad Eddie Is 'Losing It,'" Reuters, Feb. 13, 2010.

191 *Paul Slansky, an* Esquire *and* New Times *writer*: *People* Special Issue, *Carrie Fisher, Hollywood Princess*: "How the Actress Became a Novelist."

192 *Blair Sabol easily persuaded the literary agent*: Blair Sabol, interview with the author. Additional information on Al Lowman from Bill Gross, interview with the author.

192 *Carrie replaced the snarky-essays idea*: *Brian Linehan's City Lights*, 1986; Michael Gross, "Carrie Fisher, Novelist, Looks Back at the Edge," *New York Times*, Aug. 14, 1987.

193 *"She would write—in longhand"*: "How the Actress Became a Novelist."

193–94 *Carolyn See noted prominently in her review*: Carolyn See, "Heartfelt, Original Outtakes from the Life of an Actress," *Los Angeles Times*, July 27, 1987.

194 *"That's sexist" and untrue*: *Larry King Live*, 1990.

196 *Carrie, in May 1987, flew to Israel*: A neighbor of Carrie Fisher's, conversation with the author; Fisher, *My Girls*, 208–209.

196 *Bruce Wagner was along as well*: A neighbor of Carrie Fisher's, conversation with the author; various articles including Matt Thorne, "Bruce Wagner in Hollywood," *Los Angeles Review of Books*, March 9, 2014.

197 *"She's tremendously forgiving"*: Bruce Wagner to Mimi Avins, in unpublished interview portion supplied to author.

198 *"Everyone knows Carrie Fisher for her portrait"*: See, "Heartfelt, Original Outtakes from the Life of an Actress."

198 *"a cult classic"*: *Kirkus Reviews*, Aug. 5, 1987; *Washington Post, San Jose Mercury News,* and *Publishers Weekly,* found on Amazon page for *Postcards.*

199 *"bounced into the bathroom"*: Gross, "Carrie Fisher, Novelist, Looks Back at the Edge."

199 *"thinking she was hysterically funny"*: Michael Gross, interview with the author.

199 *"She is an interviewer's delight"*: Stephanie Mansfield, "Carrie Fisher's Candid Conversations," *Washington Post,* Aug. 13, 1987.

202 *"I would be snorting heroin"*: Carrie to Diane Sawyer, *Primetime,* Dec. 21, 2000.

202 *Debbie was off on a national tour:* Alvin Klein, "THEATER; Debbie Reynolds Re-Creates 'Molly,'" *New York Times,* April 1, 1990.

203 *"We'd have long meetings and brainstorm"*: Nina Jacobson in conversation with the *Los Angeles Times* writer Mimi Avins, shared with the author.

203 *Nina, at that point and soon after:* Human Rights Campaign, "Nina Jacobson Receives the HRC Visibility Award," YouTube, posted March 20, 2016, www.youtube .com/watch?v=27L2NnO2LRc.

203 *extremely funny off-screen:* Jared Cowan, "Director Joe Dante Looks Back at Working with Carrie Fisher on *The 'Burbs,*" *L.A. Weekly,* Dec. 29, 2016.

205 *there were aspects of Richard Dreyfuss:* Lacher, "Princess Carrie."

207 *"I didn't give Paul the peace he needed"*: A confidante of Carrie Fisher's, interview with the author.

207 *"If you're going out with me"*: Sherryl Connelly, "After Troubled Times, Fisher Buoyed by Wit, Friendships," *Baltimore Sun,* Sept. 14, 1990.

207 *"I like to talk and I like exchanges"*: Lacher, "Princess Carrie."

208 *something that 50 percent of people with bipolar disorder do:* Dr. Dean Parker, interview with the author.

208 *"When you're high, it's tremendous"*: Kay Redfield Jamison, quoted in Benedict Carey, "Carrie Fisher Puts Pen and Voice in Service of Bipolar Pride," *New York Times,* Dec. 28, 2016.

208 *"I have often asked myself whether"*: Kay Redfield Jamison, *An Unquiet Mind: A Memoir of Moods and Madness* (New York: Knopf, 1995), 217–18. In addition, see Frederick K. Goodwin and Kay Redfield Jamison, *Manic-Depressive Illness: Bipolar Disorders and Recurrent Depression,* 2nd ed. (New York: Oxford University Press, 2007).

209 *Surrender the Pink got some excellent reviews:* Jon Anderson, "Another Seriously Funny Fisher Novel," *Chicago Tribune,* Sept. 24, 1990.

211 *"colder than a well-digger's butt"*: Carrie said this in various interviews, and it's included in Melissa Hellstern, *Getting Along Famously* (New York: Dutton Adult, 2008), 139.

212 *"we felt bad for not being famous"*: Nina Jacobson in conversation with the *Los Angeles Times* writer Mimi Avins, shared with the author.

212 *Carrie had a unique mission:* Connelly, "After Troubled Times, Fisher Buoyed by Wit, Friendships."

214 *"a born screenwriter"*: Joan Juliet Buck, *Vanity Fair,* Aug. 1990.

214 *Mike Nichols had briefly wanted:* A friend of Carrie Fisher's, interview with the author.

215 *"Annette was going with Ed Begley Jr. then"*: Suzanne Finstad interview with Carrie Fisher, unused material for Finstad's biography *Warren Beatty: A Private Man* (New York: Harmony, 2005). Finstad provided the transcript for the author.

215 *"I feel the argument weighed heavier"*: Connelly, "After Troubled Times, Fisher Buoyed by Wit, Friendships."

215 *Lillian Burns Sidney insisted on vetting*: Confidential confidante of Debbie Reynolds's.

216 *But Meryl Streep's was the performance*: Hal Hinson, "Postcards from the Edge," *Washington Post*, Sept. 14, 1990; Owen Gleiberman, "Postcards from the Edge," *Entertainment Weekly*, Sept. 14, 1990.

217 *Eddie Fisher was spending four weeks*: Dollie F. Ryan, "Eddie Fisher Lived 'on the Edge': Hollywood: The Singer-Actor Has Some Sobering Reflections on His Mistakes and Substance Abuse," *Los Angeles Times*, Nov. 9, 1990.

219 *"You're having a pissing contest"*: Jess Cagle, "Whoopi Goldberg Duels with Disney," *Entertainment Weekly*, May 29, 1992.

8. "WHEN I LOVE, I LOVE FOR MILES"

Author interviews and conversations with Trish Lande, Michael Childers, a confidential entertainment writer, six confidential friends of Carrie's, Bruce Cohen, Albert Brooks, Bruce Vilanch, Richard Dreyfuss, Marcia Clark, Carol Caldwell, Judge Scott Gordon, Will Trinkle, Selina Cadell, Sherryl Connelly, Michelle Phillips, Matthew Diamond, Betsy Rapoport, Sydny Miner, and Tony Taccone.

221 *Kevin Huvane and Bryan Lourd*: James Andrew Miller, *Powerhouse: The Untold Story of Hollywood's Creative Artists Agency* (New York: Custom House, 2016).

222 *"pies cooling on the window sill"*: Many references, including Carrie Fisher, *Postcards from the Edge* (New York: Simon & Schuster, 1987).

224 *became extremely ill in the last stages*: Will Trinkle, interview with the author.

225 *"Julian threw up what must have been about a pint"*: Carrie Fisher, *Shockaholic* (New York: Simon & Schuster, 2012), 116.

226 *A birth announcement was sent to friends*: Birth announcement supplied to author by a friend of Carrie Fisher's.

226–27 *1700 Coldwater Canyon*: Leslie Bennetts, "Debbie Reynolds in the Desert," *Vanity Fair*, Oct. 1994; accounts of previous owners and inhabitants in many articles.

231 *Leslie Bennetts later wrote that tactfully avoiding*: Bennetts, "Debbie Reynolds in the Desert."

233 *Plugging the book a month later*: *Charlie Rose*, April 5, 1994.

235 *it earned some of the kind of praise*: Michael Dorris, "Captivating, Complicated Cora Sharpe," review of *Delusions of Grandma*, by Carrie Fisher, *Los Angeles Times*, March 17, 1994; "Carrie Fisher's 'Grandma' Too Much of a Good Thing," *Hartford Courant*, March 20, 1994.

235 *"I wept when I first went"*: Bennetts, "Debbie Reynolds in the Desert."

235 *The hotel would eventually fail*: John Willen, "Mismanagement Troubles Doomed Debbie Reynolds Hotel," *Las Vegas Sun*, July 31, 1998; Bill Kohlaase, "Despite Misfortune with Marriage and Money, Unsinkable Debbie Always Kept Her Chin Up," *Los Angeles Times*, Jan. 13, 1997.

236 *Carrie sent her mother a big check*: Bennetts, "Debbie Reynolds in the Desert."

236 *"There's something that happens"*: Ibid.

237 *imploring her friend Albert Brooks*: Albert Brooks, interview with the author.

237 *Debbie was hospitalized for a week*: Reynolds, *Unsinkable*, 176.

237 Been There, Done That *was quite brutal*: Eddie Fisher, *Been There, Done That*, with David Fisher (New York: St. Martin's Press, 1999).

238 *"I'm having my DNA fumigated!"*: Carrie Fisher, *Wishful Drinking* (New York: Simon & Schuster, 2008), 67; Jim Slotek, "Carrie Fisher Struggled with Depression, Addiction," *Toronto Sun*, Dec. 27, 2016; many other places.

238 *"I saw my mom"*: Carrie Fisher, *Shockaholic* (New York: Simon & Schuster, 2012), 137.

239 *they had forged a friendship in 1998*: Carrie Fisher, "Star Wars Actress Carrie Fisher Reveals Her Bizarre Friendship with Elizabeth Taylor, the Woman Who Stole Her Father from Her Mother," *Daily Mail*, Nov. 6, 2011.

240 *"I got in trouble in school"*: Sarah Paulson, "Billie Lourd's New Life," *Town and Country*, Aug. 1, 2017.

240 *"Carrie always talked to Billie like an adult"*: Ibid.

9. "I AM MENTALLY ILL. I CAN SAY THAT"

Author interviews and conversations with Bill LaVallee, Roy Teeluck, Marcia Clark, Maggie, Terri Cheney, Alice Spivak, Jim Hart, Stephanie Miller, Selina Cadell, Frank Coraci, Jörn Weisbrodt, Salman Rushdie, Richard Dreyfuss, Bruce Cohen, Marya Hornbacher, Joanne Doan, Betsy Rapoport, Murat Theatre lecture tour official, and three anonymous friends of Carrie's.

243 *when Carrie was having her house photographed*: Carrie to a friend.

244 *The Pacific Group was run*: Official bio of Clancy Imislund and various AA cognoscenti. (Imislund was called by this author, and he initially agreed to be interviewed just about Carrie's charity work with his Midnight Mission—"I was her [AA] sponsor!" Then at the outset of the appointed-time interview, he declined.)

245 *The move in favor of stricture loosening*: Various websites and Bill LaVallee, interview with the author.

248 *"If you ever touch my darling Heather"*: Kyle Swenson, "Carrie Fisher's Gross but Supremely Satisfying Warning to a Hollywood Sexual Harasser," *Washington Post*, Oct. 17, 2017.

249 *possibly to none more so*: "James Blunt and Carrie Fisher: The Odd Couple," *Independent*, Feb. 12, 2006.

252 *"Oh, I'm sorry," she says*: Carrie Fisher, *The Best Awful* (New York: Simon & Schuster, 2005), 2.

253 *"You've totally taken all the charm"*: Ibid., 6.

253 *"refus[ing] to take her bipolar medication"*: Ibid., 2.

257 *In 2002, Rufus's addiction to crystal meth*: Anthony DeCurtis, "Rufus Wainwright Journeys to 'Gay Hell' and Back," *New York Times*, Aug. 31, 2003; Ed Power, "Rufus: The Drugs, the Madness, the Redemption," *Independent*, Feb. 28, 2014.

258 *She was like a taming older sister*: Carrie and Courtney Love on *Conversations from the Edge*, YouTube.

258   *she befriended a low-key, dignified young actress*: Sarah Paulson, "Billie Lourd's New Life," *Town and Country*, Aug. 1, 2017.

259   *she went out with L.A.'s famous helicopter-pilot newsman*: "Carrie Fisher Wishes Transgender Ex-boyfriend the Best of Luck," *U.K. Express*, June 20, 2013.

259   *She met one of her most consequential*: "The Mystery of Hollywood's Dead Republican," *New York Times*, April 26, 2005.

260   *When Hillary Clinton was introduced*: Bruce Cohen, interview with the author.

260   *"Suzanne hadn't gone back on all her medications"*: Fisher, *The Best Awful*, 72.

261   *"still trying to act as if"*: Carrie in interview with *bp Magazine*, first issue 2004.

261   *"Something was breaking"*: Carrie to Diane Sawyer, *Primetime*, Dec. 21, 2000.

266   *"The manic depressive's battle"*: Mimi Avins, "Carrie Fisher Takes Reality for a Spin," *Los Angeles Times*, Jan. 24, 2004.

266   *It would be four years before Jane Pauley*: "Jane Pauley Shares Her Story," Books on *Dateline*, NBC News, Sept. 4, 2004.

266   *Catherine Zeta-Jones opened up about hers*: Lara Salahi, "Catherine Zeta-Jones Sheds Light on Bipolar II Disorder," CBS, April 14, 2011.

266   *Demi Lovato admitted that she had been diagnosed*: "Demi Lovato Opens Up About Her Bipolar Diagnosis," *Extra TV*, Nov. 30, 2016.

266   *Mariah Carey was able to admit*: Diane Herbst, "Mariah Carey and Bipolar Disorder: Overcoming the Stigma of Her Diagnosis," *PsyCom*, May 23, 2018.

266   *Britney Spears, who also experienced*: Caitlin McBride, "Britney Spears Opens Up on Bipolar Disorder: 'I Turn into a Different Person,'" *Independent*, Dec. 23, 2013.

267   *the designer Kate Spade tragically died*: Ashley Welch, "Kate Spade's Death Prompts Questions About Bipolar Disorder," CBS News, June 11, 2018.

267   *Jill Messick, who helped bring*: Evgenia Peretz, "How Jill Messick's Suicide Reflects the Tragedies of the #MeToo Era," *Vanity Fair*, Oct. 18, 2018.

267   *Margot Kidder was found walking*: Jennifer Bowles, "Actress Found Wandering in a Daze Was Writing Autobiography of Troubles," AP, April 25, 1996.

269   *"You can outlast anything"*: Carrie Fisher, interview quoted in Mary Ann McDonnell and Janet Wozniak, *Positive Parenting for Bipolar Kids: How to Identify, Treat, Manage, and Rise to the Challenge* (New York: Bantam, 2008).

269   *"Carrie is funny, wise"*: Gavin de Becker to Mimi Avins, in an unpublished interview portion supplied to author.

269   *"Carrie is a warrior"*: Bruce Wagner to Mimi Avins, in an unpublished interview portion supplied to author.

10. THE WARRIOR IN THE WAR ZONE

Author interviews and conversations with Bruce Vilanch, Bruce Cohen, Betsy Rapoport, Tony Taccone, Susan Lovett, Steve Callaghan, Sean Daniel, four confidential friends of Carrie's, a confidential theater worker, Kerri Kolen, Marsha Mason, Kathleen Cairns, Todd Haimes, Dr. James Phelps, Salman Rushdie, Ron Raines, Richard Dreyfuss, Guy Strobel, Fenton Bailey, Randy Barbato, and David Zentz.

271   *At the 1989 ceremony, she was a presenter*: Marco Dog, "Carrie Fisher and Martin Short on the Oscars," YouTube, posted Sept. 8, 2013, www.youtube.com/watch?v =oSwAuslFL8A.

272 *He was very tired, but he and Carrie stayed up*: Carrie to friends, reported to the author.

272 *Her brother, Todd, has reported*: Todd Fisher, *My Girls: A Lifetime with Carrie and Debbie* (New York: William Morrow, 2018), 294.

273 *"I'm lucky to have you in my life"*: An email to Betsy Rapoport, shared with the author.

274 *As soon as she recovered*: Ibid.

275 *"But I HAVEN'T lost [Greg]"*: Ibid.

275 *"If Carrie and I could have been lovers"*: Tape-recorded tribute at Women in Film and Video Awards ceremony, April 13, 2005, on video provided by Women in Film and Video, Washington, D.C., chapter.

278 *Arney and his team watched Carrie's pitch*: Christie D'Zurilla, "Carrie Fisher's 'Wishful Drinking,' Created at Geffen, Was a Feat of 'Incredible Strength,'" *Los Angeles Times*, Dec. 27, 2016.

278 *"Her appeal crossed all boundaries"*: Ibid.

278 *"Beverly Hills yard sale"*: Charles McNulty, "Carrie Fisher's 'Wishful Drinking' Shows That When It's Her Story on Stage, She Brings It Home," *Los Angeles Times*, Nov. 17, 2006.

279 *Carrie made a featured appearance on* 30 Rock: Constance Grady, "Carrie Fisher's 30 Rock Episode Hilariously Skewered Hollywood's Sexism and Ageism," *Vox*, Dec. 28, 2016.

282 *the patter and Carrie's empathic touch*: Ben Brantley, "Just Me and My Celebrity Shadows," *New York Times*, Oct. 4, 2009.

283 *"She has the gift"*: Ibid.

286 *"There hadn't been a note"*: Carrie Fisher, *Shockaholic* (New York: Simon & Schuster, 2012), 118.

286 *"For the first time in my life"*: Ibid., 16.

286 *"pretty much 24–7"*: Ibid., 17–18.

287 *there were fewer effective treatments*: Dr. James Phelps, interview with the author.

287 *Kitty Dukakis, the now-eighty-two-year-old wife*: Katharine Q. Seelye, "Kitty Dukakis, a Beneficiary of Electroshock Therapy, Emerges as Its Evangelist," *New York Times*, Dec. 31, 2016.

288 *"Given Kitty's experience, I can't support"*: Ibid.

288 *"It is not an exaggeration"*: Katherine Kitty Dukakis, "Katherine Kitty Dukakis on ECT," *Psych Central*, Oct. 8, 2018; Kitty Dukakis and Larry Tye, *Shock: The Healing Power of Electroconvulsive Therapy* (New York: Avery, 2006).

288 Entertainment Weekly *called it "drolly hysterical"*: "Carrie Fisher Brings WISHFUL DRINKING Back to Berkeley Rep's Roda Theater 7/9–23," *Broadway World*, July 9, 2009.

288 *"Fisher knows how to write"*: Robert Hurwitt, "Review: 'Wishful Drinking' Fisher's Tell-All," *SFGate*, Feb. 21, 2008.

288 *"Addiction, mental illness, movie-star parents"*: "Carrie Fisher Brings WISHFUL DRINKING Back to Berkeley Rep's Roda Theater 7/9–23."

289 *"you don't think she's trivializing"*: Brantley, "Just Me and My Celebrity Shadows."

290 *"One of the things that baffles me"*: Carrie Fisher, *Wishful Drinking* (New York: Simon & Schuster, 2008), 159.

290 *"was mortgaged to the skies"*: Carrie Fisher, *The Princess Diarist* (New York: Blue Rider Press, 2016), 219.

291 *"pretty slight, padded out with big type"*: Charles McGrath, "Princess Leia's Wit Tames the Dark Side," *New York Times*, Jan. 1, 2009.

291 *Boyd had been a heroin addict*: Scott Johnson, "The Heroin-Addict Actress, the Interventionist and a Grieving Mother's Court Fight: 'She Didn't Want to Die,'" *Hollywood Reporter*, Dec. 8, 2016.

293 *Three months after Haimes's meeting*: Confidential friend of Carrie Fisher's.

293 *Later she would say she wished*: Alan Duke, "Conrad Murray Sentenced to Four Years Behind Bars," CNN, Nov. 30, 2011.

293 *medically administered by his doctor*: Ibid.

293 *"I could swear that I could see things"*: Fisher, *Shockaholic*, 117.

294 *In fact, they could have kissed Carrie*: Brantley, "Just Me and My Celebrity Shadows."

295 *Robin Williams came backstage one night*: A confidante of Carrie Fisher's.

295 *Carrie remembered their meeting after the play*: "Carrie Fisher on Robin Williams: He Opened Up to Me About Bipolar Disorder," *Hollywood Reporter*, Aug. 13, 2014.

297 *would-be actress named Amy Breliant*: Johnson, "Heroin-Addict Actress, the Interventionist and a Grieving Mother's Court Fight."

299 *It was good, she said*: Jessie Heyman, "Carrie Fisher Loses 50 Pounds on Jenny Craig; 'Star Wars' Actress Reaches Weight Loss Goal," *Huffington Post*, Sept. 2, 2011.

299 *"Was I always funny?"*: *Bright Lights: Starring Carrie Fisher and Debbie Reynolds*, directed by Alexis Bloom and Fisher Stevens (New York: HBO, 2017).

300 *Eddie died soon after*: Raquel Maria Dillon, "Eddie Fisher Dies; 5 Marriages Included Debbie Reynolds, Liz Taylor," *Seattle Times*, Sept. 23, 2010.

300 *Amy Breliant, the young actress*: Johnson, "Heroin-Addict Actress, the Interventionist and a Grieving Mother's Court Fight."

301 *They loved her in Sydney*: Maria Noakes, "A Toast to Carrie Fisher's Wishful Drinking," *Perth Now*, Nov. 15, 2010.

301 *she gave a deeply thoughtful interview*: Lauren Paige Kennedy, "20 Questions for Carrie Fisher," *WebMD*, Nov. 3, 2010.

301 *"My mother, she loved us"*: Ibid.

302 *"No wonder she's mentally ill"*: Fisher, *Shockaholic*, 2.

303 *She decried the self-starving culture*: Ibid., 29.

303 *Of her friend Michael Jackson's death*: Ibid., 73.

303 *When she spoke of things Michael*: *The Smoking Gun*, June 16, 2004.

304 *Carrie was profoundly disgusted*: Fisher, *Shockaholic*, 64.

304 *The Chandlers eventually received $15 million*: Nick Allen, "Michael Jackson: Father of Jordan Chandler Shoots Himself Dead," *Telegraph*, Nov. 17, 2009.

304 *Now she said that Kennedy's question*: Fisher, *Shockaholic*, 45.

304 *"just another missed opportunity"*: Ibid., 113.

304 Shockaholic *was released on November 1, 2011*: William Kist, "Carrie Fisher and Rick Reilly Write the Funniest Books to Cap the Year," *Plain Dealer*, Jan. 3, 2012.

305 *During one of her book tour visits*: Houston PBS, season 11, episode 4, Sept. 17, 2012, via YouTube.

305 *"Carrie was so real"*: Sharon Horgan, "Carrie Fisher Was So Real It Was Dangerous," *Guardian*, Jan. 3, 2017.

306 *Carrie was being informed*: Johnson, "Heroin-Addict Actress, the Interventionist

and a Grieving Mother's Court Fight"; Tim Kenneally, "Carrie Fisher Heroin OD Lawsuit Moves Toward Trial," *The Wrap*, October 28, 2016.

11. WORKING THROUGH ANYTHING

Author conversations and interviews with Steve Callaghan, three confidential sources, Donavan Freberg, Alexis Bloom, Salman Rushdie, Richard Dreyfuss, Sarah Chandonnet, Tony Taccone, Dr. James Phelps, and Julie Fast. Regarding feminism in Hollywood, author conversations with Callie Khouri, Cathy Schulman of Women in Film, Geena Davis, and ten other Hollywood professionals involved in the film industry feminism fight.

307   *Her friend Tracey Ullman*: Mimi Avins, in unpublished interview supplied to author.
307   *"Everything was wrong with Gary"*: Terry Gross, *Fresh Air*, NPR, Nov. 2016.
308   *"He would sit like Winston Churchill"*: Ibid.
308   *On August 23, 2012, attorneys*: "Carrie Fisher's Heroin House of Horrors! Her Dark Secrets Revealed," *Radar Online*, Dec. 29, 2016.
309   *it was reported that Carrie's assistant Garret Edington*: Ibid.
309   *In the "third amended complaint"*: Ibid.
309   *"during the last week of June"*: Ibid.
310   *On the boat, Carrie performed*: Josh Grossberg, "Carrie Fisher Briefly Hospitalized After Suffering Bipolar Incident Aboard Cruise Ship," *E! News*, Feb. 26, 2013.
311   *"I was in a very severe manic state"*: "Carrie Fisher Hospitalized After Bizarre Behavior on Cruise Ship," *People*, Feb. 26, 2013.
311   *Seroquel, which is helpful to many people*: Dr. James Phelps and Julie Fast, interviews with the author.
311   *"This is not a neat disease"*: "Carrie Fisher Hospitalized After Bizarre Behavior on Cruise Ship."
311   *She met with Steven Soderbergh*: John Katsilometes, "Debbie Reynolds Says She Wanted More of Liberace the Showman in 'Candelabra,'" The Kats Report, *Las Vegas Sun*, May 23, 2013.
312   *In February, the tabloid the* Daily Mail: "Carrie Fisher Caught Acting Erratically as She Laughs Off Concerns of a Drug Relapse," *Daily Mail*, Feb. 20, 2014.
313   *His Kylo Ren—fitted out in glorious metal*: David Kamp, "Cover Story: *Star Wars: The Last Jedi*, the Definitive Preview," *Vanity Fair*, Summer 2017.
314   *"He made us all feel"*: Chris Gardner, "Carrie Fisher on Robin Williams," *Hollywood Reporter*, Aug. 14, 2014.
315   *Once she got onstage, her introductory words*: "*Catastrophe* Creator and Star Recounts Carrie Fisher's Final TV Shoot," *Hollywood Reporter*, Aug. 3, 2017.
316   *"It was a writers' show"*: Tribeca, "CATASTROPHE Stars Sharon Horgan and Carrie Fisher Talked Writing for Women at Tribeca 2016," YouTube, posted April 20, 2016, www.youtube.com/watch?v=ZOjRtuWhEcc.
316   *It took a while for Carrie, Sharon, and Rob to "become pals"*: Ibid.
316   *"She was, she said, Mickey Mouse"*: Sharon Horgan, "Carrie Fisher Was So Real It Was Dangerous," *Guardian*, Jan. 3, 2017.
317   *At some point in late 2014*: Alexis Bloom, in conversation with the author.
317   *Alexis says that under no circumstances*: Ibid.

318   *Most moving was footage of Debbie's receipt: Bright Lights: Starring Carrie Fisher and Debbie Reynolds*, directed by Alexis Bloom and Fisher Stevens (New York: HBO, 2017).

318   *Alexis saw the melancholy in Carrie*: Matt Grobar, "'Bright Lights' Directors Alexis Bloom and Fisher Stevens on Two Hollywood Icons Who Never Stopped Performing," *Deadline Hollywood*, June 25, 2017. Additional material on the making of the documentary: "Inside Bright Lights: The Final Curtain for Debbie Reynolds and Carrie Fisher," VF.com, Jan. 6, 2017.

319   *"I just admire my mother"*: Gross, *Fresh Air*.

320   *"I think it's a stupid conversation"*: "Let's Revisit Amy Robach's Interview with Carrie Fisher," *TVNewser*, Dec. 27, 2016.

320   *"They don't want to hire all of me"*: "Carrie Fisher on Diets, Demons, and Her Dramatic Star Wars Reinvention," *Good Housekeeping*, Nov. 2016.

320   *"There are not a lot of choices"*: "CATASTROPHE Stars Sharon Horgan and Carrie Fisher Talked Writing for Women at Tribeca 2016."

320   *As far back as 2004, the actress Geena Davis*: Geena Davis, interviews with the author in 2006 and 2015.

321   *Women in Film, partnering with*: Cathy Schulman (2015), Callie Khouri (2015), and ten other activists for feminism in the industry, interviews with the author; various websites and press releases from Sundance Institute and USC Annenberg School for Communication; Cynthia Littleton, "Study: Female Directors Face Strong Bias in Landing Studio Films," *Variety*, April 22, 2015.

321   *The disparity, said the rare female*: Nicole Sazegar, "5 Kathryn Bigelow Quotes on How to Shut Down Sexism in Any Industry," *Entity Magazine*, Sept. 18, 2017.

321   *Then came the hacking of Sony Studios' internal emails*: Madeline Berg, "Everything You Need to Know About the Hollywood Pay Gap," *Forbes*, Nov. 12, 2015.

321   *Patricia Arquette, upon accepting her Oscar*: "Patricia Arquette Uses Oscars Speech to Call for Equal Pay for Women," *Guardian*, Feb. 22, 2015.

321   *Cate Blanchett made the same point*: "Cate Blanchett: Pay Everyone the Same and 'Get On with It,'" *New Zealand Herald*, Nov. 30, 2015.

321   *At the same event, Reese Witherspoon launched*: Charlotte Alter, "Reese Witherspoon Slams Sexist Red Carpet Questions, Encourages Journalists to #AskHerMore," *Time*, Feb. 25, 2015.

322   *One of the sharpest, fiercest*: Schumer's "Last Fuckable Day" on TV and internet; Bruce Handy, "An Oral History of Amy Schumer's 'Last Fuckable Day' Sketch," VF.com, May 3, 2016.

322   *On the heels of this*: Ben Child, "Maggie Gyllenhaal: At 37 I Was 'Too Old' for Role Opposite 55-Year-Old Man," *Guardian*, April 22, 2015.

322   *And in May, at the Cannes*: Alyssa Bailey, "Emily Blunt Takes On Cause for Women Everywhere: Flats," *Guardian*, May 19, 2015.

322   *"This is what fifty-seven looks like"*: Joanne Conrath Bamberger, "Frances McDormand Is My New Hero After Saying 'This Is What 57 Really Looks Like,'" *Broad Side*, May 2015.

322   *Meryl Streep announced that she was funding*: "Meryl Streep Backs Screenwriter Lab for Women over 40," Women in Hollywood site, Feb. 12, 2016.

322   *In a Carrie Fisher–style moment*: Ashley Lee, "Jennifer Lawrence Pens Essay: 'Why Do I Make Less Than My Male Co-stars?,'" *Hollywood Reporter*, Oct. 13, 2015.

323 *Tina Fey particularly admired*: Zach Johnson, "Tina Fey Remembers Carrie Fisher's 'Honest Writing' and 'Razor-Sharp Wit,'" *E! News*, Dec. 28, 2016.

323 *Sometimes she didn't hide her pain*: Merope Mills, "My Time with Carrie Fisher, a Hurricane of Energy, Charisma, and Foul Language," *Guardian*, Dec. 29, 2016.

324 *In November 2015—just a month before*: Gregg Kilday, "Debbie Reynolds' Charitable Work Earned Her the Academy's Hersholt Award," *Hollywood Reporter*, Nov. 17, 2015.

326 *"British professor who will be able"*: Mills, "My Time with Carrie Fisher, a Hurricane of Energy, Charisma, and Foul Language."

12. A YEAR FROM HELL, A YEAR OF FINAL KINDNESS

Author interviews and conversations with Selina Cadell, Sarah Chandonnet, an anonymous confidante, a friend of Margot Kidder's, Orian Williams, Vincent Spano, Richard Dreyfuss, three anonymous friends of Carrie's, Bruce Cohen, Salman Rushdie, and Michelle Mendelsohn.

327 *"This whole year was the year from hell"*: Terry Gross, *Fresh Air*, NPR, Nov. 2016.

328 *"this incredible archaeological find"*: Simon Hattenstone, "Carrie Fisher on Harrison Ford: 'I Love Him; I'll Always Feel Something for Him,'" *Guardian*, Nov. 20, 2016.

329 *"I've spent so many years"*: Gross, *Fresh Air*.

329 *during the longer intervals in L.A.*: David Kamp, "Cover Story: Star Wars: The Last Jedi, the Definitive Preview," *Vanity Fair*, Summer 2017.

330 *The lawyers for Gianna Breliant*: Official filing, *Gianna Breliant v. Warren Boyd, Commerce Resources, Carrie Fisher, et al.*, Superior Court, County of Los Angeles, North Central District: third amended complaint; Michael Cieply, "Judge Agrees to Seal Carrie Fisher's Video Deposition in Drug Death Case Involving the Real 'Cleaner,'" *Deadline Hollywood*, Aug. 16, 2016.

330 *"Storm Troopers, Wookies"*: Brittany N. Ellis, "Humanists Honor Star Wars Actress Carrie Fisher," *Harvard Crimson*, April 19, 2016.

330 *"The Harvard Pops Orchestra played"*: Jeffrey Blackwell, "Carrie Fisher of 'Star Wars' Fame Continues the Battle," *Harvard Gazette*, April 19, 2016.

332 *On April 30, Carrie was a guest*: Megan Carpentier, "White House Correspondents' Dinner: Star Power, but According to Whom?," *Guardian*, April 30, 2016.

332 *she touchingly ended the conversation*: Merope Mills, "My Time with Carrie Fisher, a Hurricane of Energy, Charisma, and Foul Language," *Guardian*, Dec. 29, 2016.

332 *She had copiously apologized*: Ibid.

332 *"I can't help you with your homework"*: Carrie Fisher, "Tell Me Your Story, I'll Tell You Mine," *Guardian*, June 10, 2016.

333 *"Now the reaction I sometimes get is disappointment"*: Carrie Fisher, *The Princess Diarist* (New York: Blue Rider Press, 2016), 227.

333 *"how proud I am of her"*: Fisher, *The Princess Diarist*, 244.

334 *"For my mother—for being too stubborn"*: Fisher, *The Princess Diarist*, 249.

334 *At some point after the middle of 2016*: Author interview with a close friend of Kidder's.

334 *She empathized with the advice seeker*: Carrie Fisher, "Ask Carrie Fisher: My Husband Has Been Seeing Prostitutes. Can I Trust Him Again?," *Guardian*, Sept. 6, 2016.

336 *"Being around Carrie was an irreplaceable gift"*: Kamp, "Cover Story: *Star Wars: The Last Jedi*, the Definitive Preview."

336 *A month earlier, in August*: Cieply, "Judge Agrees to Seal Carrie Fisher's Video Deposition in Drug Death Case Involving the Real 'Cleaner.'"

336 *Immediately after the deposition*: Ibid.

338 *On October 24, three days after*: Tim Kenneally, "Carrie Fisher Heroin OD Lawsuit Moves Toward Trial," *Wrap*, Oct. 28, 2016; Peter Kiefer, "Carrie Fisher Faces Trial in Heroin-Related Wrongful Death Lawsuit," *Hollywood Reporter*, Oct. 28, 2016; Ted Johnson, "Judge Refuses to Remove Carrie Fisher from Wrongful Death Lawsuit," *Variety*, Oct. 28, 2016.

338 *Carrie issued this statement*: Ibid.

339 *thanks to the executive director Fred Roos*: Author interview with anonymous source.

342 *At the end of a bit of an argument*: Jamie Blynn, "Todd Fisher's New Book Details Last Exchange with Sister Carrie Fisher Before She Was on Life Support," *US Weekly*, May 30, 2018.

342 *Carrie's final* Guardian *advice column*: Carrie Fisher, "Ask Carrie Fisher: I'm Bipolar—How Do You Feel at Peace with Mental Illness?," *Guardian*, Nov. 30, 2016.

343 *"when she was going up"*: Sharon Horgan, "Carrie Fisher Was So Real It Was Dangerous," *Guardian*, Jan. 3, 2017.

344 *She made an even stronger version*: "Carrie Fisher Draws from Her Personal Journals in 'The Princess Diarist,'" *All Things Considered*, NPR, Nov. 22, 2016.

344 *"Be kind. Don't hurt other people"*: Andy Greene, "Carrie Fisher on LSD, Death, and Sex with Han Solo," *Rolling Stone*, Nov. 28, 2016.

345 *During one of their last days shooting*: Rob Delaney, "I Revered Carrie Fisher Until I Met Her. Then I Loved Her," *Guardian*, Dec. 28, 2016.

345 *In late November,* Rolling Stone *asked Carrie*: Greene, "Carrie Fisher on LSD, Death, and Sex with Han Solo."

345 *Right after her death*: "Addict Carrie Fisher 'High as a Kite' Before Her Death, Claims Source," *Radar*, Dec. 27, 2016; Kate Sheehy, "Carrie Fisher Reportedly Had Drug Relapse Before Death," *New York Post*, Dec. 27, 2016.

346 *she made a "handshake deal"*: Dana Harris, "Carrie Fisher Was About to Announce Stage Show 'Wishful Drinking Strikes Back: From Star Wars to, Uh, Star Wars!' (Exclusive)," *IndieWire*, Dec. 27, 2016.

346 *On December 17, she appeared as a guest*: Lucy Mapstone, "Graham Norton: Carrie Fisher Nearly Cancelled Her Final Interview with Me," *Independent*, Sept. 28, 2017.

346 *she had a restaurant dinner with Sharon Horgan*: Rushdie, interview with the author; "Sharon Horgan Remembers Her Last Dinner with Carrie Fisher," *Late Night with Seth Meyers*, YouTube, posted June 6, 2017, www.youtube.com/watch?v=xfpJbpa02ns.

347 *Todd had told the Associated Press*: Christopher Mele, "Carrie Fisher in Intensive Care After Medical Incident on Plane," *New York Times*, Dec. 23, 2016.

347–48 *In quickly subsequent statements*: Antoinette Bueno, "Exclusive: Carrie Fisher in Intensive Care After Heart Attack," *ET*, Dec. 23, 2016.

348 *"Carrie is in stable condition"*: "Debbie Reynolds Says Daughter in Stable Condition," *Washington Post*, Dec. 25, 2016.

349 *"She was setting me up"*: "Todd Fisher on Life with Carrie and Debbie," *Sunday Morning*, CBS, June 24, 2018.

351 *The funeral for Debbie and Carrie*: "Carrie Fisher and Debbie Reynolds Buried Together in Los Angeles," *Guardian*, Jan. 6, 2017.

352 *a memorial "show" was held*: Embry Roberts, "Carrie Fisher and Debbie Reynolds Remembered by Family, Friends at Memorial 'Show,'" *Today Show*, March 26, 2017; Jayme Deerwester, "All the Details of Carrie and Debbie's Memorial Service," *USA Today*, March 25, 2017; www.debbiereynolds.com.

354 *the internet came alive with the long-delayed results*: Bryan Alexander, "Heroin, Cocaine Found in Carrie Fisher's System," *USA Today*, June 19, 2017.

355 *"My mom battled drug addiction"*: Scott Stump, "Billie Lourd Speaks Out on Addiction After Autopsy Says Carrie Fisher Had Cocaine in System," *USA Today*, June 19, 2017.

356 *"If it weren't for Carrie Fisher"*: Patrick Kennedy, statement released by his office.

356 *"Onscreen, at least, Carrie Fisher has come back"*: Nate Jones, "How 'Star Wars: The Last Jedi' Handles Carrie Fisher's Death," *Business Insider*, Nov. 18, 2017.

357 *"We'll just cut right to the chase"*: Devon Ivie, "Feign Surprise When We Tell You Carrie Fisher Wrote *The Last Jedi*'s Funniest Lines," *Vulture, New York*, Dec. 23, 2017.

357 *"After death takes someone from you"*: Carrie Fisher, *Shockaholic* (New York: Simon & Schuster, 2012), 116.

357 *Billie Lourd gave permission for the outtake footage*: Owen Williams, "Star Wars, Episode IX: All You Need to Know," *Empire*, Sept. 3, 2018.

358 *"Carrie Fisher could have made things easy on herself"*: Sady Doyle, "Carrie Fisher's Most Feminist Act Was Her Frankness About Being Bipolar in a World Where Women Are Called 'Crazy,'" *Quartz*, Dec. 28, 2016.

358 *"There's a chance that there's peace"*: An email to Betsy Rapoport, shared with the author.

ACKNOWLEDGMENTS

I never met Carrie Fisher. I know: my loss! As a writer about women (and men) in the culture, sometimes the entertainment industry part and sometimes the writer-critiquing part (and, often, the obstacles-defeating part), I believe I would have come home from an interview with her like so many people quoted in this book did, thinking *My God, was she ever cool! And funny! And* real*!* Then I would have mused, as others have, *I kind of . . . think I've . . . never met anyone quite like her.*

As I said: my loss.

Having grown up in a slightly older version of the Beverly Hills Flats, Beverly High, and "Hollywood" that Carrie aristocratically inhabited in her childhood; having lived in the dangerous and ironic New York she called home (and socially conquered) in the late 1970s; having been knocked out by *Postcards*—both book and movie—and been aware, from a distance, of the social primacy of the Carrie-and-Penny parties, I understood the specialness of Carrie Fisher, and I was not unfamiliar with her world. But it was only during the last few years of her life that I got an acute revelation about her contribution to what might be called the honesty revolution, the positive "badass" female culture, and the more earnest, issues-based feminism (against body and age shaming, for example) that took over Hollywood while it was also reinforcing itself all over the country, bringing younger women to tougher and more era-appropriate demands and expectations than we had fashioned in the early '70s and then intensified in the decades since. Girls who weren't yet born when Carrie burst out as Princess Leia in the first and second *Star Wars* and were babies when the third one hit the theaters: they hoisted her image on posters by the hundreds at the January 2017 women's march. At that time—right after her shocking, freshly mourned-over death—what she had been, who she had portrayed, what she had gone through, and what she was teaching us by example: all these things tumbled together, explicitly making her the heroine and "representative," hiding in plain sight, that she'd long, implicitly, been. If that first women's march had a magical spontaneity to it, the anointing of Carrie/Leia as one of its main faces had that as well.

While Carrie's contribution to the culture was, literally and figuratively, aloft, I spent time remembering having tagged along, as a Hawthorne School girl, with my movie-magazine writer-and-editor mother from our house on Elm Drive near Carmelita to Debbie Reynolds's house around the corner on Maple between Lomitas and Sunset, and meeting the lovely Debbie at the doorstep: with baby Carrie presumably in the back. My own family was noncelebrity but industry immersed: my mother's brother owned Ciro's, where Debbie and her friend Jane Powell used to sneak in, underage, and learn to be sophisticated, recalls my uncle's then protégée George Schlatter—and I spent after-school hours doing my homework sitting in a banquette in the darkened, empty main room, watching Debbie and Eddie's peers, like Nat King Cole and Peggy Lee and Dean Martin and Jerry Lewis, rehearse. More than that, my family—at the same time as the Debbie-Eddie-and-Liz drama was going on—had its own version of a beautiful diva breaking up a marriage, in a literally violent, similarly near incestuous, and not unpublic way. The episode left my mother and me uncomfortably bonded (joint empathy *and* joint humiliation) as paired rejects of an adored man in a way that I presume may have colored Debbie and Carrie's relationship as well. I grew up with my plucky, ever-working, husband-dumped mother—after shock treatments had saved her from suicidal depression—writing and editing Debbie-and-Eddie stories and then Debbie-and-Eddie-and-Liz stories and then Liz-Taylor-and-her-husbands stories on typewriters in one and then the other of our houses in Beverly Hills, to both of which Eddie's subsequent wife, the lovely and cheerful Connie Stevens, came over once or twice. So jumbled pieces of Carrie's life rang a bell with my own.

All of those factors came together in early January 2017, and I started to write the proposal that, almost three years later, has turned into this book.

I was grateful to have had a glimpse—and then a plunge, and then a deeper plunge—into Carrie's life and world through the many people who were good enough to share their memories of and insights into this unique and compelling woman. In addition to those who knew her personally, at whatever age and situation in her life or depth of closeness—and I will get to the thank-yous to all of them in a moment—I thank the fellow journalists who helped me by offering me notes from their interviews with Carrie and some of her close friends: Suzanne Finstad, Mimi Avins, and Ned Zeman. I also want to thank the authorities who taught me about bipolar disorder: Dr. James Phelps, Dr. Dean Parker, Kathleen Cairns, PhD, Joanne Doan, and bipolar community members and writers Marya Hornbacher, Terri Cheney, and Julie Fast. (I tried seven times, in vain, to acquire an interview with Dr. Kay Redfield Jamison. She is a busy woman.)

I was immensely lucky to be able to work with Sarah Crichton, a vibrant, brilliant, and generous woman I had met and lunched with years earlier and had always wanted to have as my editor. Sarah, known as a woman of impeccable taste, got a two-hundred-pages-longer-than-assigned manuscript from me on October 4, 2018, and after her first (emphasis, *first*) read, she wrote the kind of praiseful letter all writers dream of—signing off with "Your delighted editor"! I was thrilled. Then we got to the heart of it, and her long and brilliant editorial letters ("The smartest I have ever read—you are lucky!" said my husband, also an author) and more than five hundred (gulp) margin-note questions called for sometimes demanding rethinking and fast rereporting, and included daunting requests. But she knew what the best editors (and shrinks and coaches) know: cheer on your writer amid those demands—to keep her from having a nervous breakdown. So, yes, I loved getting her instantaneous "Fabulous!!" and "Fantastic!!" email returns to my text changes—and in that regard we were soul mates; I'm an exclamation-mark-using cheerleader, too. She also knew enough to put aside some of her stylistic and formal demands as she read on.

To make our deadline, Sarah worked through the 2018–2019 holidays—Christmas and New Year's—and sent me emails on Sunday nights up until January 31! Her cuts made the book stronger—and when we had a "High-five! We're done!" round of drinks after we were finished with the process, we felt like old friends. Sarah is just plain terrific, and I am honored to be the author of a Sarah Crichton Book.

I am also highly honored to have worked with Jonathan Galassi, the distinguished president of Farrar, Straus and Giroux, and have been deeply grateful for his attention and his praise.

Great thanks to my agent, Suzanne Gluck, for combining power, down-to-earthness, and cut-to-the-chase honesty with great supportiveness. I am lucky that you always have my back. And to her assistant, the wonderful Andrea Blatt, who has been besieged with more than a couple of anxiety-filled emails from me and has responded with lovely, calm helpfulness.

Speaking of assistants: What in the world would I have done without Ben Rosenstock, who, at FSG, combined my versions and Sarah's versions and my *further* versions and Sarah's *further* versions? And then spent a couple of weeks putting my eons of source notes in the correct stylistic form and handling the all-important Master Copy? Ben was the manager. Thank you, Ben!

Continuing on in the assistants department, for the first year of my research, I had the help of one and then another Columbia University graduate student—Elena Burger and Kelly Wydryk—in writing to requested sources and finding non-web-available old newspaper articles about *Star Wars* and interviews with Carrie. Thank you both!

I'd also like to thank Michael Cantwell for his careful read of the manuscript. Not only was his work impeccable, but he could not have been nicer. Thank you, too, Jeff Seroy, senior vice president of publicity and marketing at FSG, and Brian Gittis, assistant director of publicity, for getting my book "out there." Gratitude, as well, to the production manager, Peter Richardson, and the designer, Abby Kagan.

Since the fact of Carrie Fisher becoming a major writer was essential to the story of her life, I want to thank the editors who worked with her who agreed to be interviewed by me about their work process with her: Sydny Miner, Trishe Lande, Betsy Rapoport, Kerri Kolen, and the wonderful publishing executive Susan Kamil, who, years ago, was my editor on my first—learning the ropes—nonfiction book.

My friend Elisa Petrini was extraordinarily helpful in advice and counsel at so many critical points. My husband, John Kelly, kept saying, after hearing snippets of my phone interviews in our mutual home office, "Was that [conversation] as good as it sounded?" My friend Carol Ardman was a cheerleader. My sister Liz Weller was nothing less than indispensable to my peace of mind and confidence in so many ways, as well as always offering me accommodations in L.A.

I interviewed many people who knew Carrie Fisher—both deeply well and not so well but at important junctures. Their names are attributed in the text whenever they supplied a quote or an observation (I'm wonky that way), and some insisted on being anonymous, so I am respecting that. Their names are also listed in each chapter citation of the source notes, often multiple times. Some were critically important and supportive and helped me find other sources, and I could not be more grateful. Of these and the others: your insights, large and small, fit together in a tapestry and tell, I sincerely hope, the story of a rich, unique, accomplished, and complicated life.

I thank everyone who helped me understand and describe this woman who stood for so much that we have lived, have seen, have suffered through, and have needed to reach for and go to. Her honesty was refreshing, endearing, and, today in America, a needed North Star.

I send enduring condolences and enormous respect to her family.

Sheila Weller, New York City, May 6, 2019

INDEX

A NOTE ABOUT THE AUTHOR

Sheila Weller is the author of the *New York Times* bestseller *Girls Like Us: Carole King, Joni Mitchell, Carly Simon—and the Journey of a Generation* and of the acclaimed family memoir *Dancing at Ciro's: A Family's Love, Loss, and Scandal on the Sunset Strip*, as well as *The News Sorority, Marrying the Hangman, Raging Heart,* and *Saint of Circumstance*. Her investigative articles on women's issues and cultural history—for publications such as *Vanity Fair, Glamour,* and *The New York Times*—have won her six Newswomen's Club of New York Front Page Awards, two National Women's Political Caucus Exceptional Merit in Media Awards, and a National Headliner Award. She grew up in Beverly Hills, graduated from UC Berkeley, and lives in Manhattan.